TEMPLES...
CHOKER

D1450657

STORY
BEN McCOOL
benmccool.com

ART/DESIGN
BEN TEMPLESMITH

templesmith.com

LETTERS
TOM B LONG
tombgraphics.com

FONTS
COMICRAFT
comicraft.com

IMAGE COMICS, INC.
WWW.IMAGECOMICS.COM

Robert Kirkman — Chief Operating Officer
Erik Larsen — Chief Financial Officer
Todd McFarlane — President
Marc Silvestri — Chief Executive Officer
Jim Valentino — Vice-President
Eric Stephenson — Publisher
Todd Martinez — Sales & Licensing Coordinator
Jennifer de Guzman — PR & Marketing Director
Branwyn Bigglestone — Accounts Manager

Emily Miller — Administrative Assistant
Jamie Parreno — Marketing Assistant
Sarah deLaine — Events Coordinator
Kevin Yuen — Digital Rights Coordinator
Tyler Shainline — Production Manager
Drew Gill — Art Director
Jonathan Chan — Senior Production Artist
Monica Garcia — Production Artist
Vincent Kukua — Production Artist
Jana Cook — Production Artist

Crime noir is awesome.

Soon after I started reading "adult" fiction (I guess I was around 11 at the time) I started noticing these really cool-looking detective novels dotted around the library my mum worked in (and still does, actually). Dark, moody covers featuring shifty characters doing sleazy things; immediately, I wanted in. From Raymond Chandler to Ed McBain, this stuff captivated me. It would be a number of years before I was fully able to appreciate the sophistication of these works (particularly in terms of tone and atmosphere) but straight off the bat I was hooked by the idea of guys who do bad things being responsible for catching people who do worse things—the "antihero" fascinated me.

As time went by, I started reading more contemporary works, particularly by the likes of James Ellroy and Lawrence Block, and my interest in the genre only intensified. Once I hit 18, I was almost exclusively reading crime fiction (only science fiction managed to occasionally sway my attention); narrow-minded, perhaps, but I was as happy as a pig in shit. I'd frequently spend weekends at home with a case of cheap lager and the writings of Mickey Spillane—never before had being a stony-broke student seemed like such luxury!

Twisted science fiction worked as an ideal interlude to the crime stories I was ingesting: though not as reliant on ambience, it offered up bucketloads of peculiar ideas that made my mind boggle. I was in awe of the journeys into outlandish worlds authors like Philip K. Dick were steering me through, and the more I read, the more intense my yearning for zanier, crazier adventures became. The sheer level of imagination involved in these stories astounded me.

Eventually, I decided that there might be more to life than just crime and sci-fi, and started "cheating" on my two usual genres. I myself was developing an interest in writing, and figured I should diversify; indulge in some of the other good stuff out there. I was soon reading everything from horror to history, and game for pretty much anything else.

But crime and science fiction were still top of the heap. And all I wanted to do was splice 'em together and create a story of my own...

Cut forward to 2008 and a chance meeting with a certain Mr. Templesmith: It was the eve of San Diego Comic-Con, and Ben was throwing a rather splendid warm-up party. He didn't know who the bloody hell I was, but seemingly embraced my dreadful jokes and insatiable thirst for Guinness. I was flattered; after all, he's one of the top artists in the biz. Better yet, after telling him that I was a writer looking to "properly" break into comics (I'd had a few little odds and sods published already) he said he'd take a look at some of my stuff. I couldn't believe it—why would this talented bastard who'd worked with some of the industry's elite want to do anything with me? But I jumped on the chance, sent him a synopsis for what would eventually become the very book you hold in your hands, and voila! A creative team was born.

Yeah, I got lucky. Real lucky.

This was my very first mini-series, and boy, did I have fun writing it. Looking back, there are a few things I might've done differently, a few parts I'd change altogether, but heck, I've got nothing but fine memories of putting CHOKER together. Seeing it come to life was a treat, and I was barely able to contain my joy when pages of Ben's art started to roll in; the kooky slimeballs and misfits that inhabit Shotgun City, a noir world fueled with cyberpunk sensibilities, were evolving before my very eyes and my brain was ready to explode with exhilaration.

(Yeah. You guessed it. I'm an excitable kinda guy.)

Anyway, that's the background behind this devious tale of debauchery—now it's time for you to get stuck into the world of Johnny Jackson and CHOKER.

And remember...

Crime noir is awesome. So is science fiction. And I'll be damned if comics isn't the perfect medium for both of 'em.

—Ben McCool, New York City, April 2012.

There are three things you need to know.

1. Ben McCool likes a beer.

This is actually how we met and how this collected edition of CHOKER has finally made it into your hot little hands. I met Ben, several years ago now, while we were both rather pissed, (That's inebriated to you, my American cousins, rather than angry,) and despite my addled state, I was so impressed with how Ben worked his words, the sheer force of charisma, that I just had to declare on the spot that if he wrote as well as he talked, he'd be a made man in comics and that I'd kill to do a book with him. And thus, shortly after, in a slightly more sober state, CHOKER was born.

2. Ben McCool is an immensely patient man.

This book, without a doubt, should have been done well over a year ago. Looking back on when I started this journey with Ben to when I finished it, it truly was a lifetime ago. Interspersed with divorce, making some rather poor life choices in the throes of a midlife crisis or something, deciding to hang out with some people, very unhealthy for creativity, some paralysis in a leg and even a bout of homelessness and international vagrancy. When it came to doing comics, I was useless at anything for far too long. So issue 5 took awhile and by issue 6... most people had given up.

But Ben was a patient man. Beyond patient. Since CHOKER started he's gone from strength to strength... other projects have come and gone. But CHOKER remained unfinished. Many artists may have just buggered off all together and honestly, maybe that would've been easier... but I really wanted to finish this for him, the way we started it. I HAD to. I need to apologise for taking so bloody long, both to him and to the audience. As a rule, I finish what I start, even if it takes me awhile to get there.

So a huge, huuuge thank you to all, to Image Comics, the only game in town when it comes to real comics where creators are able to own and benefit from what they create and especially Ben, for persevering with me and allowing me the time to get back to the most important thing in life for me. Comics. & this little book.

3. Ben McCool is a crafty, talented bugger.

CHOKER is one of the best books I think I've ever done. It's longer too. But I think I both lost and found myself with this project. I can look back on it now and actually appreciate what Ben did with it. His characters are bastards and heroes at the same time. Larger than life and horrifically entertaining.

I hope you find it a worthy read.

-Ben Templesmith, Chicago, April 2012

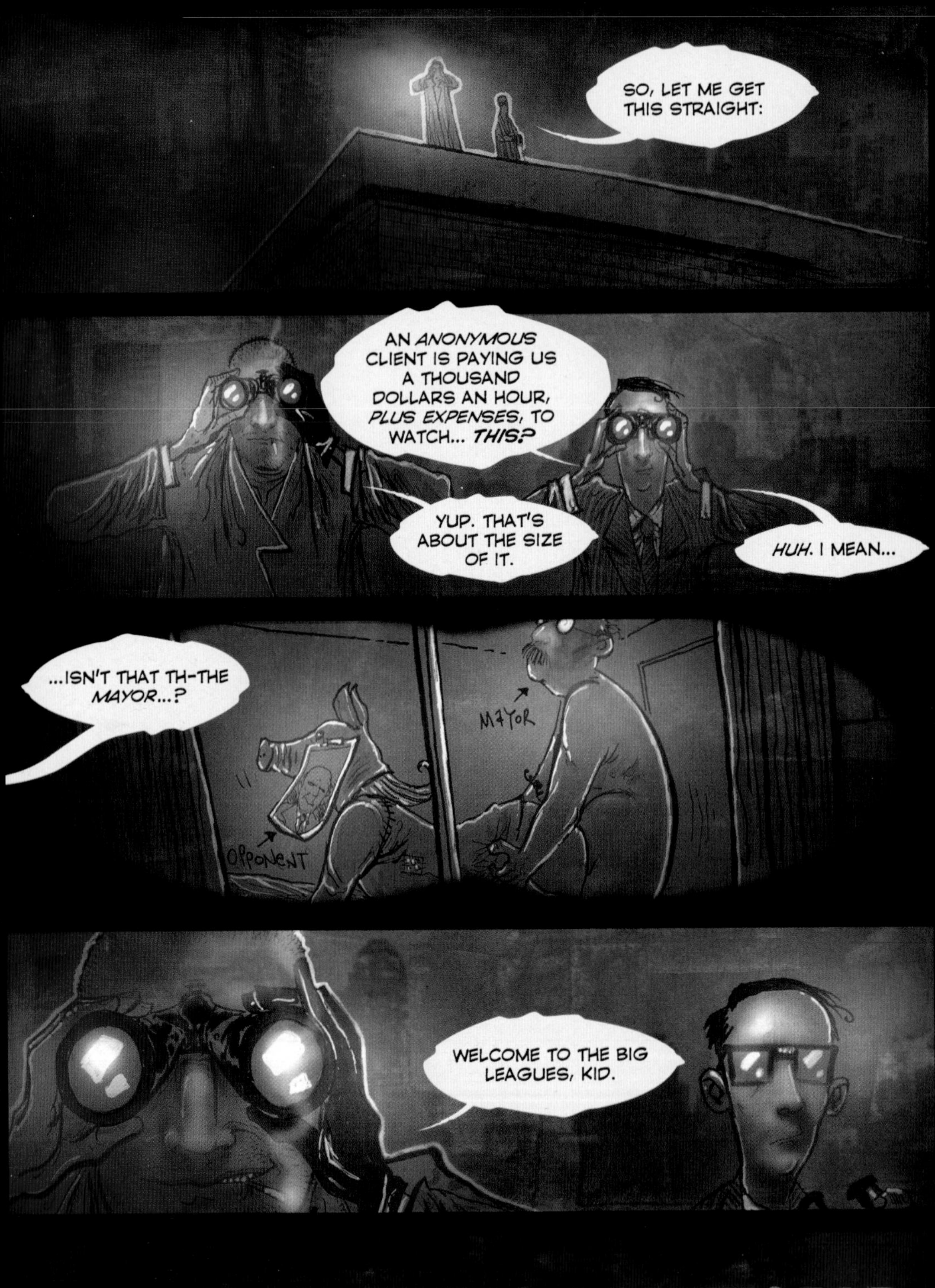
SO, LET ME GET THIS STRAIGHT:
AN *ANONYMOUS* CLIENT IS PAYING US A THOUSAND DOLLARS AN HOUR, *PLUS EXPENSES,* TO WATCH... ***THIS?***
YUP. THAT'S ABOUT THE SIZE OF IT.
HUH. I MEAN...
...ISN'T THAT TH-THE *MAYOR*...?
MAYOR
OPPONENT
WELCOME TO THE BIG LEAGUES, KID.

BIG BAD CITY, BIG BAD WORLD.

WORDS: BEN MCCOOL

ART/LETTERS: BEN TEMPLESMITH

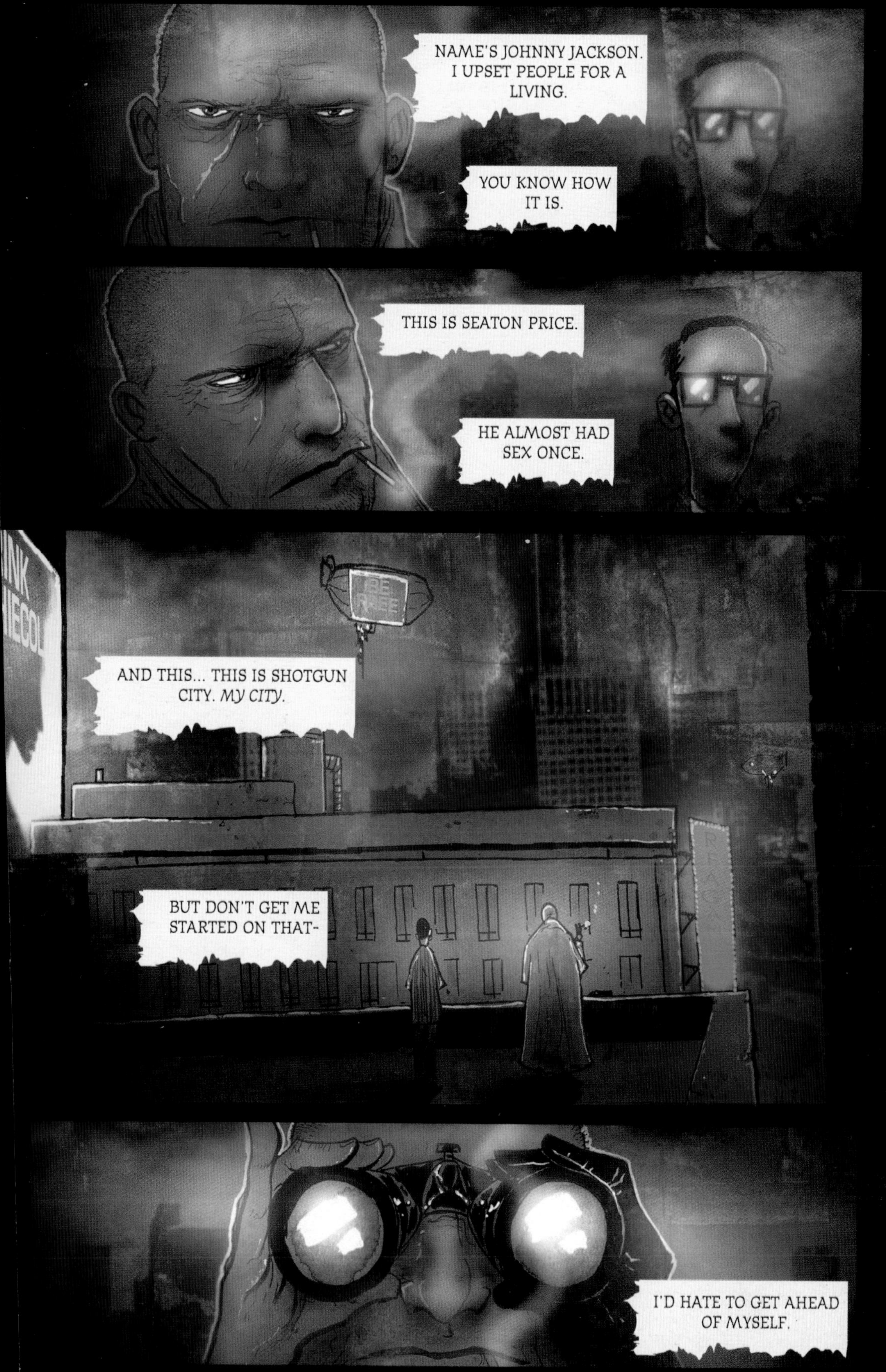
NAME'S JOHNNY JACKSON. I UPSET PEOPLE FOR A LIVING.
YOU KNOW HOW IT IS.
THIS IS SEATON PRICE.
HE ALMOST HAD SEX ONCE.
AND THIS... THIS IS SHOTGUN CITY. *MY CITY.*
BUT DON'T GET ME STARTED ON THAT-
I'D HATE TO GET AHEAD OF MYSELF.

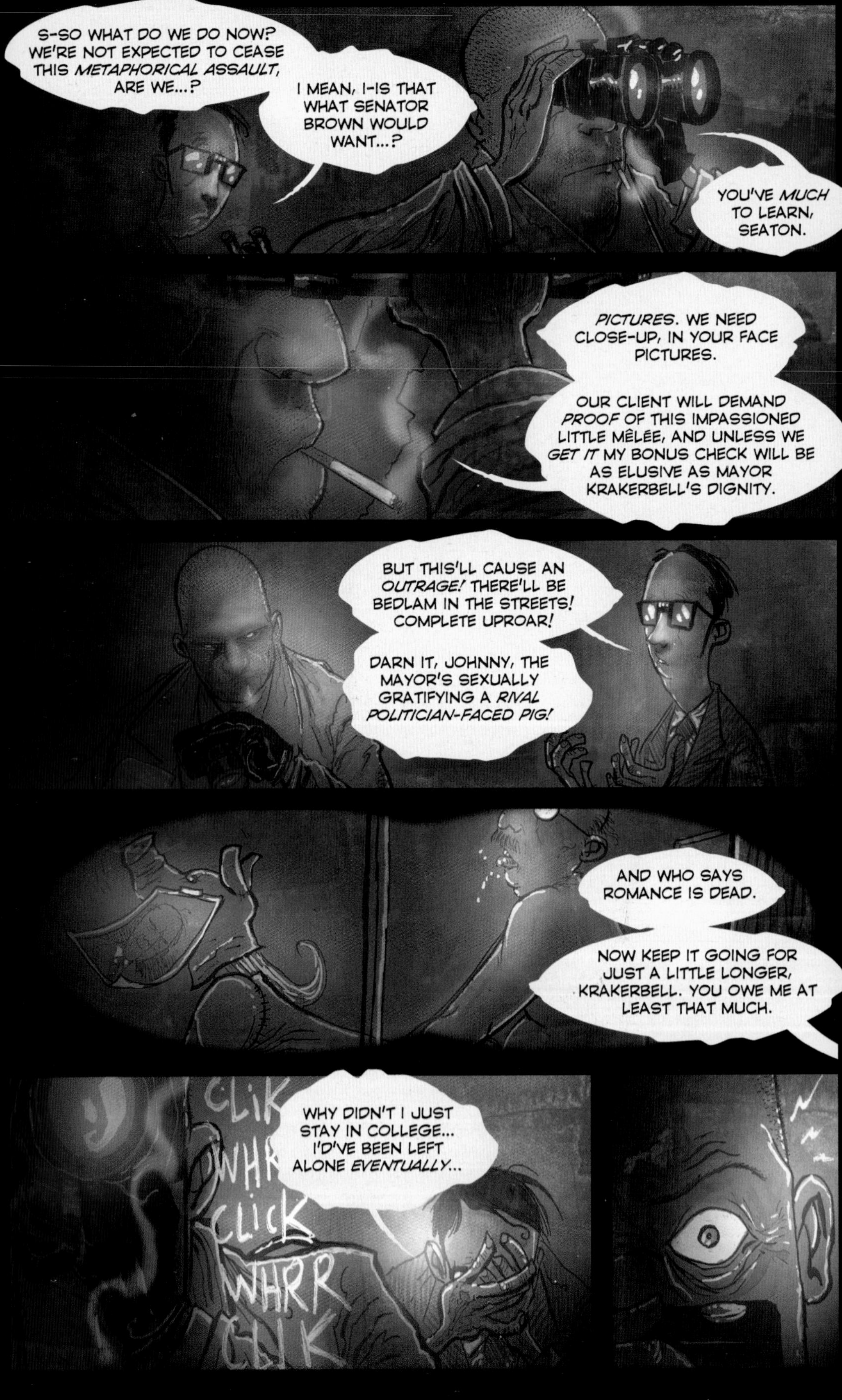
S-SO WHAT DO WE DO NOW? WE'RE NOT EXPECTED TO CEASE THIS *METAPHORICAL ASSAULT*, ARE WE...?
I MEAN, I-IS THAT WHAT SENATOR BROWN WOULD WANT...?
YOU'VE *MUCH* TO LEARN, SEATON.
PICTURES. WE NEED CLOSE-UP, IN YOUR FACE PICTURES.
OUR CLIENT WILL DEMAND *PROOF* OF THIS IMPASSIONED LITTLE MÊLÉE, AND UNLESS WE *GET IT* MY BONUS CHECK WILL BE AS ELUSIVE AS MAYOR KRAKERBELL'S DIGNITY.
BUT THIS'LL CAUSE AN *OUTRAGE!* THERE'LL BE BEDLAM IN THE STREETS! COMPLETE UPROAR!
DARN IT, JOHNNY, THE MAYOR'S SEXUALLY GRATIFYING A *RIVAL POLITICIAN-FACED PIG!*
AND WHO SAYS ROMANCE IS DEAD.
NOW KEEP IT GOING FOR JUST A LITTLE LONGER, KRAKERBELL. YOU OWE ME AT LEAST THAT MUCH.
CLIK
WHR
CLICK
WHRR
CLIK
WHY DIDN'T I JUST STAY IN COLLEGE... I'D'VE BEEN LEFT ALONE *EVENTUALLY*...

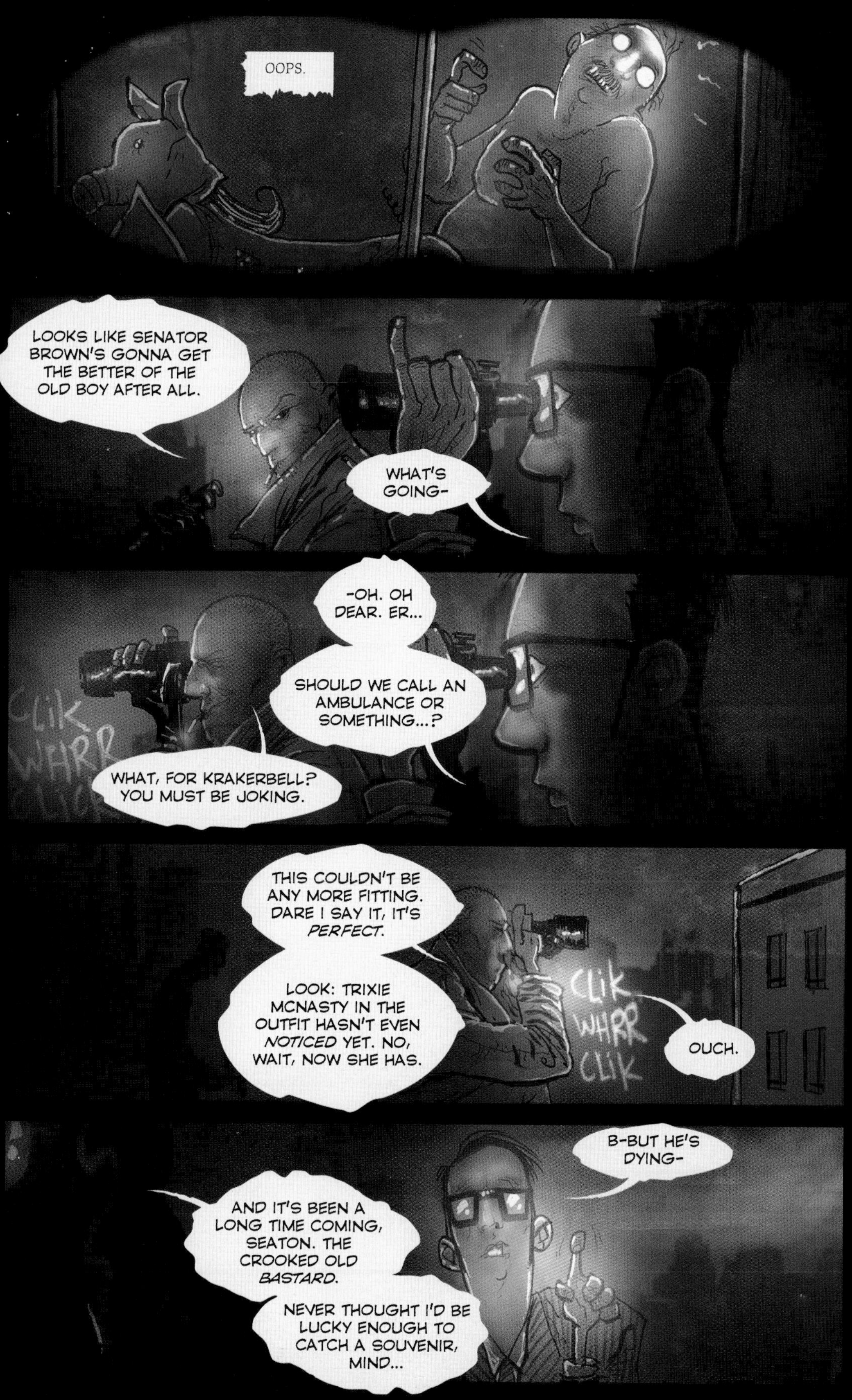
OOPS.
LOOKS LIKE SENATOR BROWN'S GONNA GET THE BETTER OF THE OLD BOY AFTER ALL.
WHAT'S GOING-
-OH. OH DEAR. ER...
SHOULD WE CALL AN AMBULANCE OR SOMETHING...?
CLIK WHRR CLIK
WHAT, FOR KRAKERBELL? YOU MUST BE JOKING.
THIS COULDN'T BE ANY MORE FITTING. DARE I SAY IT, IT'S *PERFECT*.
LOOK: TRIXIE MCNASTY IN THE OUTFIT HASN'T EVEN *NOTICED* YET. NO, WAIT, NOW SHE HAS.
CLIK WHRR CLIK
OUCH.
B-BUT HE'S DYING-
AND IT'S BEEN A LONG TIME COMING, SEATON. THE CROOKED OLD *BASTARD*.
NEVER THOUGHT I'D BE LUCKY ENOUGH TO CATCH A SOUVENIR, MIND...

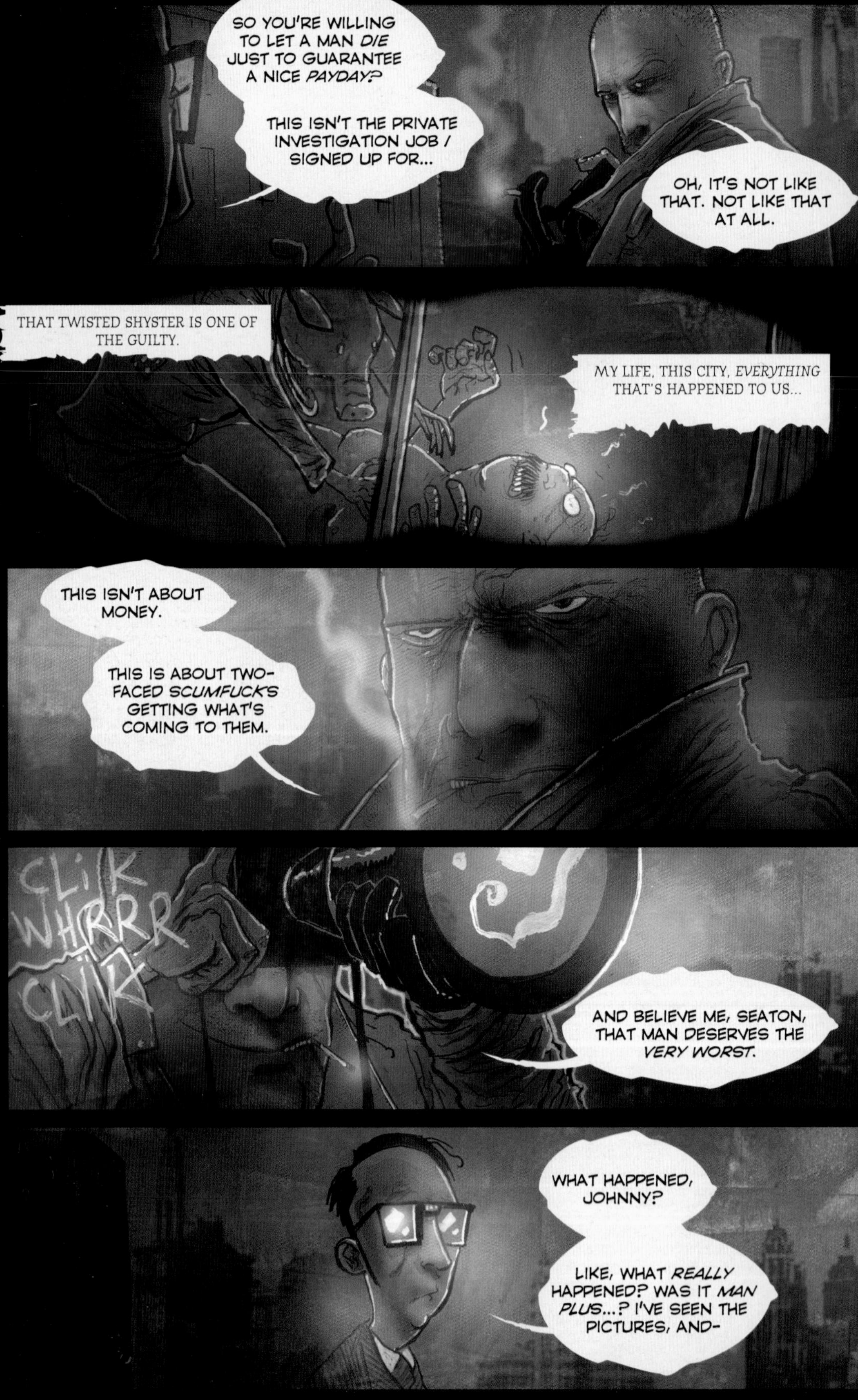
SO YOU'RE WILLING TO LET A MAN *DIE* JUST TO GUARANTEE A NICE *PAYDAY*?
THIS ISN'T THE PRIVATE INVESTIGATION JOB I SIGNED UP FOR...
OH, IT'S NOT LIKE THAT. NOT LIKE THAT AT ALL.
THAT TWISTED SHYSTER IS ONE OF THE GUILTY.
MY LIFE, THIS CITY, *EVERYTHING* THAT'S HAPPENED TO US...
THIS ISN'T ABOUT MONEY.
THIS IS ABOUT TWO-FACED *SCUMFUCKS* GETTING WHAT'S COMING TO THEM.
CLIK
WHRRR
CLIK
AND BELIEVE ME, SEATON, THAT MAN DESERVES THE *VERY WORST*.
WHAT HAPPENED, JOHNNY?
LIKE, WHAT *REALLY* HAPPENED? WAS IT *MAN PLUS*...? I'VE SEEN THE PICTURES, AND-

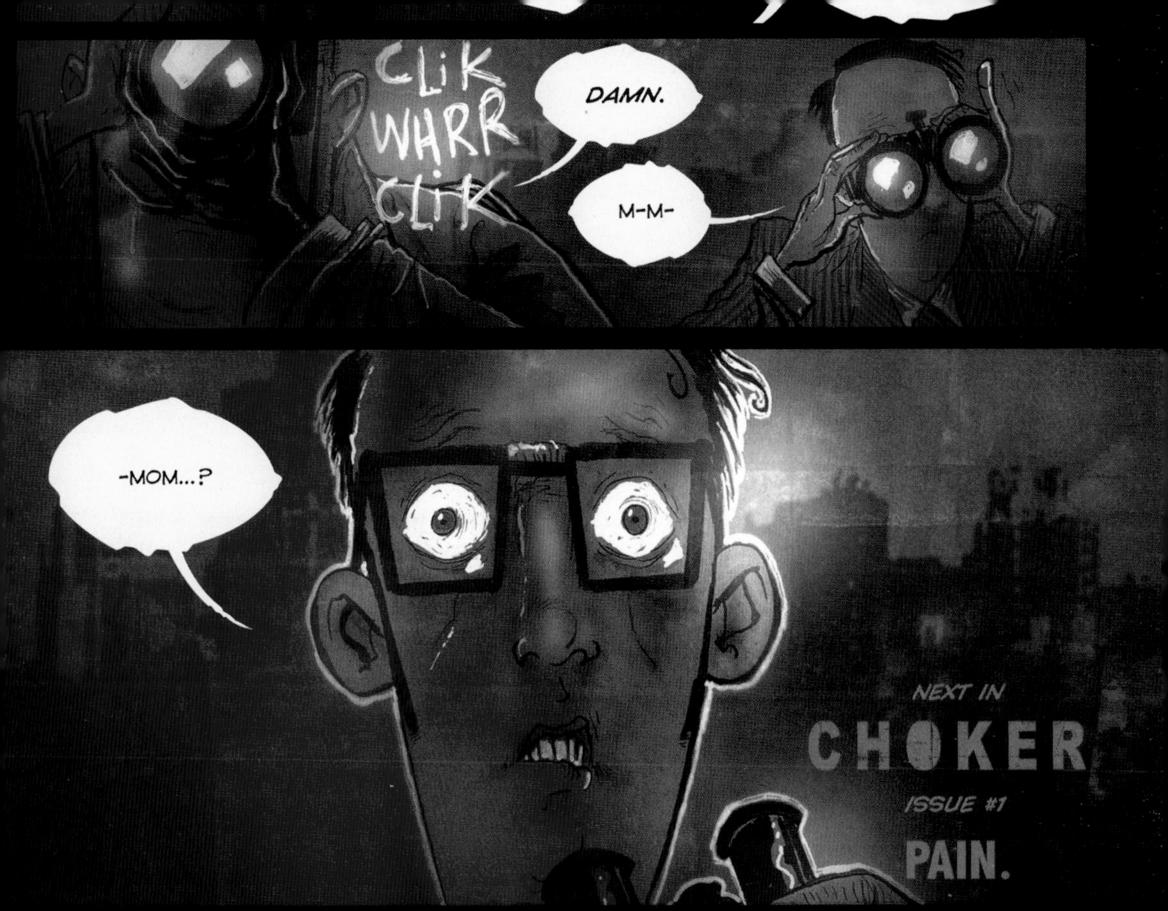
CLIK
WHRR
CLIK
DAMN.
M-M-
-MOM...?
NEXT IN
CHOKER
ISSUE #1
PAIN.

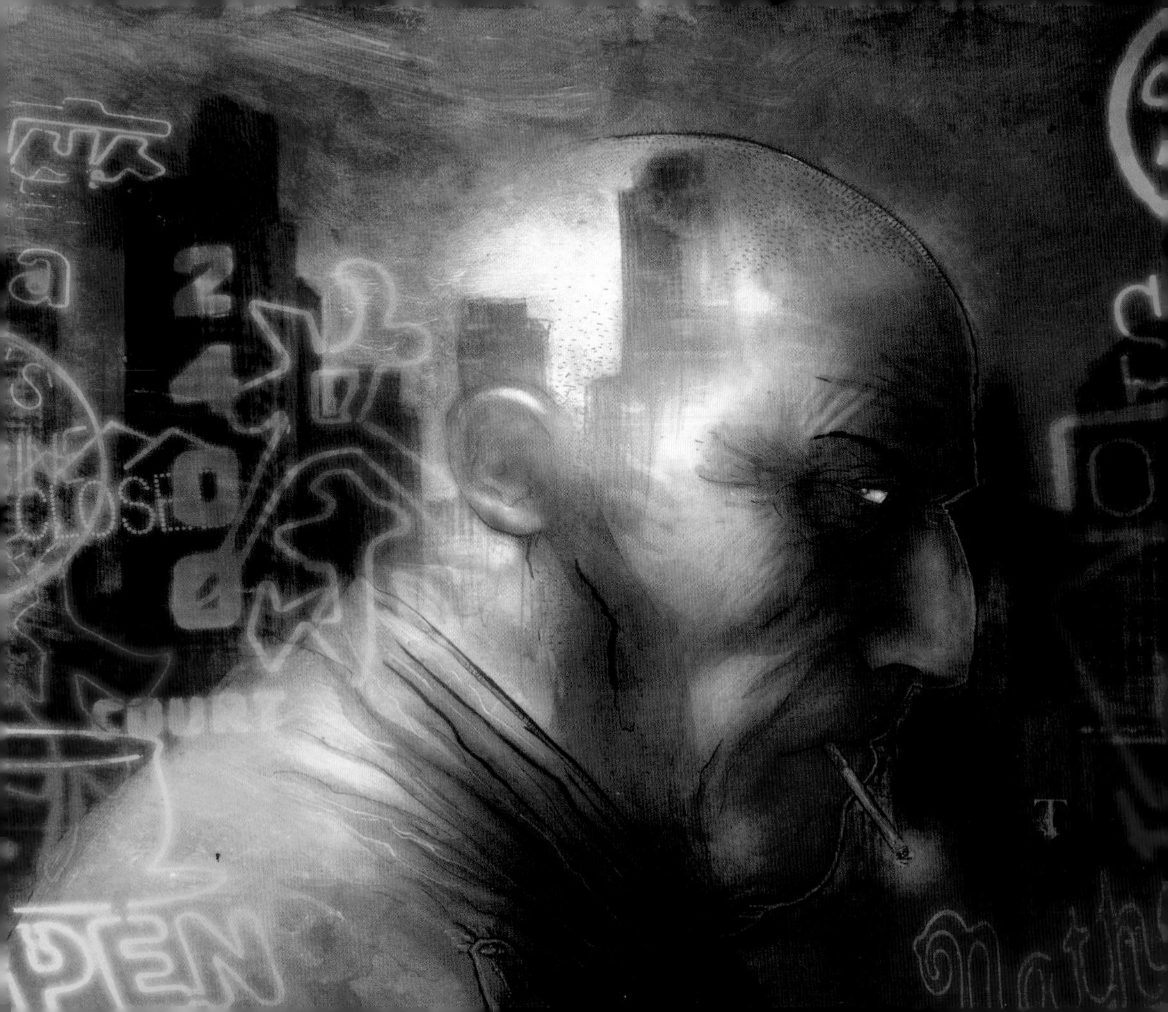

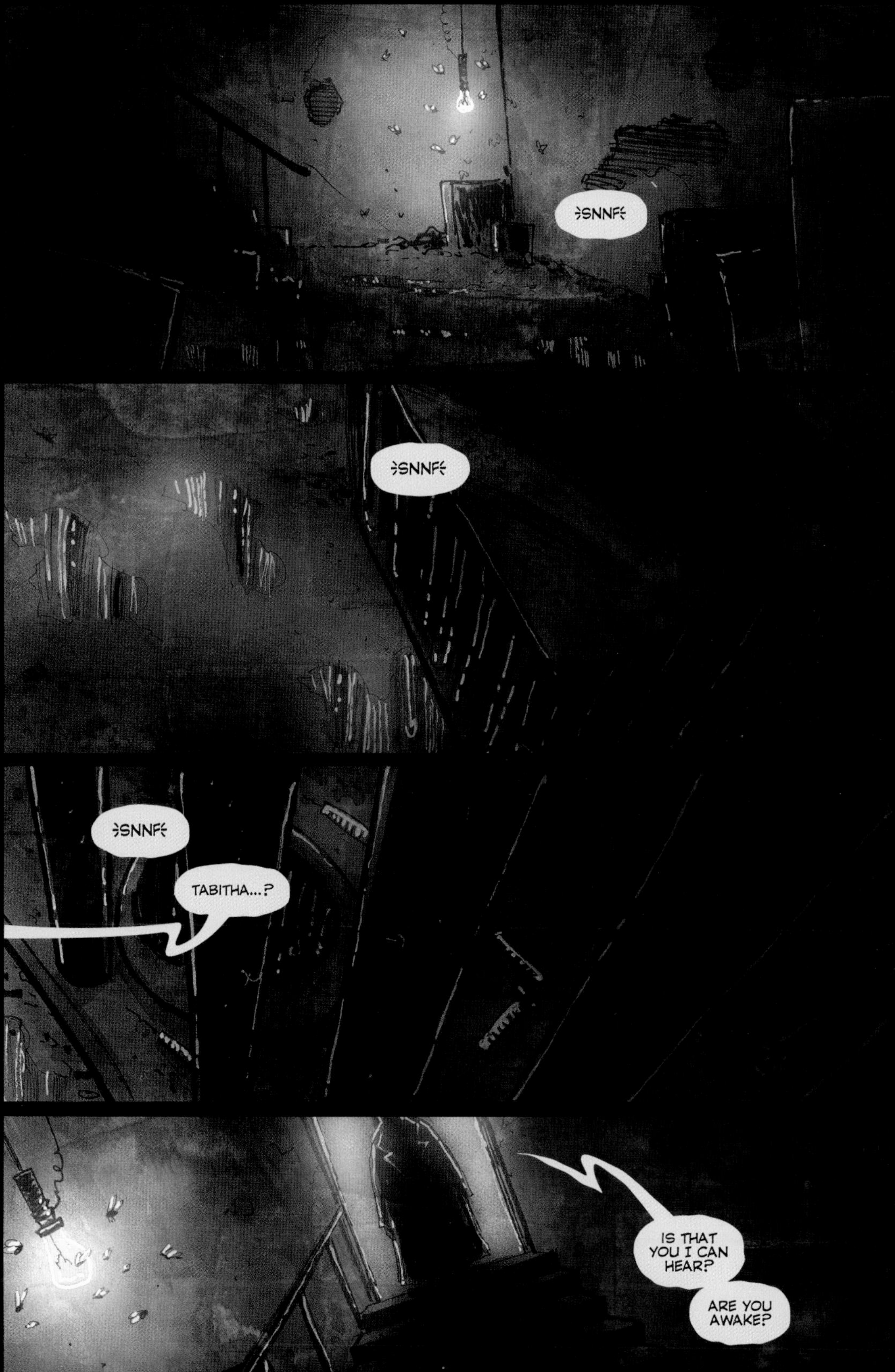
SNNF
SNNF
SNNF
TABITHA...?
IS THAT YOU I CAN HEAR?
ARE YOU AWAKE?

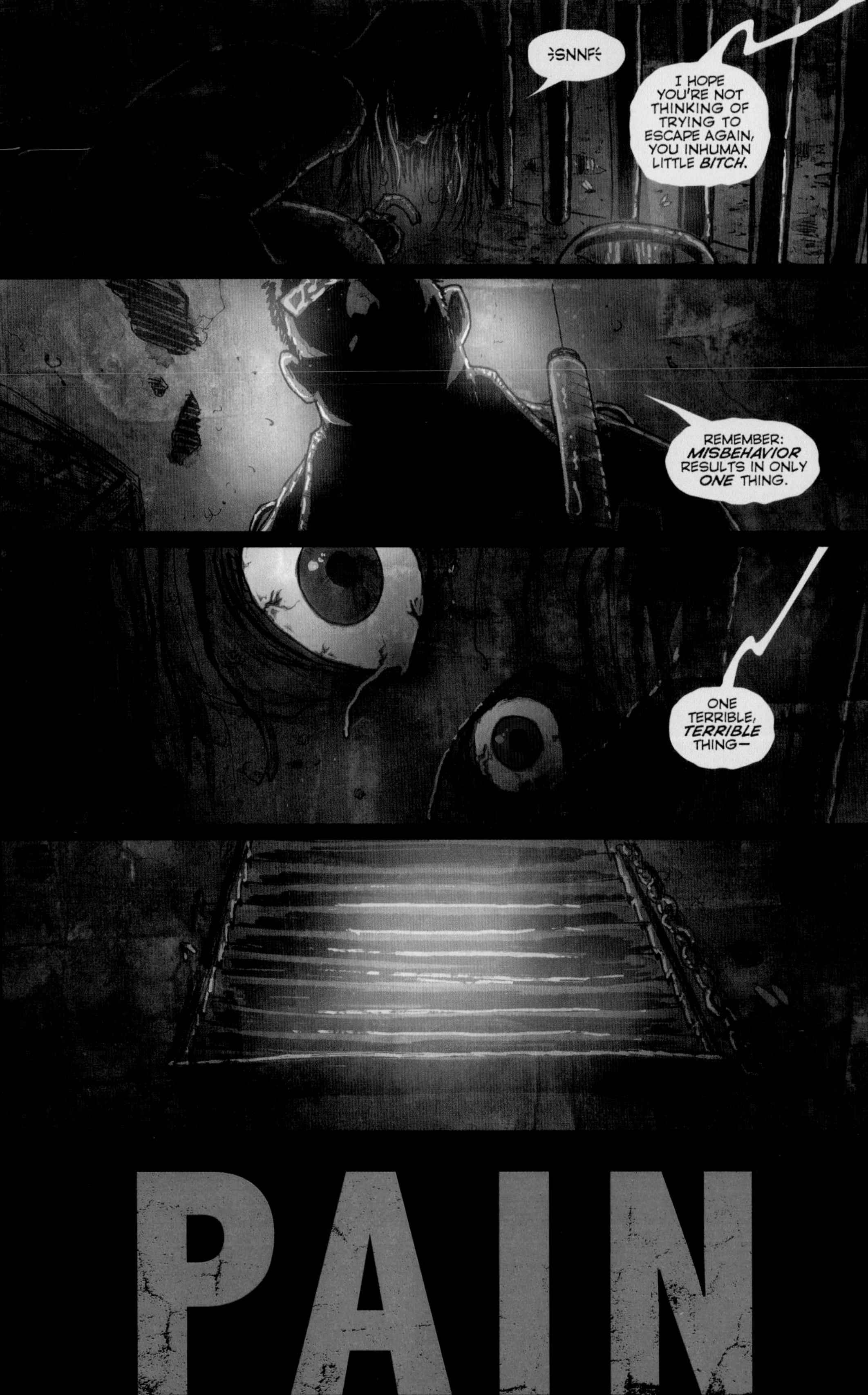

SNNF
I HOPE YOU'RE NOT THINKING OF TRYING TO ESCAPE AGAIN, YOU INHUMAN LITTLE *BITCH*.
REMEMBER: *MISBEHAVIOR* RESULTS IN ONLY *ONE* THING.
ONE TERRIBLE, *TERRIBLE* THING—
PAIN

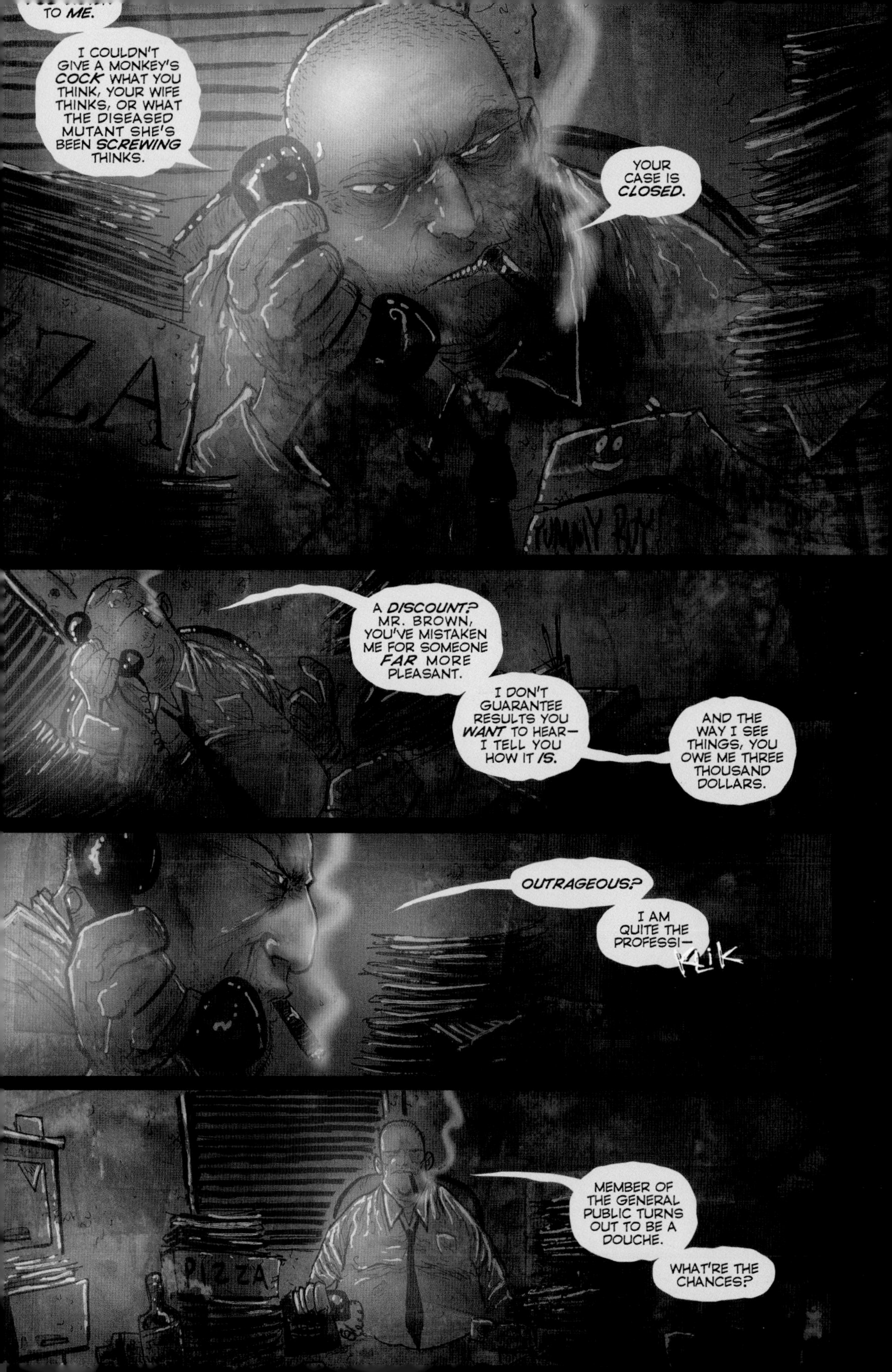
TO ME.
I COULDN'T GIVE A MONKEY'S COCK WHAT YOU THINK, YOUR WIFE THINKS, OR WHAT THE DISEASED MUTANT SHE'S BEEN SCREWING THINKS.
YOUR CASE IS CLOSED.
A DISCOUNT? MR. BROWN, YOU'VE MISTAKEN ME FOR SOMEONE FAR MORE PLEASANT.
I DON'T GUARANTEE RESULTS YOU WANT TO HEAR— I TELL YOU HOW IT IS.
AND THE WAY I SEE THINGS, YOU OWE ME THREE THOUSAND DOLLARS.
OUTRAGEOUS?
I AM QUITE THE PROFESSI—
KLIK
PIZZA
MEMBER OF THE GENERAL PUBLIC TURNS OUT TO BE A DOUCHE.
WHAT'RE THE CHANCES?

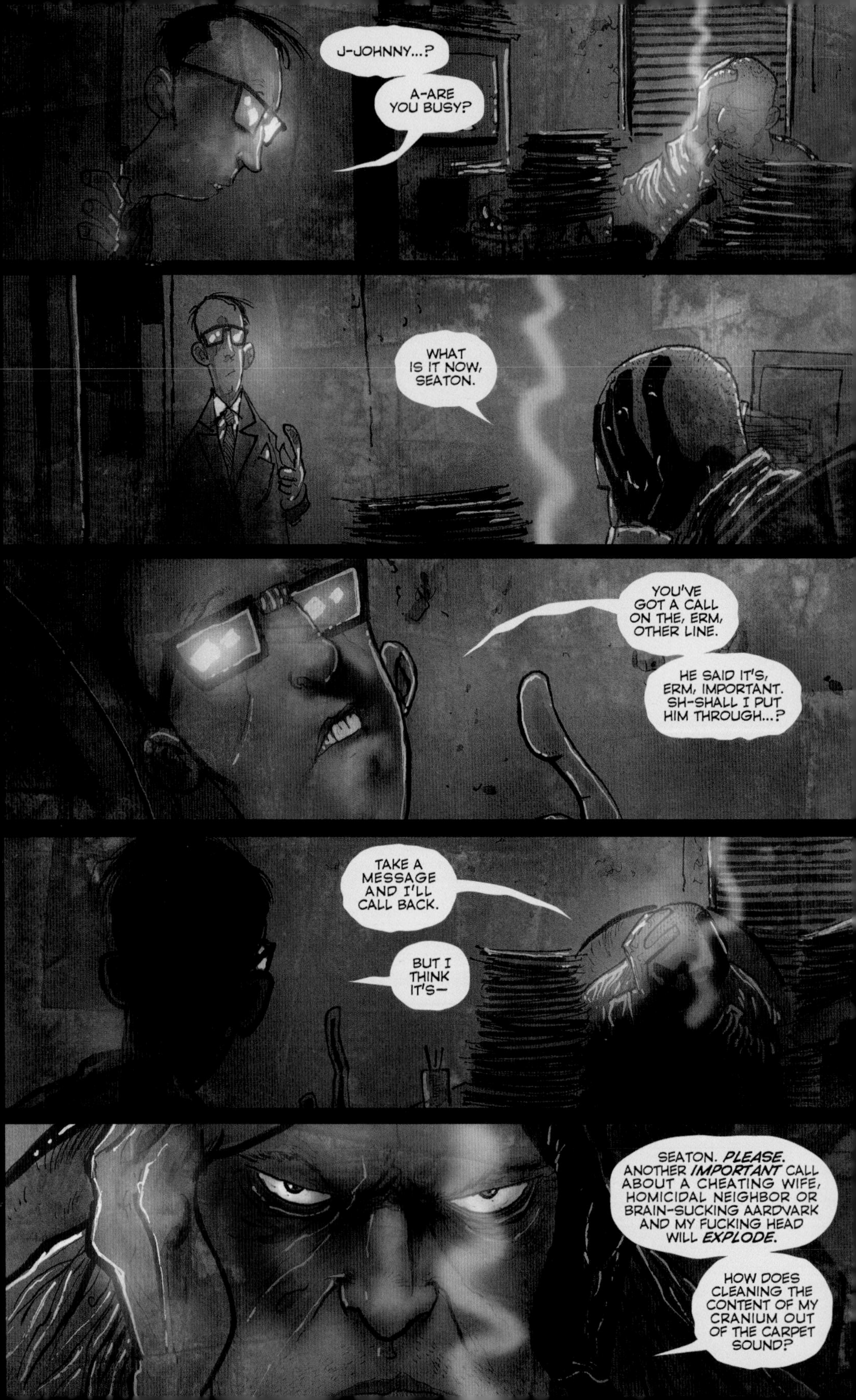
J-JOHNNY...?
A-ARE YOU BUSY?
WHAT IS IT NOW, SEATON.
YOU'VE GOT A CALL ON THE, ERM, OTHER LINE.
HE SAID IT'S, ERM, IMPORTANT. SH-SHALL I PUT HIM THROUGH...?
TAKE A MESSAGE AND I'LL CALL BACK.
BUT I THINK IT'S—
SEATON. *PLEASE.* ANOTHER *IMPORTANT* CALL ABOUT A CHEATING WIFE, HOMICIDAL NEIGHBOR OR BRAIN-SUCKING AARDVARK AND MY FUCKING HEAD WILL *EXPLODE.*
HOW DOES CLEANING THE CONTENT OF MY CRANIUM OUT OF THE CARPET SOUND?

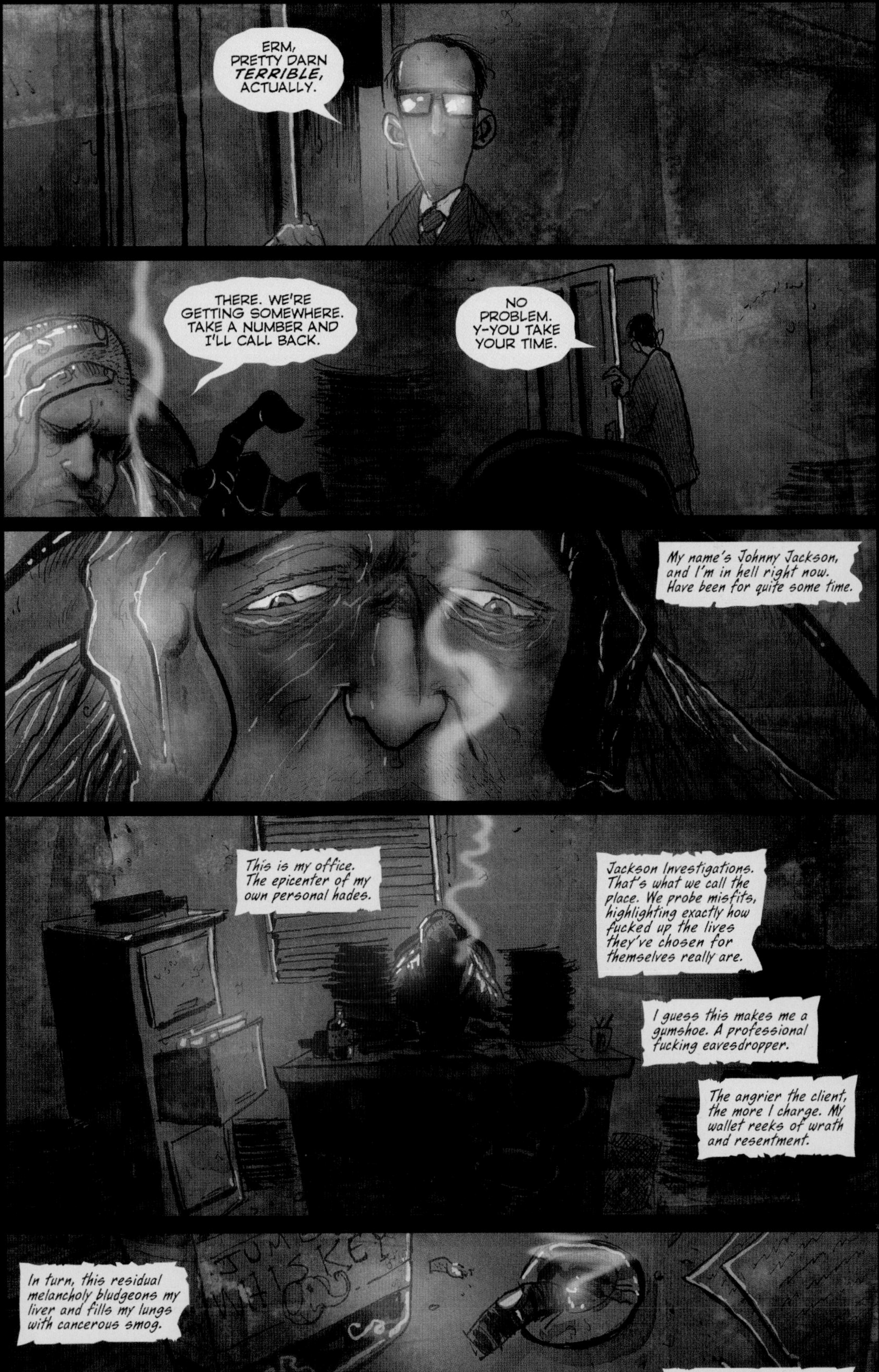

ERM, PRETTY DARN *TERRIBLE,* ACTUALLY.
THERE. WE'RE GETTING SOMEWHERE. TAKE A NUMBER AND I'LL CALL BACK.
NO PROBLEM. Y-YOU TAKE YOUR TIME.
My name's Johnny Jackson, and I'm in hell right now. Have been for quite some time.
This is my office. The epicenter of my own personal hades.
Jackson Investigations. That's what we call the place. We probe misfits, highlighting exactly how fucked up the lives they've chosen for themselves really are.
I guess this makes me a gumshoe. A professional fucking eavesdropper.
The angrier the client, the more I charge. My wallet reeks of wrath and resentment.
In turn, this residual melancholy bludgeons my liver and fills my lungs with cancerous smog.
A fair trade, you could say.

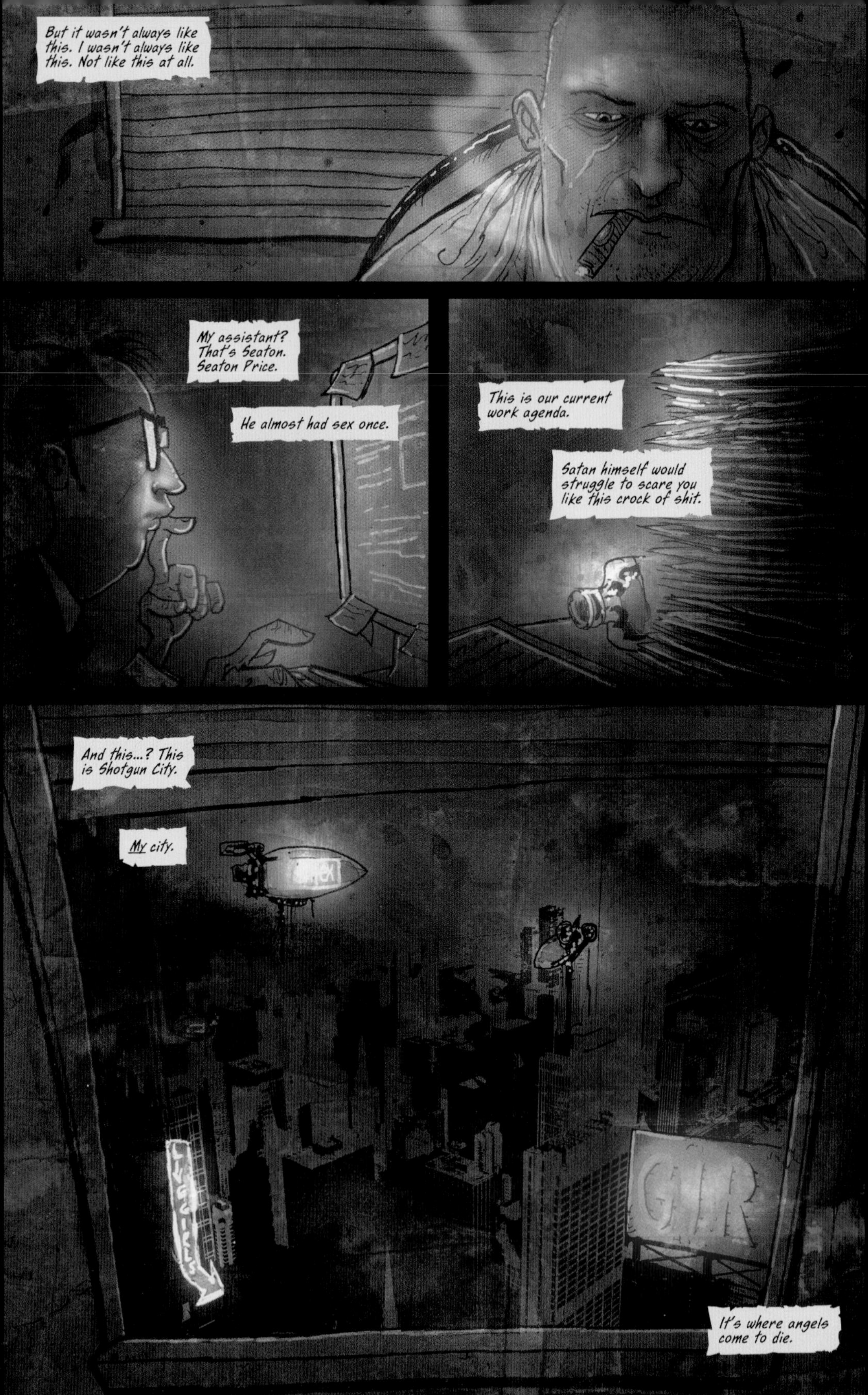
But it wasn't always like this. I wasn't always like this. Not like this at all.
My assistant? That's Seaton. Seaton Price.
He almost had sex once.
This is our current work agenda.
Satan himself would struggle to scare you like this crock of shit.
And this...? This is Shotgun City.
My city.
It's where angels come to die.

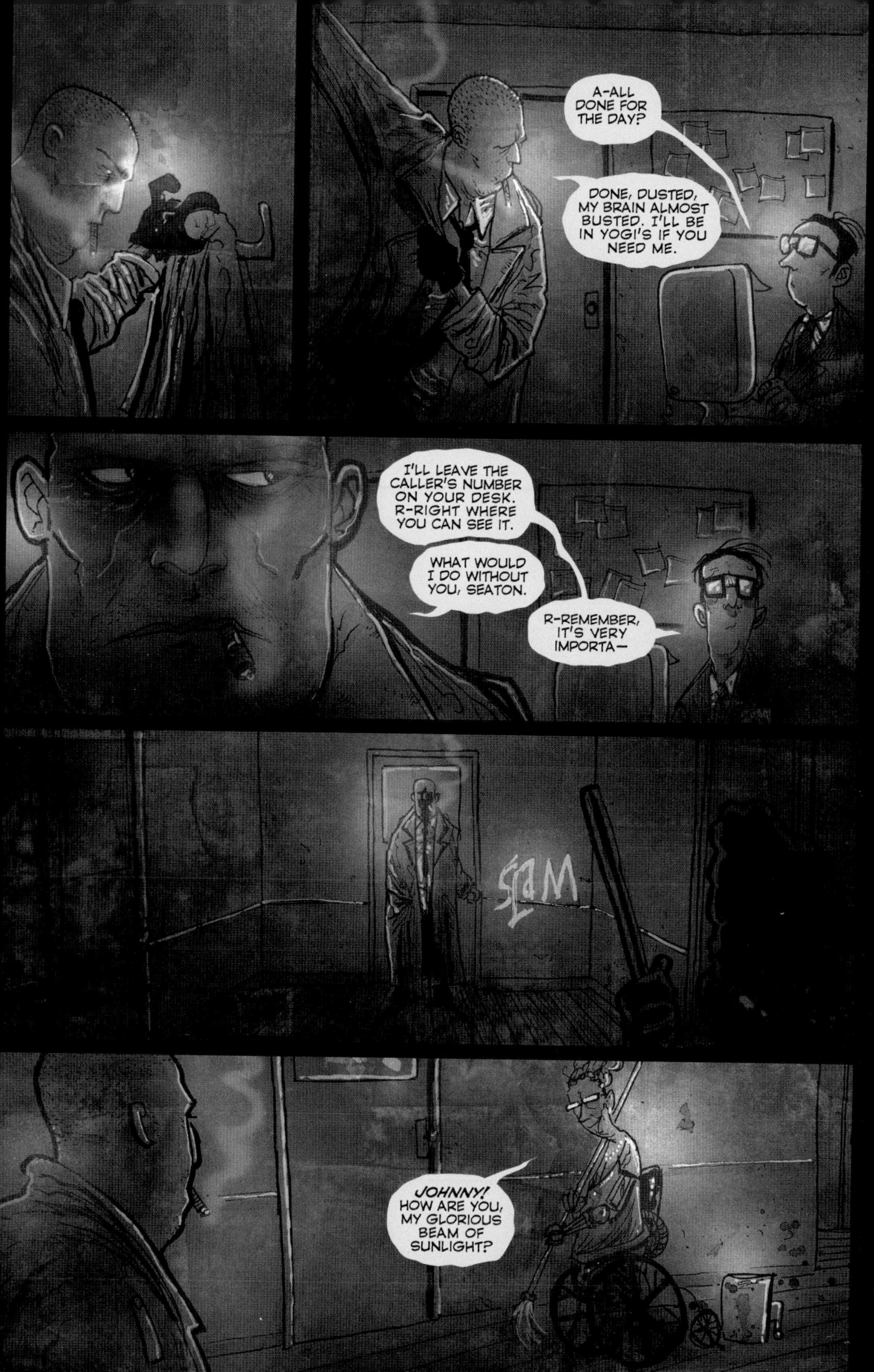
A-ALL DONE FOR THE DAY?
DONE, DUSTED, MY BRAIN ALMOST BUSTED. I'LL BE IN YOGI'S IF YOU NEED ME.
I'LL LEAVE THE CALLER'S NUMBER ON YOUR DESK. R-RIGHT WHERE YOU CAN SEE IT.
WHAT WOULD I DO WITHOUT YOU, SEATON.
R-REMEMBER, IT'S VERY IMPORTA—
SLAM
JOHNNY! HOW ARE YOU, MY GLORIOUS BEAM OF SUNLIGHT?

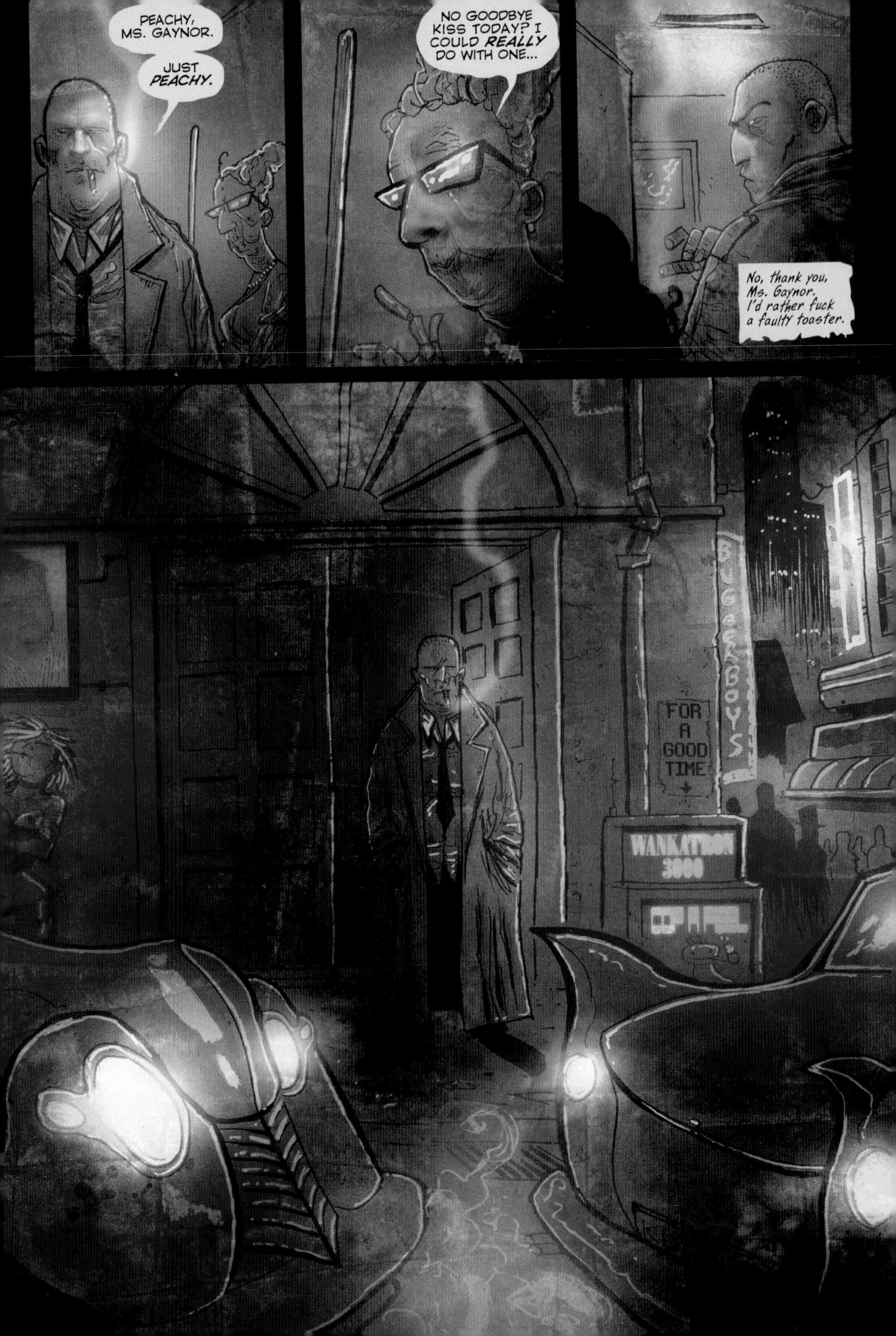
PEACHY, MS. GAYNOR.
JUST *PEACHY.*
NO GOODBYE KISS TODAY? I COULD *REALLY* DO WITH ONE...
No, thank you, Ms. Gaynor. I'd rather fuck a faulty toaster.
BUGGERBOYS
FOR A GOOD TIME
WANKATRON 3000

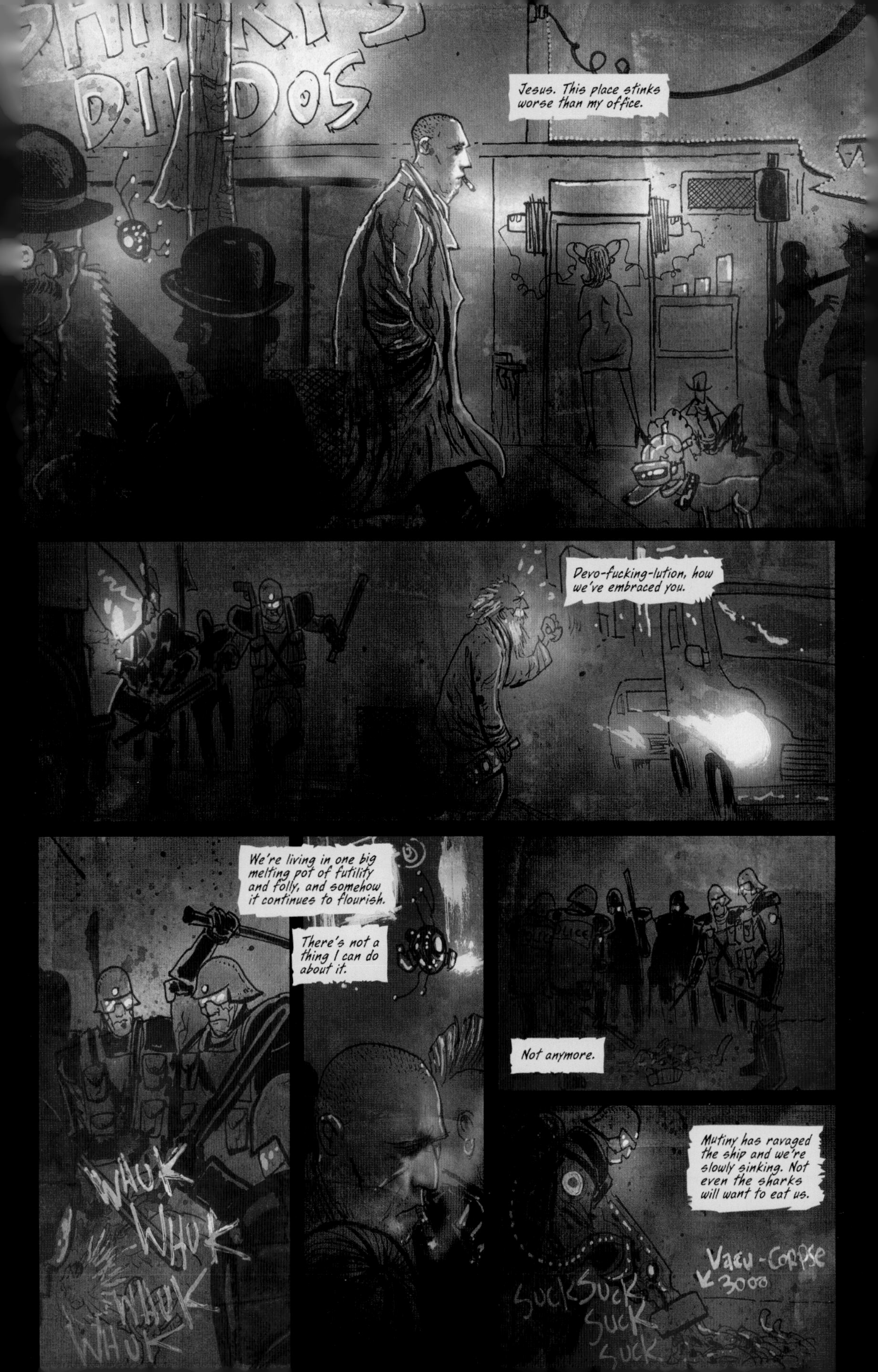
Jesus. This place stinks worse than my office.
Devo-fucking-lution, how we've embraced you.
We're living in one big melting pot of futility and folly, and somehow it continues to flourish.
There's not a thing I can do about it.
WHUK
WHUK
WHUK
WHUK
Not anymore.
Mutiny has ravaged the ship and we're slowly sinking. Not even the sharks will want to eat us.
Vacu-Corpse 3000
SUCK SUCK
SUCK
SUCK

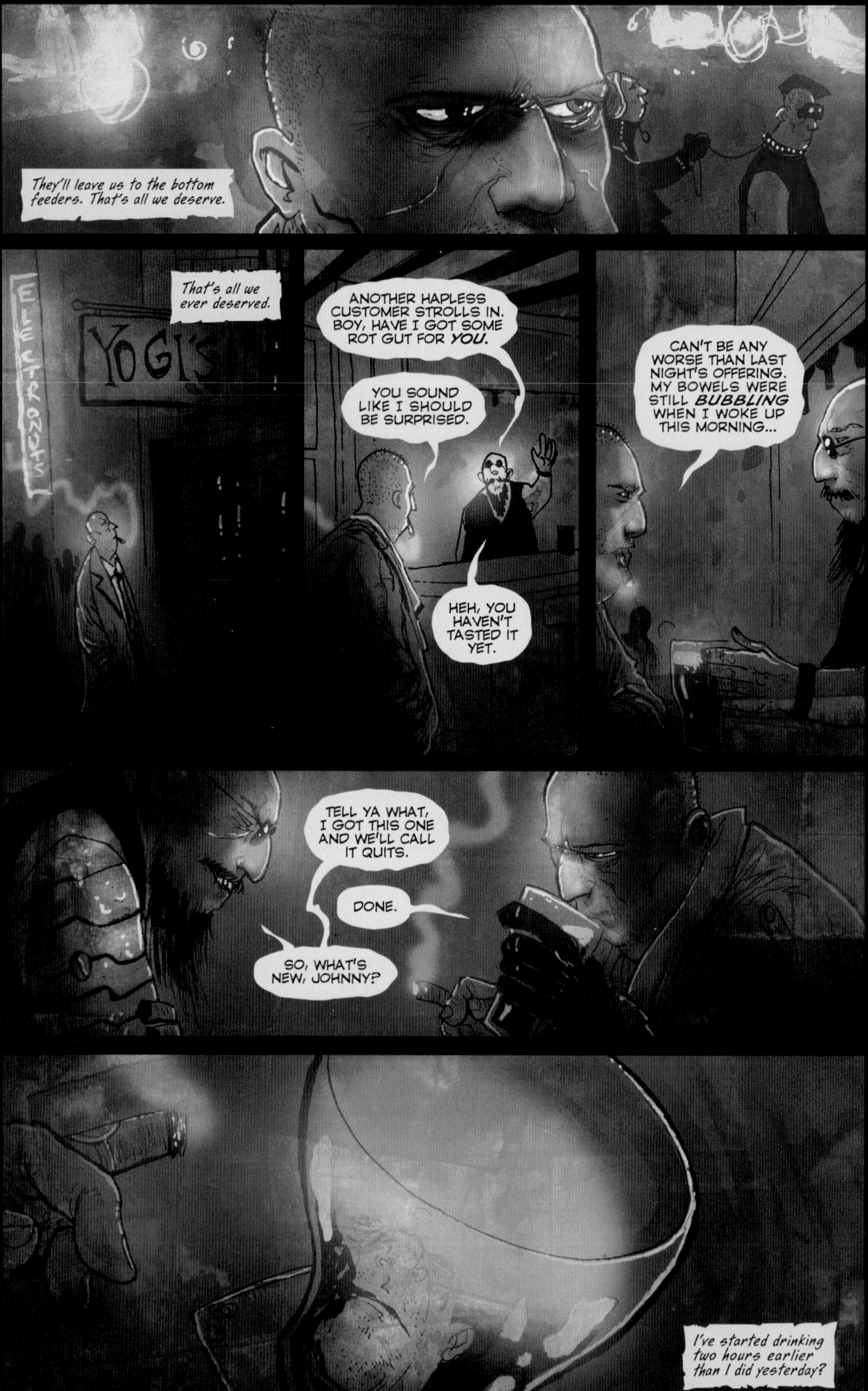
They'll leave us to the bottom feeders. That's all we deserve.
That's all we ever deserved.
YOGI'S
ELECTRONICS
ANOTHER HAPLESS CUSTOMER STROLLS IN. BOY, HAVE I GOT SOME ROT GUT FOR *YOU*.
YOU SOUND LIKE I SHOULD BE SURPRISED.
HEH, YOU HAVEN'T TASTED IT YET.
CAN'T BE ANY WORSE THAN LAST NIGHT'S OFFERING. MY BOWELS WERE STILL *BUBBLING* WHEN I WOKE UP THIS MORNING...
TELL YA WHAT, I GOT THIS ONE AND WE'LL CALL IT QUITS.
DONE.
SO, WHAT'S NEW, JOHNNY?
I've started drinking two hours earlier than I did yesterday?

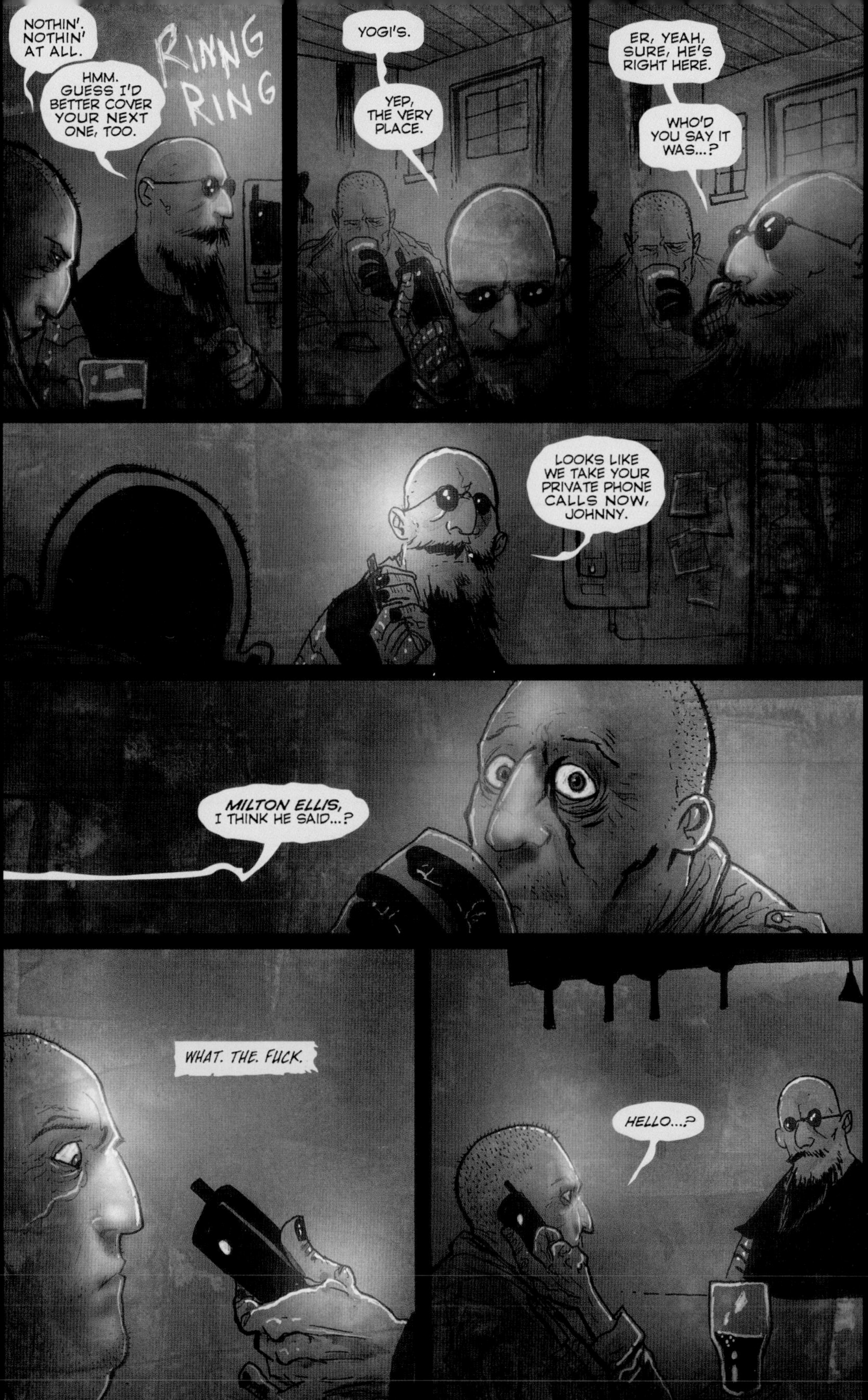
NOTHIN'. NOTHIN' AT ALL.
HMM. GUESS I'D BETTER COVER YOUR NEXT ONE, TOO.
RINNG RING
YOGI'S.
YEP, THE VERY PLACE.
ER, YEAH, SURE, HE'S RIGHT HERE.
WHO'D YOU SAY IT WAS...?
LOOKS LIKE WE TAKE YOUR PRIVATE PHONE CALLS NOW, JOHNNY.
MILTON ELLIS, I THINK HE SAID...?
WHAT. THE. FUCK.
HELLO...?

YOU'RE A TOUGH MAN TO GET HOLD OF, JOHNNY.
ESPECIALLY AS *YOU* DON'T RETURN PHONE CALLS.
CH-*CHIEF*...?
I'M SORRY, I WAS—
NO NEED TO APOLOGIZE. I KNEW WHERE TO FIND YOU. AND BESIDES, I'M SURE YOU'RE BEING KEPT AS *BUSY* AS CAN BE.
JACKSON INVESTIGATIONS MUST BE CLEANING UP IN THESE *CURIOUS TIMES*, RIGHT?
RIGHT.
ER, IS THERE SOMETHING—
—YOU CAN DO FOR ME? *PERHAPS* SO, JOHNNY.
AND IN RETURN, THERE ARE SEVERAL THINGS *I* CAN DO FOR YOU.

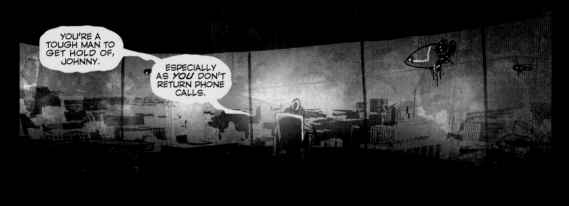

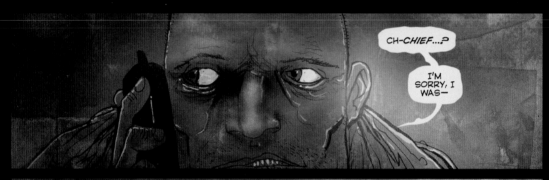

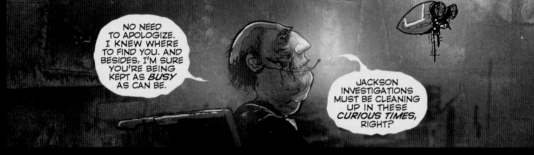

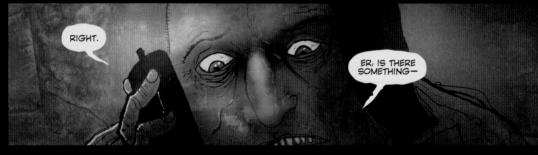

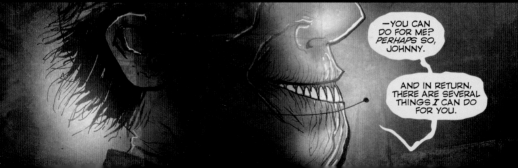

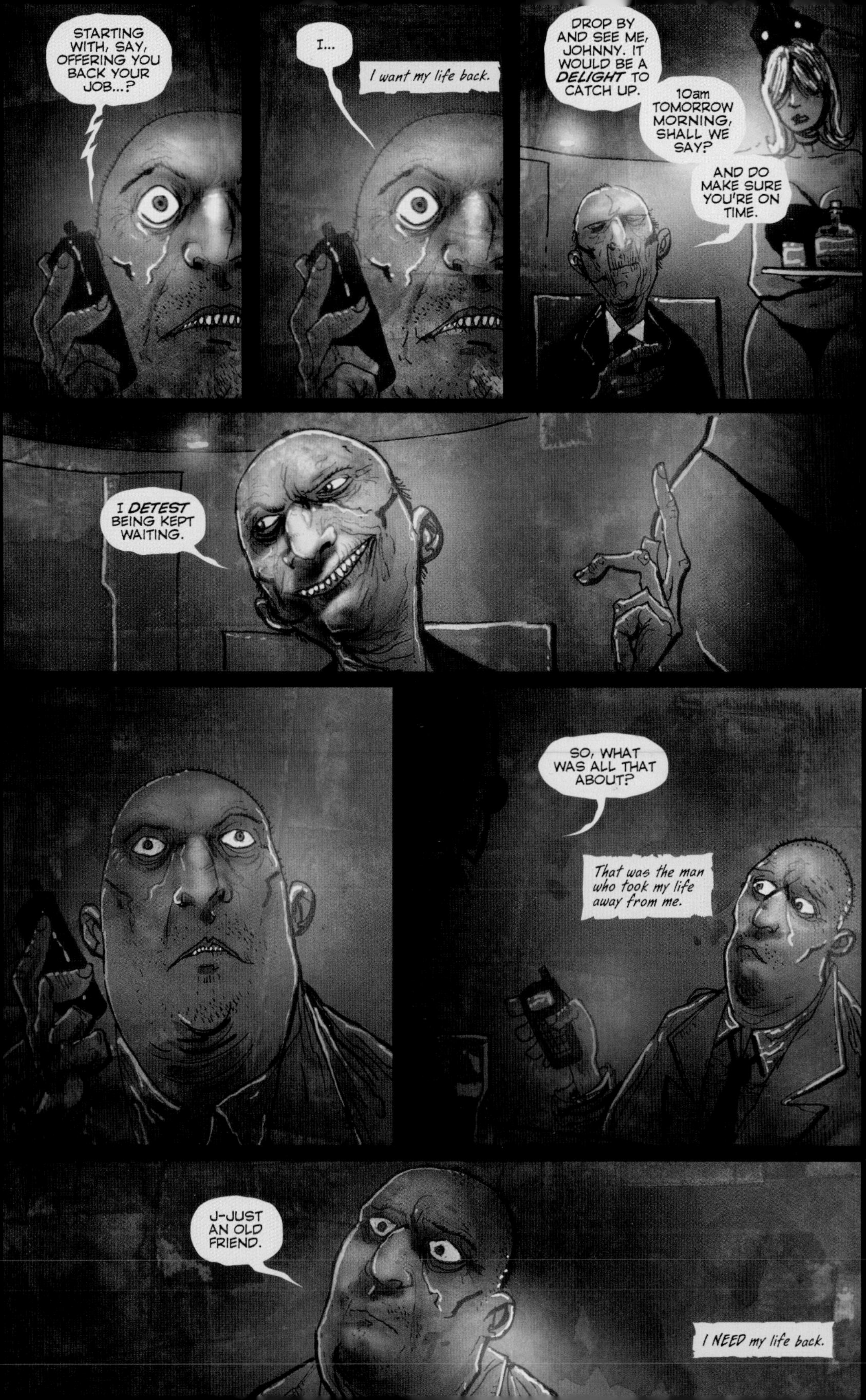
STARTING WITH, SAY, OFFERING YOU BACK YOUR JOB...?
I...
I want my life back.
DROP BY AND SEE ME, JOHNNY. IT WOULD BE A DELIGHT TO CATCH UP.
10am TOMORROW MORNING, SHALL WE SAY?
AND DO MAKE SURE YOU'RE ON TIME.
I DETEST BEING KEPT WAITING.
SO, WHAT WAS ALL THAT ABOUT?
That was the man who took my life away from me.
J-JUST AN OLD FRIEND.
I NEED my life back.

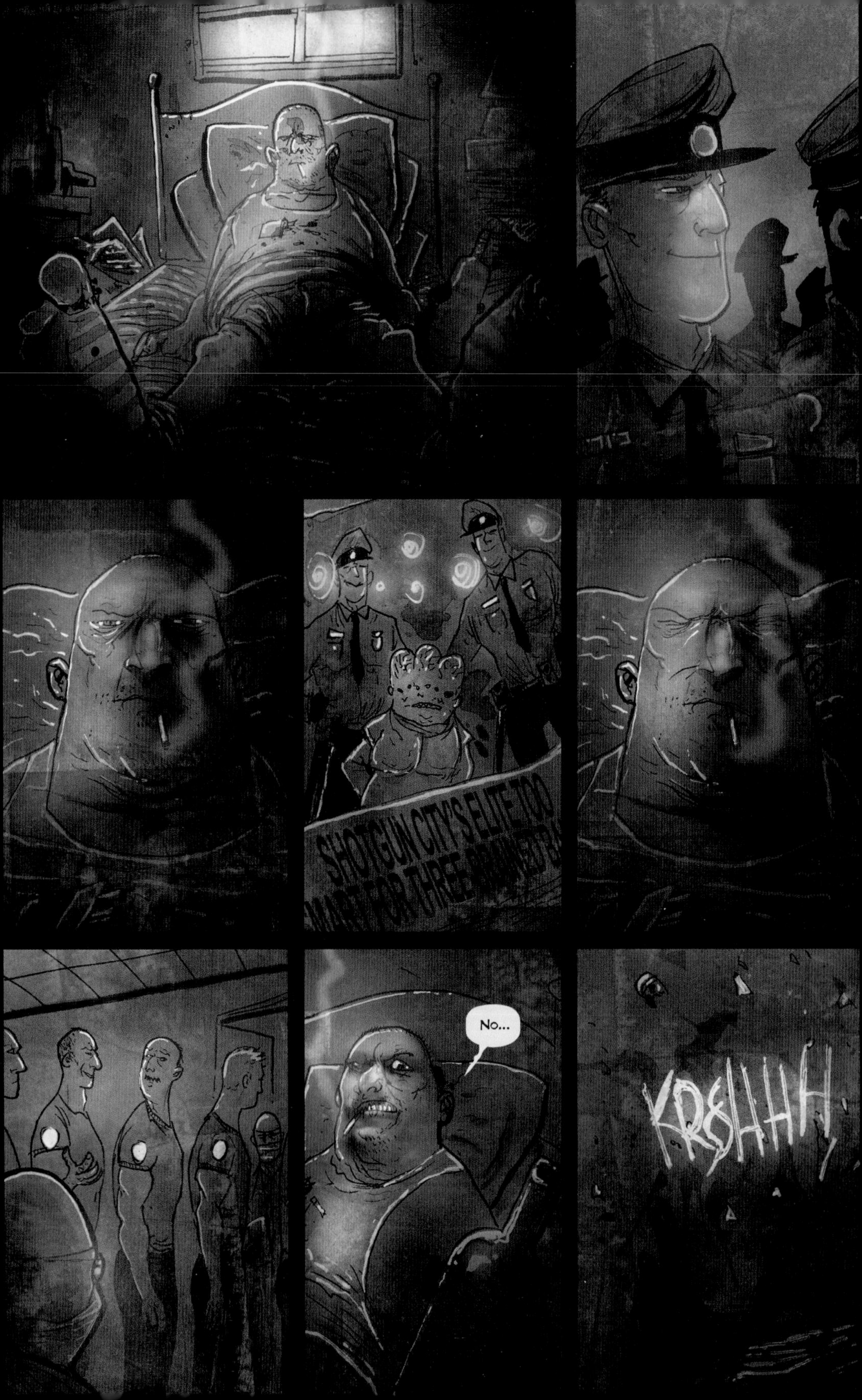
SHOTGUN CITY'S ELITE TOO
MART FOR THREE-BRAINED B
No...
KRSHHH

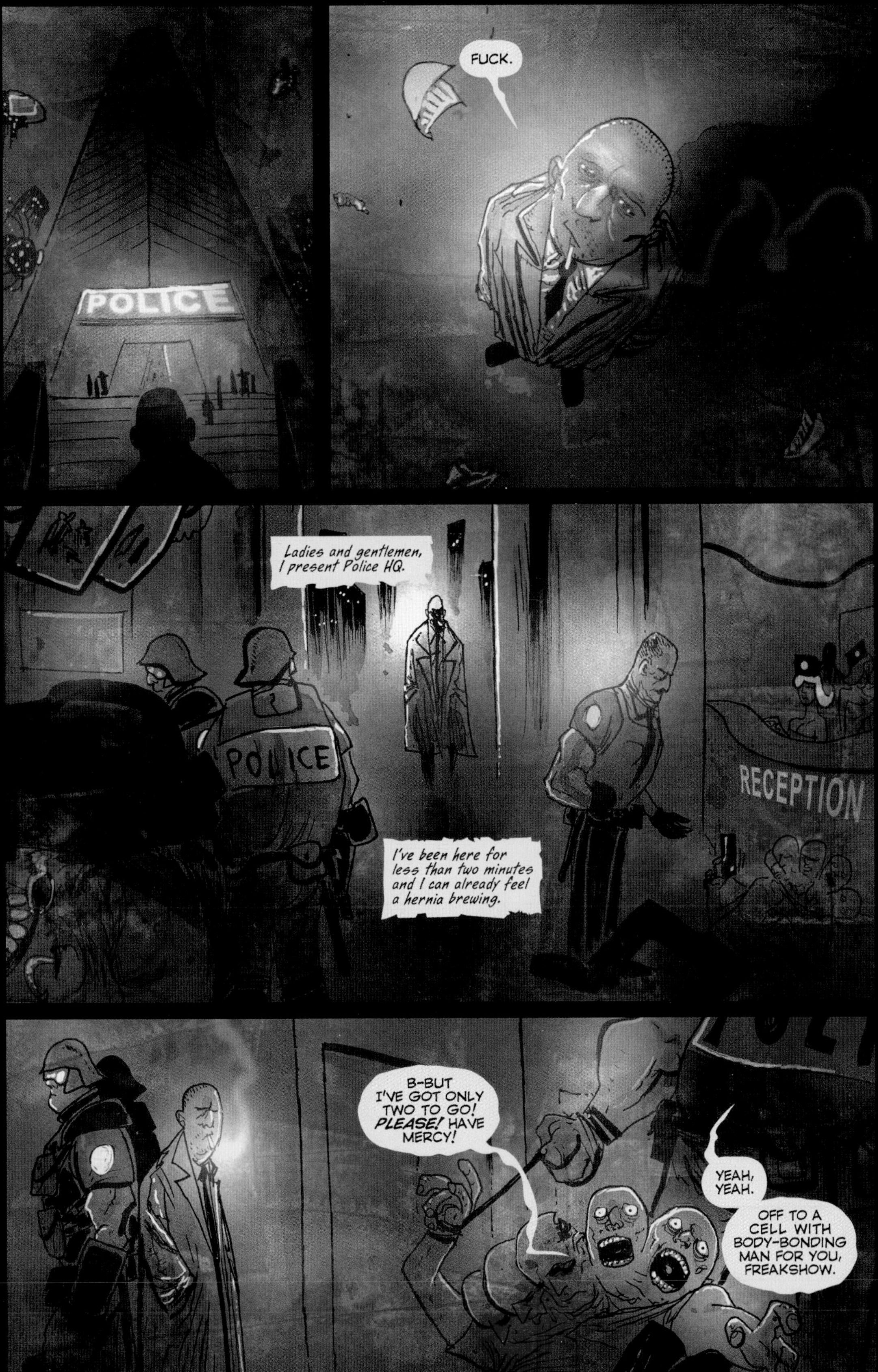
POLICE
FUCK.
Ladies and gentlemen, I present Police HQ.
POLICE
RECEPTION
I've been here for less than two minutes and I can already feel a hernia brewing.
B-BUT I'VE GOT ONLY TWO TO GO! PLEASE! HAVE MERCY!
YEAH, YEAH.
OFF TO A CELL WITH BODY-BONDING MAN FOR YOU, FREAKSHOW.

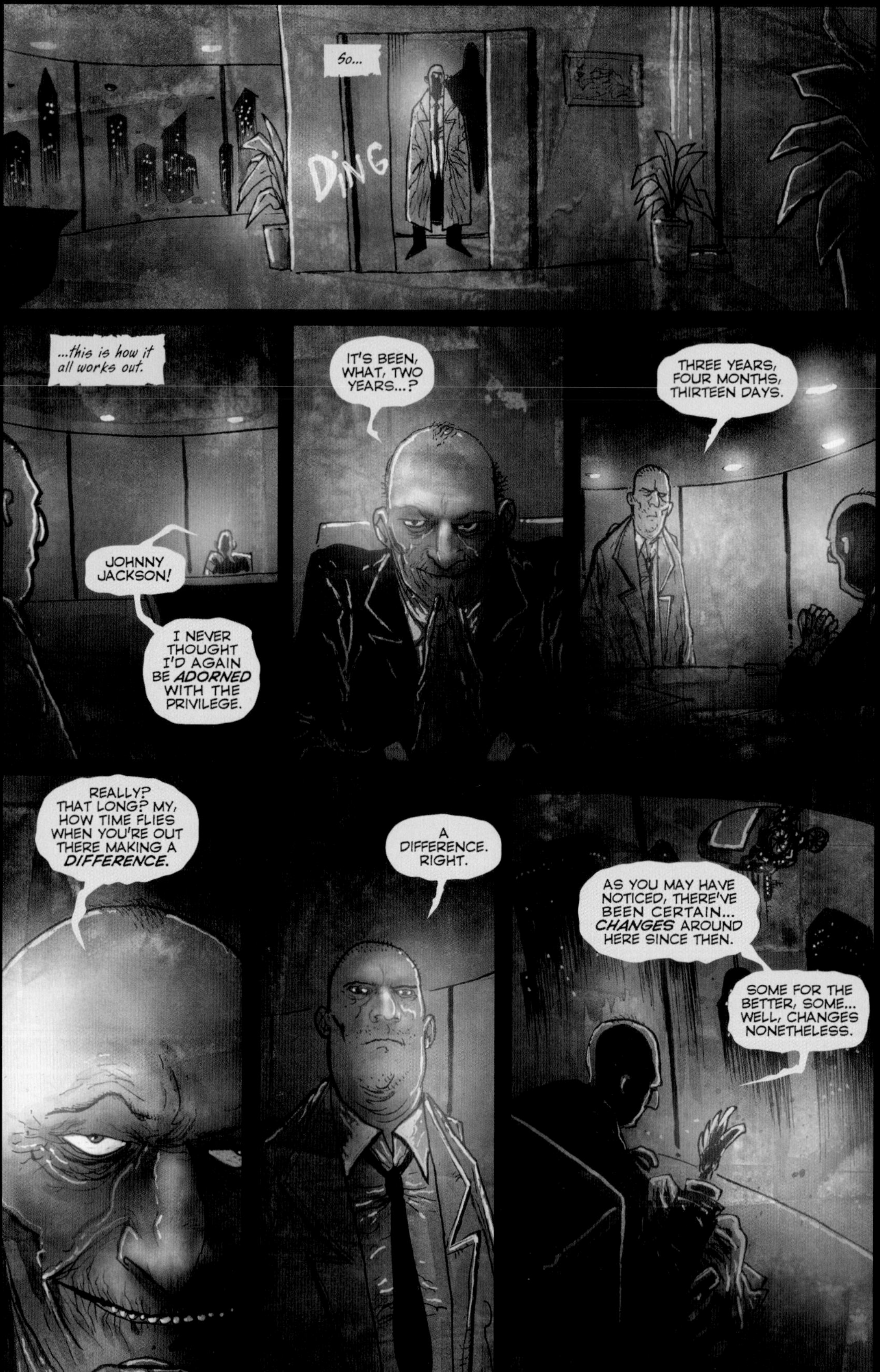
So...
DING
...this is how it all works out.
JOHNNY JACKSON!
I NEVER THOUGHT I'D AGAIN BE *ADORNED* WITH THE PRIVILEGE.
IT'S BEEN, WHAT, TWO YEARS...?
THREE YEARS, FOUR MONTHS, THIRTEEN DAYS.
REALLY? THAT LONG? MY, HOW TIME FLIES WHEN YOU'RE OUT THERE MAKING A *DIFFERENCE*.
A DIFFERENCE. RIGHT.
AS YOU MAY HAVE NOTICED, THERE'VE BEEN CERTAIN... *CHANGES* AROUND HERE SINCE THEN.
SOME FOR THE BETTER, SOME... WELL, CHANGES NONETHELESS.

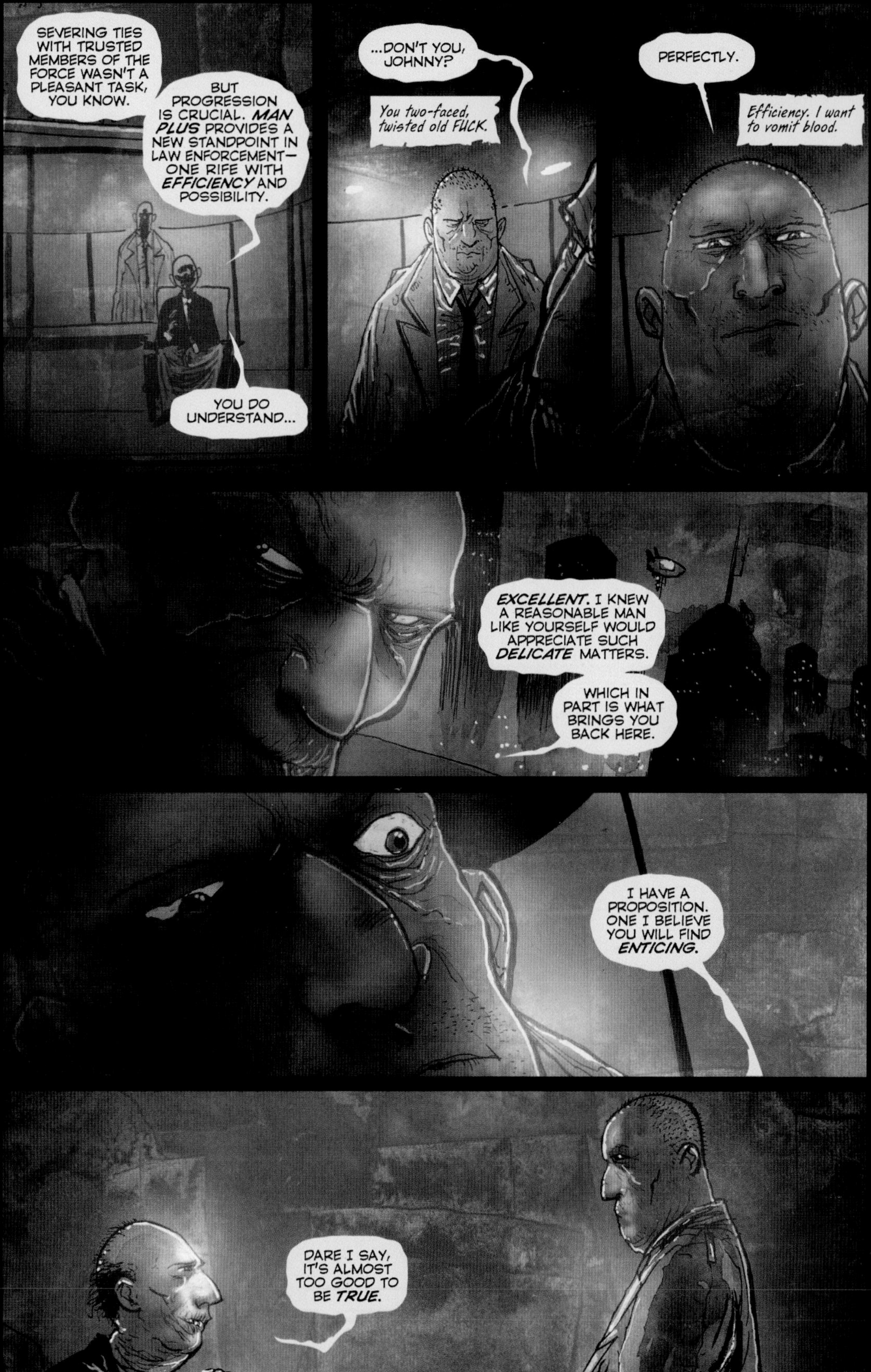
SEVERING TIES WITH TRUSTED MEMBERS OF THE FORCE WASN'T A PLEASANT TASK, YOU KNOW.
BUT PROGRESSION IS CRUCIAL. MAN PLUS PROVIDES A NEW STANDPOINT IN LAW ENFORCEMENT— ONE RIFE WITH EFFICIENCY AND POSSIBILITY.
YOU DO UNDERSTAND...
...DON'T YOU, JOHNNY?
You two-faced, twisted old FUCK.
PERFECTLY.
Efficiency. I want to vomit blood.
EXCELLENT. I KNEW A REASONABLE MAN LIKE YOURSELF WOULD APPRECIATE SUCH DELICATE MATTERS.
WHICH IN PART IS WHAT BRINGS YOU BACK HERE.
I HAVE A PROPOSITION. ONE I BELIEVE YOU WILL FIND ENTICING.
DARE I SAY, IT'S ALMOST TOO GOOD TO BE TRUE.

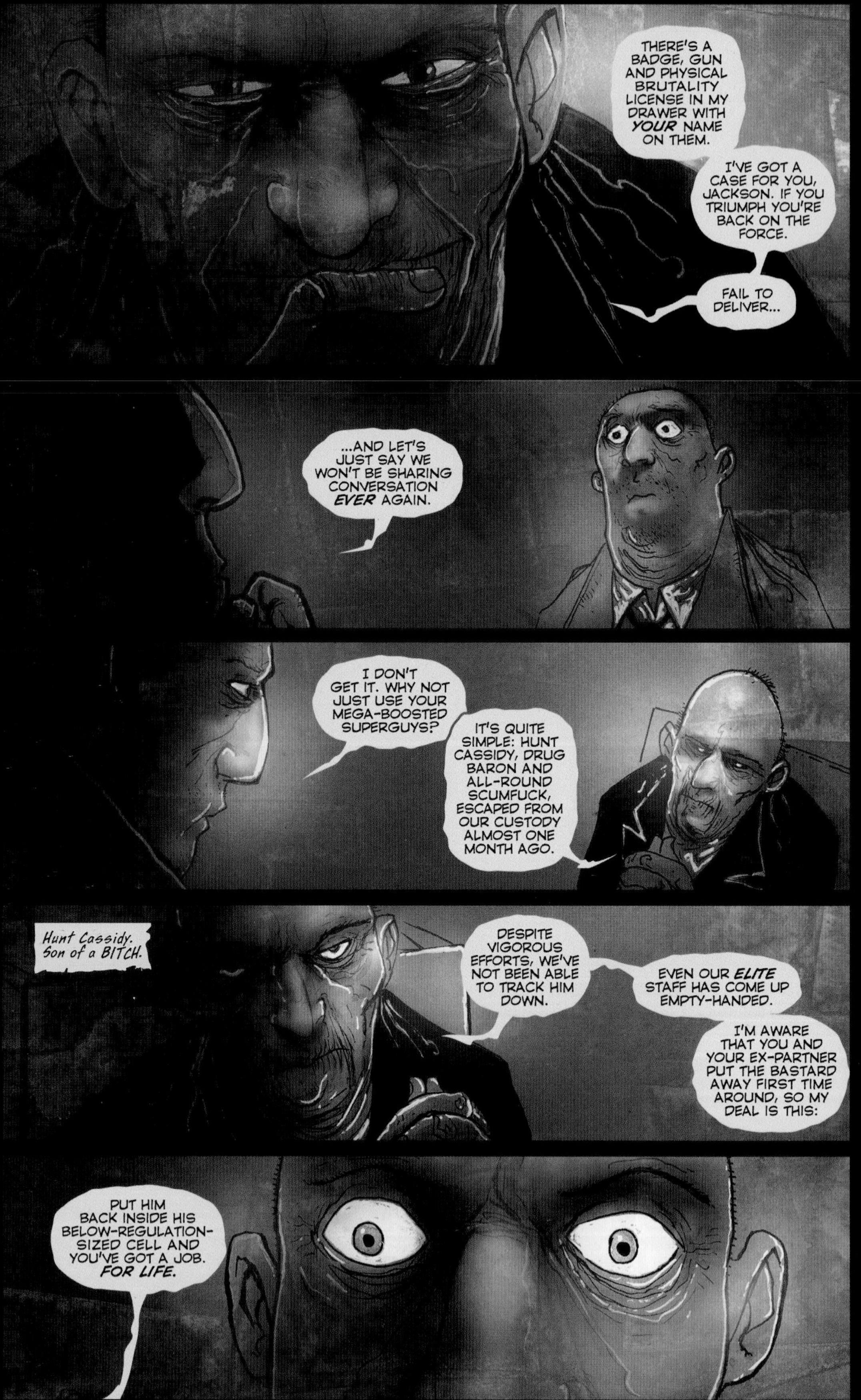

THERE'S A BADGE, GUN AND PHYSICAL BRUTALITY LICENSE IN MY DRAWER WITH *YOUR* NAME ON THEM.
I'VE GOT A CASE FOR YOU, JACKSON. IF YOU TRIUMPH YOU'RE BACK ON THE FORCE.
FAIL TO DELIVER...
...AND LET'S JUST SAY WE WON'T BE SHARING CONVERSATION *EVER* AGAIN.
I DON'T GET IT. WHY NOT JUST USE YOUR MEGA-BOOSTED SUPERGUYS?
IT'S QUITE SIMPLE: HUNT CASSIDY, DRUG BARON AND ALL-ROUND SCUMFUCK, ESCAPED FROM OUR CUSTODY ALMOST ONE MONTH AGO.
Hunt Cassidy. Son of a BITCH.
DESPITE VIGOROUS EFFORTS, WE'VE NOT BEEN ABLE TO TRACK HIM DOWN.
EVEN OUR *ELITE* STAFF HAS COME UP EMPTY-HANDED.
I'M AWARE THAT YOU AND YOUR EX-PARTNER PUT THE BASTARD AWAY FIRST TIME AROUND, SO MY DEAL IS THIS:
PUT HIM BACK INSIDE HIS BELOW-REGULATION-SIZED CELL AND YOU'VE GOT A JOB. *FOR LIFE.*

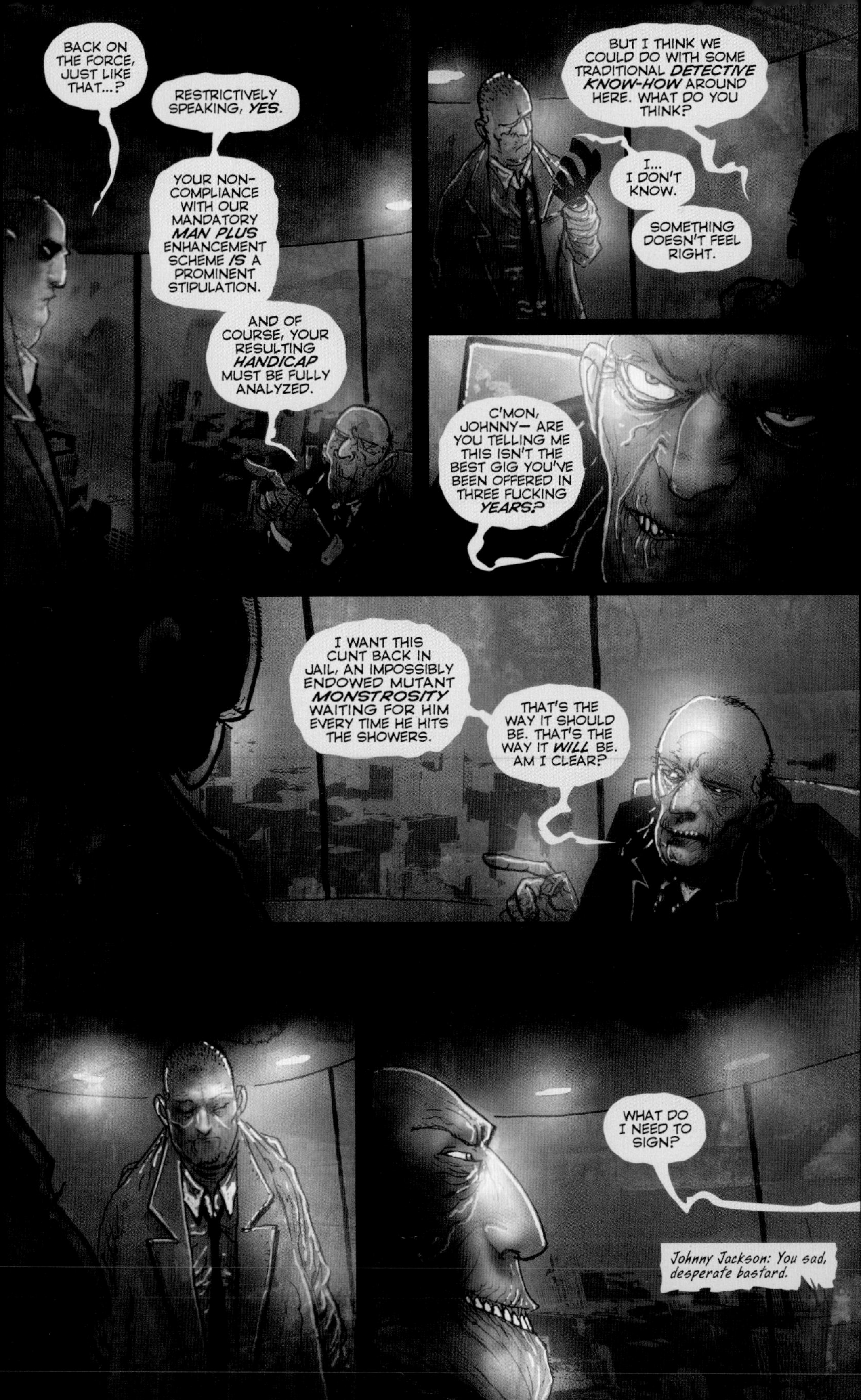
BACK ON THE FORCE, JUST LIKE THAT...?
RESTRICTIVELY SPEAKING, **YES**.
YOUR NON-COMPLIANCE WITH OUR MANDATORY **MAN PLUS** ENHANCEMENT SCHEME **IS** A PROMINENT STIPULATION.
AND OF COURSE, YOUR RESULTING **HANDICAP** MUST BE FULLY ANALYZED.
BUT I THINK WE COULD DO WITH SOME TRADITIONAL **DETECTIVE KNOW-HOW** AROUND HERE. WHAT DO YOU THINK?
I... I DON'T KNOW.
SOMETHING DOESN'T FEEL RIGHT.
C'MON, JOHNNY— ARE YOU TELLING ME THIS ISN'T THE BEST GIG YOU'VE BEEN OFFERED IN THREE FUCKING **YEARS?**
I WANT THIS CUNT BACK IN JAIL, AN IMPOSSIBLY ENDOWED MUTANT **MONSTROSITY** WAITING FOR HIM EVERY TIME HE HITS THE SHOWERS.
THAT'S THE WAY IT SHOULD BE. THAT'S THE WAY IT **WILL** BE. AM I CLEAR?
WHAT DO I NEED TO SIGN?
Johnny Jackson: You sad, desperate bastard.

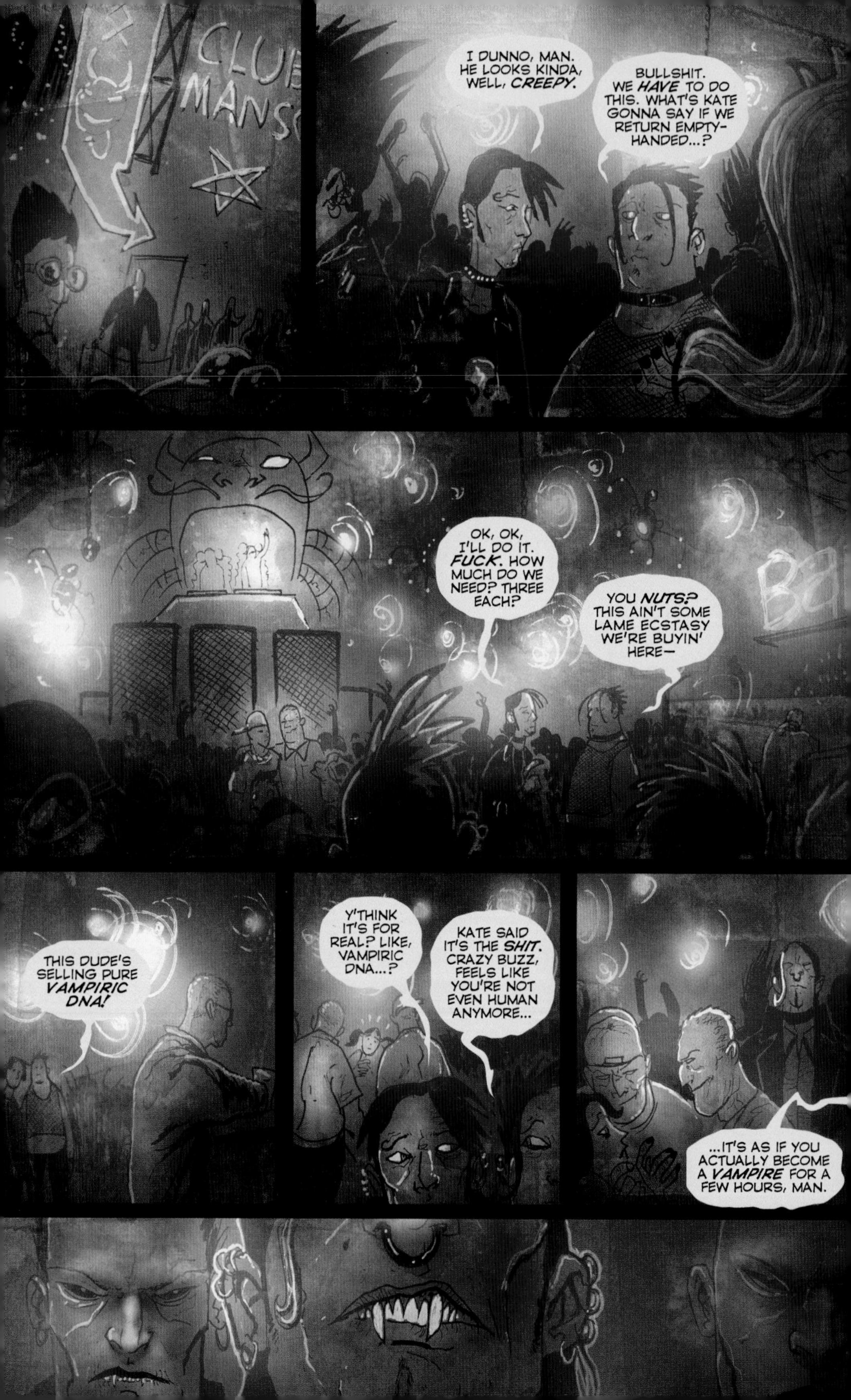
CLUB MANS
I DUNNO, MAN. HE LOOKS KINDA, WELL, *CREEPY*.
BULLSHIT. WE *HAVE* TO DO THIS. WHAT'S KATE GONNA SAY IF WE RETURN EMPTY-HANDED...?
OK, OK, I'LL DO IT. *FUCK*. HOW MUCH DO WE NEED? THREE EACH?
YOU *NUTS?* THIS AIN'T SOME LAME ECSTASY WE'RE BUYIN' HERE—
THIS DUDE'S SELLING PURE *VAMPIRIC DNA!*
Y'THINK IT'S FOR REAL? LIKE, VAMPIRIC DNA...?
KATE SAID IT'S THE *SHIT*. CRAZY BUZZ, FEELS LIKE YOU'RE NOT EVEN HUMAN ANYMORE...
...IT'S AS IF YOU ACTUALLY BECOME A *VAMPIRE* FOR A FEW HOURS, MAN.

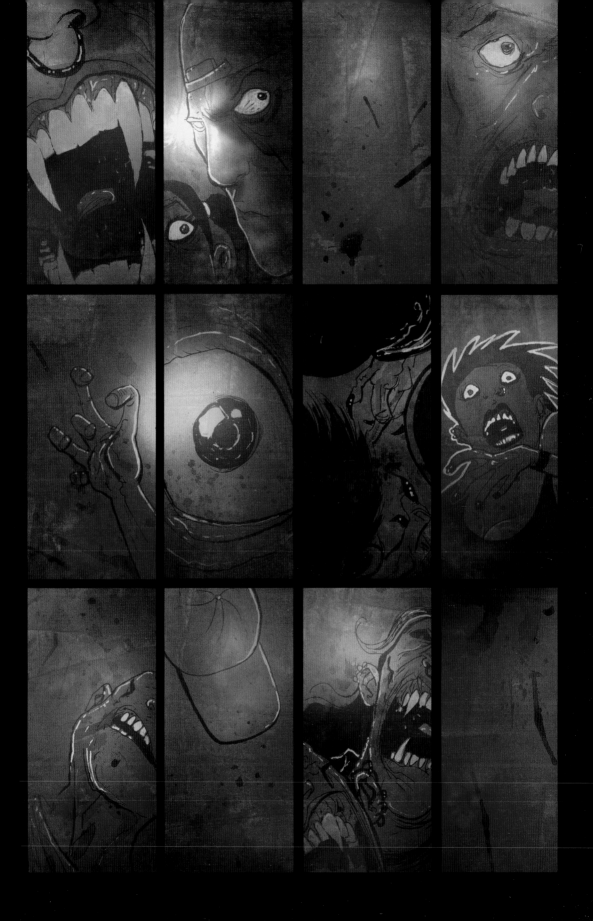

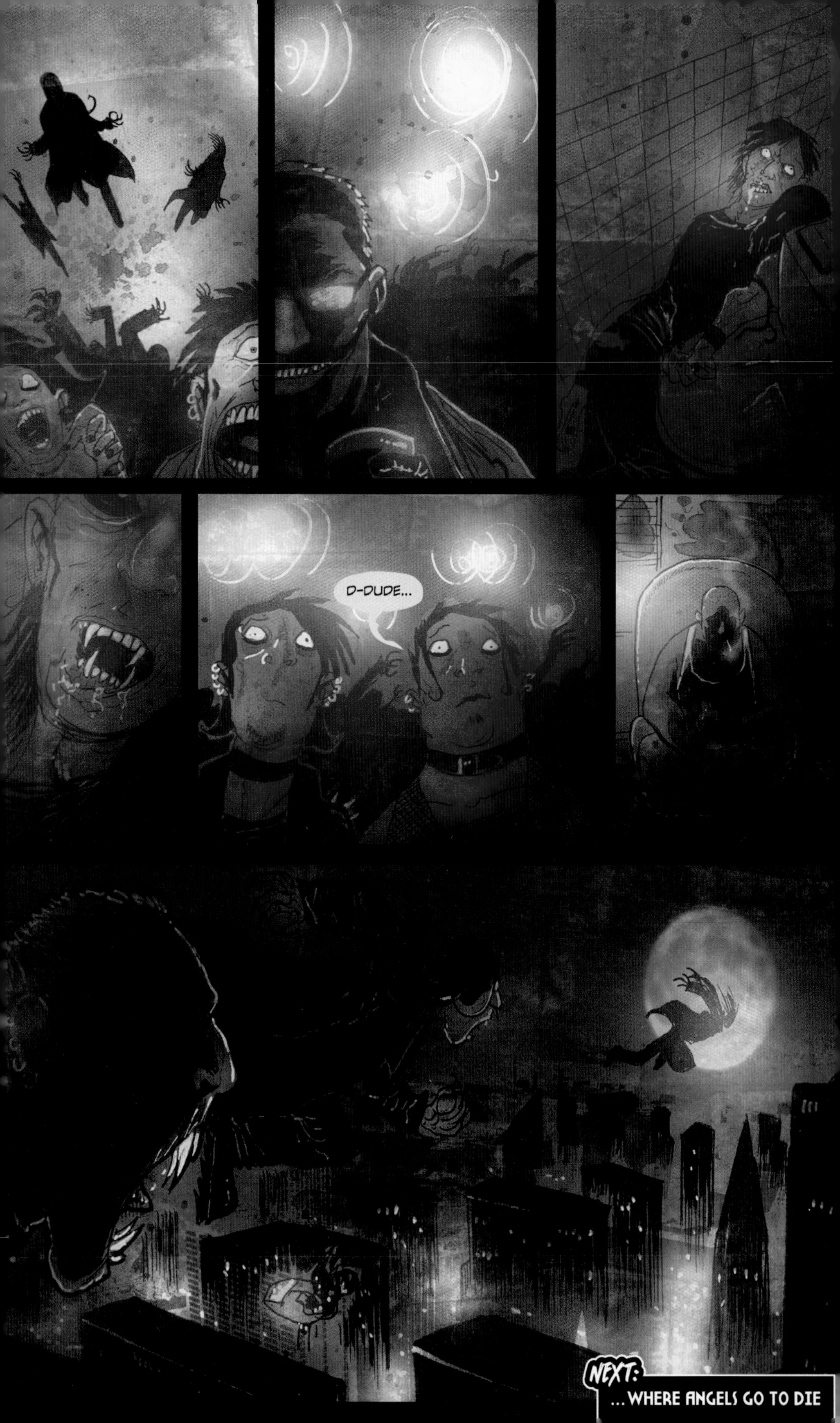
D-DUDE...
NEXT:
...WHERE ANGELS GO TO DIE

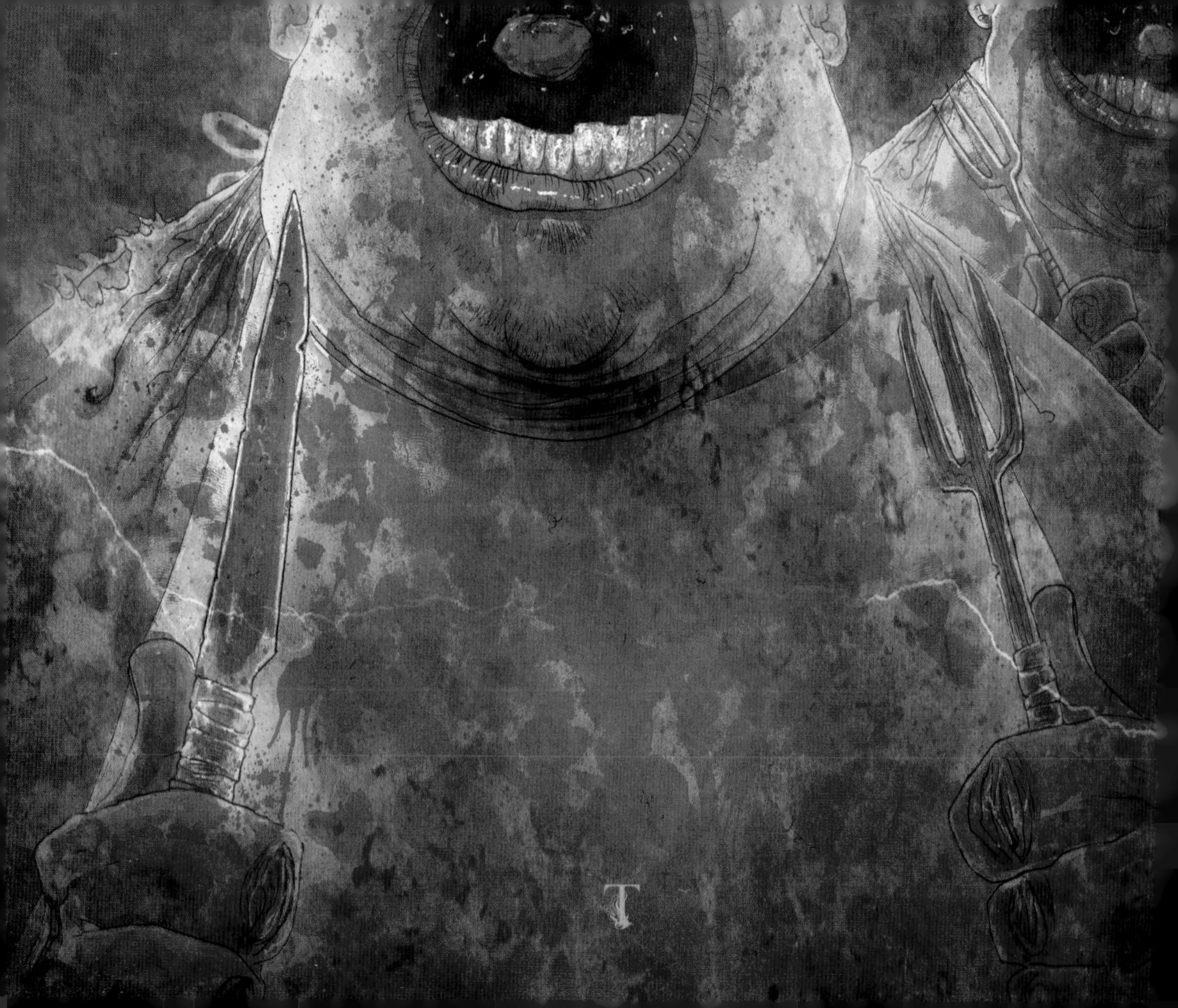

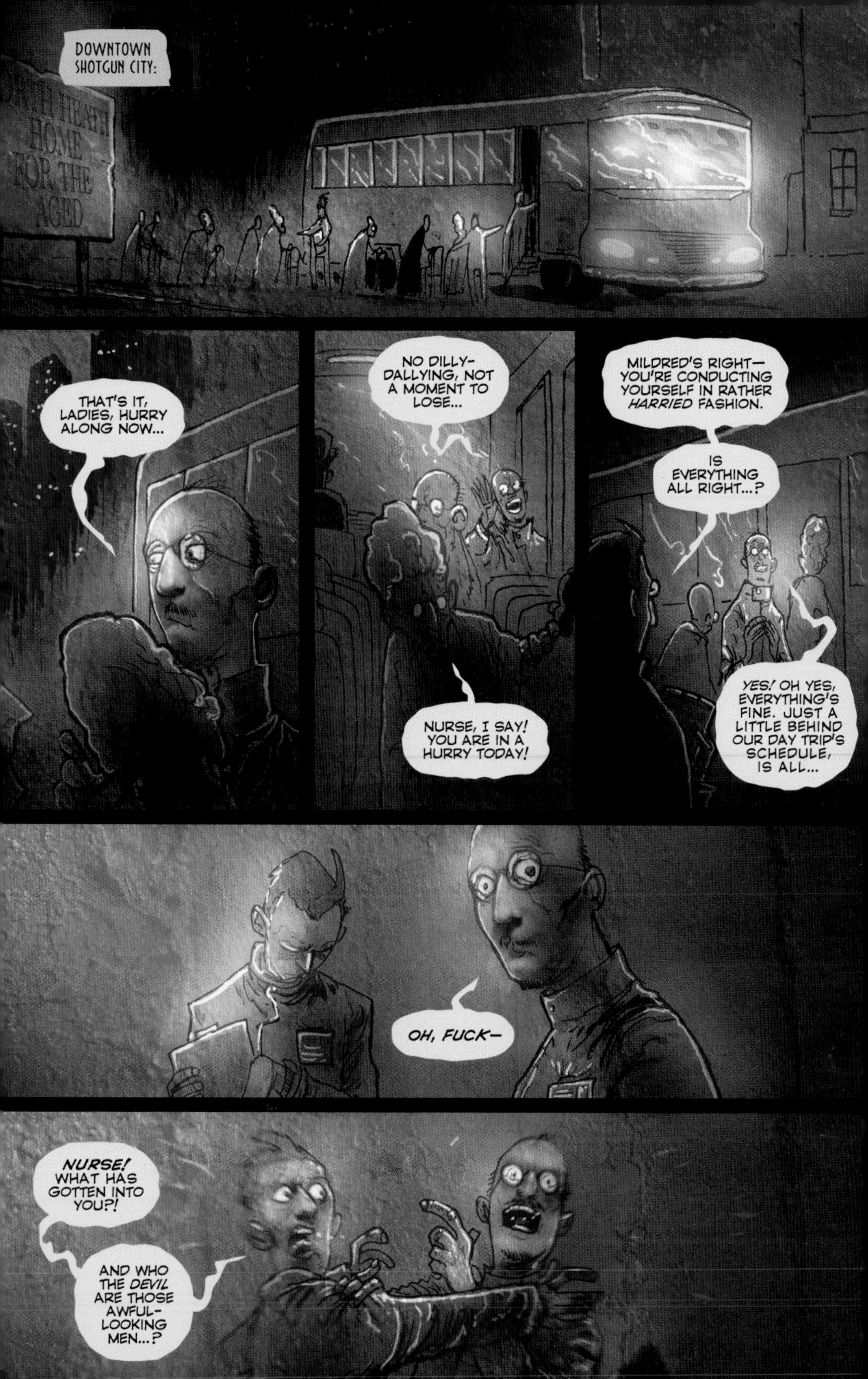
DOWNTOWN SHOTGUN CITY:
THAT'S IT, LADIES, HURRY ALONG NOW...
NO DILLY-DALLYING, NOT A MOMENT TO LOSE...
NURSE, I SAY! YOU ARE IN A HURRY TODAY!
MILDRED'S RIGHT—YOU'RE CONDUCTING YOURSELF IN RATHER *HARRIED* FASHION.
IS EVERYTHING ALL RIGHT...?
YES! OH YES, EVERYTHING'S FINE. JUST A LITTLE BEHIND OUR DAY TRIP'S SCHEDULE, IS ALL...
OH, FUCK—
NURSE! WHAT HAS GOTTEN INTO YOU?!
AND WHO THE *DEVIL* ARE THOSE AWFUL-LOOKING MEN...?

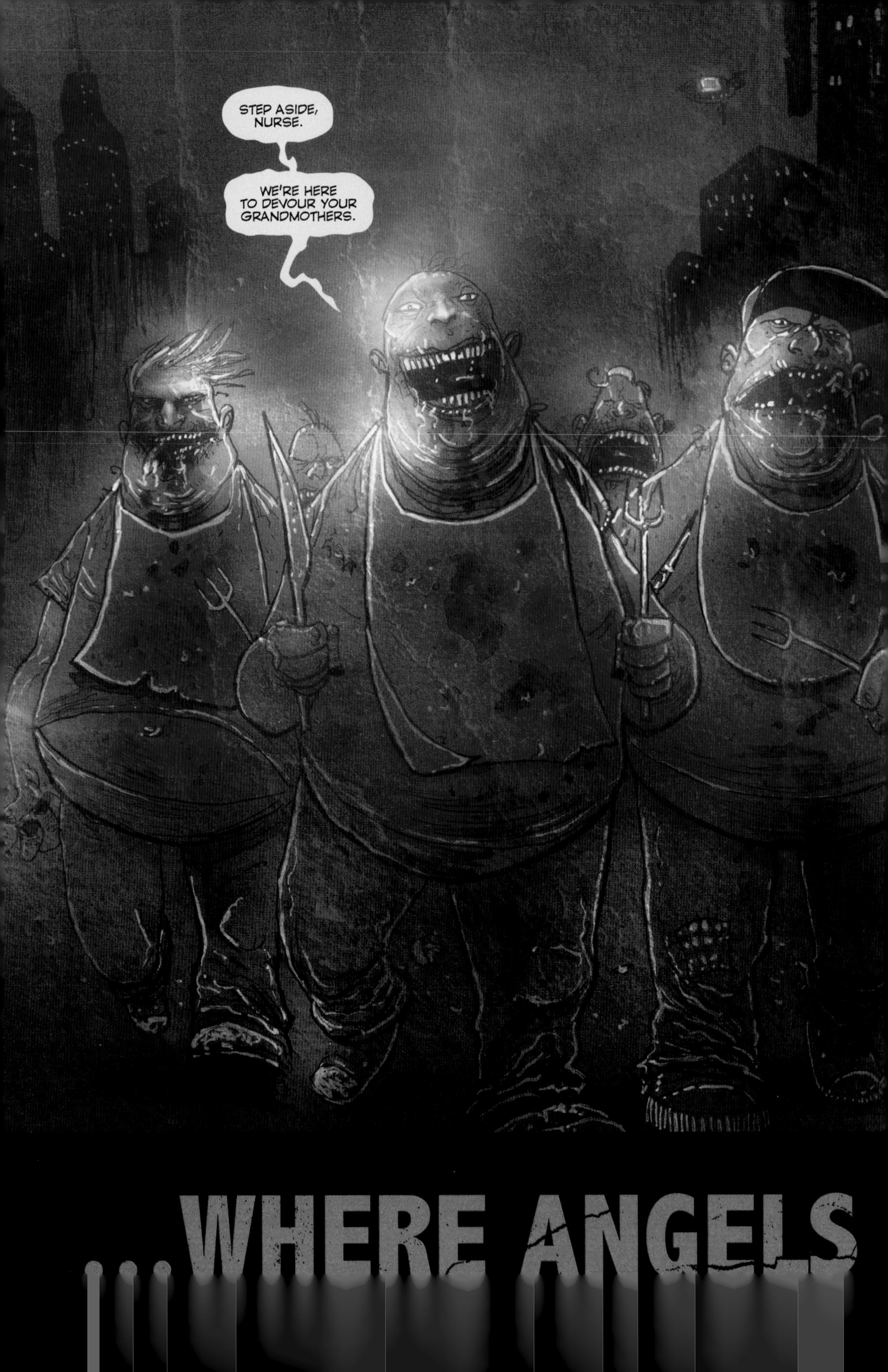
STEP ASIDE, NURSE.
WE'RE HERE TO DEVOUR YOUR GRANDMOTHERS.
...WHERE ANGELS

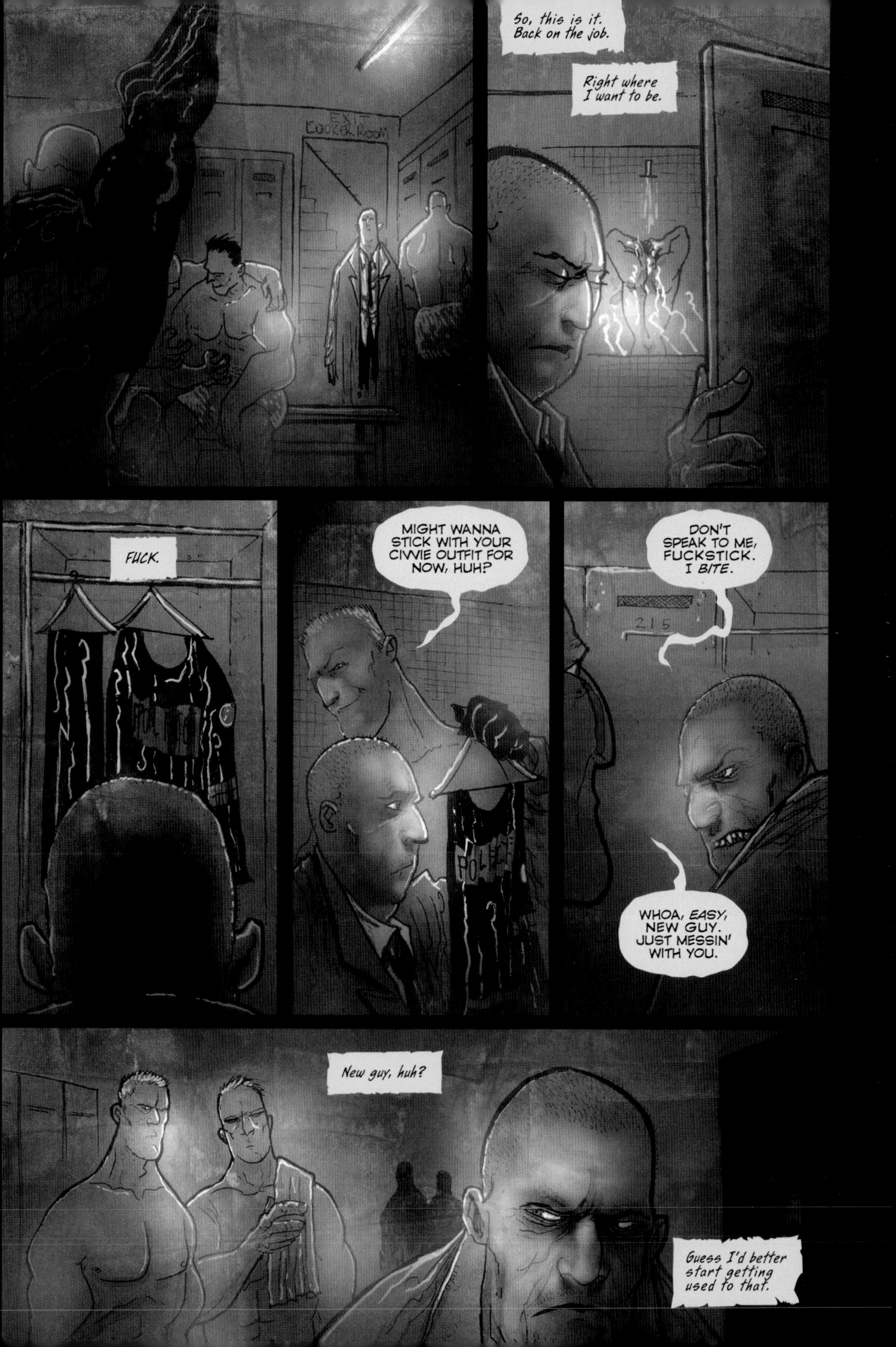
EXIT
LOCKER ROOM
So, this is it. Back on the job.
Right where I want to be.
FUCK.
MIGHT WANNA STICK WITH YOUR CIVVIE OUTFIT FOR NOW, HUH?
DON'T SPEAK TO ME, FUCKSTICK. I *BITE*.
215
WHOA, *EASY*, NEW GUY. JUST MESSIN' WITH YOU.
New guy, huh?
Guess I'd better start getting used to that.

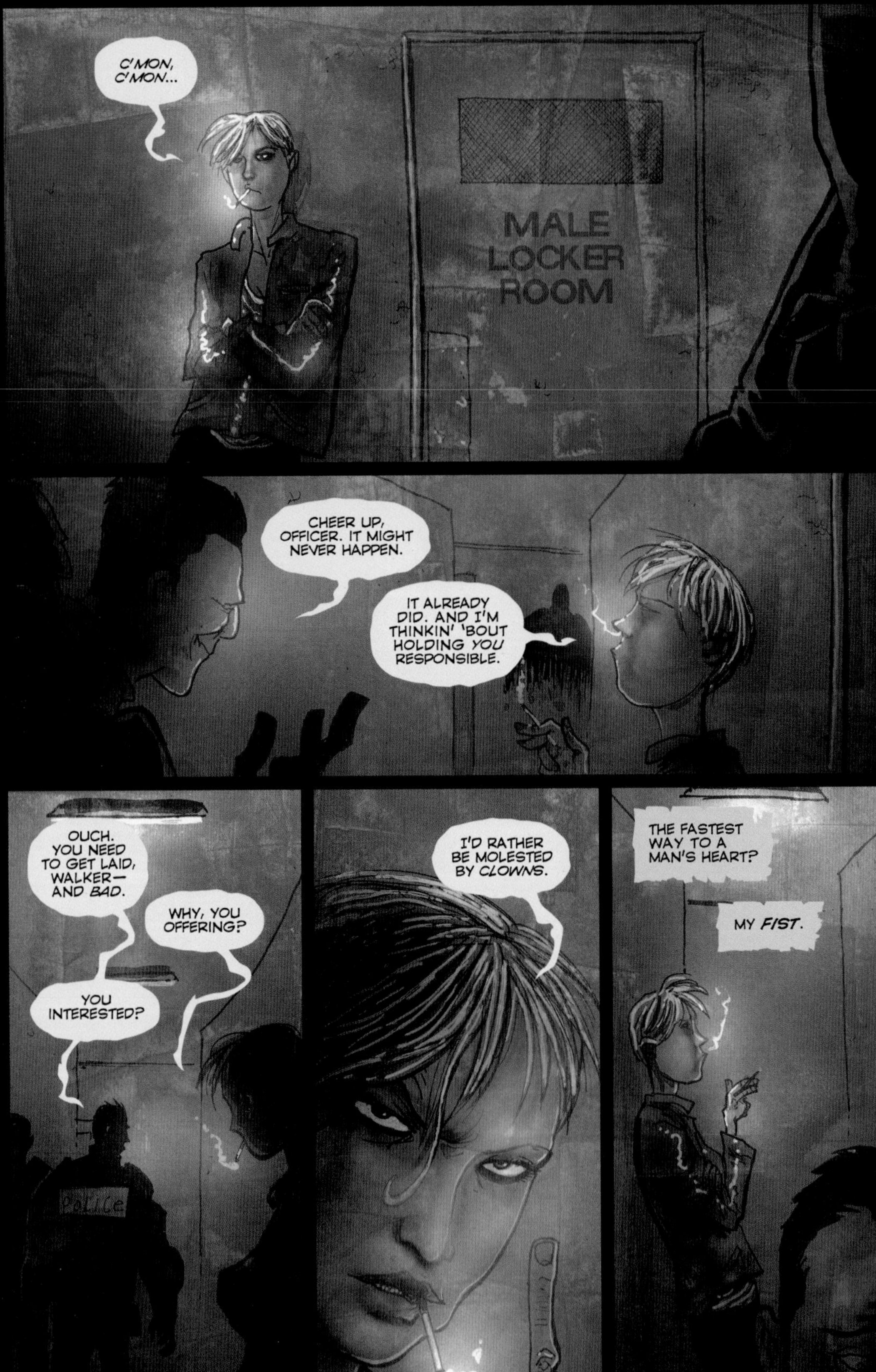

C'MON, C'MON...
MALE LOCKER ROOM
CHEER UP, OFFICER. IT MIGHT NEVER HAPPEN.
IT ALREADY DID. AND I'M THINKIN' 'BOUT HOLDING *YOU* RESPONSIBLE.
OUCH. YOU NEED TO GET LAID, WALKER— AND *BAD*.
WHY, YOU OFFERING?
YOU INTERESTED?
POLICE
I'D RATHER BE MOLESTED BY *CLOWNS*.
THE FASTEST WAY TO A MAN'S HEART?
MY *FIST*.

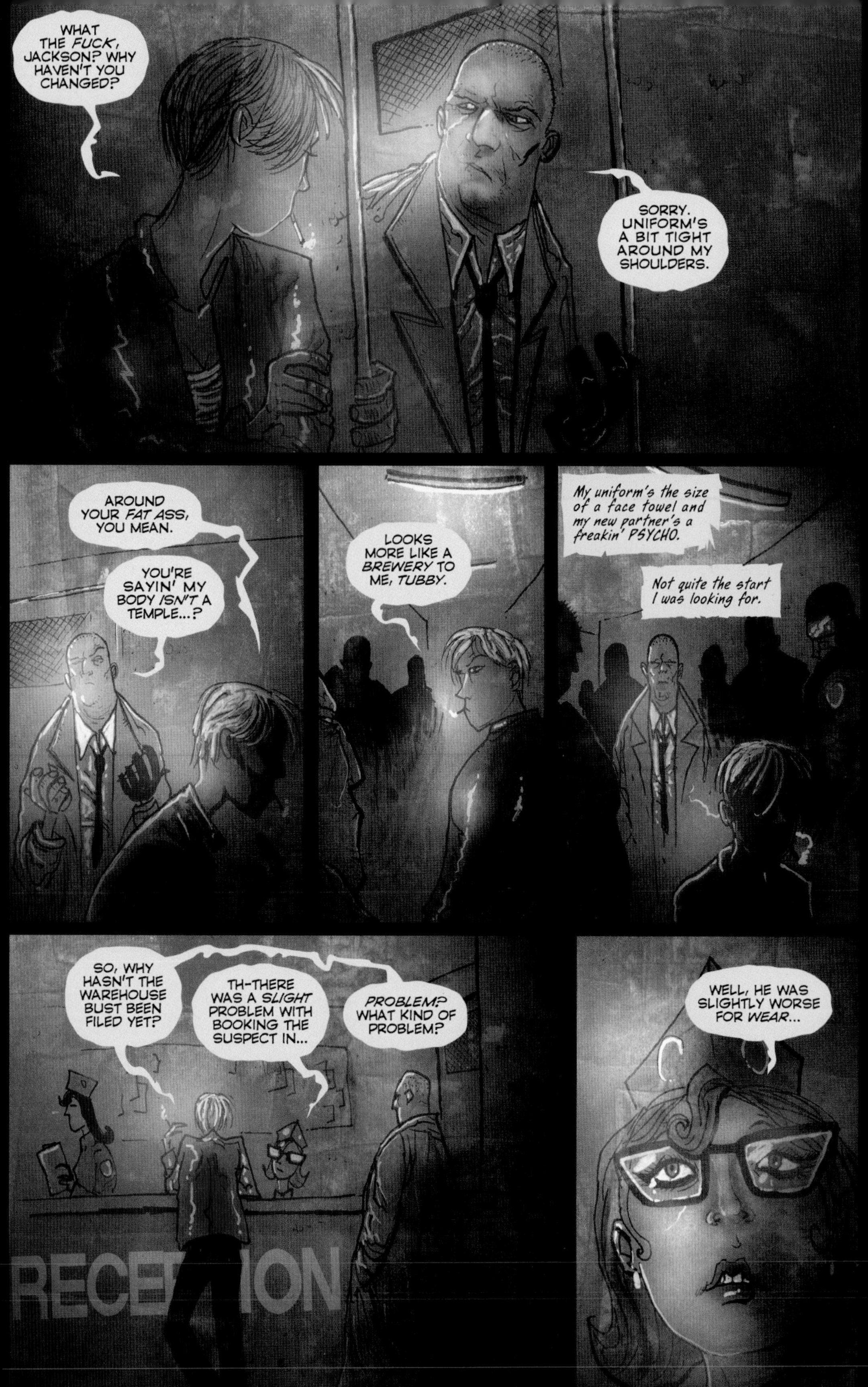
WHAT THE FUCK, JACKSON? WHY HAVEN'T YOU CHANGED?
SORRY. UNIFORM'S A BIT TIGHT AROUND MY SHOULDERS.
AROUND YOUR FAT ASS, YOU MEAN.
YOU'RE SAYIN' MY BODY ISN'T A TEMPLE...?
LOOKS MORE LIKE A BREWERY TO ME, TUBBY.
My uniform's the size of a face towel and my new partner's a freakin' PSYCHO.
Not quite the start I was looking for.
SO, WHY HASN'T THE WAREHOUSE BUST BEEN FILED YET?
TH-THERE WAS A SLIGHT PROBLEM WITH BOOKING THE SUSPECT IN...
PROBLEM? WHAT KIND OF PROBLEM?
RECEPTION
WELL, HE WAS SLIGHTLY WORSE FOR WEAR...

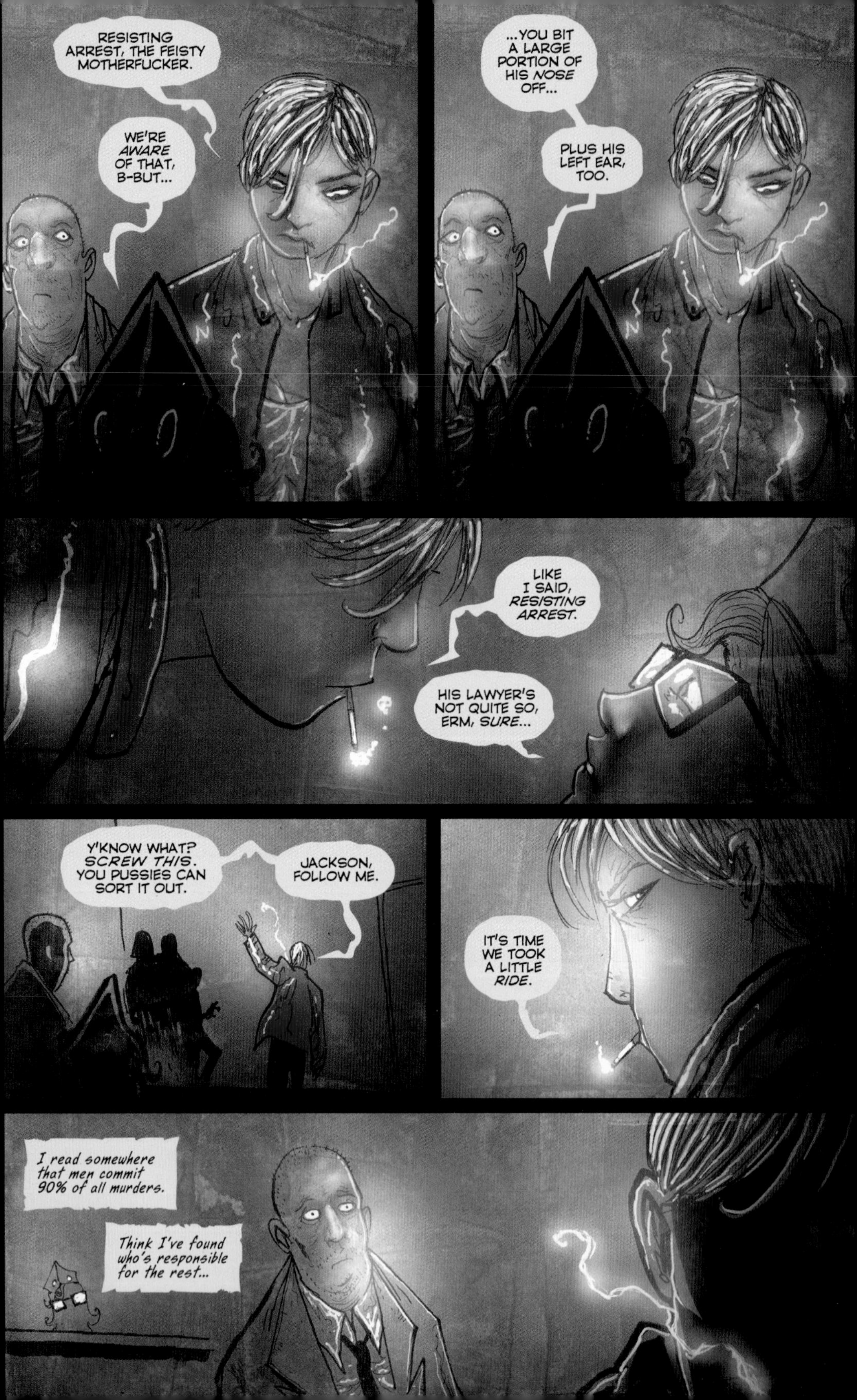
RESISTING ARREST, THE FEISTY MOTHERFUCKER.
WE'RE *AWARE* OF THAT, B-BUT...
...YOU BIT A LARGE PORTION OF HIS *NOSE* OFF...
PLUS HIS LEFT EAR, TOO.
LIKE I SAID, *RESISTING ARREST*.
HIS LAWYER'S NOT QUITE SO, ERM, *SURE*...
Y'KNOW WHAT? *SCREW THIS*. YOU PUSSIES CAN SORT IT OUT.
JACKSON, FOLLOW ME.
IT'S TIME WE TOOK A LITTLE *RIDE*.
I read somewhere that men commit 90% of all murders.
Think I've found who's responsible for the rest...

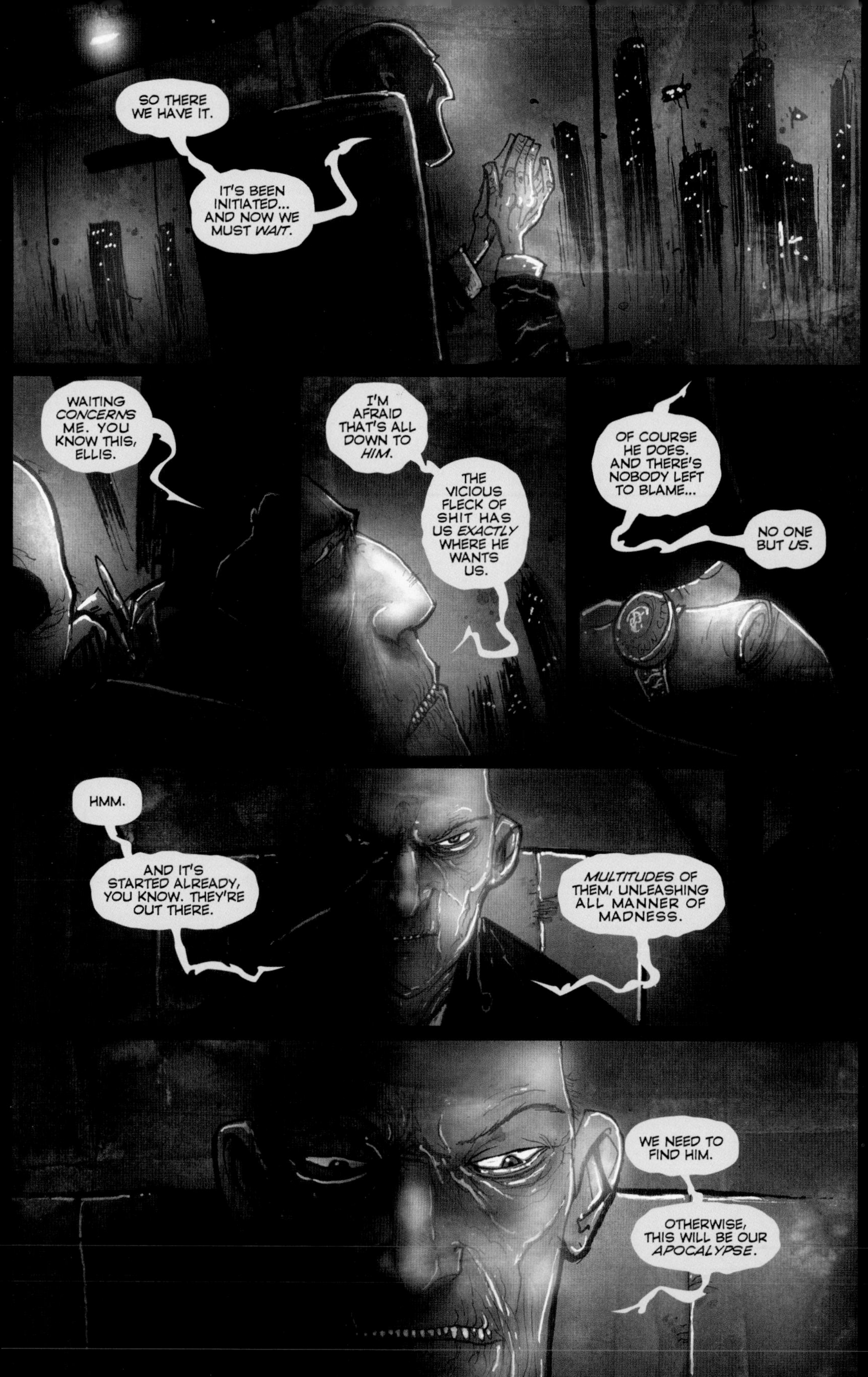
SO THERE WE HAVE IT.
IT'S BEEN INITIATED... AND NOW WE MUST *WAIT*.
WAITING *CONCERNS* ME. YOU KNOW THIS, ELLIS.
I'M AFRAID THAT'S ALL DOWN TO *HIM*.
THE VICIOUS FLECK OF SHIT HAS US *EXACTLY* WHERE HE WANTS US.
OF COURSE HE DOES. AND THERE'S NOBODY LEFT TO BLAME...
NO ONE BUT *US*.
HMM.
AND IT'S STARTED ALREADY, YOU KNOW. THEY'RE OUT THERE.
MULTITUDES OF THEM, UNLEASHING ALL MANNER OF MADNESS.
WE NEED TO FIND HIM.
OTHERWISE, THIS WILL BE OUR *APOCALYPSE*.

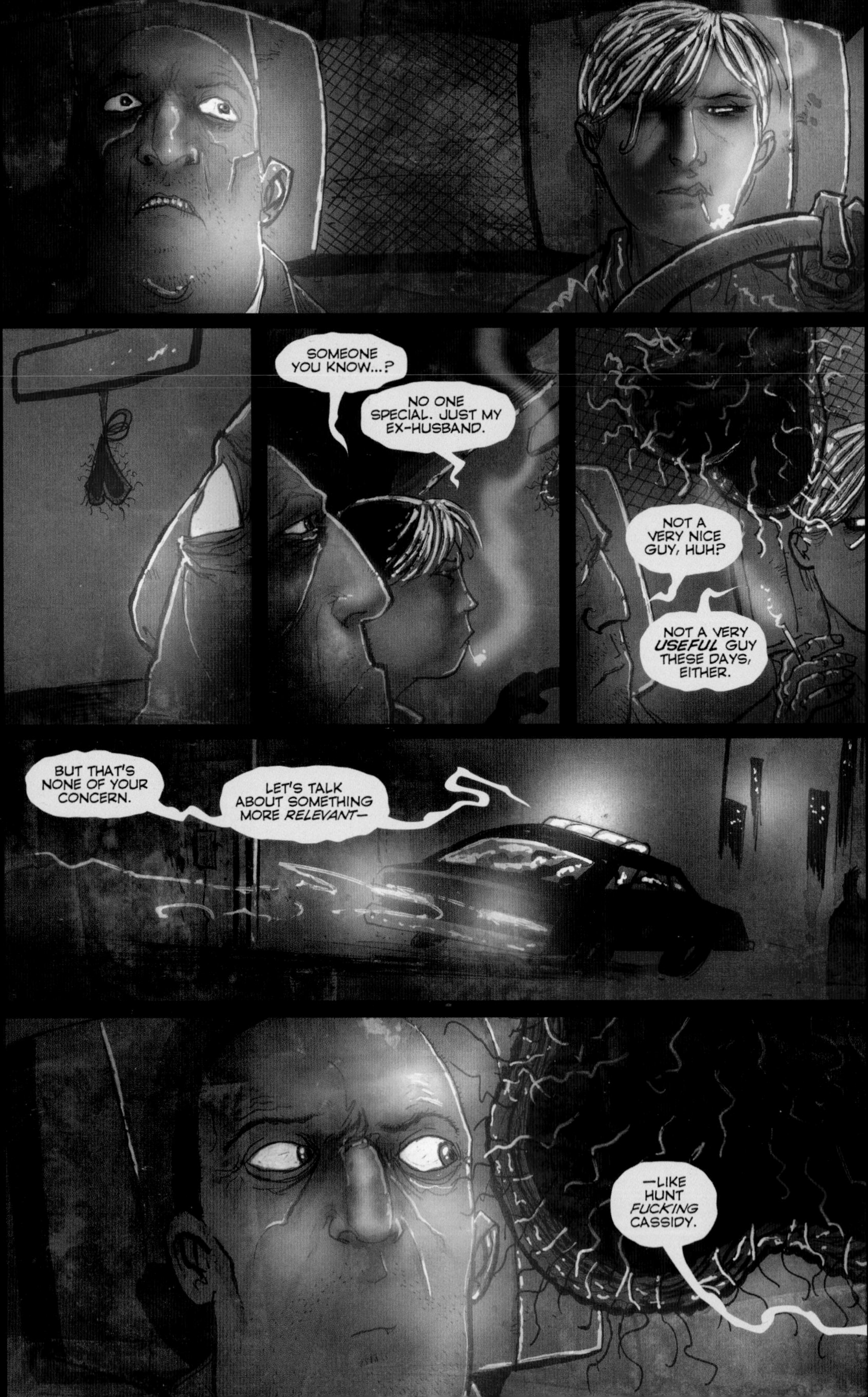
SOMEONE YOU KNOW...?
NO ONE SPECIAL. JUST MY EX-HUSBAND.
NOT A VERY NICE GUY, HUH?
NOT A VERY *USEFUL* GUY THESE DAYS, EITHER.
BUT THAT'S NONE OF YOUR CONCERN.
LET'S TALK ABOUT SOMETHING MORE *RELEVANT*—
—LIKE HUNT *FUCKING* CASSIDY.

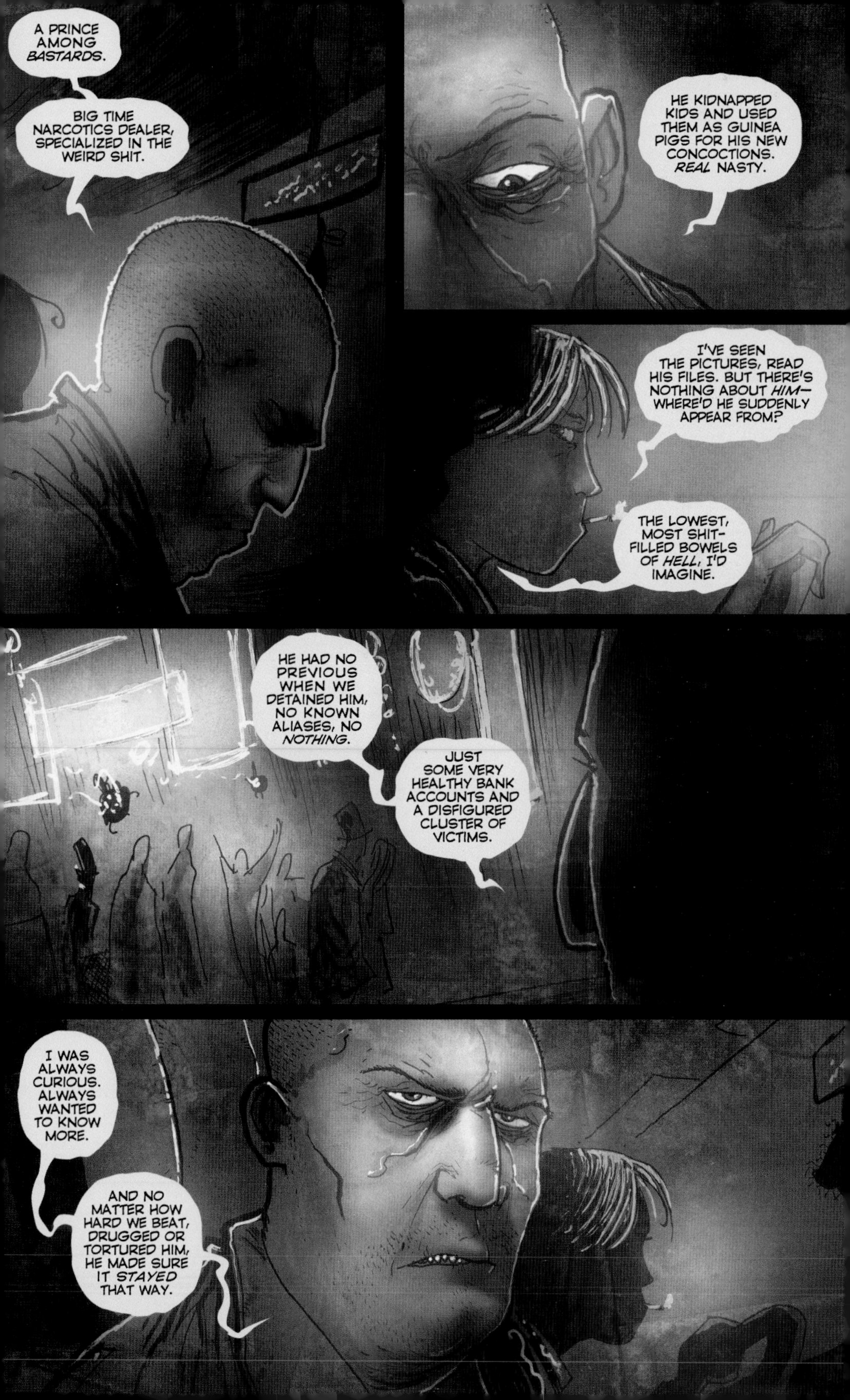
A PRINCE AMONG *BASTARDS*.
BIG TIME NARCOTICS DEALER, SPECIALIZED IN THE WEIRD SHIT.
HE KIDNAPPED KIDS AND USED THEM AS GUINEA PIGS FOR HIS NEW CONCOCTIONS. *REAL* NASTY.
I'VE SEEN THE PICTURES, READ HIS FILES. BUT THERE'S NOTHING ABOUT *HIM*— WHERE'D HE SUDDENLY APPEAR FROM?
THE LOWEST, MOST SHIT-FILLED BOWELS OF *HELL*, I'D IMAGINE.
HE HAD NO PREVIOUS WHEN WE DETAINED HIM, NO KNOWN ALIASES, NO *NOTHING*.
JUST SOME VERY HEALTHY BANK ACCOUNTS AND A DISFIGURED CLUSTER OF VICTIMS.
I WAS ALWAYS CURIOUS. ALWAYS WANTED TO KNOW MORE.
AND NO MATTER HOW HARD WE BEAT, DRUGGED OR TORTURED HIM, HE MADE SURE IT *STAYED* THAT WAY.

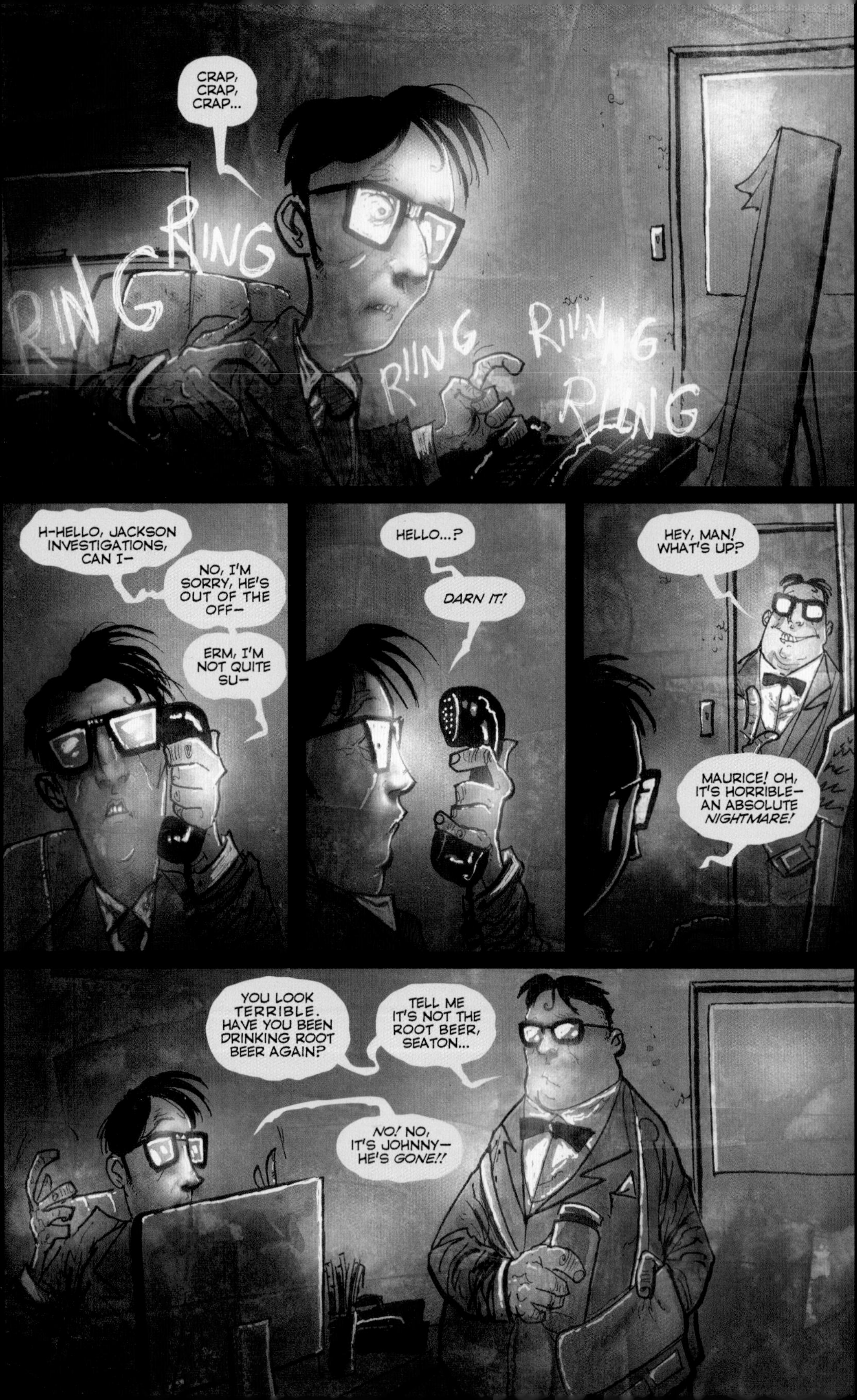
CRAP, CRAP, CRAP...
RING RING
RIING RIING RING
H-HELLO, JACKSON INVESTIGATIONS, CAN I-
NO, I'M SORRY, HE'S OUT OF THE OFF-
ERM, I'M NOT QUITE SU-
HELLO...?
DARN IT!
HEY, MAN! WHAT'S UP?
MAURICE! OH, IT'S HORRIBLE— AN ABSOLUTE NIGHTMARE!
YOU LOOK TERRIBLE. HAVE YOU BEEN DRINKING ROOT BEER AGAIN?
TELL ME IT'S NOT THE ROOT BEER, SEATON...
NO! NO, IT'S JOHNNY— HE'S GONE!!

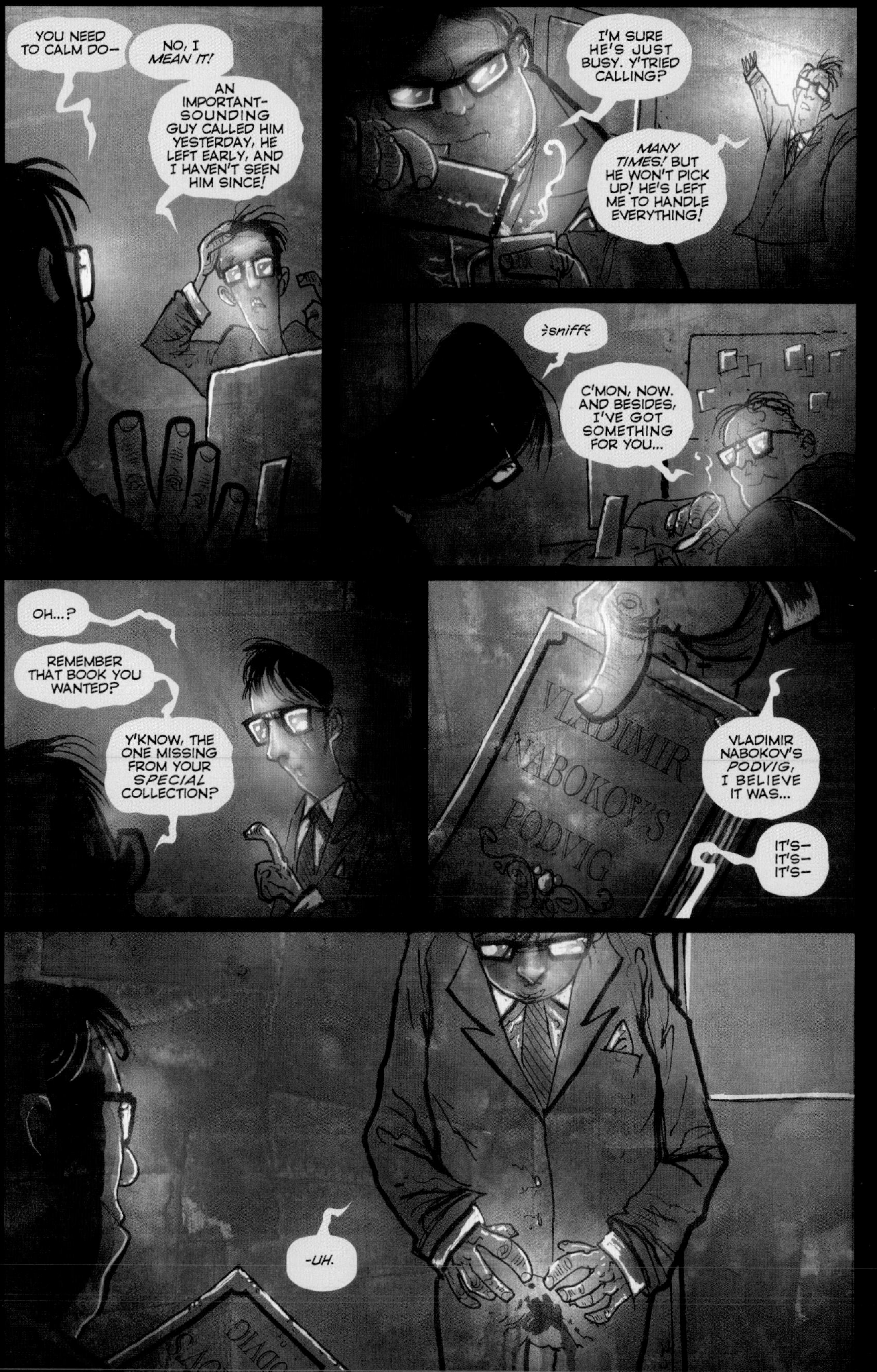
YOU NEED TO CALM DO—
NO, I *MEAN IT!*
AN IMPORTANT-SOUNDING GUY CALLED HIM YESTERDAY, HE LEFT EARLY, AND I HAVEN'T SEEN HIM SINCE!
I'M SURE HE'S JUST BUSY. Y'TRIED CALLING?
MANY TIMES! BUT HE WON'T PICK UP! HE'S LEFT ME TO HANDLE EVERYTHING!
sniff
C'MON, NOW. AND BESIDES, I'VE GOT SOMETHING FOR YOU...
OH...?
REMEMBER THAT BOOK YOU WANTED?
Y'KNOW, THE ONE MISSING FROM YOUR *SPECIAL* COLLECTION?
VLADIMIR NABOKOV'S PODVIG
VLADIMIR NABOKOV'S *PODVIG*, I BELIEVE IT WAS...
IT'S— IT'S— IT'S—
-UH.
PODVIG

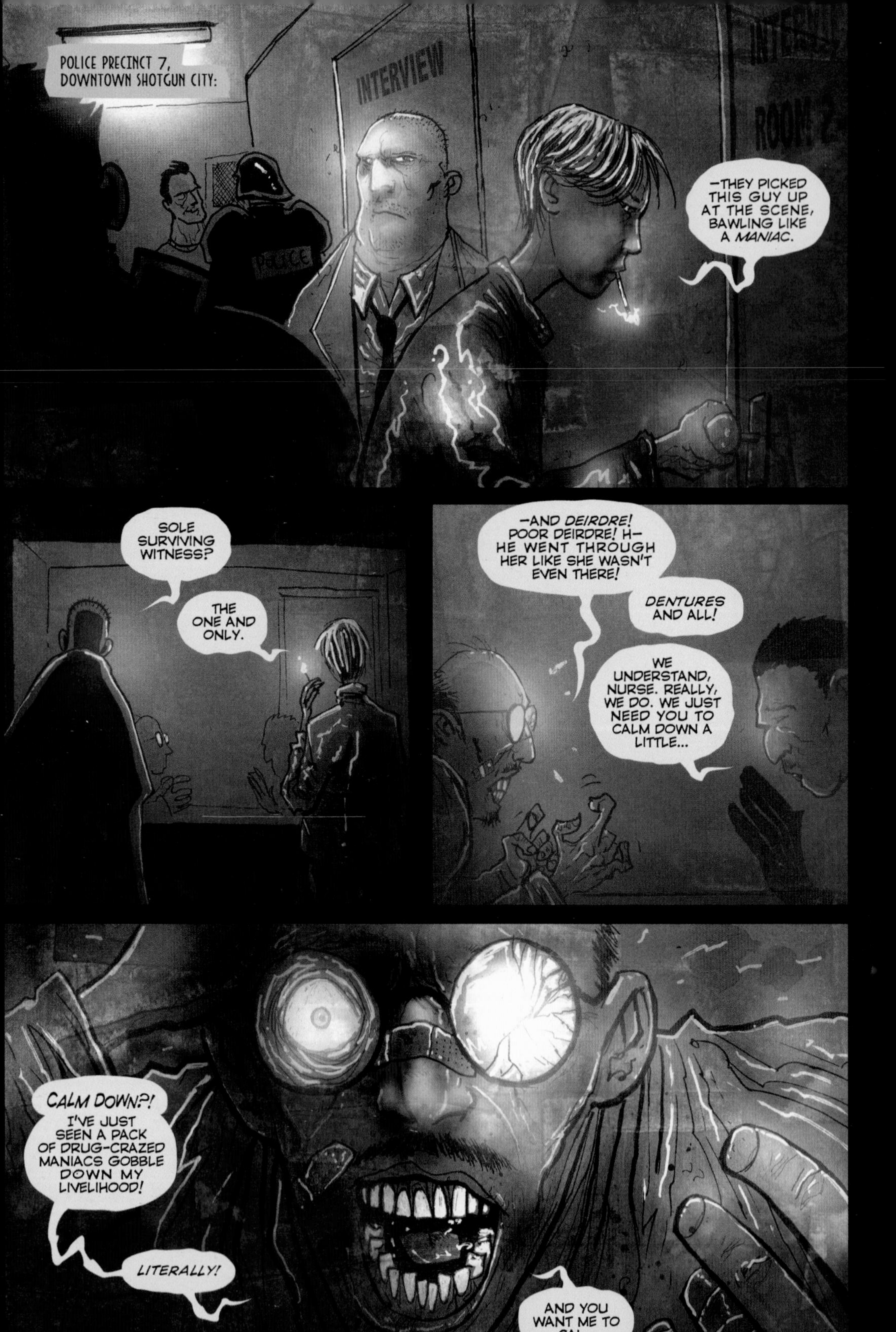
POLICE PRECINCT 7, DOWNTOWN SHOTGUN CITY:
INTERVIEW
ROOM 2
POLICE
—THEY PICKED THIS GUY UP AT THE SCENE, BAWLING LIKE A *MANIAC*.
SOLE SURVIVING WITNESS?
THE ONE AND ONLY.
—AND *DEIRDRE!* POOR DEIRDRE! H— HE WENT THROUGH HER LIKE SHE WASN'T EVEN THERE!
DENTURES AND ALL!
WE UNDERSTAND, NURSE. REALLY, WE DO. WE JUST NEED YOU TO CALM DOWN A LITTLE...
CALM DOWN?! I'VE JUST SEEN A PACK OF DRUG-CRAZED MANIACS GOBBLE DOWN MY *LIVELIHOOD!*
LITERALLY!
AND YOU WANT ME TO CAL—

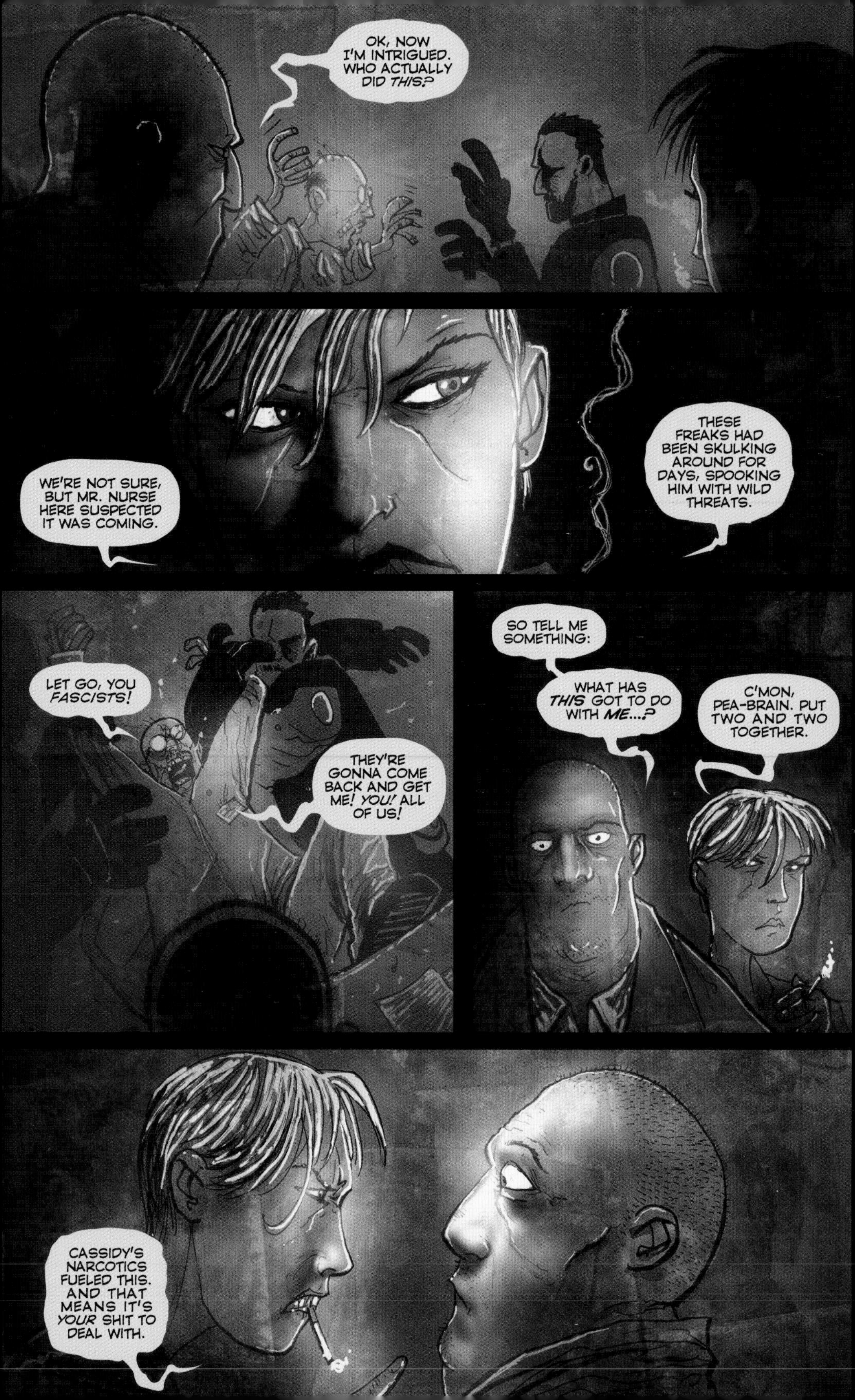
OK, NOW I'M INTRIGUED. WHO ACTUALLY DID *THIS*?
WE'RE NOT SURE, BUT MR. NURSE HERE SUSPECTED IT WAS COMING.
THESE FREAKS HAD BEEN SKULKING AROUND FOR DAYS, SPOOKING HIM WITH WILD THREATS.
LET GO, YOU *FASCISTS*!
THEY'RE GONNA COME BACK AND GET ME! *YOU!* ALL OF US!
SO TELL ME SOMETHING:
WHAT HAS ***THIS*** GOT TO DO WITH ***ME***...?
C'MON, PEA-BRAIN. PUT TWO AND TWO TOGETHER.
CASSIDY'S NARCOTICS FUELED THIS. AND THAT MEANS IT'S *YOUR* SHIT TO DEAL WITH.

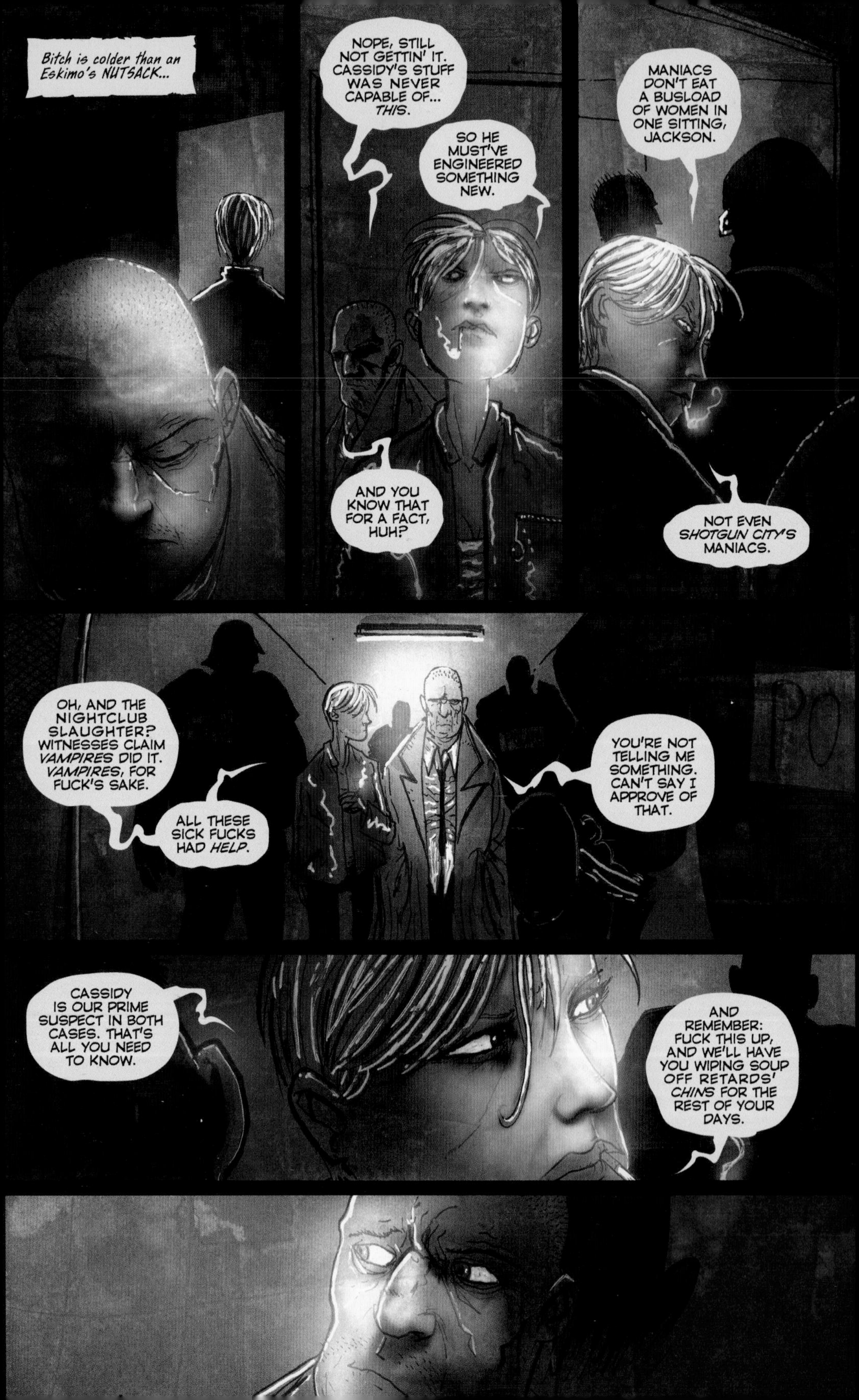
Bitch is colder than an Eskimo's NUTSACK...
NOPE, STILL NOT GETTIN' IT. CASSIDY'S STUFF WAS NEVER CAPABLE OF... THIS.
SO HE MUST'VE ENGINEERED SOMETHING NEW.
AND YOU KNOW THAT FOR A FACT, HUH?
MANIACS DON'T EAT A BUSLOAD OF WOMEN IN ONE SITTING, JACKSON.
NOT EVEN SHOTGUN CITY'S MANIACS.
OH, AND THE NIGHTCLUB SLAUGHTER? WITNESSES CLAIM VAMPIRES DID IT. VAMPIRES, FOR FUCK'S SAKE.
ALL THESE SICK FUCKS HAD HELP.
YOU'RE NOT TELLING ME SOMETHING. CAN'T SAY I APPROVE OF THAT.
CASSIDY IS OUR PRIME SUSPECT IN BOTH CASES. THAT'S ALL YOU NEED TO KNOW.
AND REMEMBER: FUCK THIS UP, AND WE'LL HAVE YOU WIPING SOUP OFF RETARDS' CHINS FOR THE REST OF YOUR DAYS.

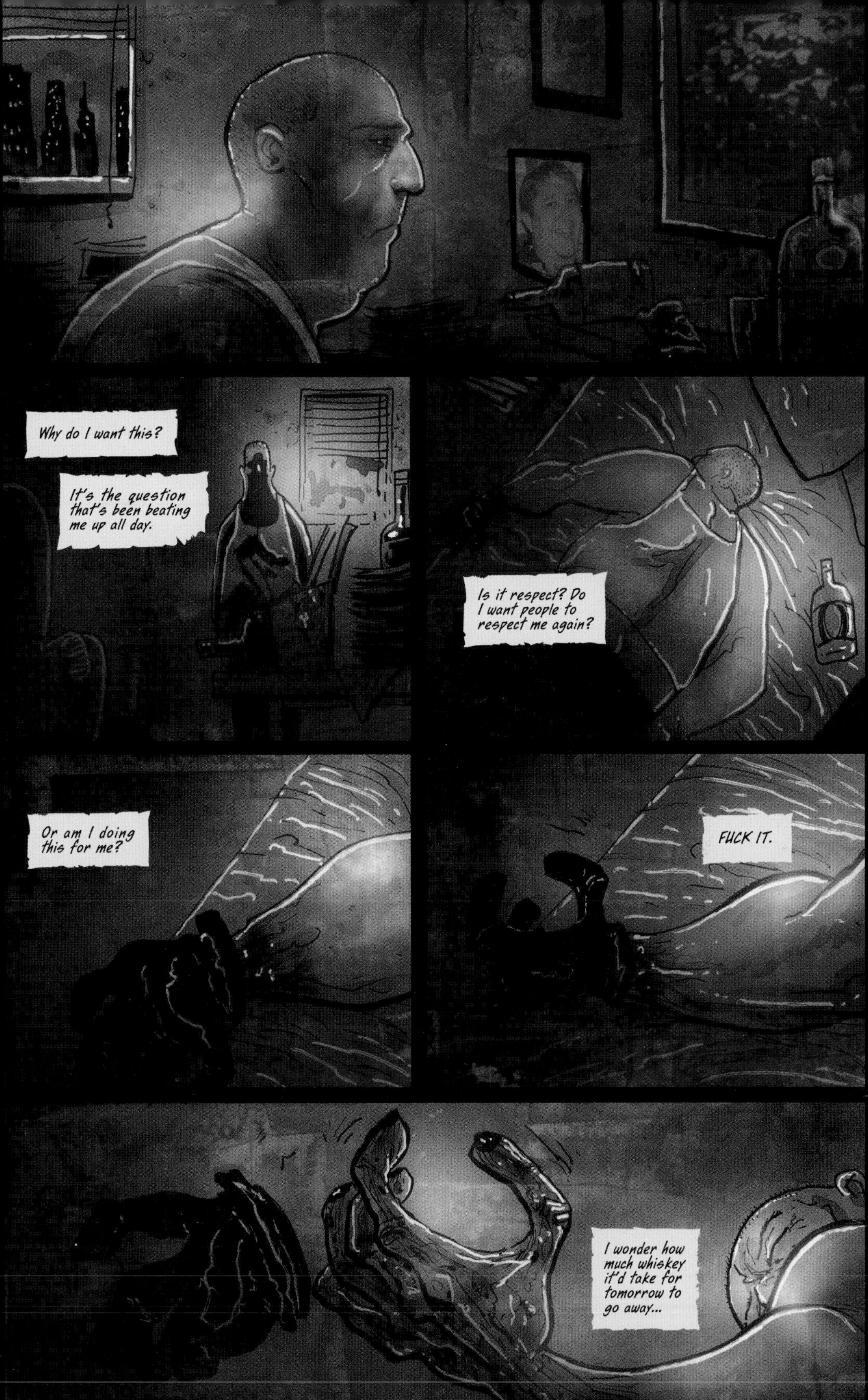
Why do I want this?
It's the question that's been beating me up all day.
Is it respect? Do I want people to respect me again?
Or am I doing this for me?
FUCK IT.
I wonder how much whiskey it'd take for tomorrow to go away...

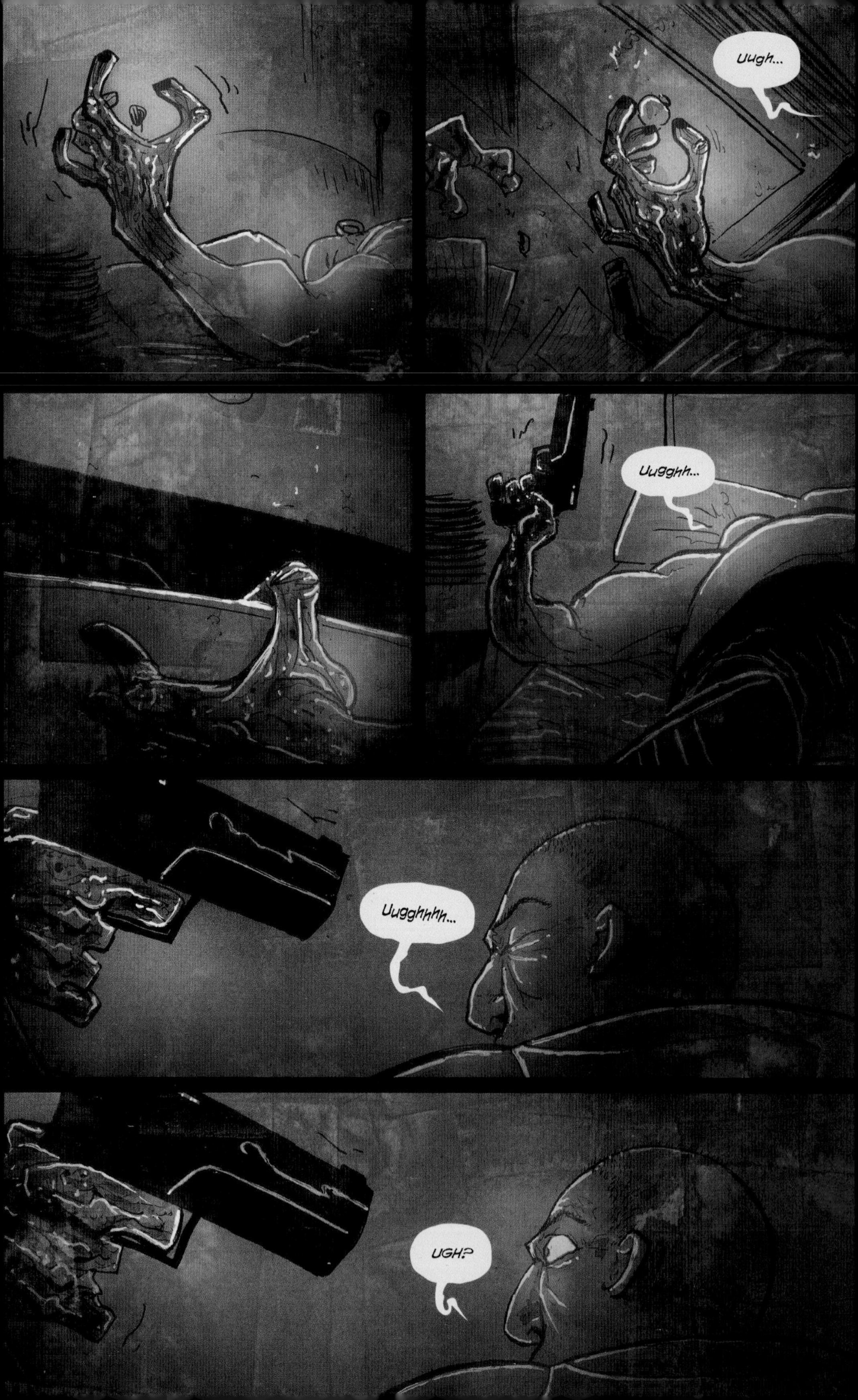
Uugh...
Uugghh...
Uugghhhh...
UGH?

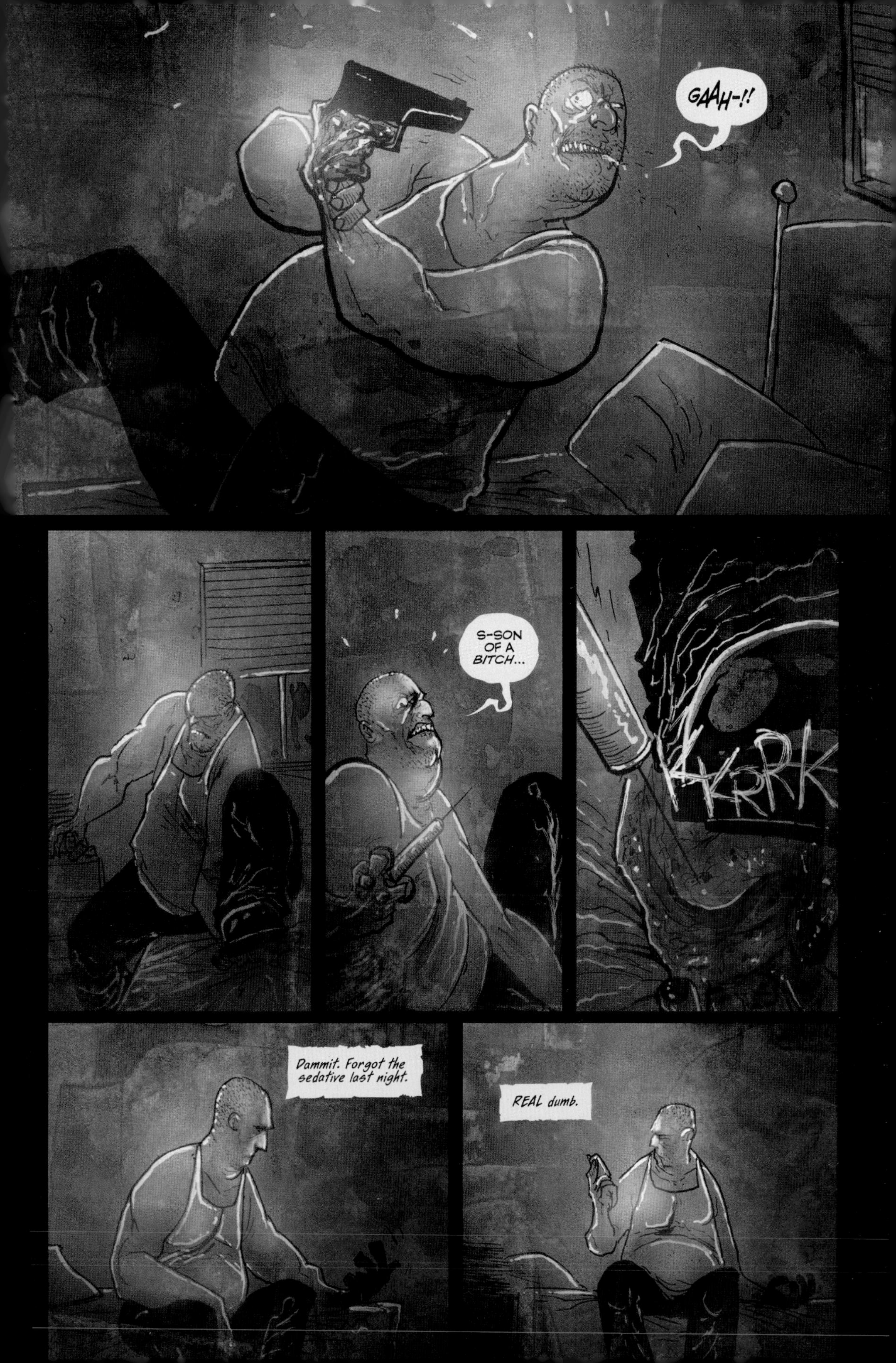
GAAH-!!
S-SON OF A BITCH...
KKRRK
Dammit. Forgot the sedative last night.
REAL dumb.

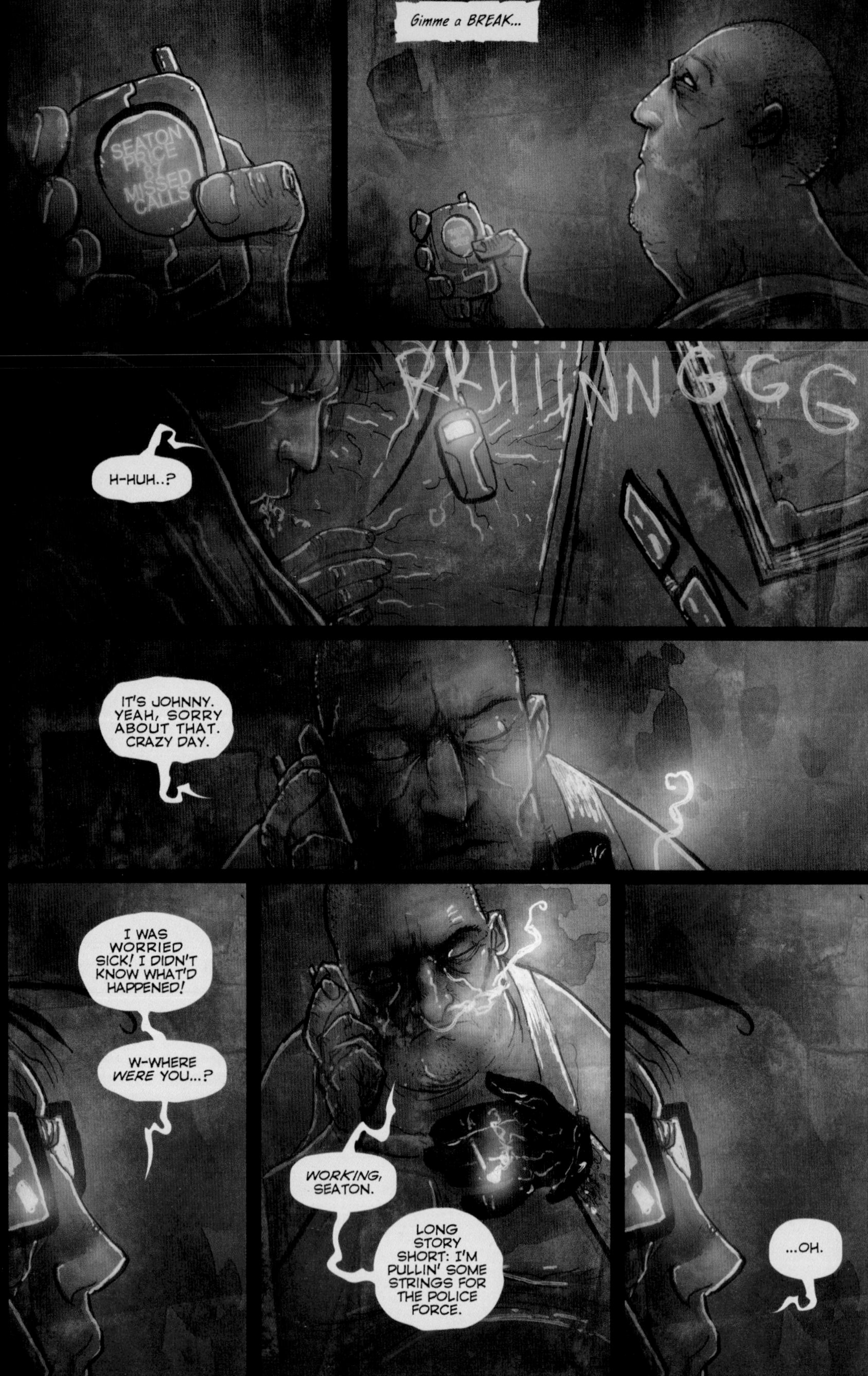

SEATON PRICE 87 MISSED CALLS
Gimme a BREAK...
RRIIINNGGG
H-HUH..?
IT'S JOHNNY. YEAH, SORRY ABOUT THAT. CRAZY DAY.
I WAS WORRIED SICK! I DIDN'T KNOW WHAT'D HAPPENED!
W-WHERE *WERE* YOU...?
WORKING, SEATON.
LONG STORY SHORT: I'M PULLIN' SOME STRINGS FOR THE POLICE FORCE.
...OH.

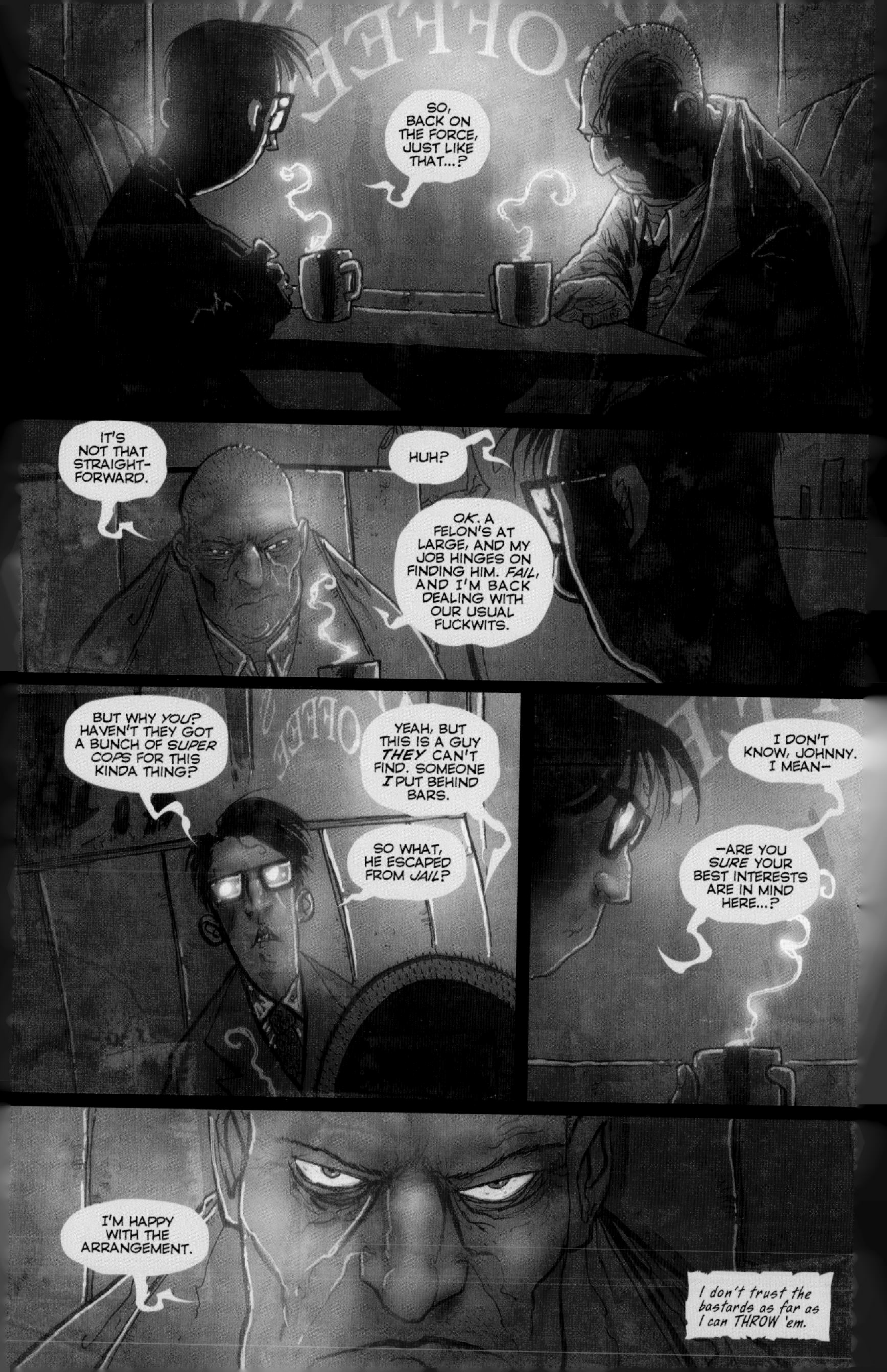

SO, BACK ON THE FORCE, JUST LIKE THAT...?
IT'S NOT THAT STRAIGHT-FORWARD.
HUH?
OK. A FELON'S AT LARGE, AND MY JOB HINGES ON FINDING HIM. FAIL, AND I'M BACK DEALING WITH OUR USUAL FUCKWITS.
BUT WHY YOU? HAVEN'T THEY GOT A BUNCH OF SUPER COPS FOR THIS KINDA THING?
YEAH, BUT THIS IS A GUY THEY CAN'T FIND. SOMEONE I PUT BEHIND BARS.
SO WHAT, HE ESCAPED FROM JAIL?
I DON'T KNOW, JOHNNY. I MEAN—
—ARE YOU SURE YOUR BEST INTERESTS ARE IN MIND HERE...?
I'M HAPPY WITH THE ARRANGEMENT.
I don't trust the bastards as far as I can THROW 'em.

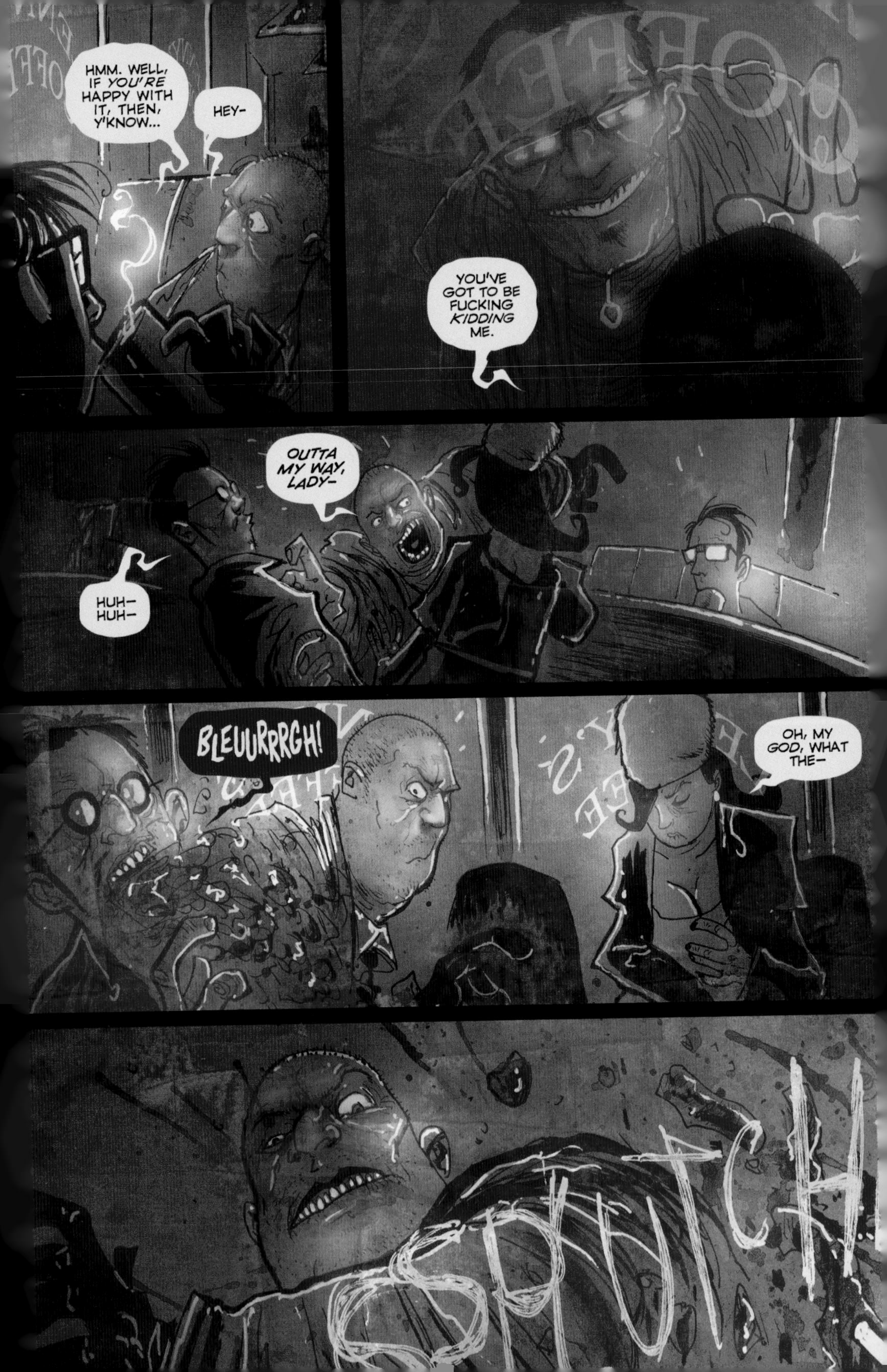
HMM. WELL, IF YOU'RE HAPPY WITH IT, THEN, Y'KNOW...
HEY-
YOU'VE GOT TO BE FUCKING KIDDING ME.
OUTTA MY WAY, LADY-
HUH-HUH-
BLEUURRRGH!
OH, MY GOD, WHAT THE-
SPLOTCH

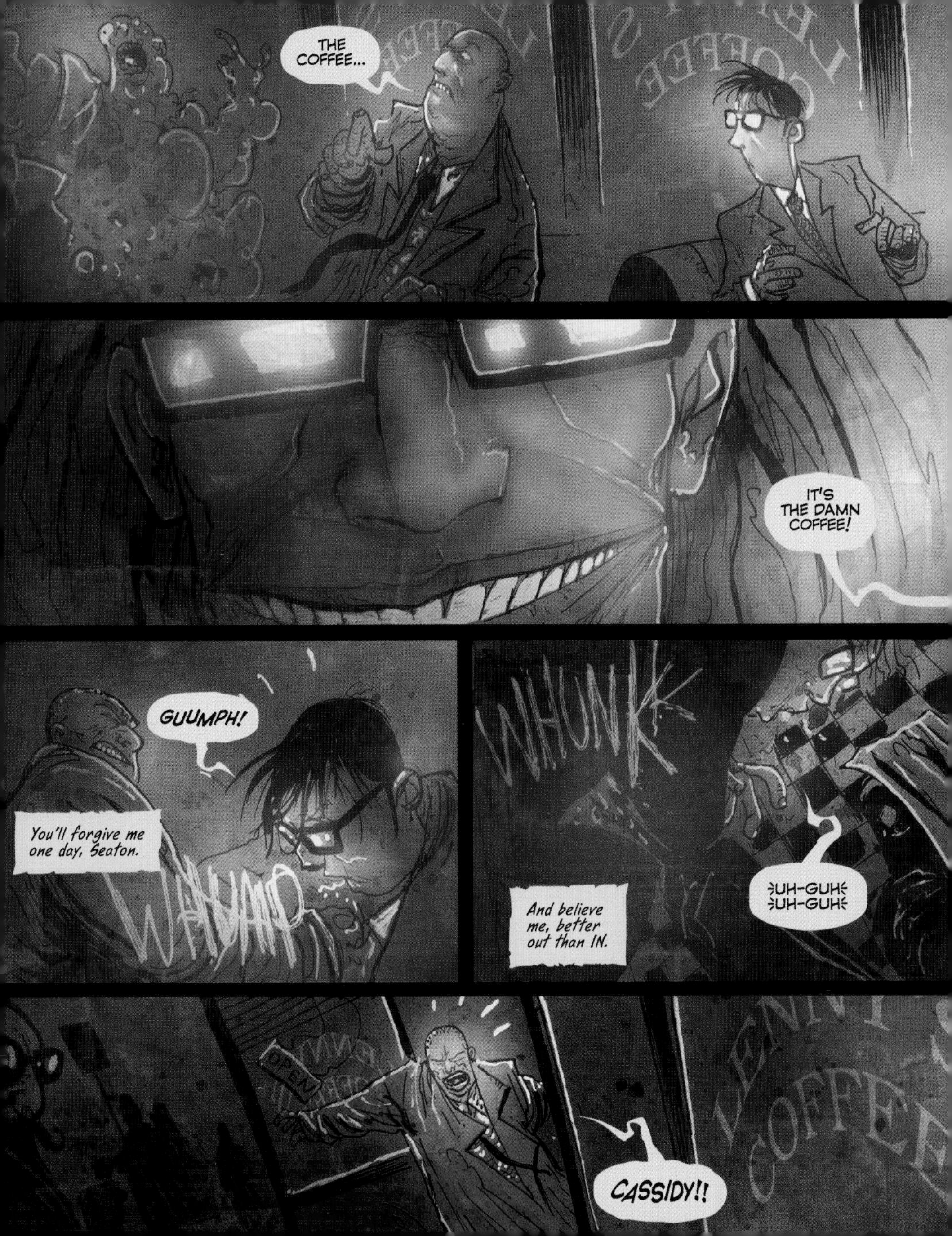
THE COFFEE...
IT'S THE DAMN COFFEE!
GUUMPH!
You'll forgive me one day, Seaton.
WHUMP
WHUNK
And believe me, better out than IN.
UH-GUH UH-GUH
OPEN
CASSIDY!!

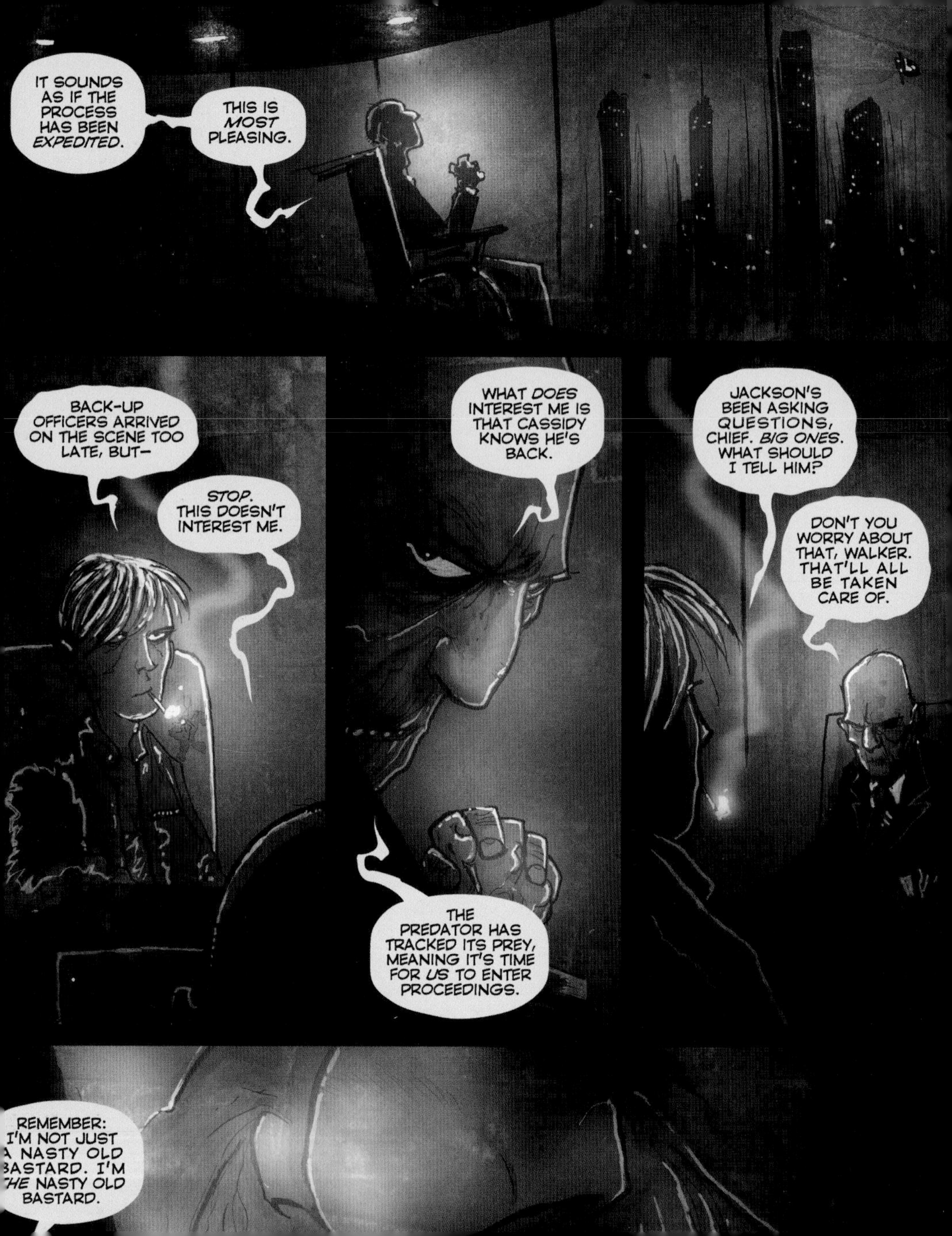
IT SOUNDS AS IF THE PROCESS HAS BEEN *EXPEDITED*.
THIS IS *MOST* PLEASING.
BACK-UP OFFICERS ARRIVED ON THE SCENE TOO LATE, BUT—
STOP. THIS DOESN'T INTEREST ME.
WHAT *DOES* INTEREST ME IS THAT CASSIDY KNOWS HE'S BACK.
THE PREDATOR HAS TRACKED ITS PREY, MEANING IT'S TIME FOR *US* TO ENTER PROCEEDINGS.
JACKSON'S BEEN ASKING QUESTIONS, CHIEF. *BIG ONES*. WHAT SHOULD I TELL HIM?
DON'T YOU WORRY ABOUT THAT, WALKER. THAT'LL ALL BE TAKEN CARE OF.
REMEMBER: I'M NOT JUST A NASTY OLD BASTARD. I'M *THE* NASTY OLD BASTARD.

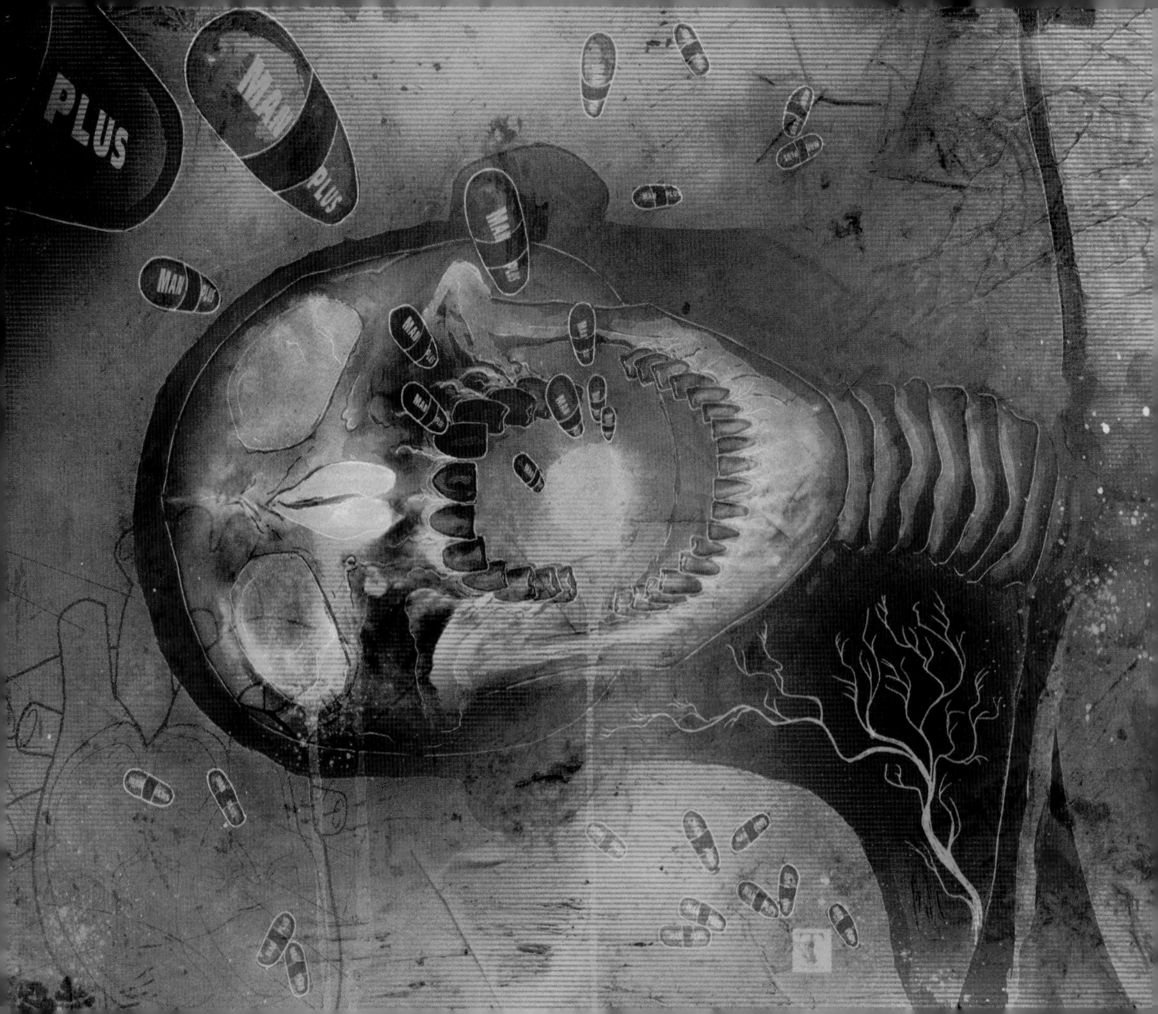
PLUS
MAN
PLUS
MAN
PLUS
MAN
PLUS

DOWN THESE MEAN STREETS A BASTARD MUST GO

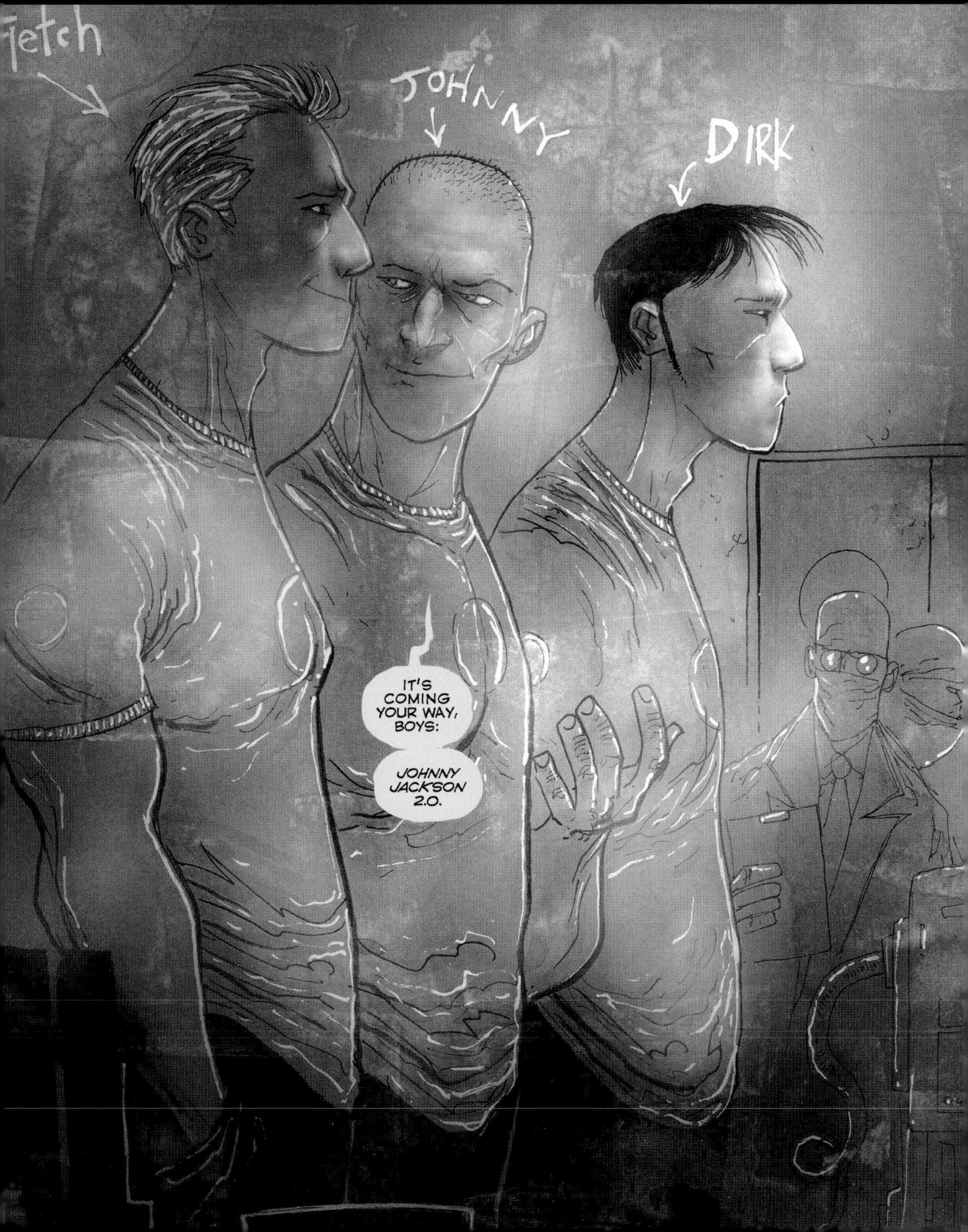
Fetch
JOHNNY
DIRK
IT'S COMING YOUR WAY, BOYS:
JOHNNY JACKSON 2.0.

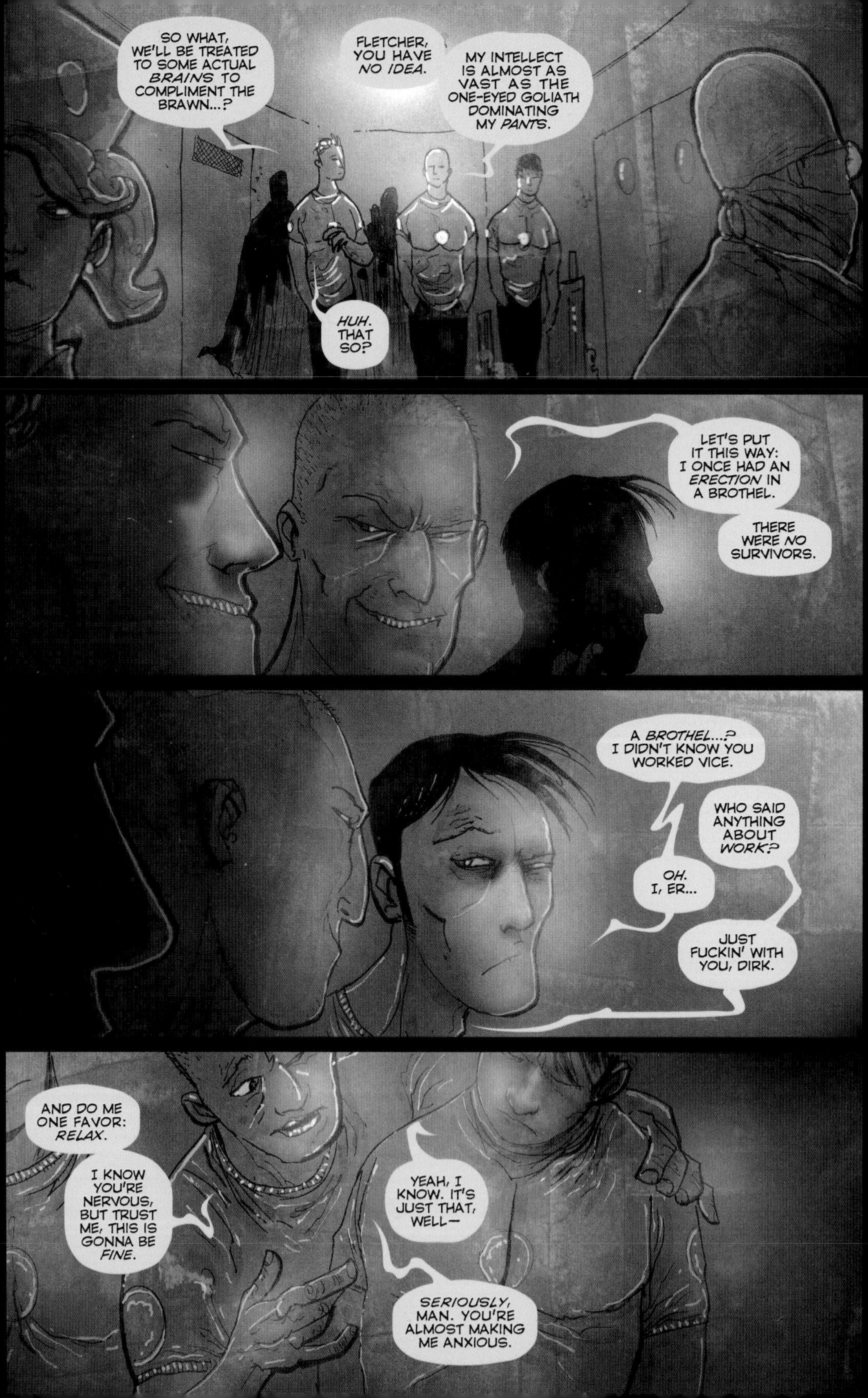
SO WHAT, WE'LL BE TREATED TO SOME ACTUAL *BRAINS* TO COMPLIMENT THE BRAWN...?
FLETCHER, YOU HAVE *NO IDEA*.
MY INTELLECT IS ALMOST AS VAST AS THE ONE-EYED GOLIATH DOMINATING MY *PANTS*.
HUH. THAT SO?
LET'S PUT IT THIS WAY: I ONCE HAD AN *ERECTION* IN A BROTHEL.
THERE WERE *NO* SURVIVORS.
A *BROTHEL*...? I DIDN'T KNOW YOU WORKED VICE.
WHO SAID ANYTHING ABOUT *WORK?*
OH. I, ER...
JUST FUCKIN' WITH YOU, DIRK.
AND DO ME ONE FAVOR: *RELAX*.
I KNOW YOU'RE NERVOUS, BUT TRUST ME, THIS IS GONNA BE *FINE*.
YEAH, I KNOW. IT'S JUST THAT, WELL—
SERIOUSLY, MAN. YOU'RE ALMOST MAKING ME ANXIOUS.

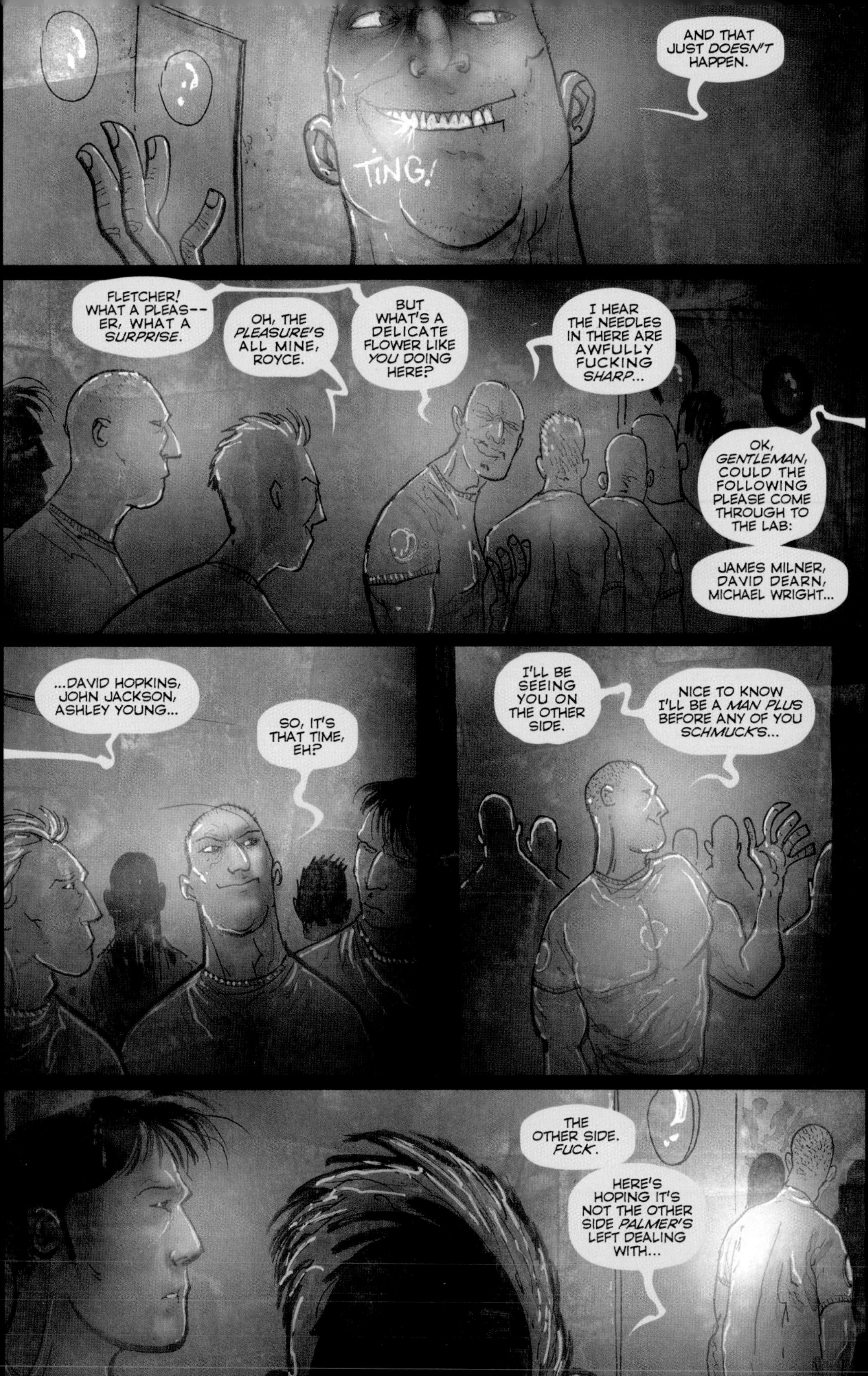

AND THAT JUST *DOESN'T* HAPPEN.
TING!
FLETCHER! WHAT A PLEAS-- ER, WHAT A *SURPRISE*.
OH, THE *PLEASURE'S* ALL MINE, ROYCE.
BUT WHAT'S A DELICATE FLOWER LIKE *YOU* DOING HERE?
I HEAR THE NEEDLES IN THERE ARE AWFULLY FUCKING *SHARP*...
OK, *GENTLEMAN*, COULD THE FOLLOWING PLEASE COME THROUGH TO THE LAB:
JAMES MILNER, DAVID DEARN, MICHAEL WRIGHT...
...DAVID HOPKINS, JOHN JACKSON, ASHLEY YOUNG...
SO, IT'S THAT TIME, EH?
I'LL BE SEEING YOU ON THE OTHER SIDE.
NICE TO KNOW I'LL BE A *MAN PLUS* BEFORE ANY OF YOU *SCHMUCKS*...
THE OTHER SIDE. *FUCK*.
HERE'S HOPING IT'S NOT THE OTHER SIDE *PALMER'S* LEFT DEALING WITH...

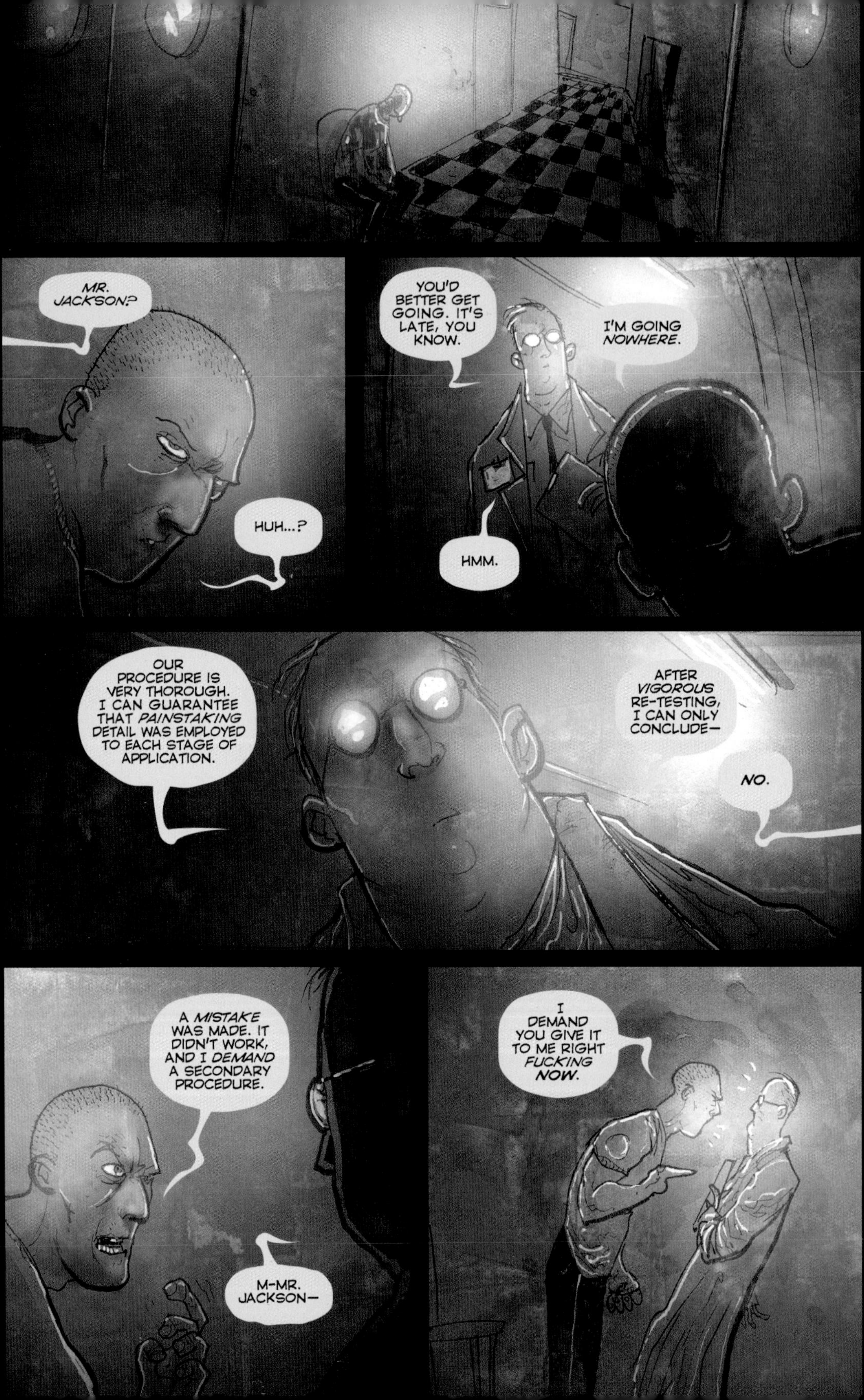
MR. JACKSON?
HUH...?
YOU'D BETTER GET GOING. IT'S LATE, YOU KNOW.
I'M GOING *NOWHERE*.
HMM.
OUR PROCEDURE IS VERY THOROUGH. I CAN GUARANTEE THAT *PAINSTAKING* DETAIL WAS EMPLOYED TO EACH STAGE OF APPLICATION.
AFTER *VIGOROUS* RE-TESTING, I CAN ONLY CONCLUDE—
NO.
A *MISTAKE* WAS MADE. IT DIDN'T WORK, AND I *DEMAND* A SECONDARY PROCEDURE.
M-MR. JACKSON—
I DEMAND YOU GIVE IT TO ME RIGHT *FUCKING NOW*.

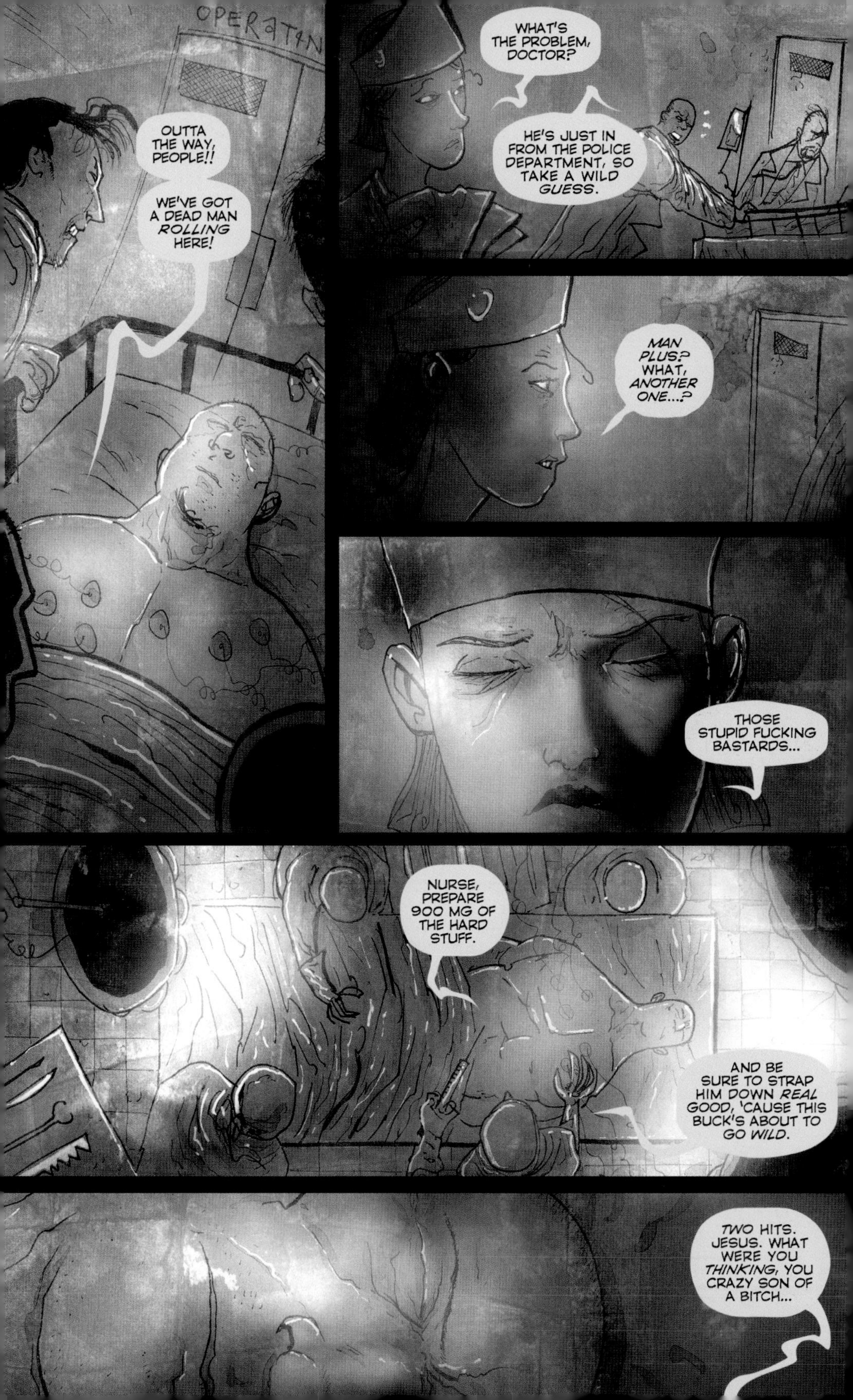
OPERATAN
OUTTA THE WAY, PEOPLE!!
WE'VE GOT A DEAD MAN *ROLLING* HERE!
WHAT'S THE PROBLEM, DOCTOR?
HE'S JUST IN FROM THE POLICE DEPARTMENT, SO TAKE A WILD *GUESS*.
MAN PLUS? WHAT, *ANOTHER ONE...?*
THOSE STUPID FUCKING BASTARDS...
NURSE, PREPARE 900 MG OF THE HARD STUFF.
AND BE SURE TO STRAP HIM DOWN *REAL* GOOD, 'CAUSE THIS BUCK'S ABOUT TO GO *WILD*.
TWO HITS. JESUS. WHAT WERE YOU *THINKING*, YOU CRAZY SON OF A BITCH...

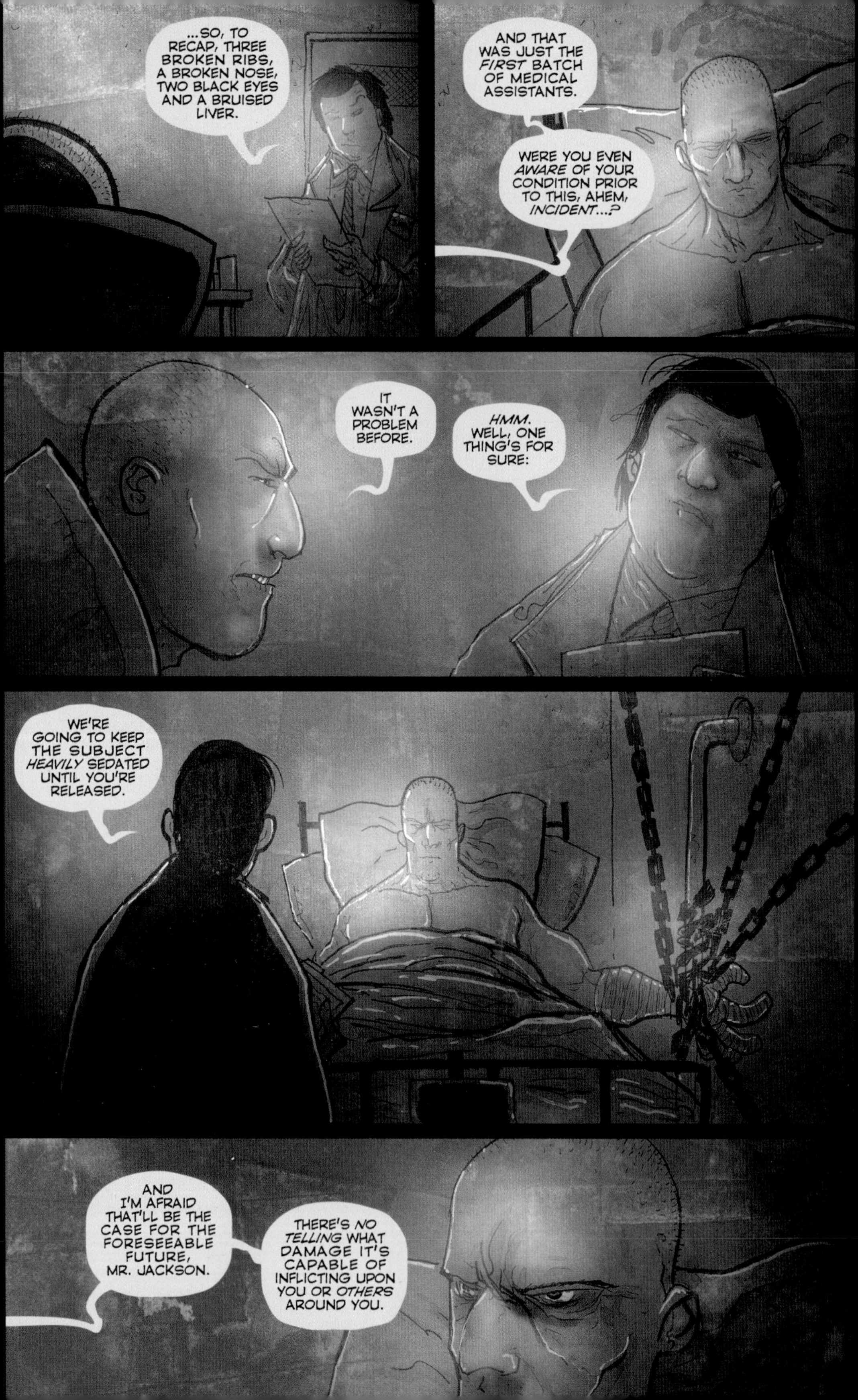
...SO, TO RECAP, THREE BROKEN RIBS, A BROKEN NOSE, TWO BLACK EYES AND A BRUISED LIVER.
AND THAT WAS JUST THE *FIRST* BATCH OF MEDICAL ASSISTANTS.
WERE YOU EVEN *AWARE* OF YOUR CONDITION PRIOR TO THIS, AHEM, *INCIDENT*...?
IT WASN'T A PROBLEM BEFORE.
HMM. WELL, ONE THING'S FOR SURE:
WE'RE GOING TO KEEP THE SUBJECT *HEAVILY* SEDATED UNTIL YOU'RE RELEASED.
AND I'M AFRAID THAT'LL BE THE CASE FOR THE FORESEEABLE FUTURE, MR. JACKSON.
THERE'S *NO TELLING* WHAT DAMAGE IT'S CAPABLE OF INFLICTING UPON YOU OR *OTHERS* AROUND YOU.

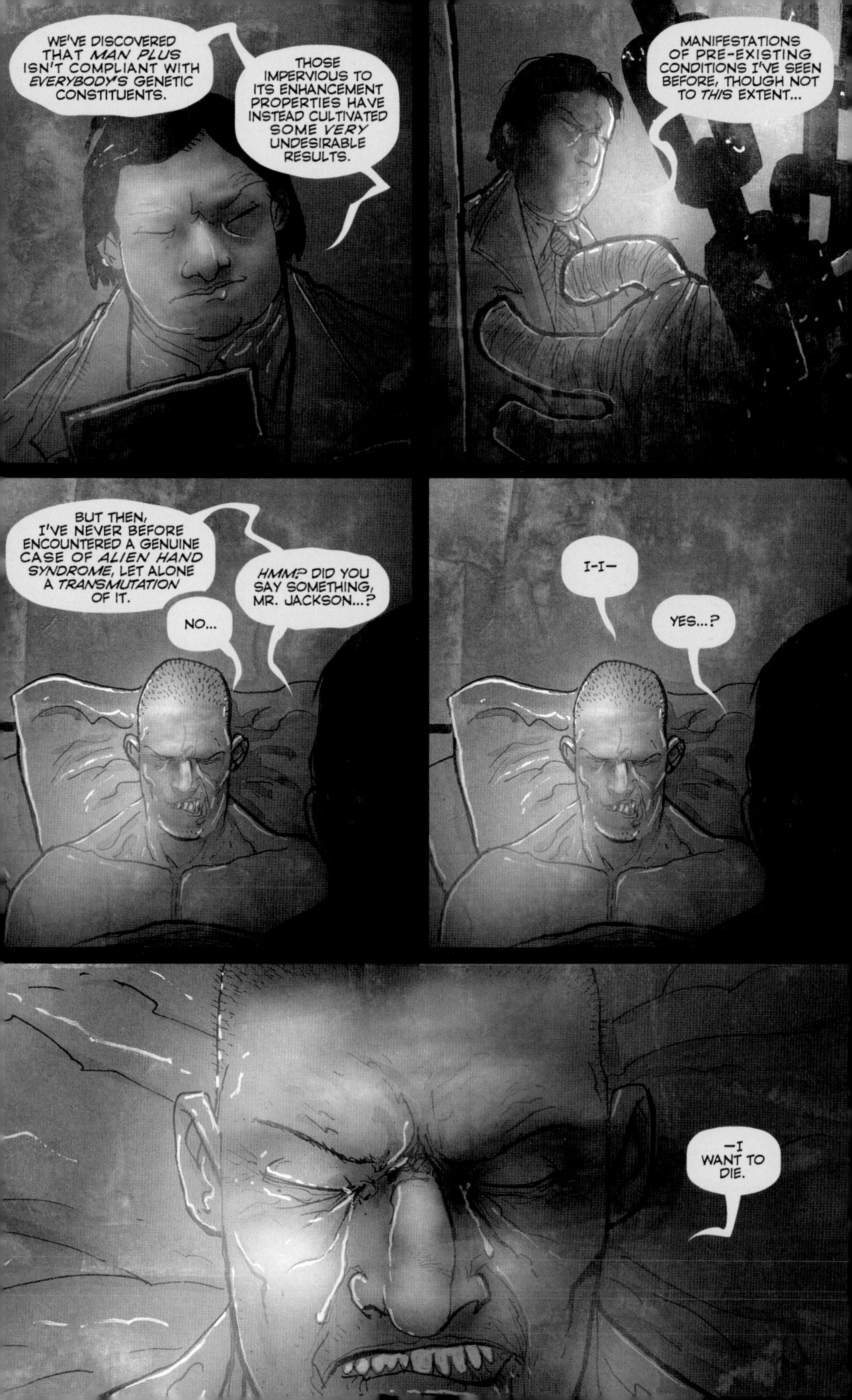
WE'VE DISCOVERED THAT MAN PLUS ISN'T COMPLIANT WITH EVERYBODY'S GENETIC CONSTITUENTS.
THOSE IMPERVIOUS TO ITS ENHANCEMENT PROPERTIES HAVE INSTEAD CULTIVATED SOME VERY UNDESIRABLE RESULTS.
MANIFESTATIONS OF PRE-EXISTING CONDITIONS I'VE SEEN BEFORE, THOUGH NOT TO THIS EXTENT...
BUT THEN, I'VE NEVER BEFORE ENCOUNTERED A GENUINE CASE OF ALIEN HAND SYNDROME, LET ALONE A TRANSMUTATION OF IT.
NO...
HMM? DID YOU SAY SOMETHING, MR. JACKSON...?
I-I—
YES...?
—I WANT TO DIE.

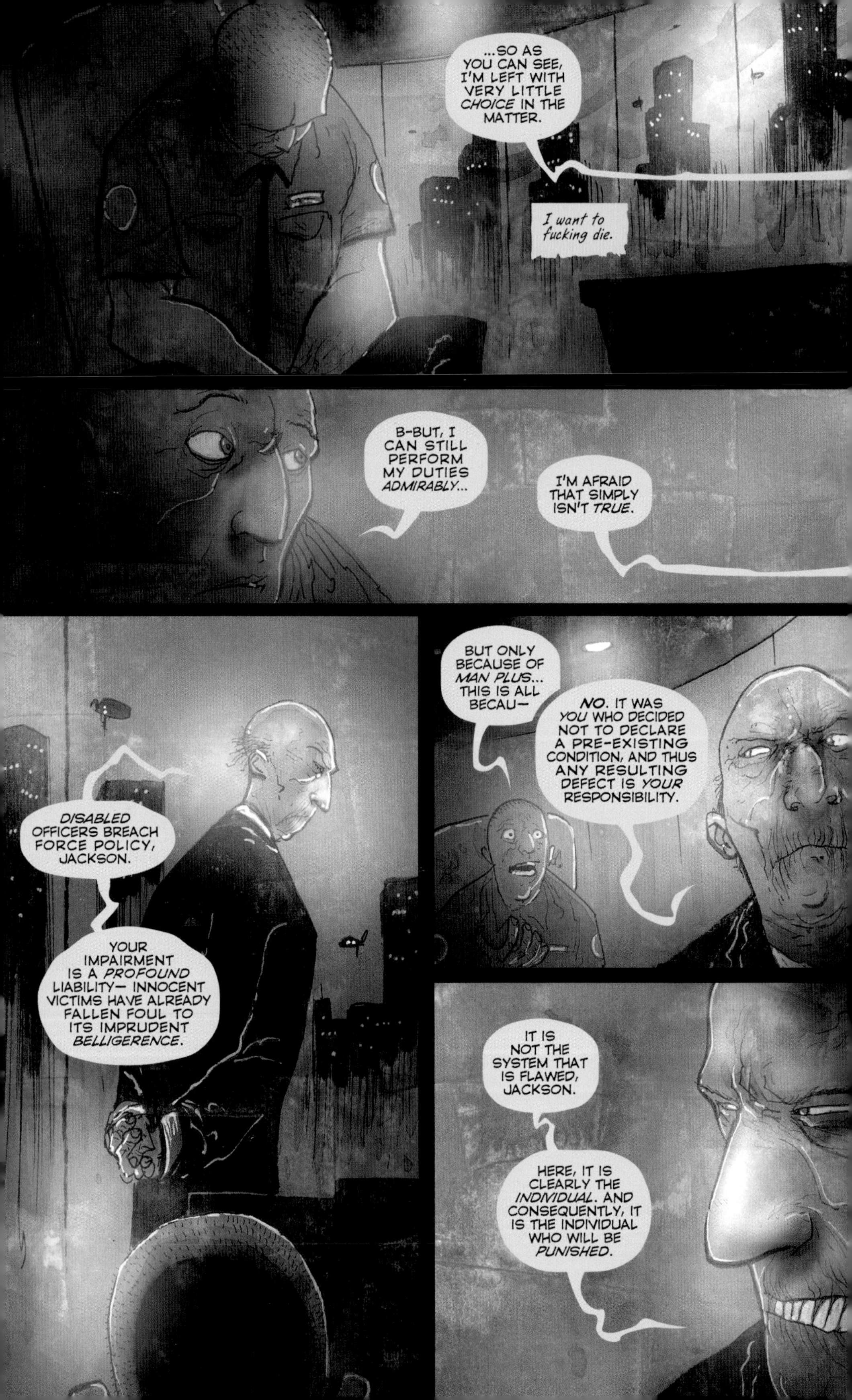
...SO AS YOU CAN SEE, I'M LEFT WITH VERY LITTLE *CHOICE* IN THE MATTER.
I want to fucking die.
B-BUT, I CAN STILL PERFORM MY DUTIES *ADMIRABLY*...
I'M AFRAID THAT SIMPLY ISN'T *TRUE*.
DISABLED OFFICERS BREACH FORCE POLICY, JACKSON.
YOUR IMPAIRMENT IS A *PROFOUND* LIABILITY— INNOCENT VICTIMS HAVE ALREADY FALLEN FOUL TO ITS IMPRUDENT *BELLIGERENCE*.
BUT ONLY BECAUSE OF *MAN PLUS*... THIS IS ALL BECAU—
NO. IT WAS *YOU* WHO DECIDED NOT TO DECLARE A PRE-EXISTING CONDITION, AND THUS ANY RESULTING DEFECT IS *YOUR* RESPONSIBILITY.
IT IS NOT THE SYSTEM THAT IS FLAWED, JACKSON.
HERE, IT IS CLEARLY THE *INDIVIDUAL*. AND CONSEQUENTLY, IT IS THE INDIVIDUAL WHO WILL BE *PUNISHED*.

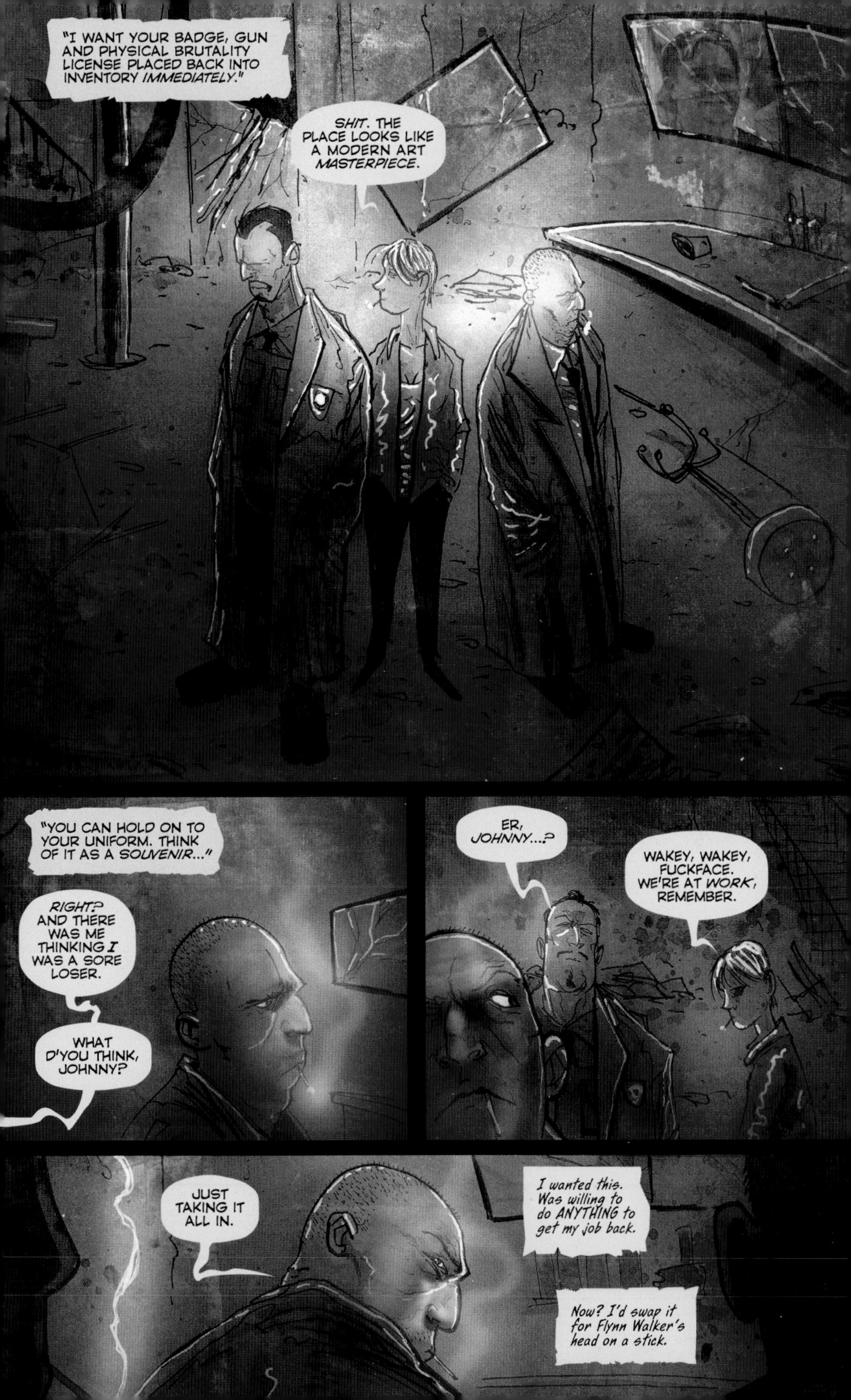
"I WANT YOUR BADGE, GUN AND PHYSICAL BRUTALITY LICENSE PLACED BACK INTO INVENTORY *IMMEDIATELY*."
SHIT. THE PLACE LOOKS LIKE A MODERN ART *MASTERPIECE*.
"YOU CAN HOLD ON TO YOUR UNIFORM. THINK OF IT AS A *SOUVENIR*..."
RIGHT? AND THERE WAS ME THINKING *I* WAS A SORE LOSER.
WHAT D'YOU THINK, JOHNNY?
ER, *JOHNNY*...?
WAKEY, WAKEY, FUCKFACE. WE'RE AT *WORK*, REMEMBER.
JUST TAKING IT ALL IN.
I wanted this. Was willing to do ANYTHING to get my job back.
Now? I'd swap it for Flynn Walker's head on a stick.

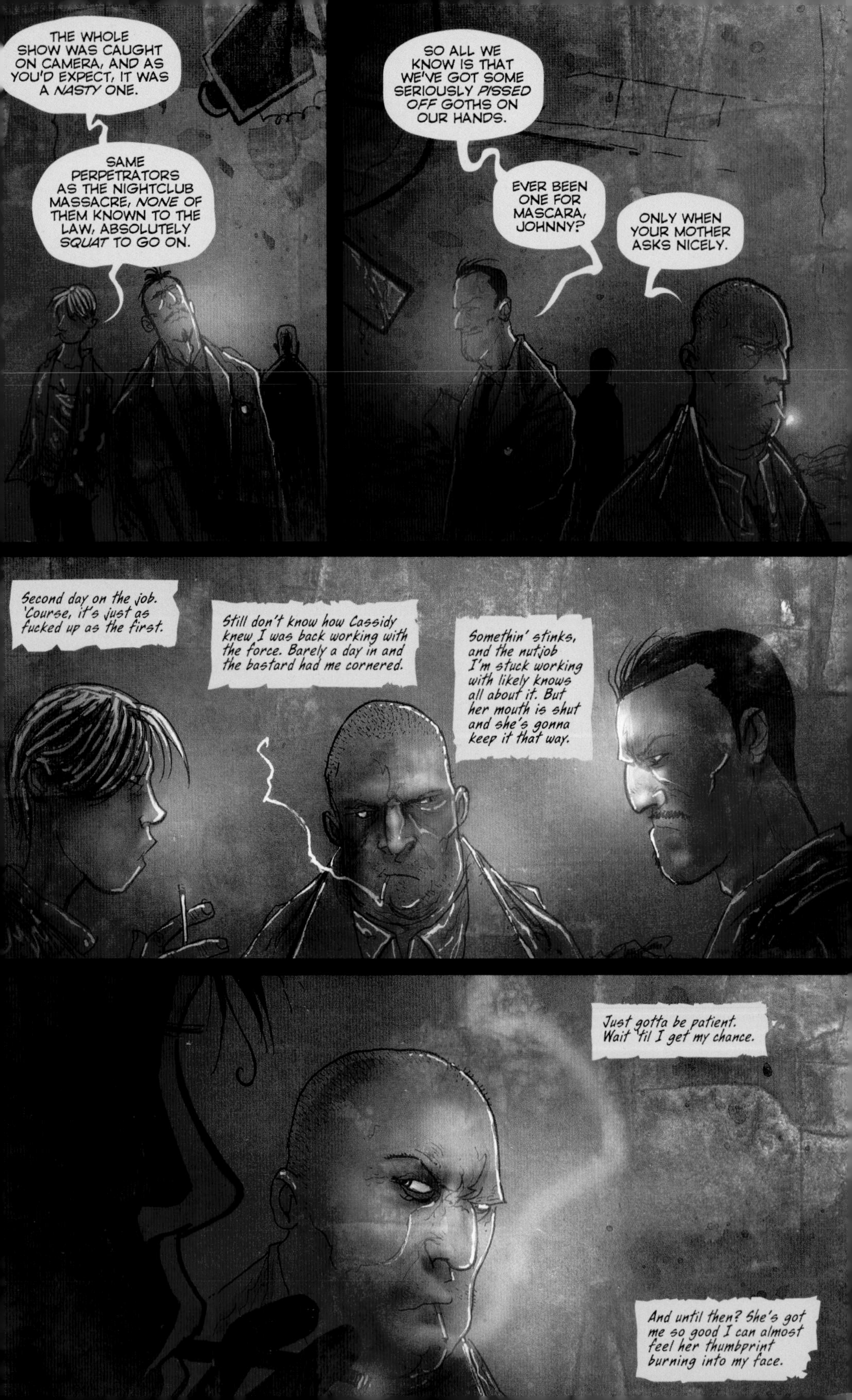
THE WHOLE SHOW WAS CAUGHT ON CAMERA, AND AS YOU'D EXPECT, IT WAS A *NASTY* ONE.
SAME PERPETRATORS AS THE NIGHTCLUB MASSACRE, *NONE* OF THEM KNOWN TO THE LAW, ABSOLUTELY *SQUAT* TO GO ON.
SO ALL WE KNOW IS THAT WE'VE GOT SOME SERIOUSLY *PISSED OFF* GOTHS ON OUR HANDS.
EVER BEEN ONE FOR MASCARA, JOHNNY?
ONLY WHEN YOUR MOTHER ASKS NICELY.
Second day on the job. 'Course, it's just as fucked up as the first.
Still don't know how Cassidy knew I was back working with the force. Barely a day in and the bastard had me cornered.
Somethin' stinks, and the nutjob I'm stuck working with likely knows all about it. But her mouth is shut and she's gonna keep it that way.
Just gotta be patient. Wait 'til I get my chance.
And until then? She's got me so good I can almost feel her thumbprint burning into my face.

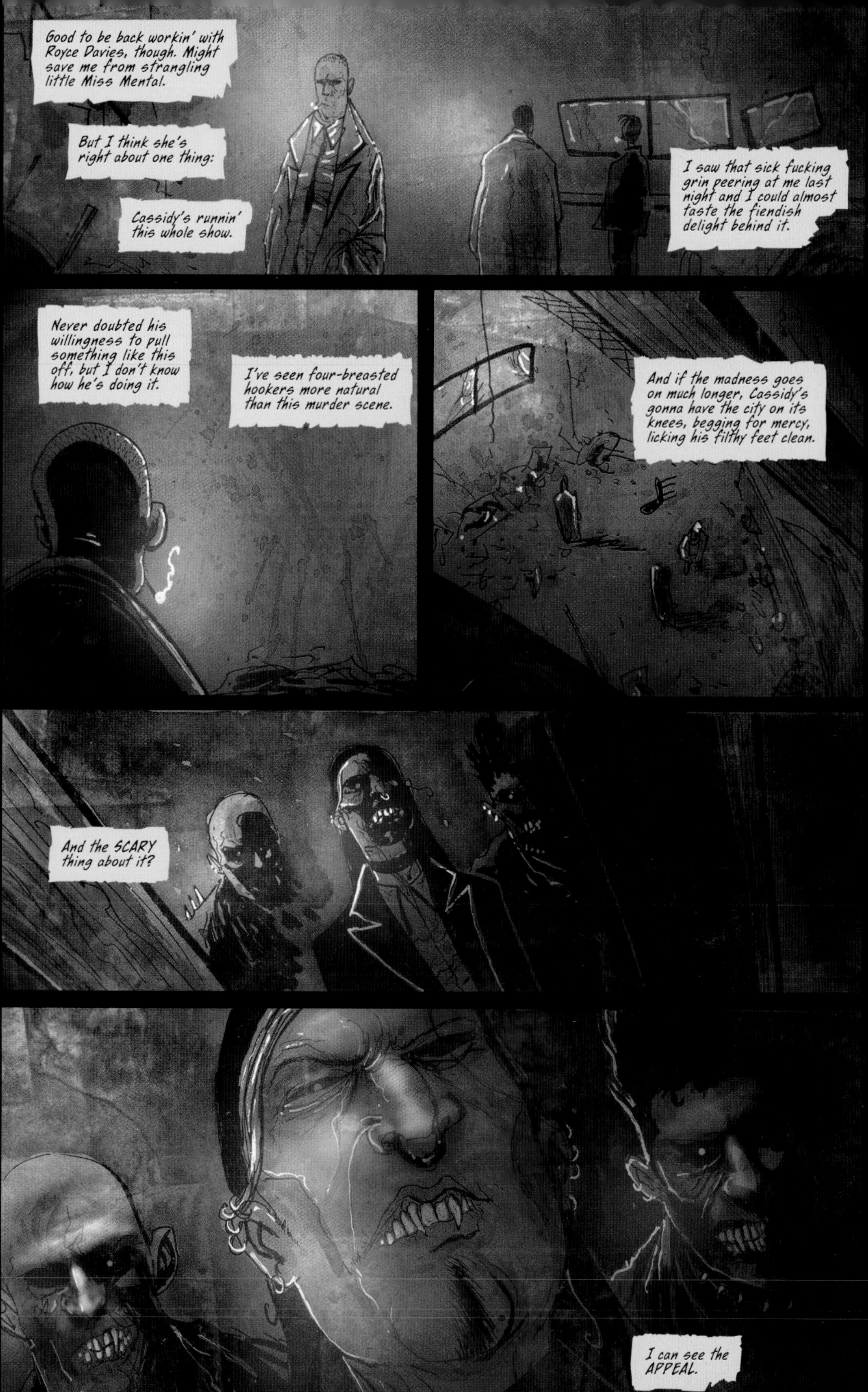
Good to be back workin' with Royce Davies, though. Might save me from strangling little Miss Mental.
But I think she's right about one thing:
Cassidy's runnin' this whole show.
I saw that sick fucking grin peering at me last night and I could almost taste the fiendish delight behind it.
Never doubted his willingness to pull something like this off, but I don't know how he's doing it.
I've seen four-breasted hookers more natural than this murder scene.
And if the madness goes on much longer, Cassidy's gonna have the city on its knees, begging for mercy, licking his filthy feet clean.
And the SCARY thing about it?
I can see the APPEAL.

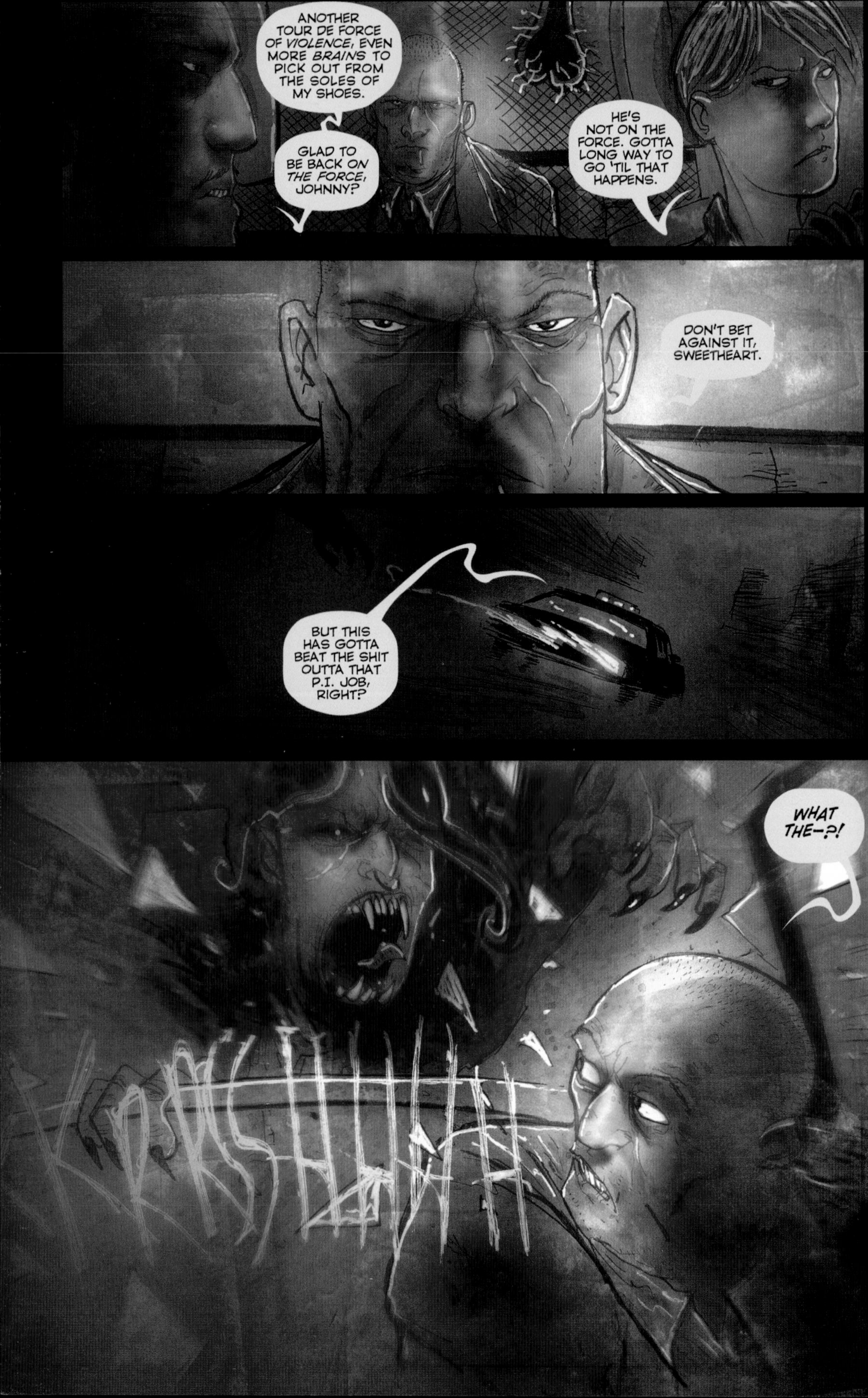
ANOTHER TOUR DE FORCE OF *VIOLENCE*, EVEN MORE *BRAINS* TO PICK OUT FROM THE SOLES OF MY SHOES.
GLAD TO BE BACK ON *THE FORCE*, JOHNNY?
HE'S NOT ON THE FORCE. GOTTA LONG WAY TO GO 'TIL THAT HAPPENS.
DON'T BET AGAINST IT, SWEETHEART.
BUT THIS HAS GOTTA BEAT THE SHIT OUTTA THAT P.I. JOB, RIGHT?
WHAT THE--?!

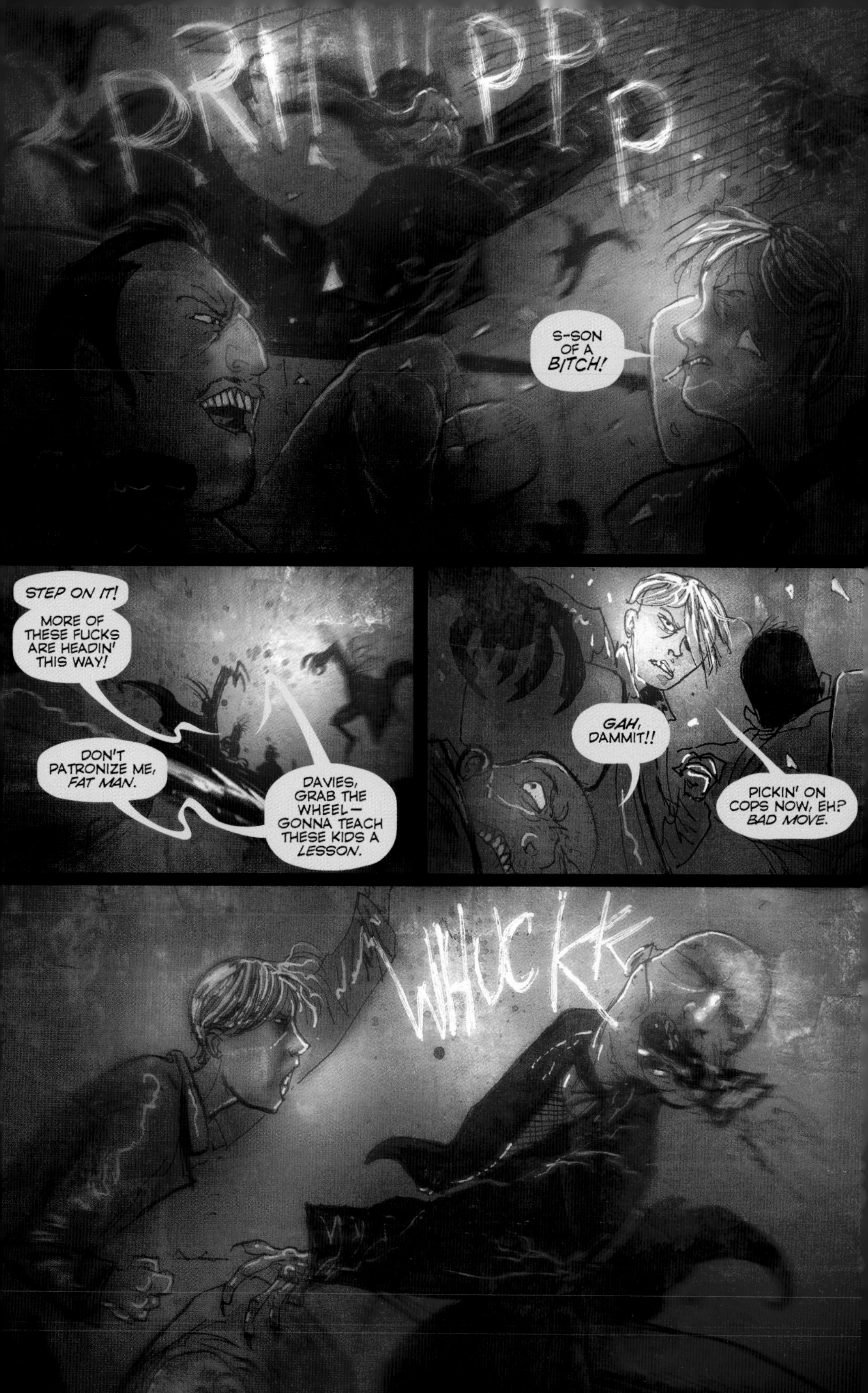
PRRTHPPPP
S-SON OF A *BITCH!*
STEP ON IT!
MORE OF THESE FUCKS ARE HEADIN' THIS WAY!
DON'T PATRONIZE ME, *FAT MAN.*
DAVIES, GRAB THE WHEEL— GONNA TEACH THESE KIDS A *LESSON.*
GAH, DAMMIT!!
PICKIN' ON COPS NOW, EH? *BAD MOVE.*
WHUCKK

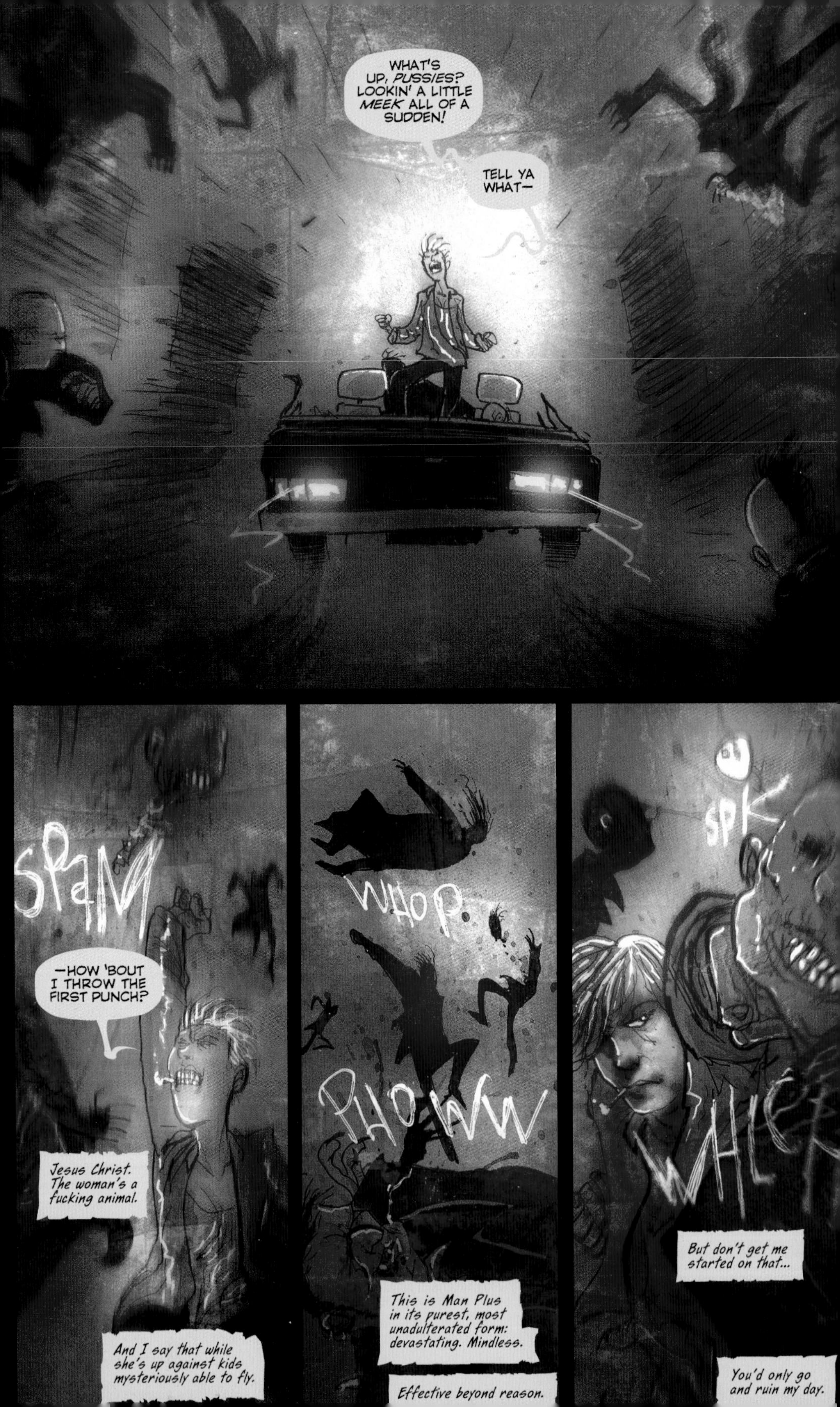
WHAT'S UP, PUSSIES? LOOKIN' A LITTLE MEEK ALL OF A SUDDEN!
TELL YA WHAT—
SPAM
—HOW 'BOUT I THROW THE FIRST PUNCH?
Jesus Christ. The woman's a fucking animal.
And I say that while she's up against kids mysteriously able to fly.
WHOP
PHOWW
This is Man Plus in its purest, most unadulterated form: devastating. Mindless.
Effective beyond reason.
SPK
But don't get me started on that...
You'd only go and ruin my day.

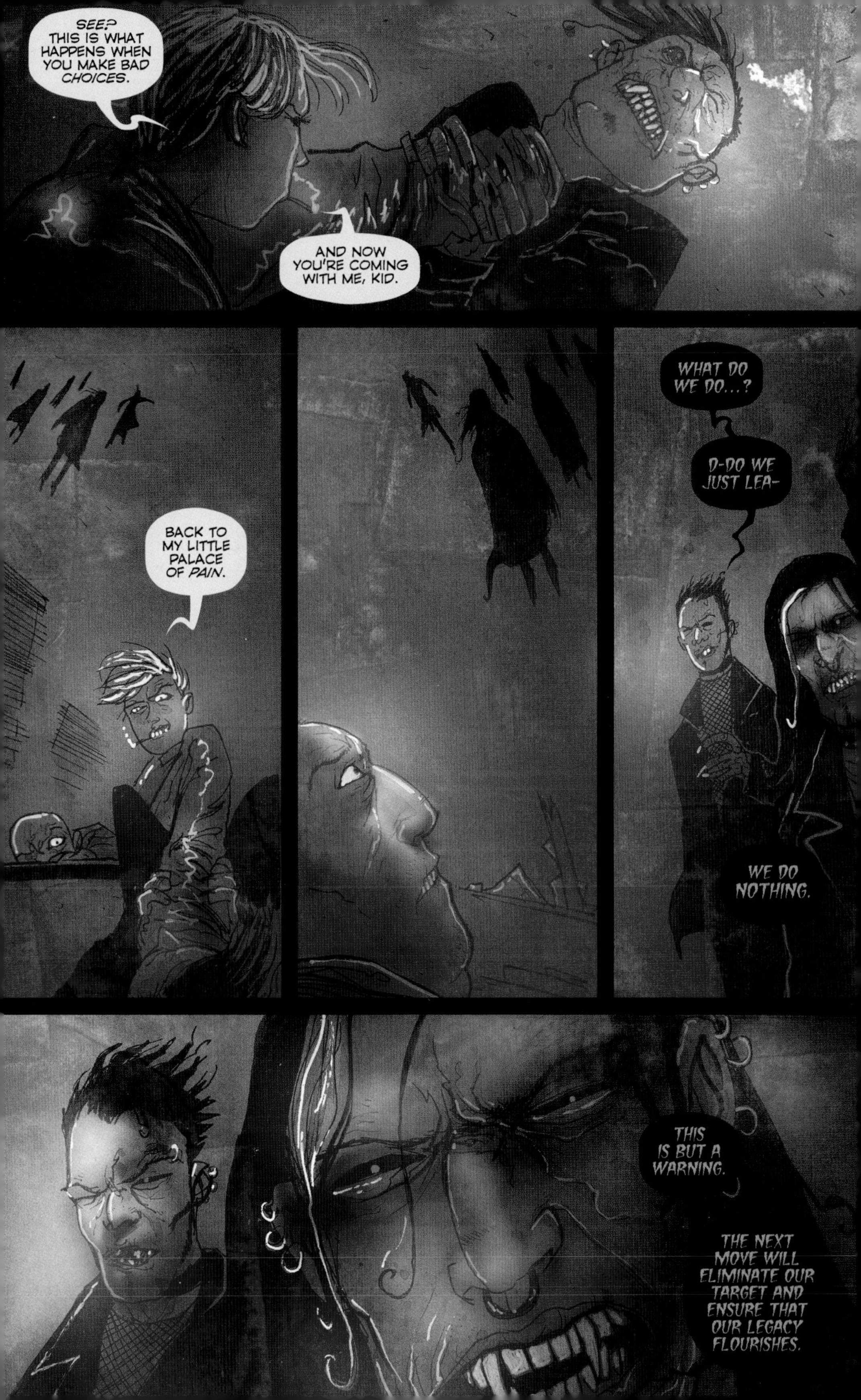
SEE? THIS IS WHAT HAPPENS WHEN YOU MAKE BAD *CHOICES*.
AND NOW YOU'RE COMING WITH ME, KID.
BACK TO MY LITTLE PALACE OF *PAIN*.
WHAT DO WE DO...?
D-DO WE JUST LEA-
WE DO NOTHING.
THIS IS BUT A WARNING.
THE NEXT MOVE WILL ELIMINATE OUR TARGET AND ENSURE THAT OUR LEGACY FLOURISHES.

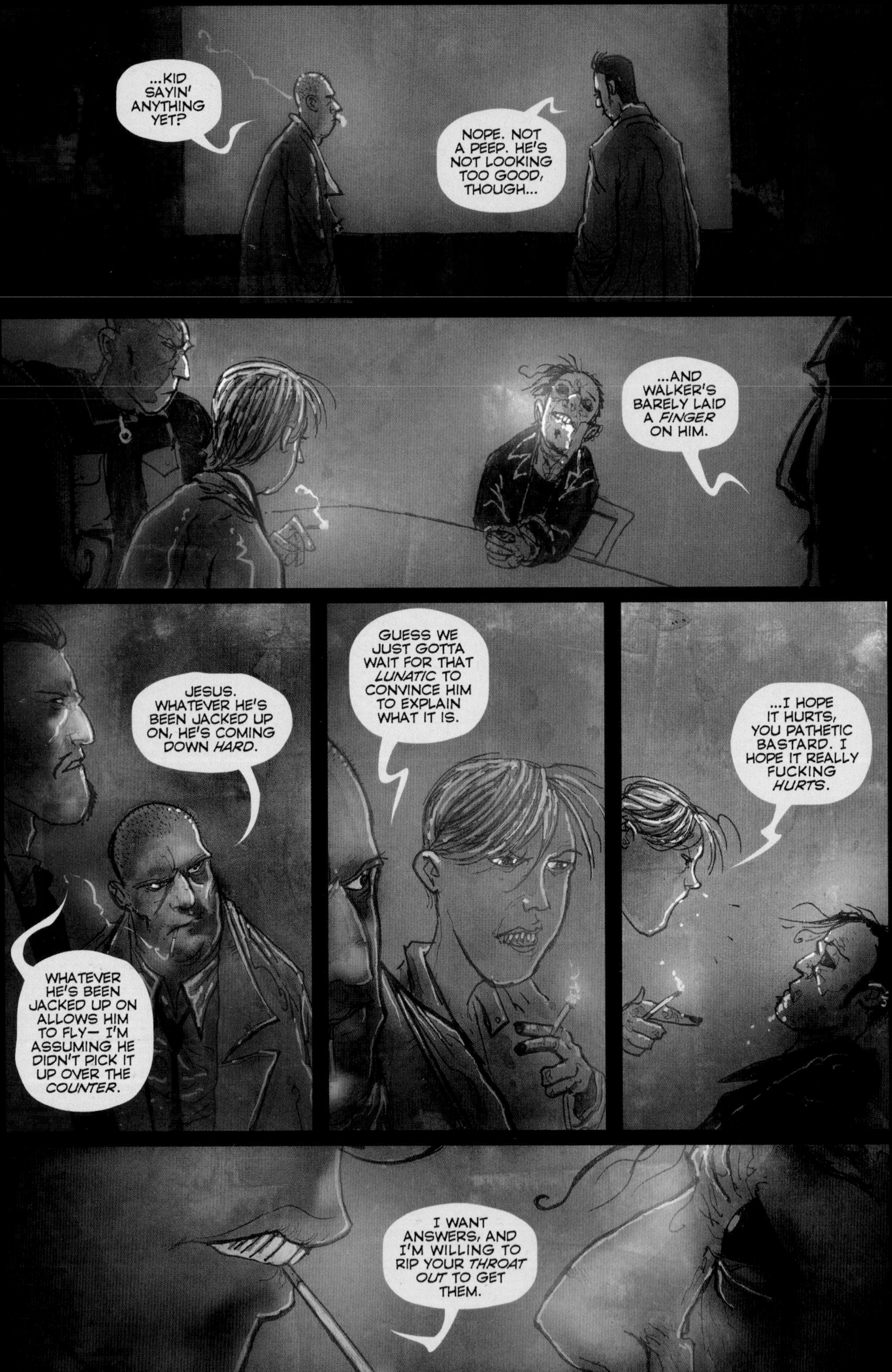
...KID SAYIN' ANYTHING YET?
NOPE. NOT A PEEP. HE'S NOT LOOKING TOO GOOD, THOUGH...
...AND WALKER'S BARELY LAID A *FINGER* ON HIM.
JESUS. WHATEVER HE'S BEEN JACKED UP ON, HE'S COMING DOWN *HARD*.
WHATEVER HE'S BEEN JACKED UP ON ALLOWS HIM TO FLY— I'M ASSUMING HE DIDN'T PICK IT UP OVER THE *COUNTER*.
GUESS WE JUST GOTTA WAIT FOR THAT *LUNATIC* TO CONVINCE HIM TO EXPLAIN WHAT IT IS.
...I HOPE IT HURTS, YOU PATHETIC BASTARD. I HOPE IT REALLY FUCKING *HURTS*.
I WANT ANSWERS, AND I'M WILLING TO RIP YOUR *THROAT OUT* TO GET THEM.

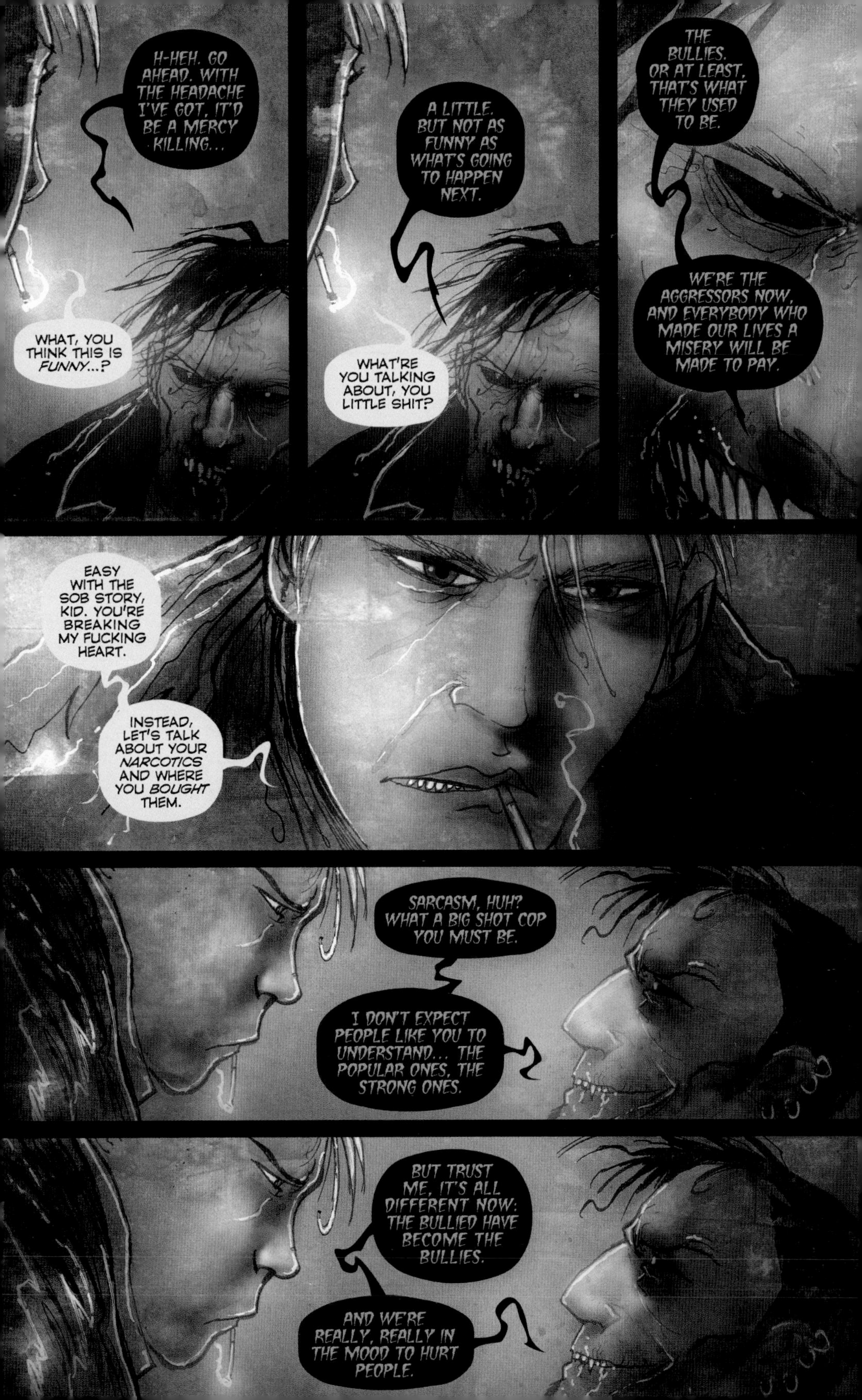
H-HEH. GO AHEAD. WITH THE HEADACHE I'VE GOT, IT'D BE A MERCY KILLING...
WHAT, YOU THINK THIS IS *FUNNY*...?
A LITTLE. BUT NOT AS FUNNY AS WHAT'S GOING TO HAPPEN NEXT.
WHAT'RE YOU TALKING ABOUT, YOU LITTLE SHIT?
THE BULLIES. OR AT LEAST, THAT'S WHAT THEY USED TO BE.
WE'RE THE AGGRESSORS NOW, AND EVERYBODY WHO MADE OUR LIVES A MISERY WILL BE MADE TO PAY.
EASY WITH THE SOB STORY, KID. YOU'RE BREAKING MY FUCKING HEART.
INSTEAD, LET'S TALK ABOUT YOUR *NARCOTICS* AND WHERE YOU *BOUGHT* THEM.
SARCASM, HUH? WHAT A BIG SHOT COP YOU MUST BE.
I DON'T EXPECT PEOPLE LIKE YOU TO UNDERSTAND... THE POPULAR ONES, THE STRONG ONES.
BUT TRUST ME, IT'S ALL DIFFERENT NOW: THE BULLIED HAVE BECOME THE BULLIES.
AND WE'RE REALLY, REALLY IN THE MOOD TO HURT PEOPLE.

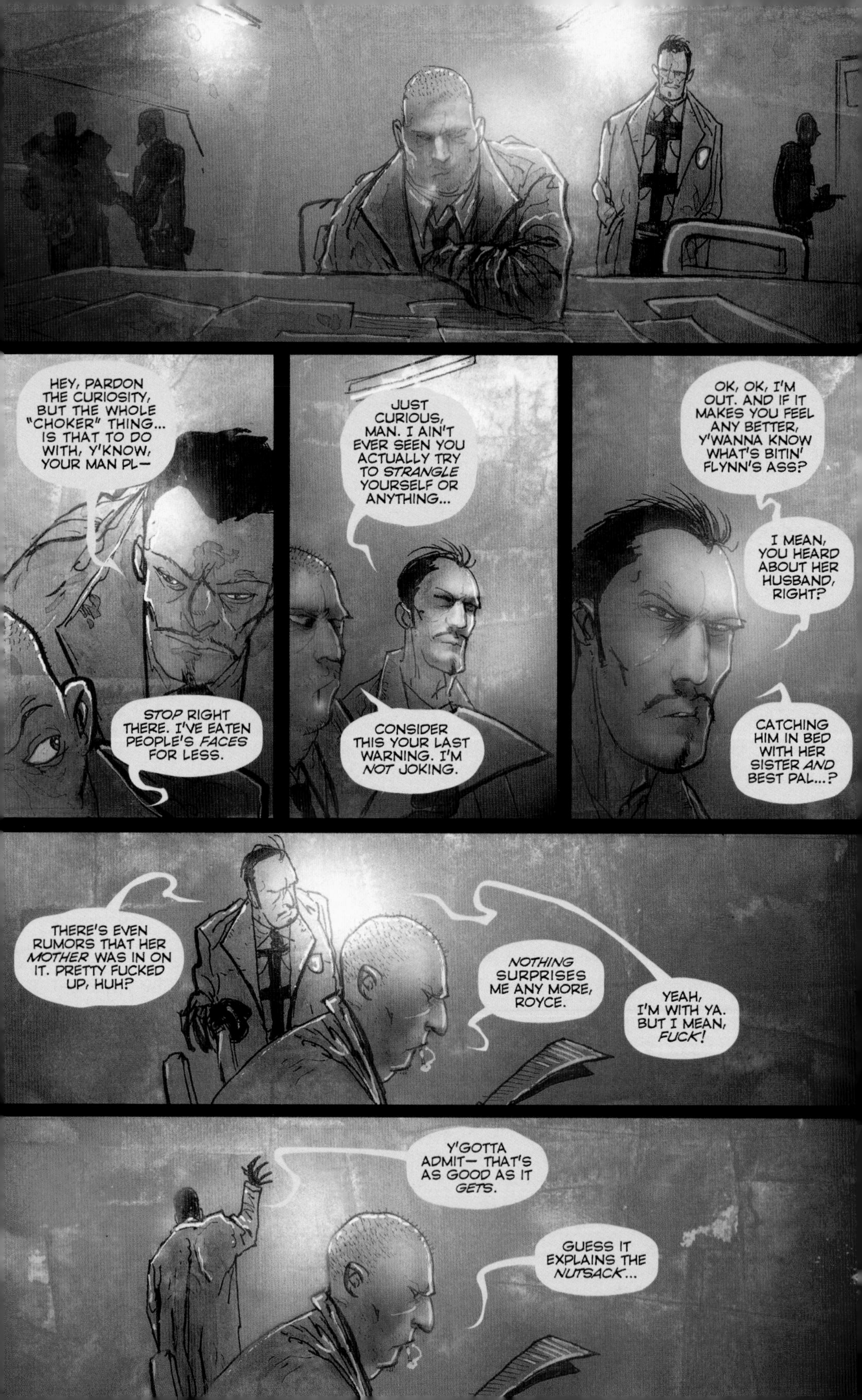
HEY, PARDON THE CURIOSITY, BUT THE WHOLE "CHOKER" THING... IS THAT TO DO WITH, Y'KNOW, YOUR MAN PL—
STOP RIGHT THERE. I'VE EATEN PEOPLE'S FACES FOR LESS.
JUST CURIOUS, MAN. I AIN'T EVER SEEN YOU ACTUALLY TRY TO STRANGLE YOURSELF OR ANYTHING...
CONSIDER THIS YOUR LAST WARNING. I'M NOT JOKING.
OK, OK, I'M OUT. AND IF IT MAKES YOU FEEL ANY BETTER, Y'WANNA KNOW WHAT'S BITIN' FLYNN'S ASS?
I MEAN, YOU HEARD ABOUT HER HUSBAND, RIGHT?
CATCHING HIM IN BED WITH HER SISTER AND BEST PAL...?
THERE'S EVEN RUMORS THAT HER MOTHER WAS IN ON IT. PRETTY FUCKED UP, HUH?
NOTHING SURPRISES ME ANY MORE, ROYCE.
YEAH, I'M WITH YA. BUT I MEAN, FUCK!
Y'GOTTA ADMIT— THAT'S AS GOOD AS IT GETS.
GUESS IT EXPLAINS THE NUTSACK...

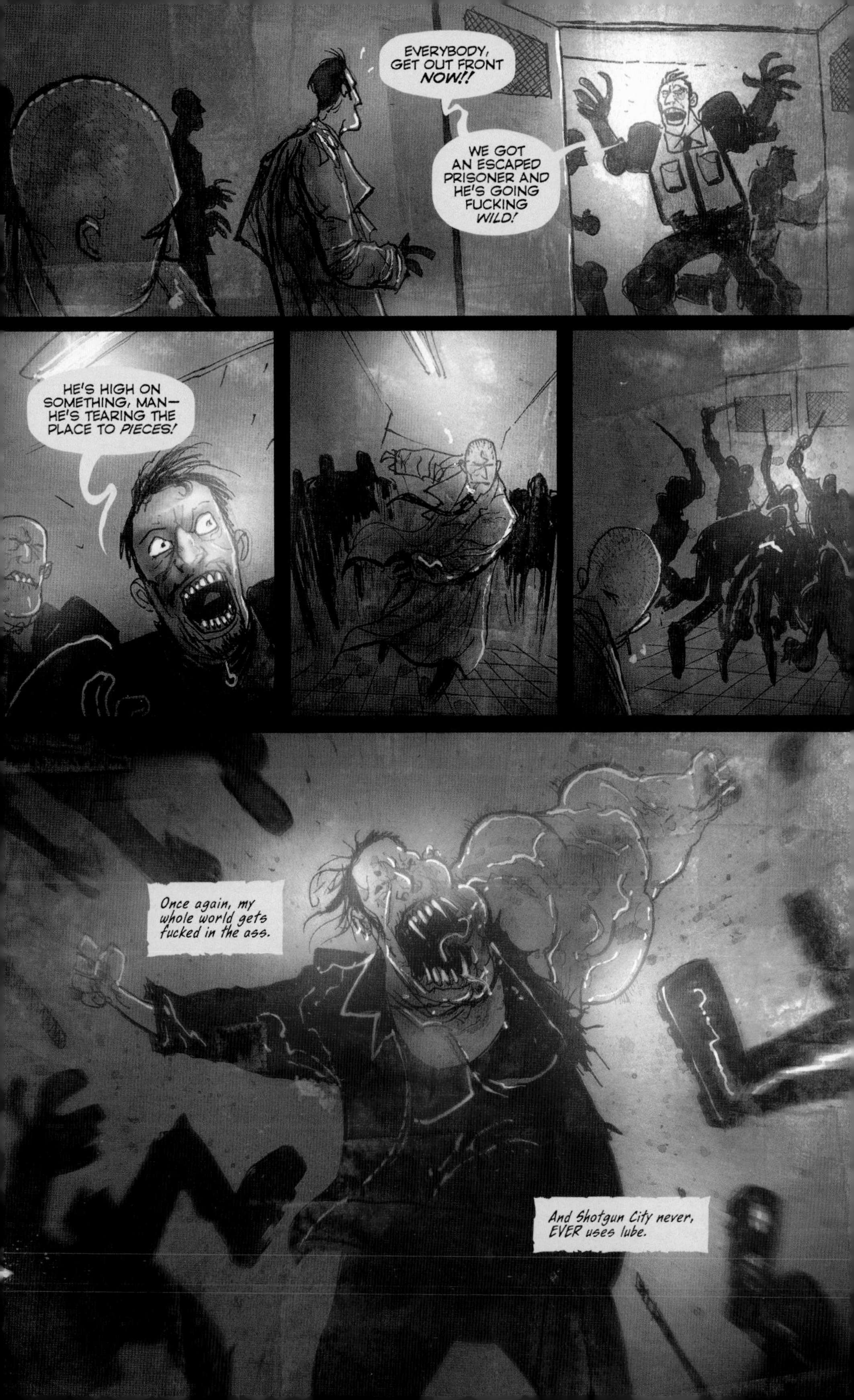

EVERYBODY, GET OUT FRONT NOW!!
WE GOT AN ESCAPED PRISONER AND HE'S GOING FUCKING WILD!
HE'S HIGH ON SOMETHING, MAN— HE'S TEARING THE PLACE TO PIECES!
Once again, my whole world gets fucked in the ass.
And Shotgun City never, EVER uses lube.

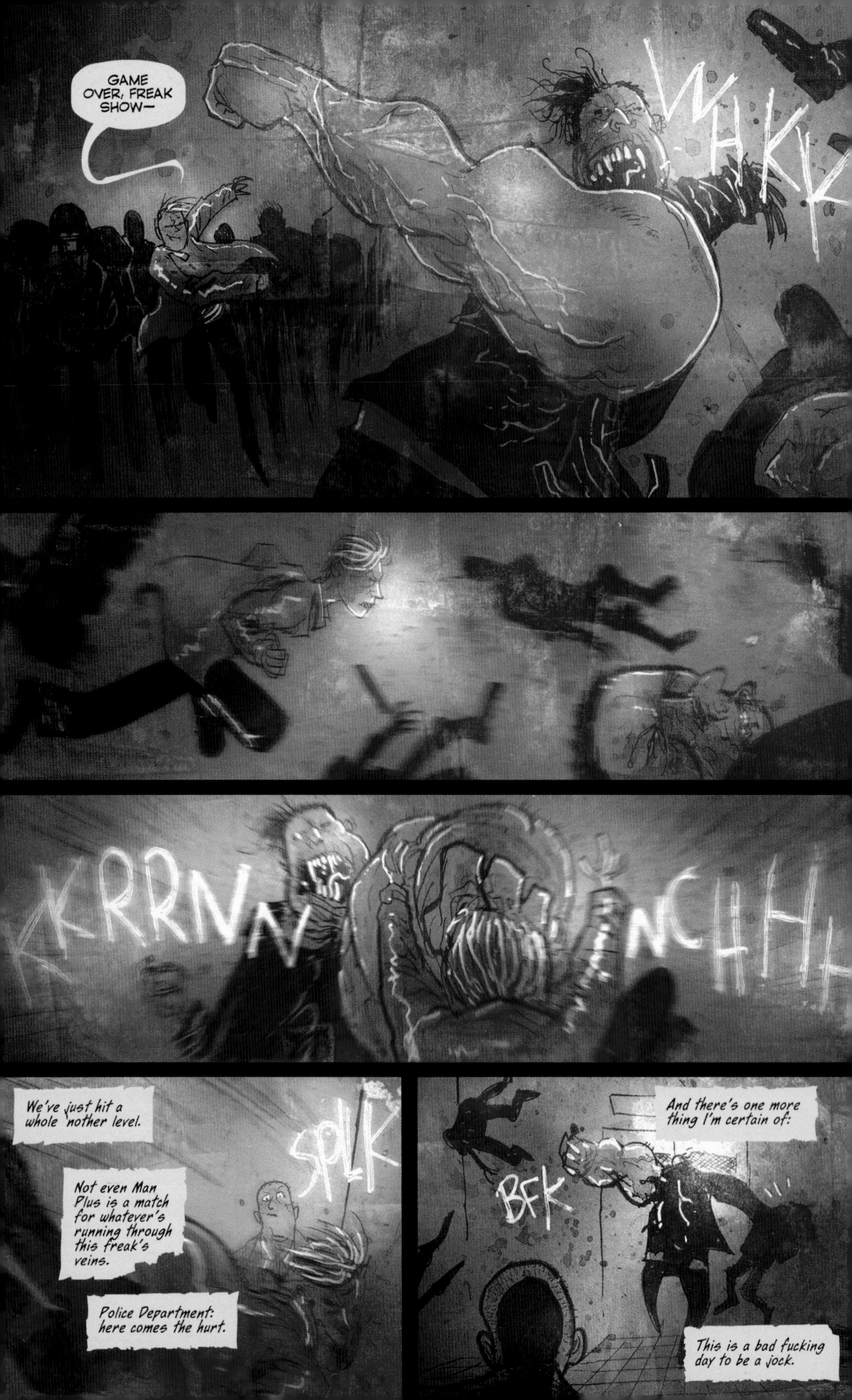

GAME OVER, FREAK SHOW—
WHKK
KKRRNNNCHH
We've just hit a whole 'nother level.
SPLK
Not even Man Plus is a match for whatever's running through this freak's veins.
Police Department: here comes the hurt.
And there's one more thing I'm certain of:
BFK
This is a bad fucking day to be a jock.

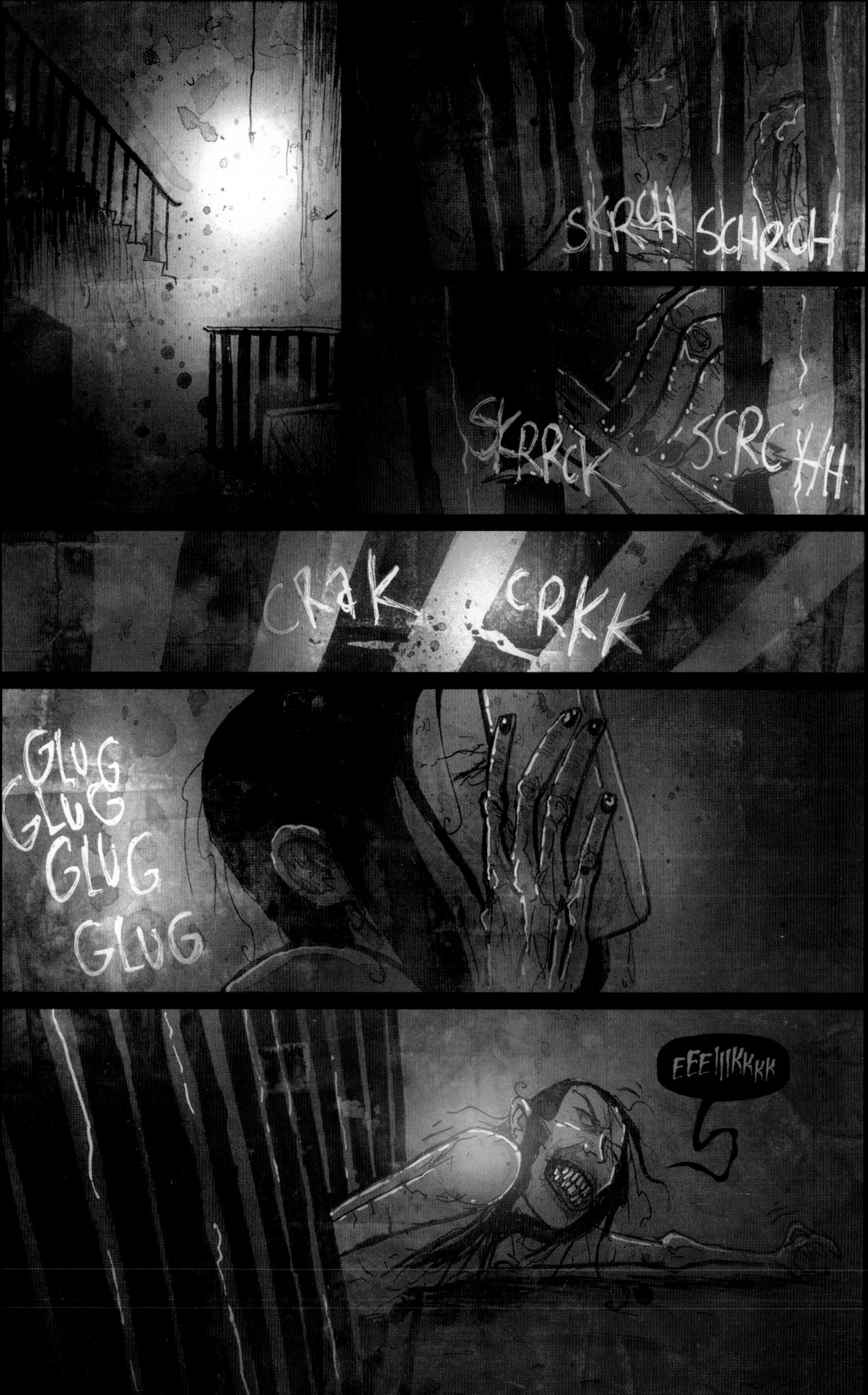
SKRCH SCHRCH
SKRRCK SCRCHH
CRAK CRKK
GLUG GLUG GLUG GLUG
EEEIIIKKKK

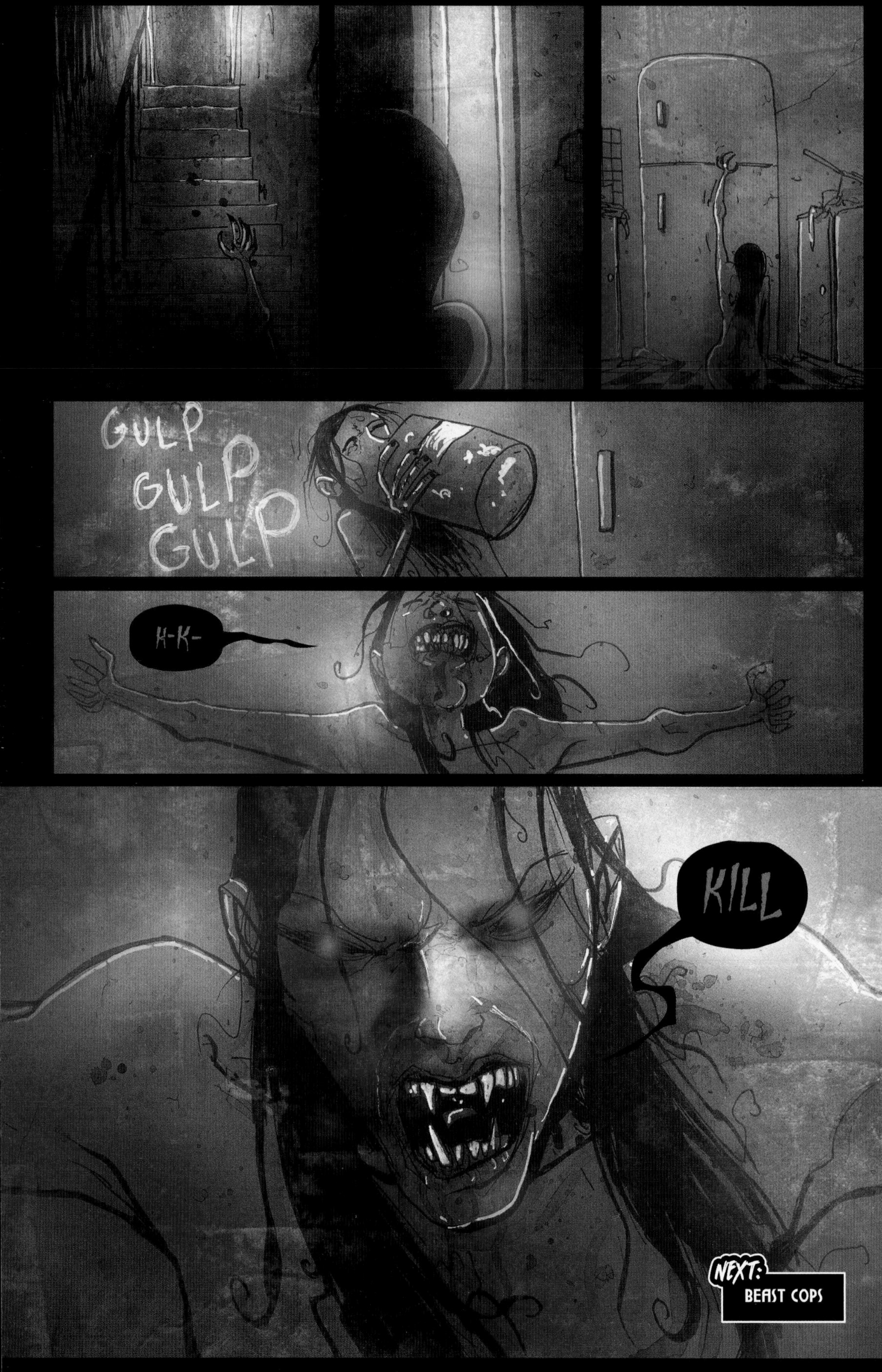
GULP
GULP
GULP
H-K-
KILL
NEXT:
BEAST COPS

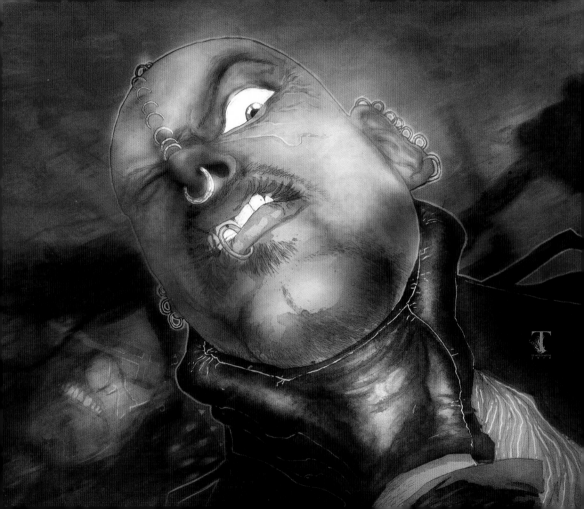

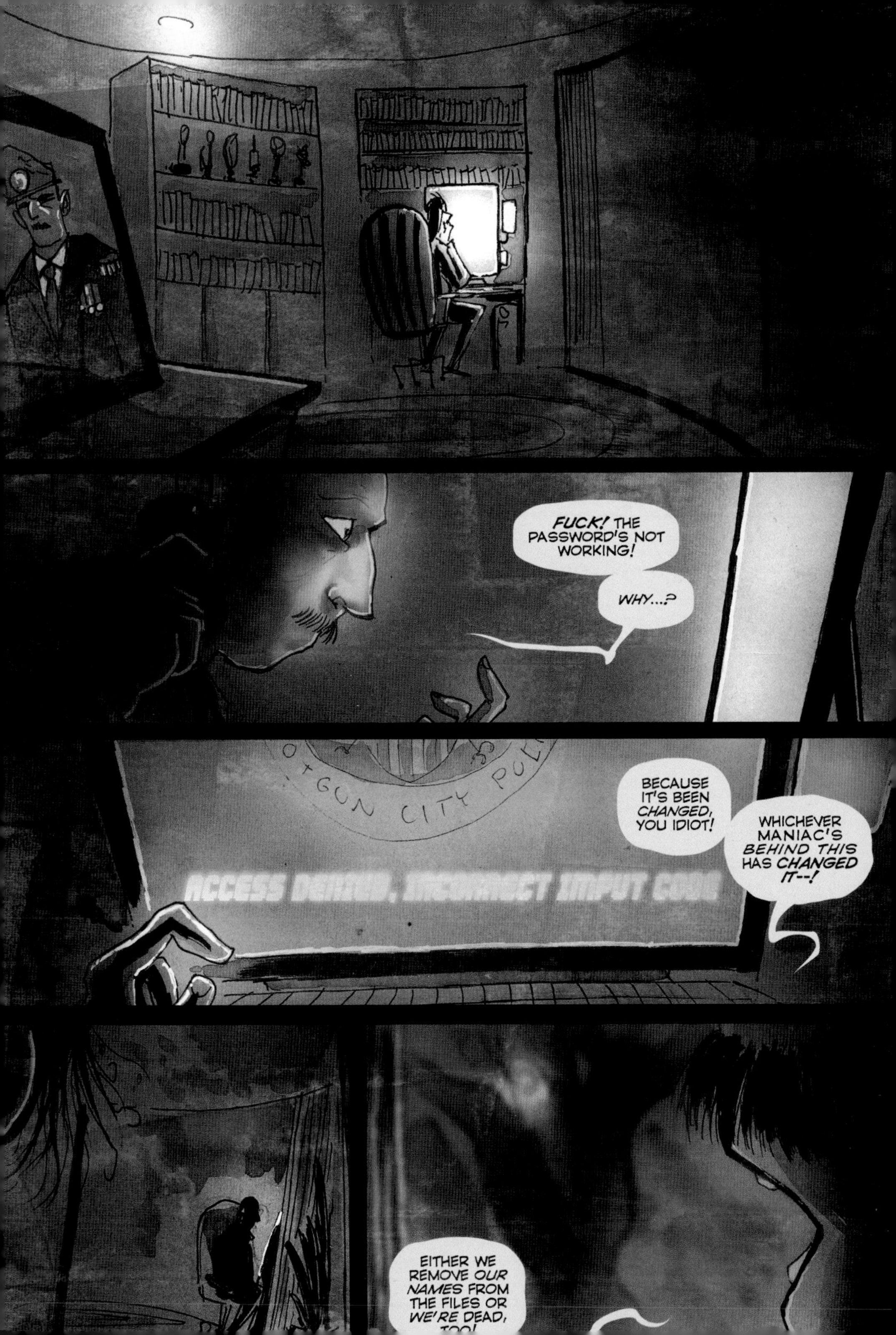

FUCK! THE PASSWORD'S NOT WORKING!
WHY...?
ACCESS DENIED, INCORRECT IMPUT CODE
BECAUSE IT'S BEEN *CHANGED,* YOU IDIOT!
WHICHEVER MANIAC'S *BEHIND THIS* HAS *CHANGED IT--!*
EITHER WE REMOVE *OUR NAMES* FROM THE FILES OR *WE'RE DEAD,* TOO!

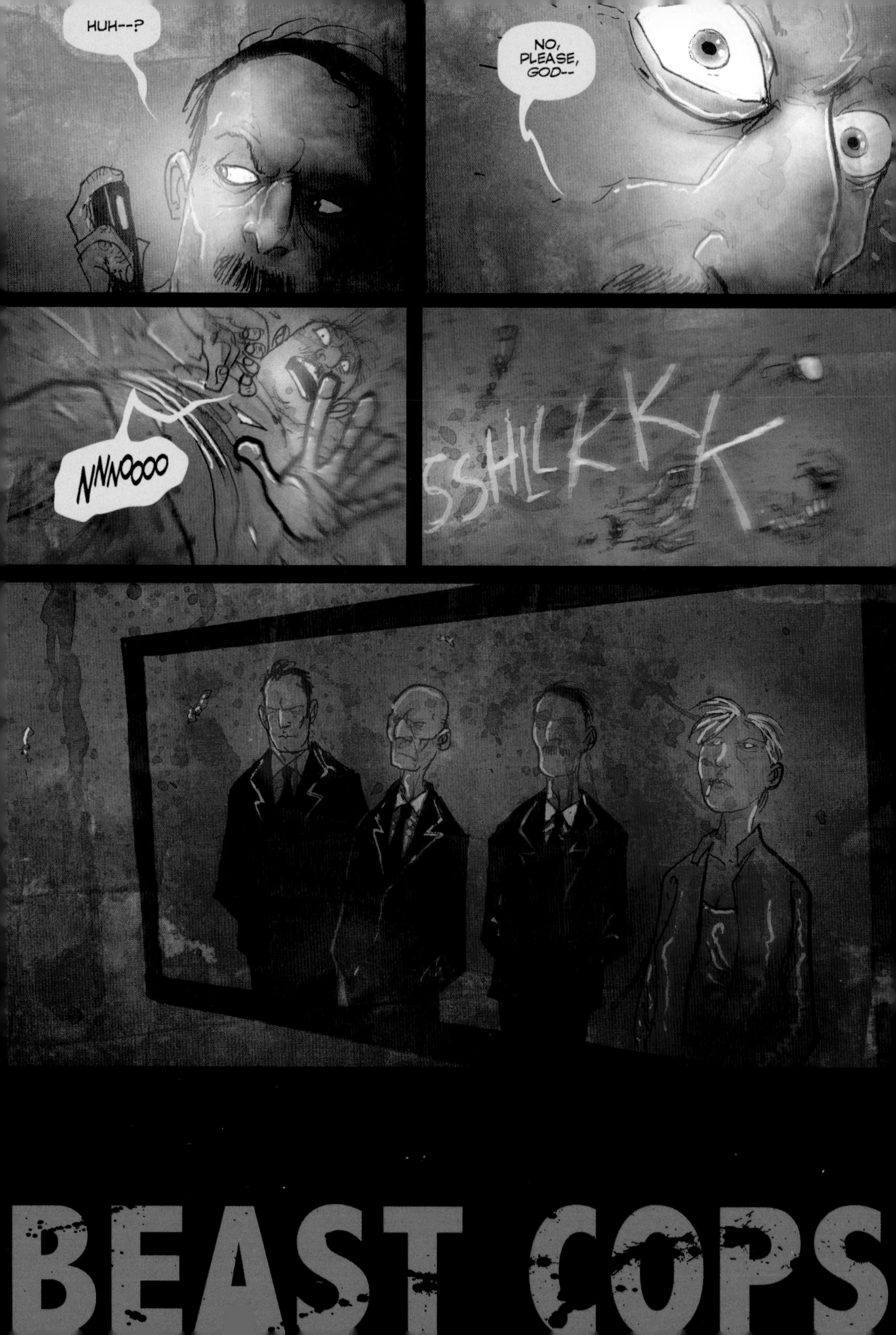
HUH--?
NO, PLEASE, GOD--
NNNOOOO
SSHLLKKK
BEAST COPS

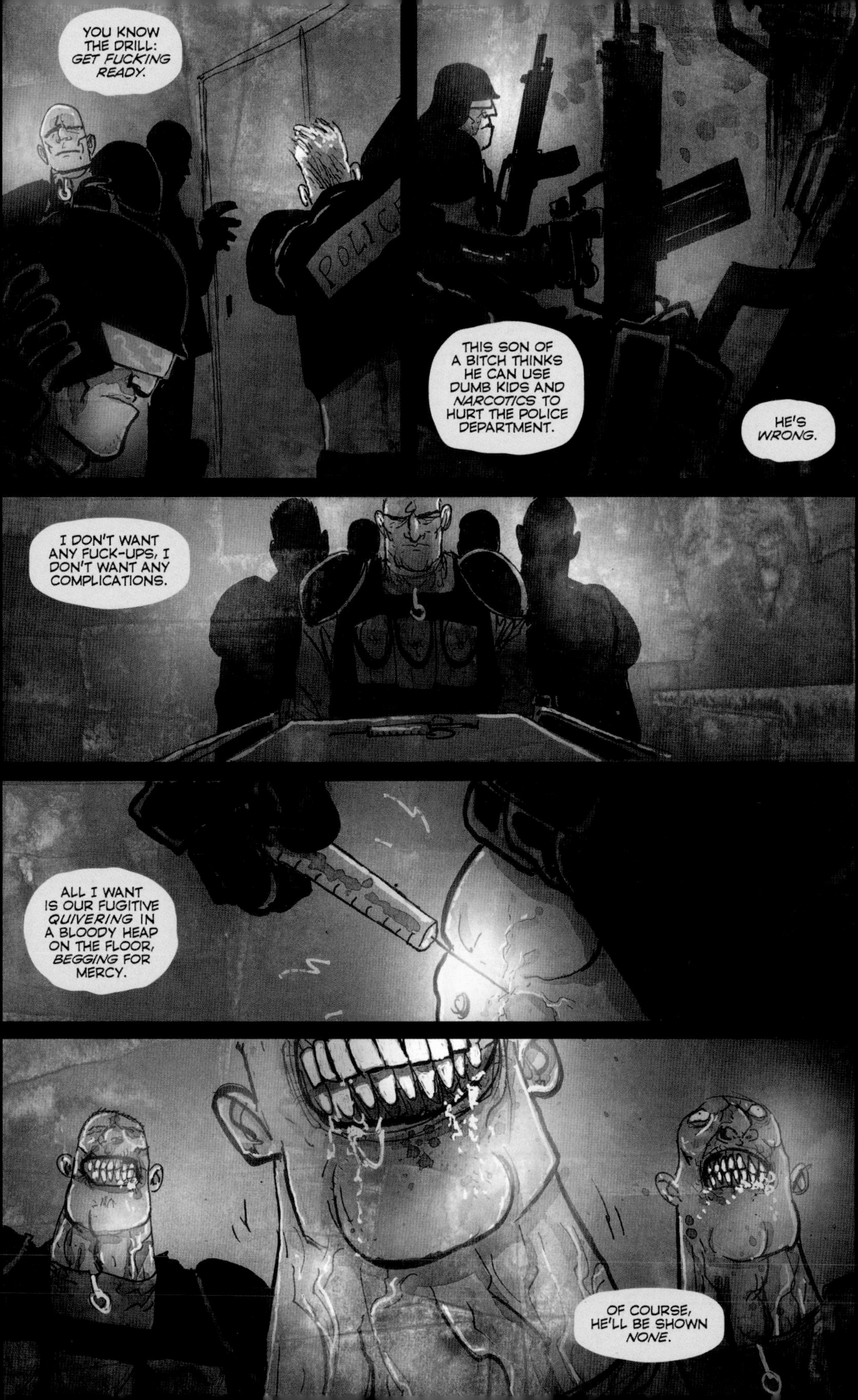
YOU KNOW THE DRILL: *GET FUCKING READY.*
POLICE
THIS SON OF A BITCH THINKS HE CAN USE DUMB KIDS AND *NARCOTICS* TO HURT THE POLICE DEPARTMENT.
HE'S *WRONG.*
I DON'T WANT ANY FUCK-UPS, I DON'T WANT ANY COMPLICATIONS.
ALL I WANT IS OUR FUGITIVE *QUIVERING* IN A BLOODY HEAP ON THE FLOOR, *BEGGING* FOR MERCY.
OF COURSE, HE'LL BE SHOWN *NONE.*

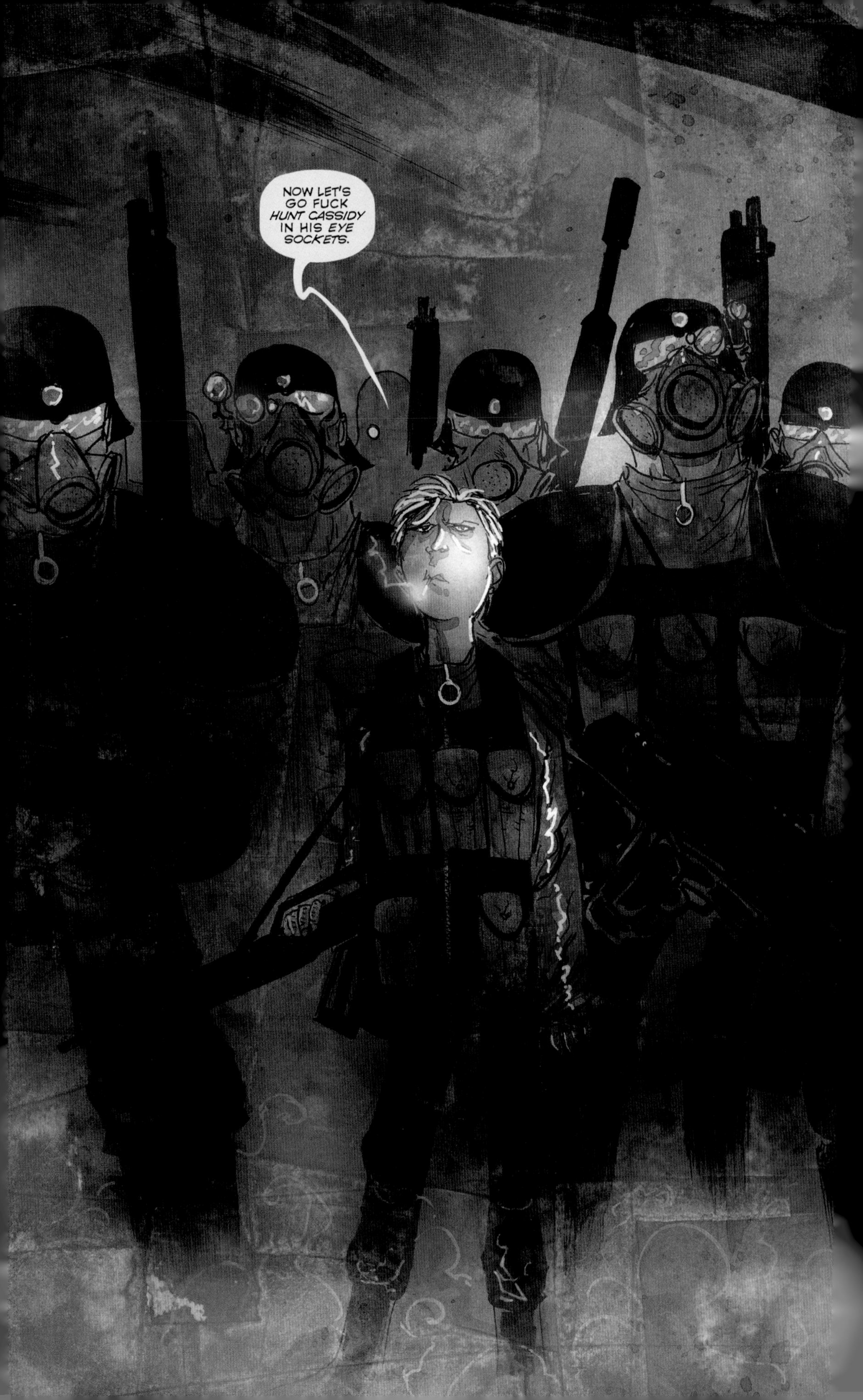
NOW LET'S GO FUCK *HUNT CASSIDY* IN HIS *EYE SOCKETS.*

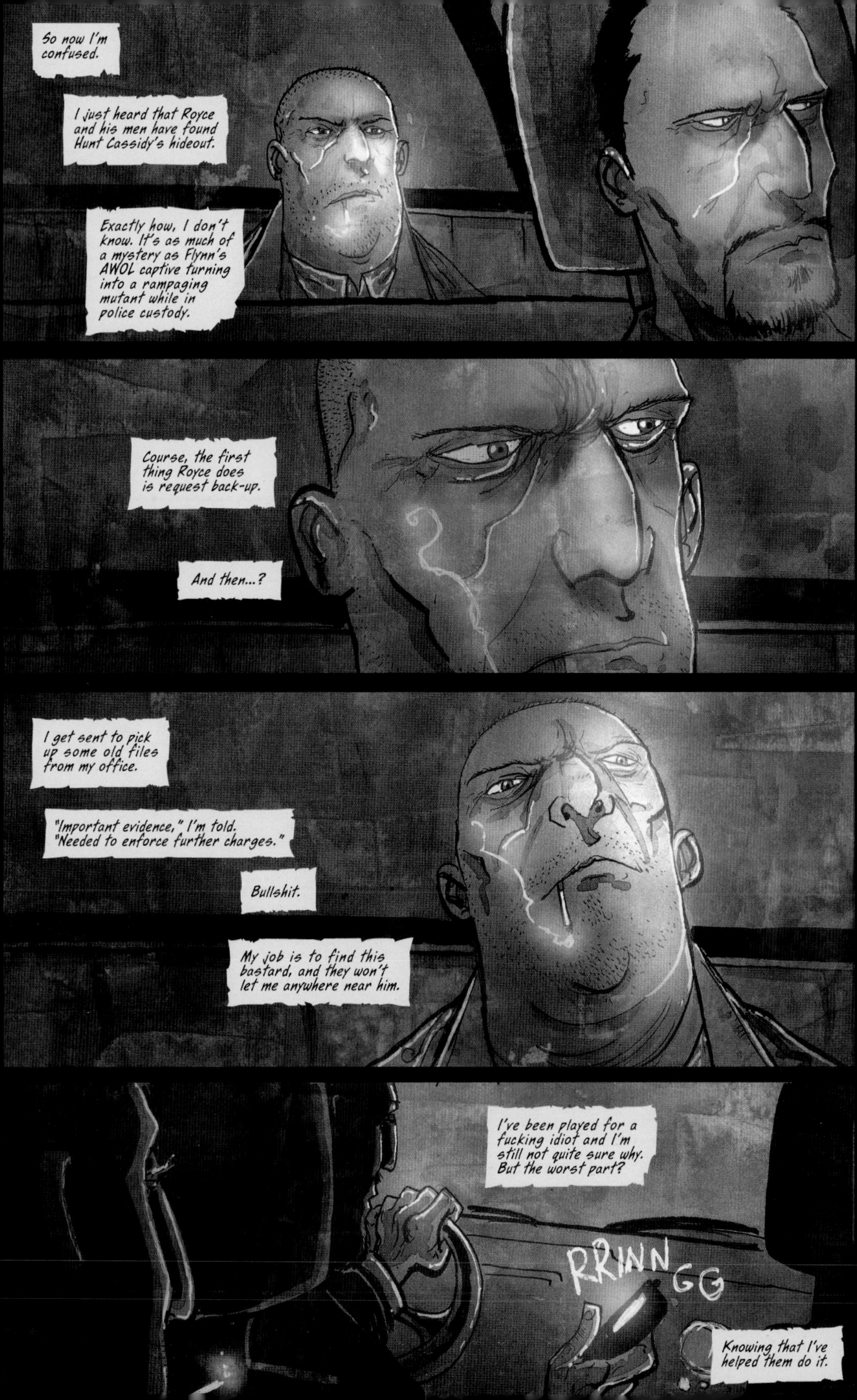
So now I'm confused.
I just heard that Royce and his men have found Hunt Cassidy's hideout.
Exactly how, I don't know. It's as much of a mystery as Flynn's AWOL captive turning into a rampaging mutant while in police custody.
Course, the first thing Royce does is request back-up.
And then...?
I get sent to pick up some old files from my office.
"Important evidence," I'm told. "Needed to enforce further charges."
Bullshit.
My job is to find this bastard, and they won't let me anywhere near him.
I've been played for a fucking idiot and I'm still not quite sure why. But the worst part?
RRINNGG
Knowing that I've helped them do it.

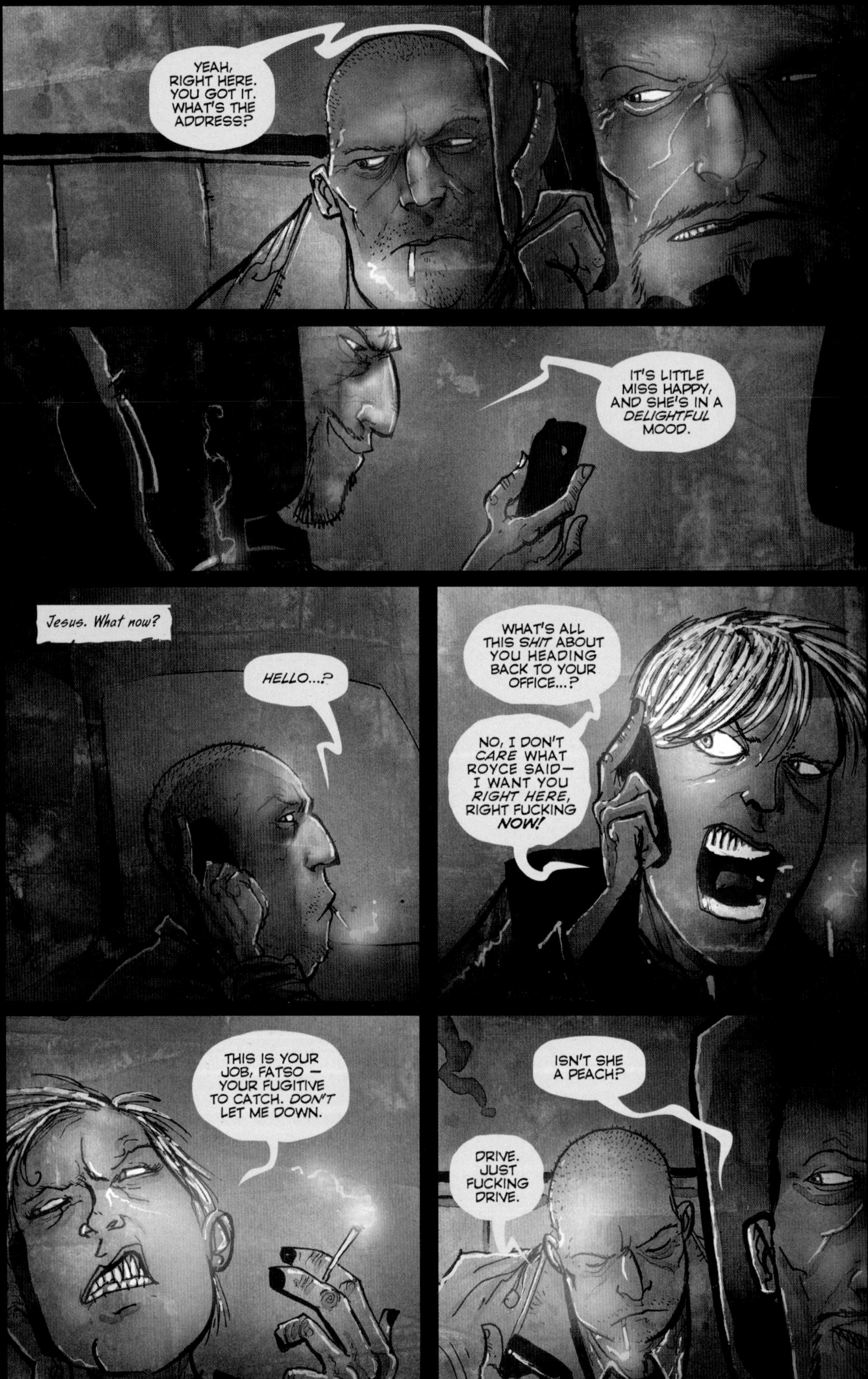
YEAH, RIGHT HERE. YOU GOT IT. WHAT'S THE ADDRESS?
IT'S LITTLE MISS HAPPY, AND SHE'S IN A *DELIGHTFUL* MOOD.
Jesus. What now?
HELLO...?
WHAT'S ALL THIS *SHIT* ABOUT YOU HEADING BACK TO YOUR OFFICE...?
NO, I DON'T *CARE* WHAT ROYCE SAID— I WANT YOU *RIGHT HERE*, RIGHT FUCKING ***NOW!***
THIS IS YOUR JOB, FATSO — YOUR FUGITIVE TO CATCH. *DON'T* LET ME DOWN.
ISN'T SHE A PEACH?
DRIVE. JUST FUCKING DRIVE.

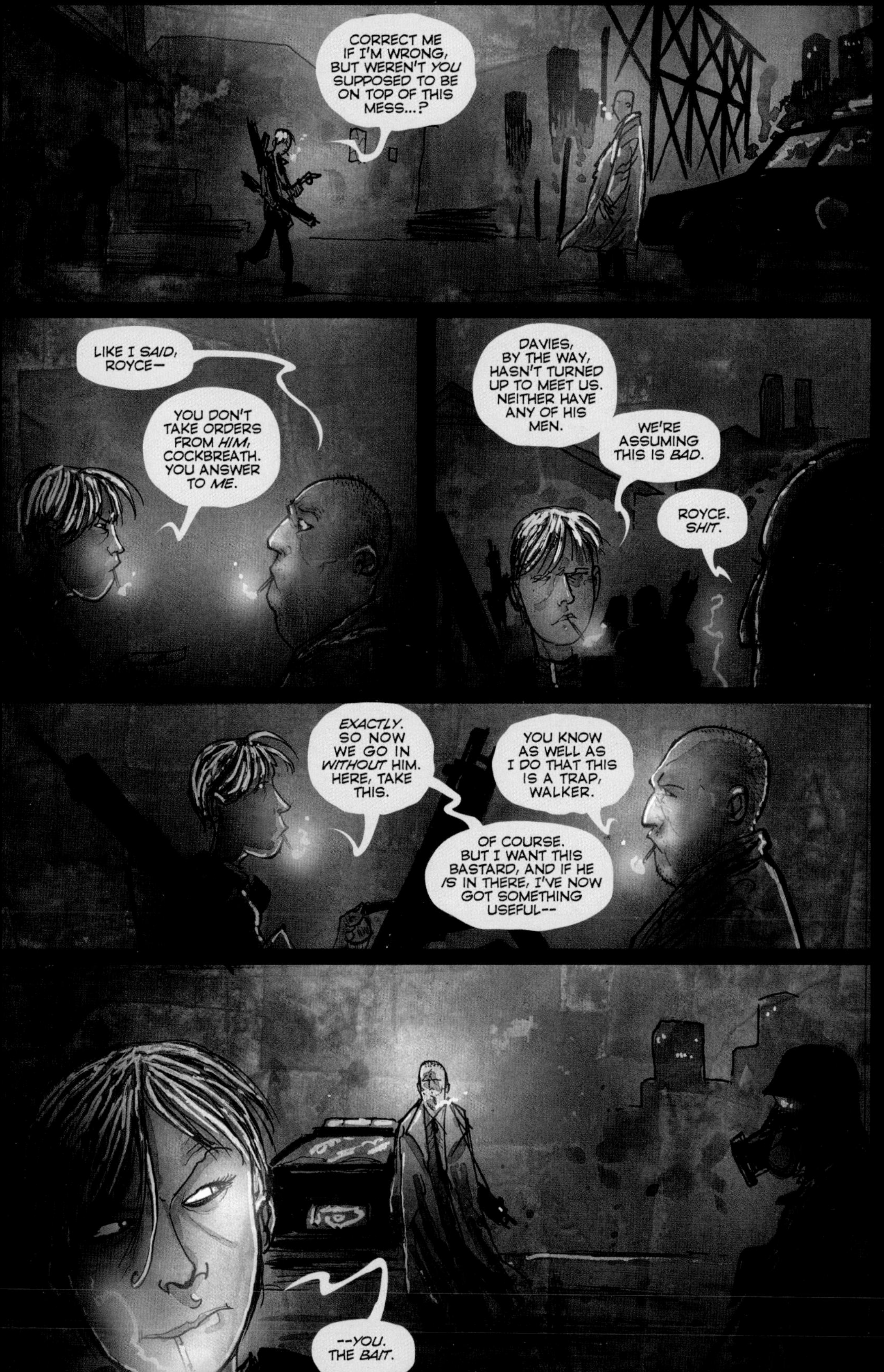
CORRECT ME IF I'M WRONG, BUT WEREN'T *YOU* SUPPOSED TO BE ON TOP OF THIS MESS...?
LIKE I *SAID*, ROYCE—
YOU DON'T TAKE ORDERS FROM *HIM*, COCKBREATH. YOU ANSWER TO *ME*.
DAVIES, BY THE WAY, HASN'T TURNED UP TO MEET US. NEITHER HAVE ANY OF HIS MEN.
WE'RE ASSUMING THIS IS *BAD*.
ROYCE. *SHIT*.
EXACTLY. SO NOW WE GO IN *WITHOUT* HIM. HERE, TAKE THIS.
YOU KNOW AS WELL AS I DO THAT THIS IS A TRAP, WALKER.
OF COURSE. BUT I WANT THIS BASTARD, AND IF HE *IS* IN THERE, I'VE NOW GOT SOMETHING USEFUL--
--YOU. THE *BAIT*.

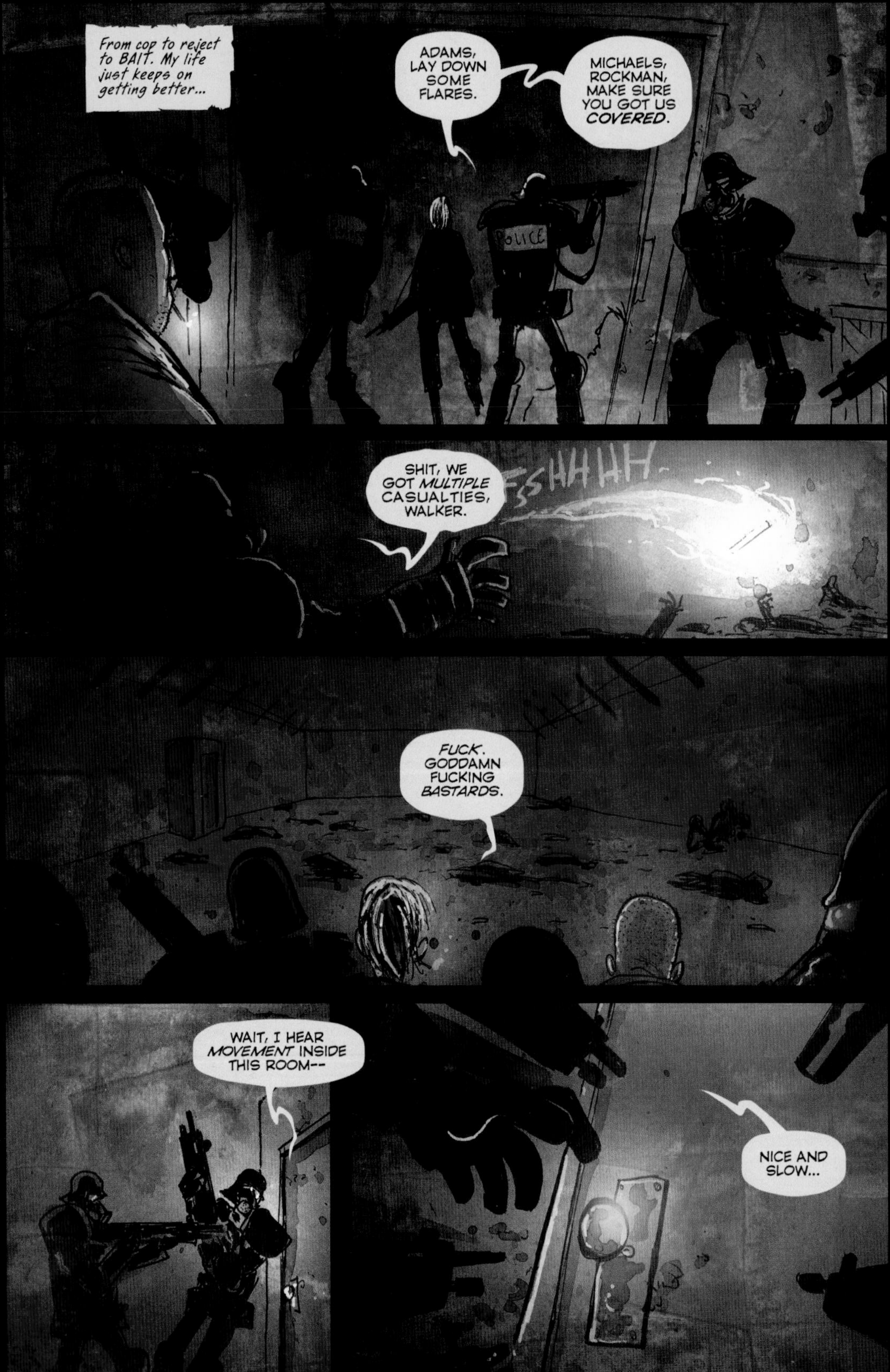
From cop to reject to BAIT. My life just keeps on getting better...
ADAMS, LAY DOWN SOME FLARES.
MICHAELS, ROCKMAN, MAKE SURE YOU GOT US *COVERED*.
POLICE
SHIT, WE GOT *MULTIPLE* CASUALTIES, WALKER.
FSHHHH
FUCK. GODDAMN FUCKING *BASTARDS*.
WAIT, I HEAR *MOVEMENT* INSIDE THIS ROOM--
NICE AND SLOW...

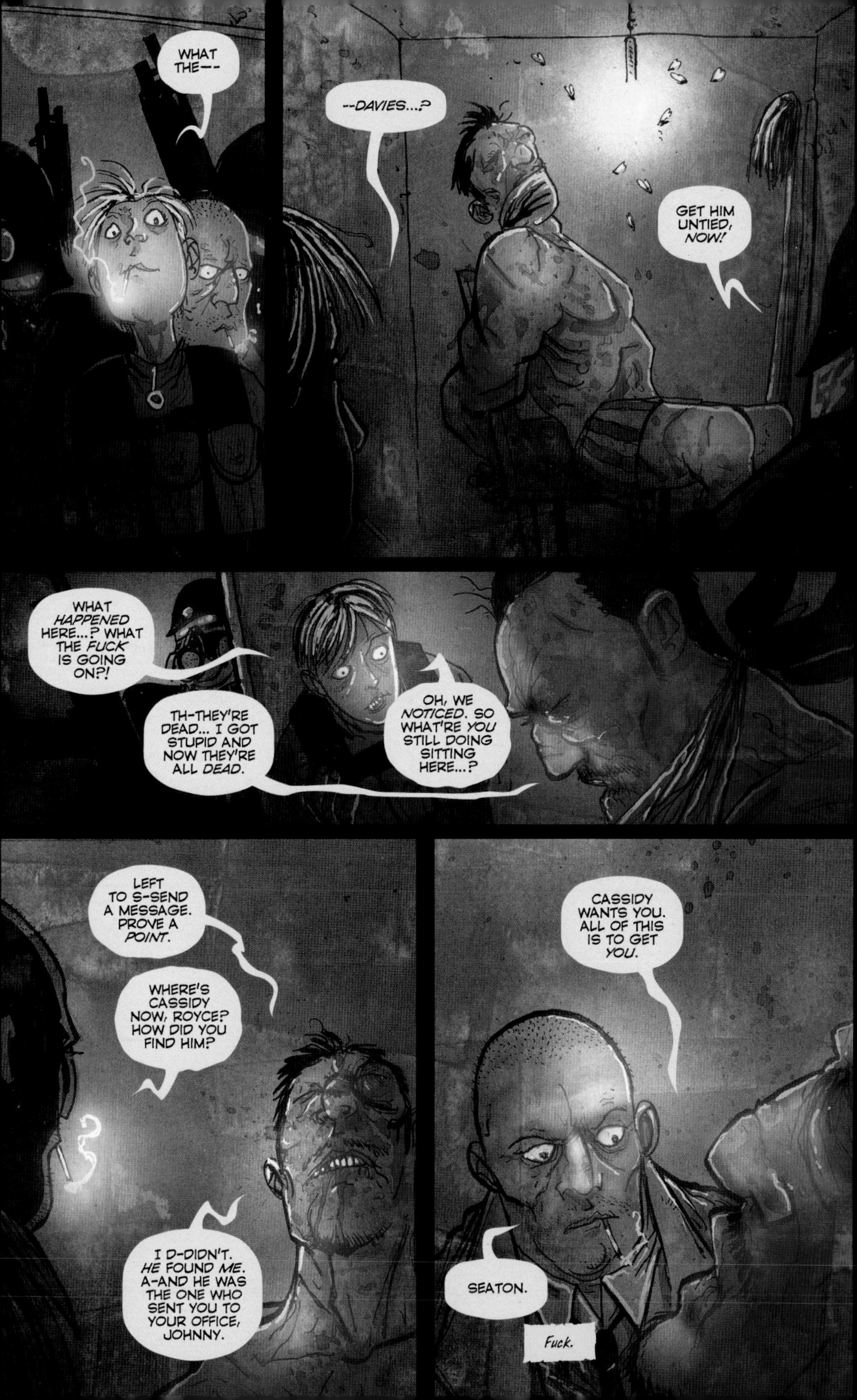
WHAT THE--
--DAVIES...?
GET HIM UNTIED, NOW!
WHAT HAPPENED HERE...? WHAT THE FUCK IS GOING ON?!
TH-THEY'RE DEAD... I GOT STUPID AND NOW THEY'RE ALL DEAD.
OH, WE NOTICED. SO WHAT'RE YOU STILL DOING SITTING HERE...?
LEFT TO S-SEND A MESSAGE. PROVE A POINT.
WHERE'S CASSIDY NOW, ROYCE? HOW DID YOU FIND HIM?
I D-DIDN'T. HE FOUND ME. A-AND HE WAS THE ONE WHO SENT YOU TO YOUR OFFICE, JOHNNY.
CASSIDY WANTS YOU. ALL OF THIS IS TO GET YOU.
SEATON.
Fuck.

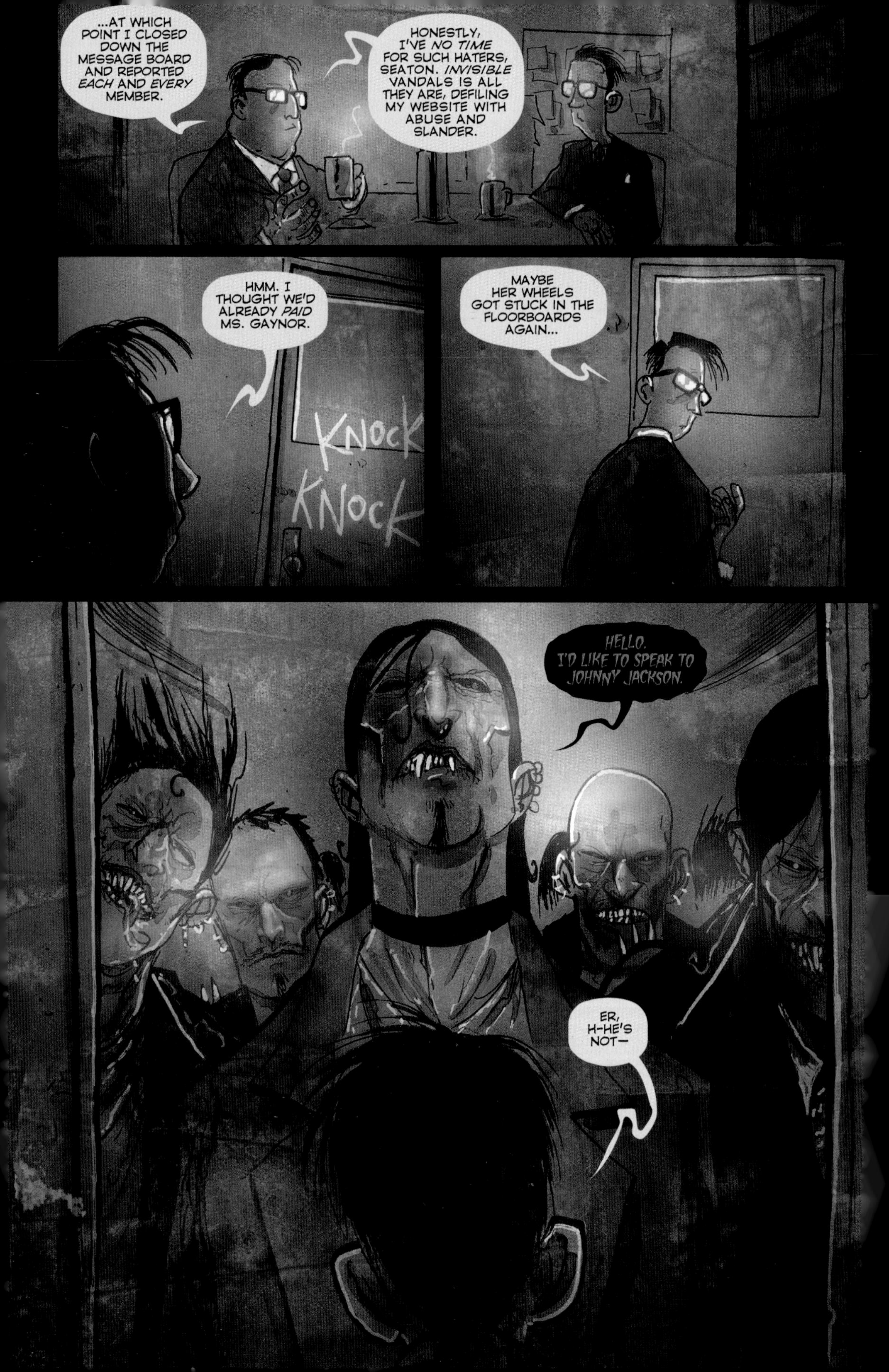
...AT WHICH POINT I CLOSED DOWN THE MESSAGE BOARD AND REPORTED *EACH* AND *EVERY* MEMBER.
HONESTLY, I'VE *NO TIME* FOR SUCH HATERS, SEATON. *INVISIBLE* VANDALS IS ALL THEY ARE, DEFILING MY WEBSITE WITH ABUSE AND SLANDER.
HMM. I THOUGHT WE'D ALREADY *PAID* MS. GAYNOR.
KNOCK
KNOCK
MAYBE HER WHEELS GOT STUCK IN THE FLOORBOARDS AGAIN...
HELLO. I'D LIKE TO SPEAK TO JOHNNY JACKSON.
ER, H-HE'S NOT—

WRONG ANSWER, YOU LITTLE FUCKING WORM.

SoK

SEATON--!

WH-WHAT DO YOU WANT...?

A FAT LOSER EX-COP, PLEASE.

GIVE US THAT AND YOU MIGHT EVEN LIVE.

B-BUT HE'S NOT HE—*UNK!*

THEN TELL ME WHERE HE IS BEFORE I RIP YOUR FACE OFF!

SMaK

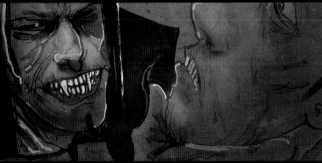

JOHNNY JACKSON DEAD. THAT'S ALL WE'RE HERE FOR.

WE'VE GOT A LITTLE UNDERSTANDING WITH A FRIEND OF HIS, SEE.

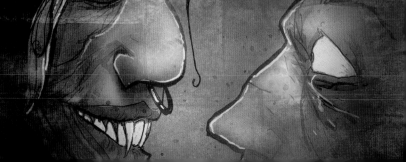

BUT WITH NO JACKSON, I'M AT SOMETHING OF A DISADVANTAGE.

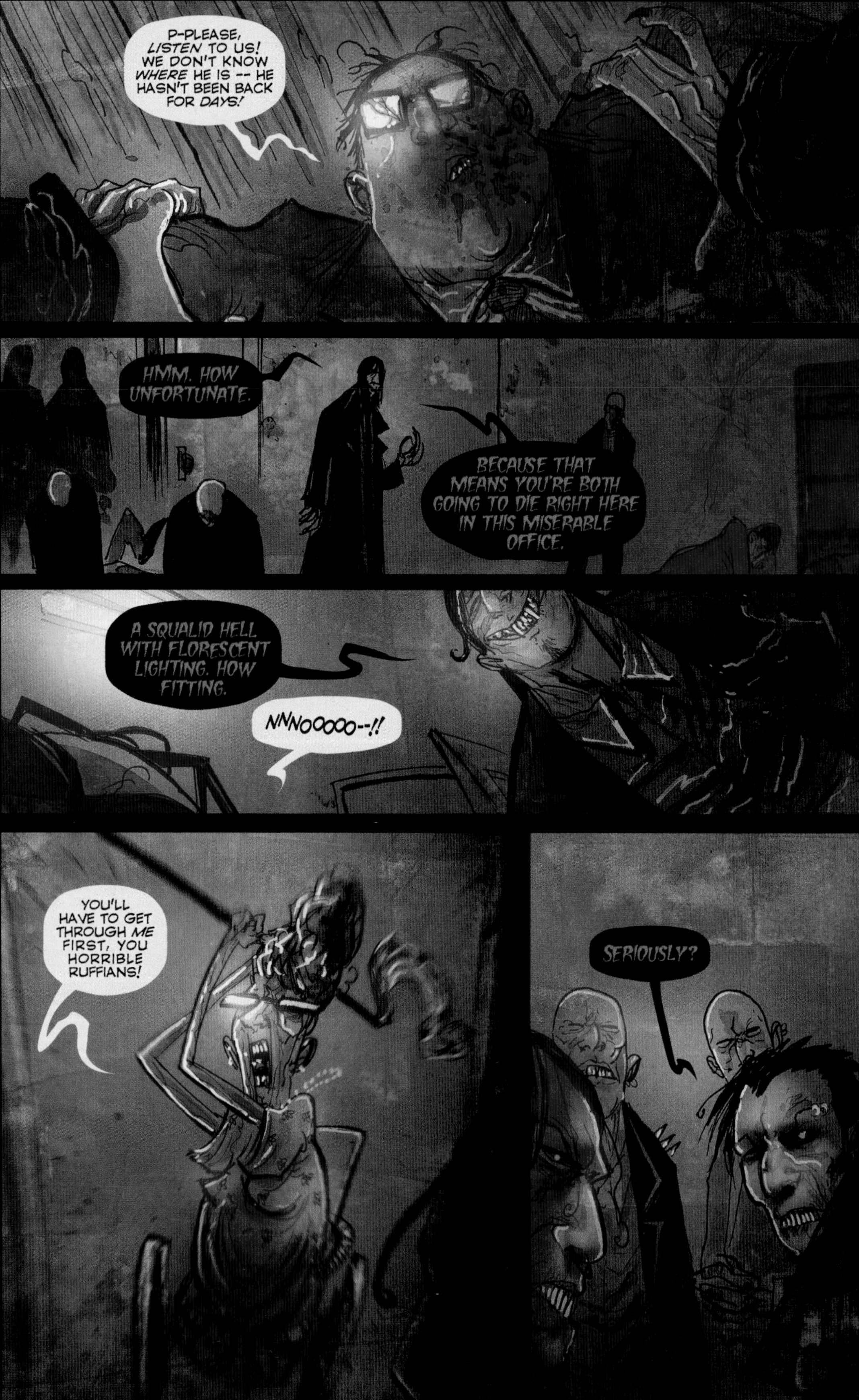
P-PLEASE, LISTEN TO US! WE DON'T KNOW WHERE HE IS -- HE HASN'T BEEN BACK FOR DAYS!
HMM. HOW UNFORTUNATE.
BECAUSE THAT MEANS YOU'RE BOTH GOING TO DIE RIGHT HERE IN THIS MISERABLE OFFICE.
A SQUALID HELL WITH FLORESCENT LIGHTING. HOW FITTING.
NNNOOOOO--!!
YOU'LL HAVE TO GET THROUGH ME FIRST, YOU HORRIBLE RUFFIANS!
SERIOUSLY?

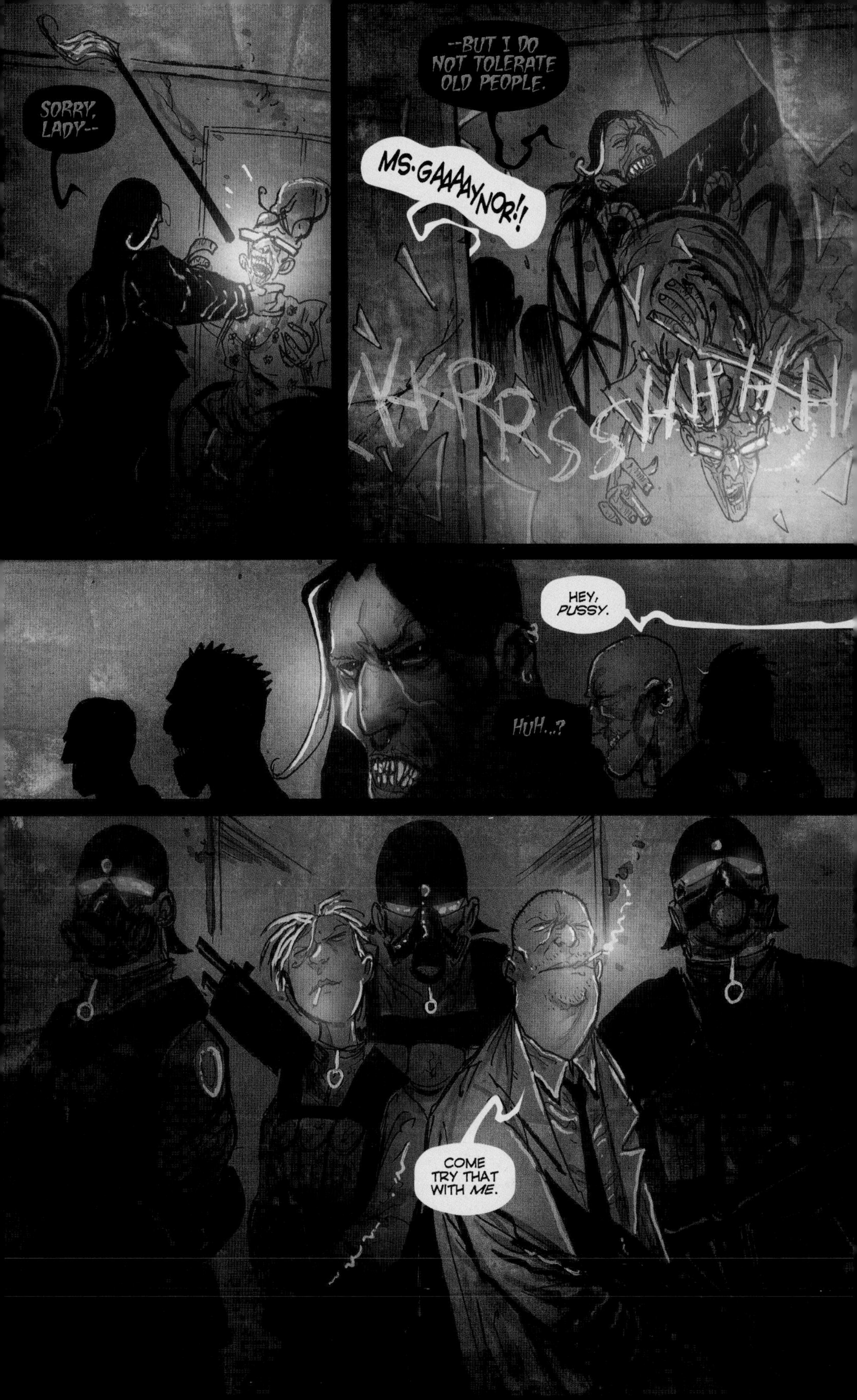
SORRY, LADY--
--BUT I DO NOT TOLERATE OLD PEOPLE.
MS·GAAAAYNOR!!
KKRRSSSHHHHH
HEY, PUSSY.
HUH...?
COME TRY THAT WITH ME.

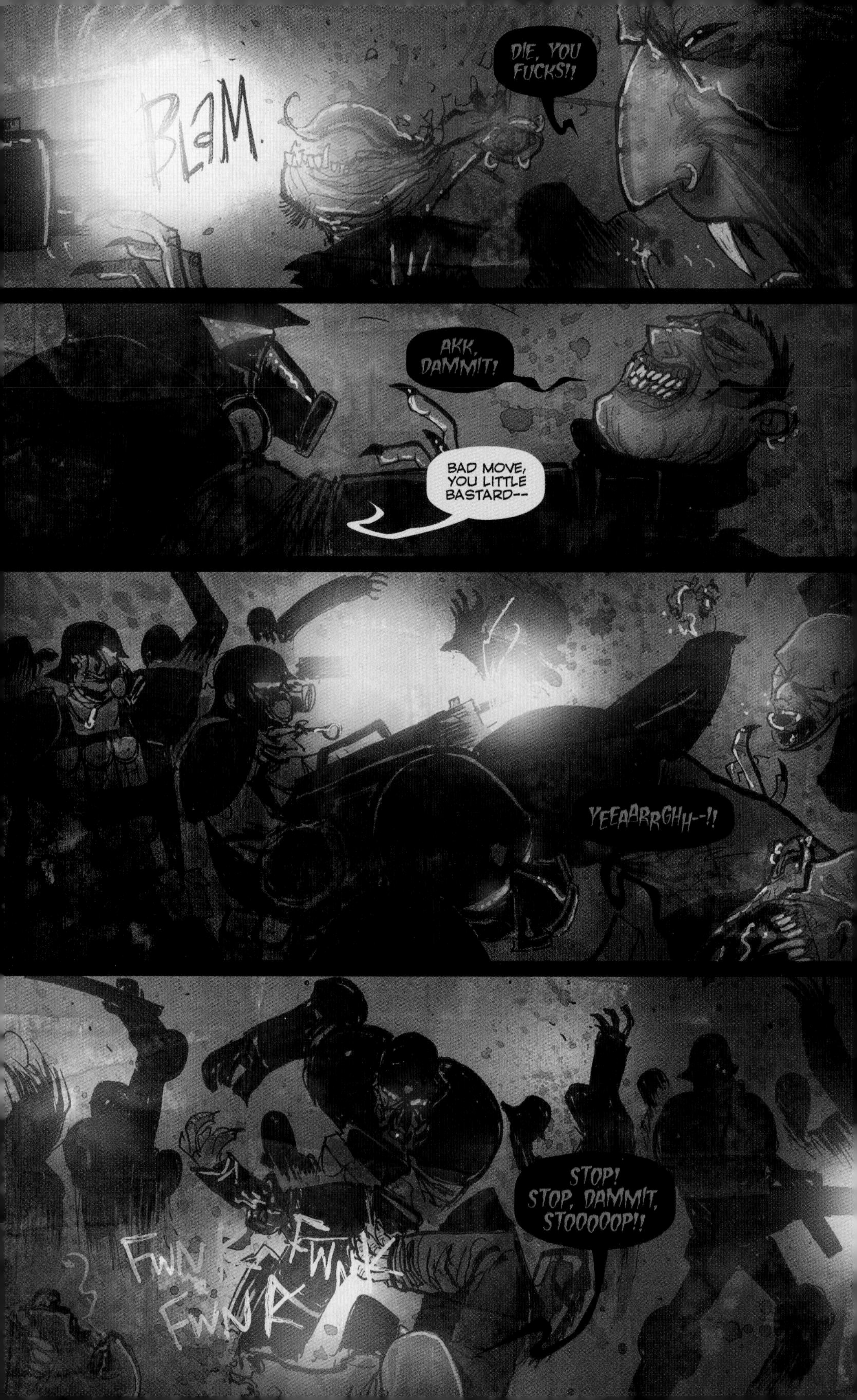
BLAM.
DIE, YOU FUCKS!!
AKK, DAMMIT!
BAD MOVE, YOU LITTLE BASTARD--
YEEAARRGHH--!!
STOP! STOP, DAMMIT, STOOOOOP!!
FWNR FWNR FWNR

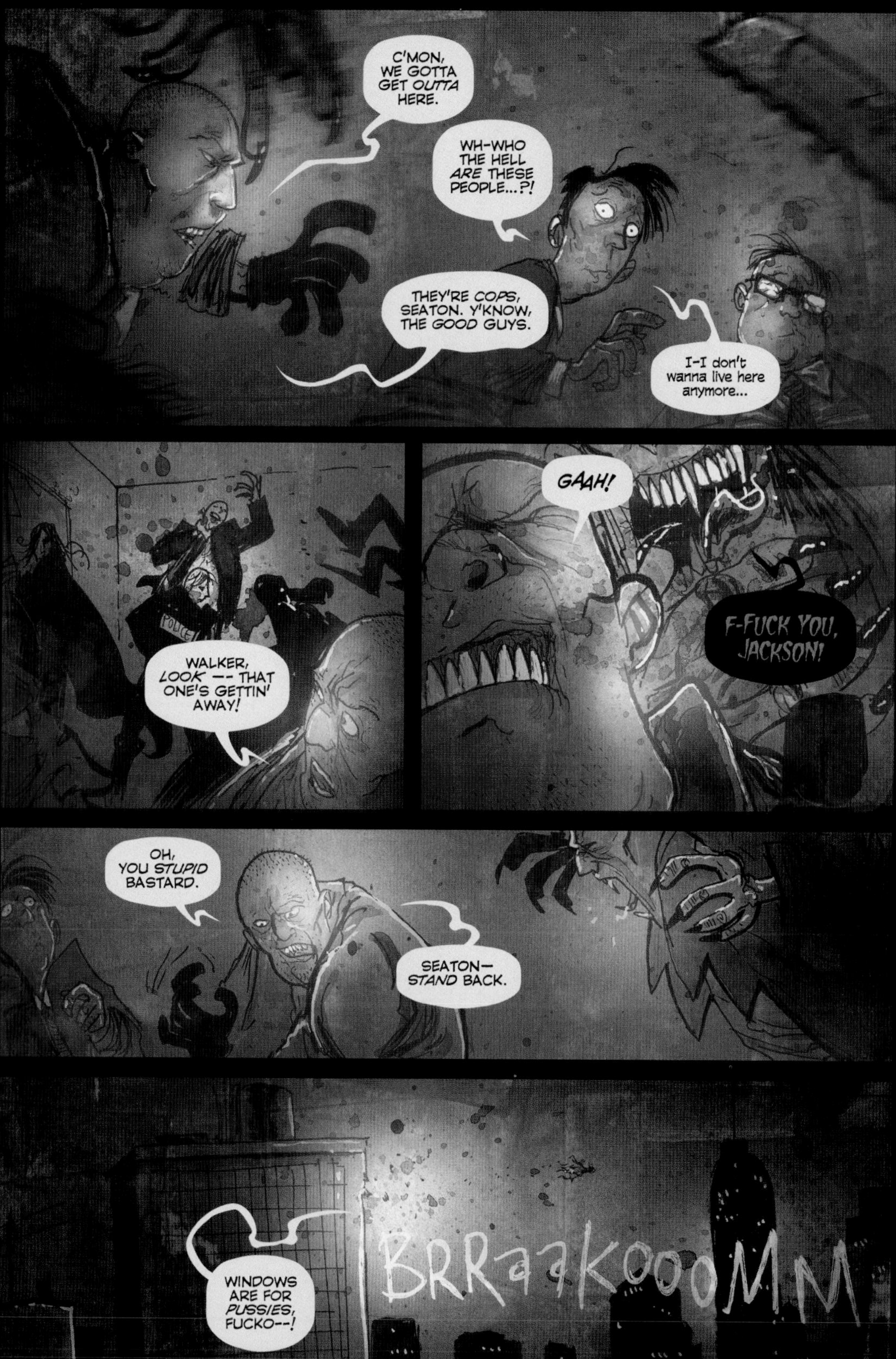
C'MON, WE GOTTA GET OUTTA HERE.
WH-WHO THE HELL ARE THESE PEOPLE...?!
THEY'RE COPS, SEATON. Y'KNOW, THE GOOD GUYS.
I-I don't wanna live here anymore...
POLICE
WALKER, LOOK -- THAT ONE'S GETTIN' AWAY!
GAAH!
F-FUCK YOU, JACKSON!
OH, YOU STUPID BASTARD.
SEATON— STAND BACK.
WINDOWS ARE FOR PUSSIES, FUCKO--!
BRRaakOOOMM

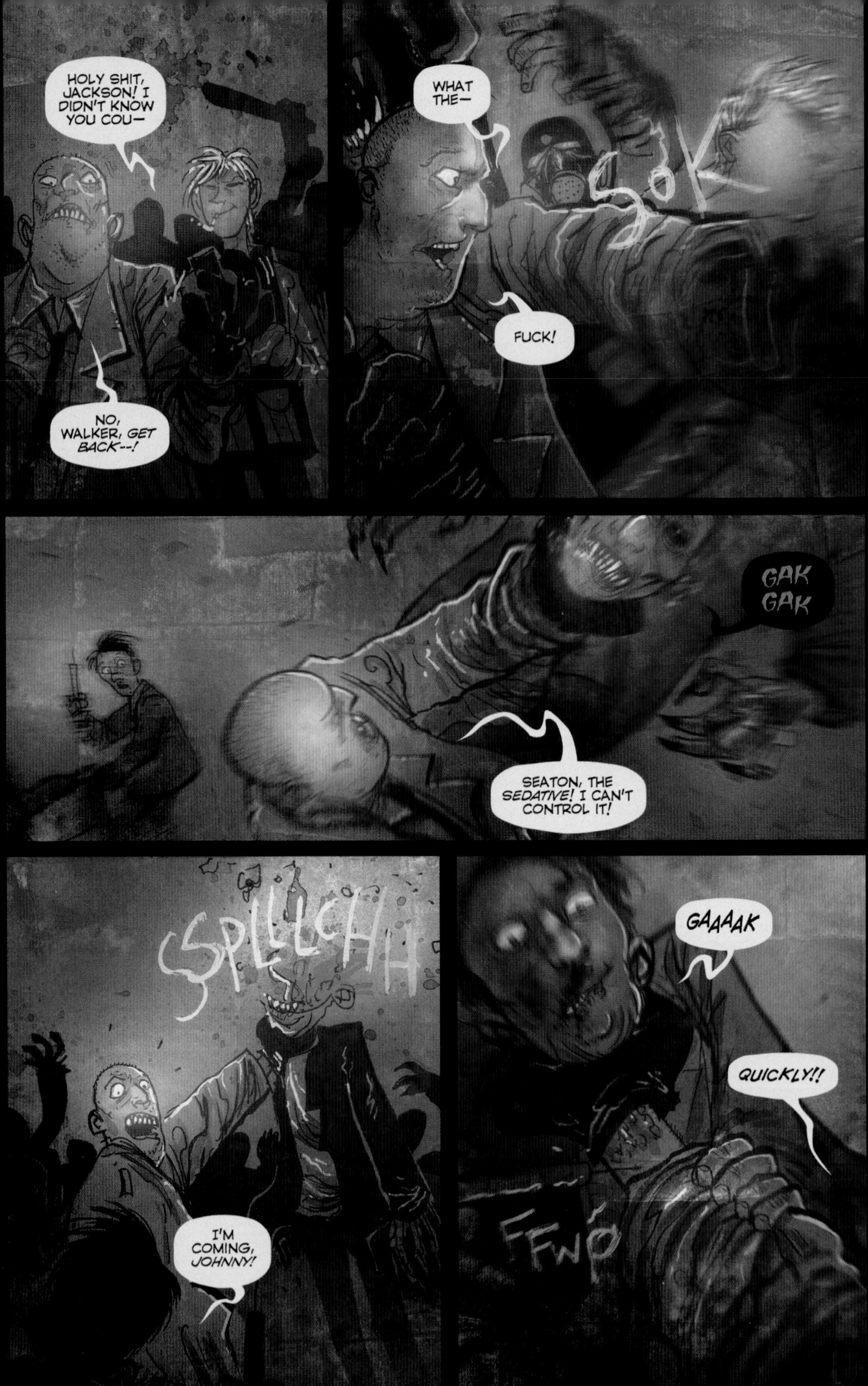
HOLY SHIT, JACKSON! I DIDN'T KNOW YOU COU—
NO, WALKER, GET BACK--!
WHAT THE—
SOK
FUCK!
GAK GAK
SEATON, THE SEDATIVE! I CAN'T CONTROL IT!
SPLLLCHH
I'M COMING, JOHNNY!
GAAAAK
QUICKLY!!
FFWP

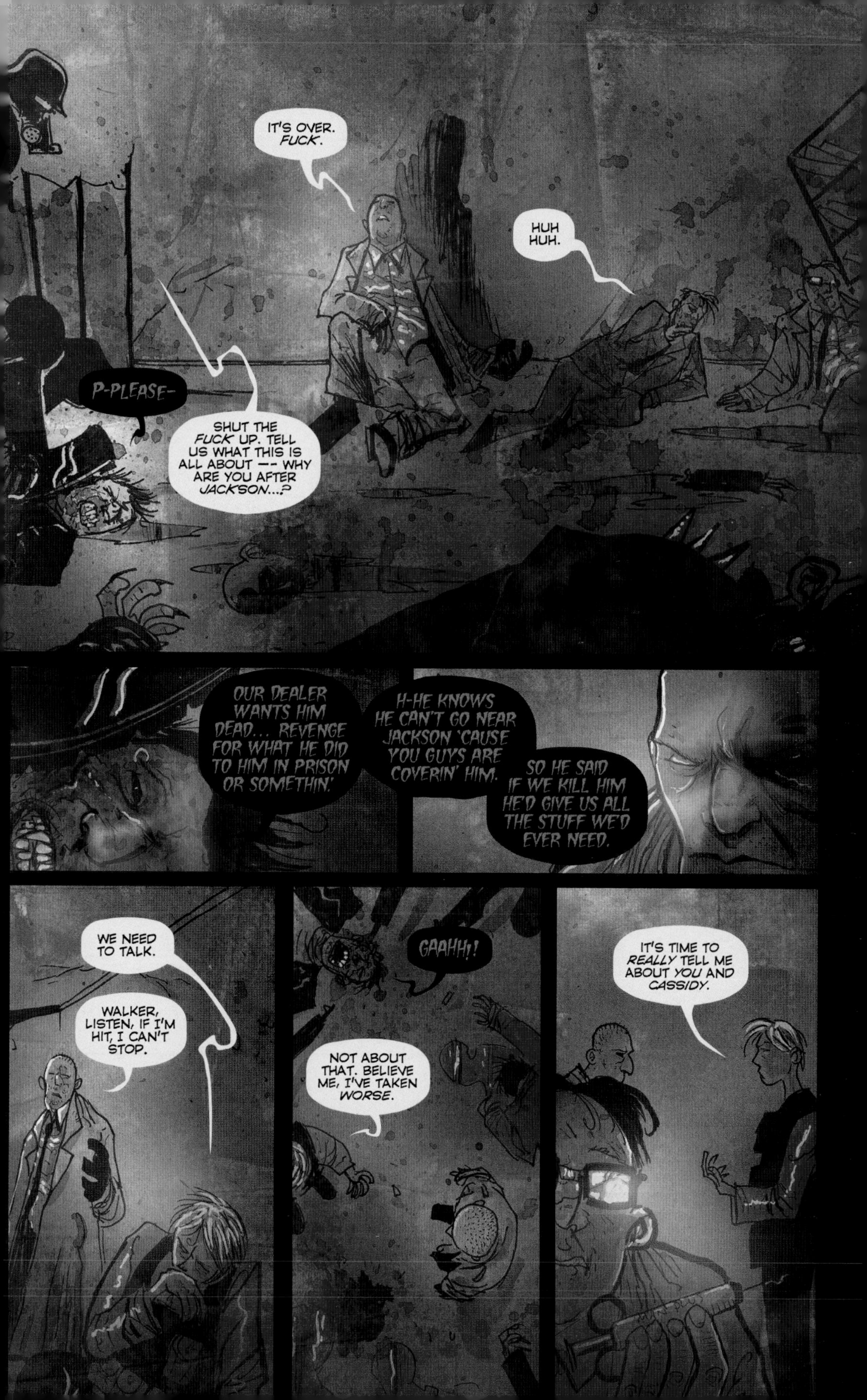
IT'S OVER. FUCK.
HUH HUH.
P-PLEASE-
SHUT THE FUCK UP. TELL US WHAT THIS IS ALL ABOUT -- WHY ARE YOU AFTER JACKSON...?
OUR DEALER WANTS HIM DEAD... REVENGE FOR WHAT HE DID TO HIM IN PRISON OR SOMETHIN'.
H-HE KNOWS HE CAN'T GO NEAR JACKSON 'CAUSE YOU GUYS ARE COVERIN' HIM.
SO HE SAID IF WE KILL HIM HE'D GIVE US ALL THE STUFF WE'D EVER NEED.
WE NEED TO TALK.
WALKER, LISTEN, IF I'M HIT, I CAN'T STOP.
GAAHH!!
NOT ABOUT THAT. BELIEVE ME, I'VE TAKEN WORSE.
IT'S TIME TO REALLY TELL ME ABOUT YOU AND CASSIDY.

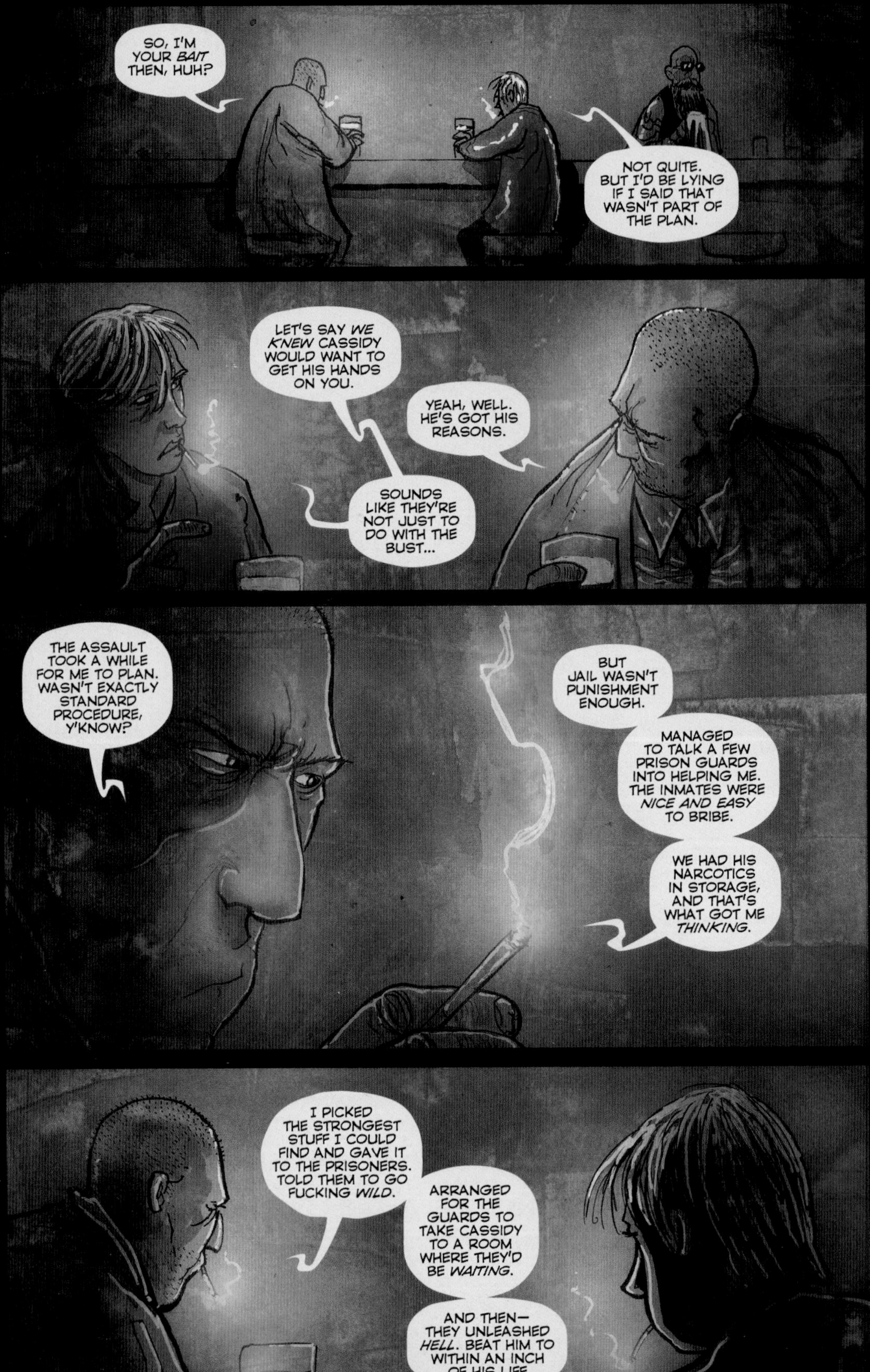

SO, I'M YOUR *BAIT* THEN, HUH?
NOT QUITE. BUT I'D BE LYING IF I SAID THAT WASN'T PART OF THE PLAN.
LET'S SAY *WE KNEW* CASSIDY WOULD WANT TO GET HIS HANDS ON YOU.
YEAH, WELL. HE'S GOT HIS REASONS.
SOUNDS LIKE THEY'RE NOT JUST TO DO WITH THE BUST...
THE ASSAULT TOOK A WHILE FOR ME TO PLAN. WASN'T EXACTLY STANDARD PROCEDURE, Y'KNOW?
BUT JAIL WASN'T PUNISHMENT ENOUGH.
MANAGED TO TALK A FEW PRISON GUARDS INTO HELPING ME. THE INMATES WERE *NICE AND EASY* TO BRIBE.
WE HAD HIS NARCOTICS IN STORAGE, AND THAT'S WHAT GOT ME *THINKING*.
I PICKED THE STRONGEST STUFF I COULD FIND AND GAVE IT TO THE PRISONERS. TOLD THEM TO GO FUCKING *WILD*.
ARRANGED FOR THE GUARDS TO TAKE CASSIDY TO A ROOM WHERE THEY'D BE *WAITING*.
AND THEN— THEY UNLEASHED *HELL*. BEAT HIM TO WITHIN AN INCH OF HIS LIFE.

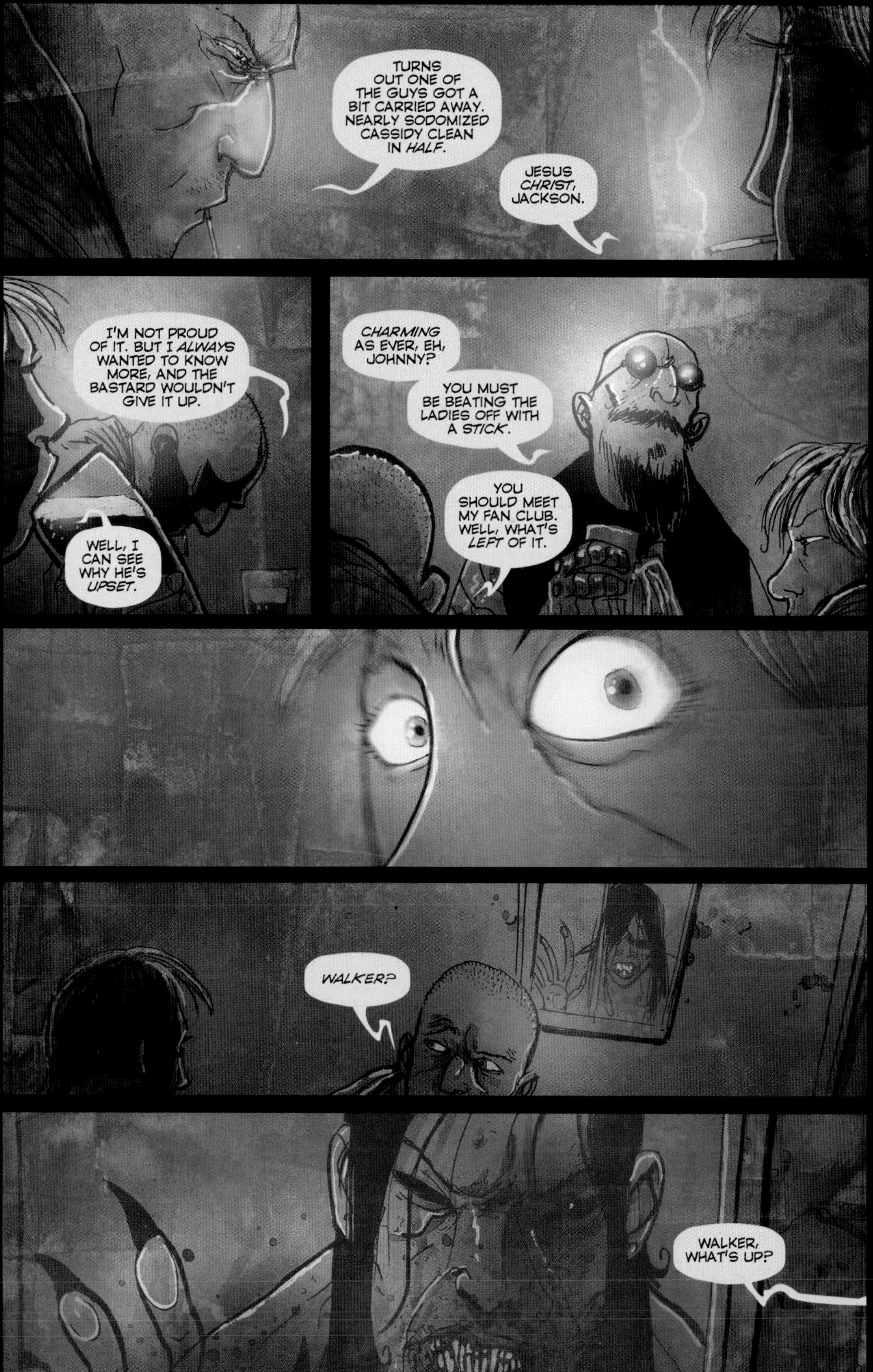
TURNS OUT ONE OF THE GUYS GOT A BIT CARRIED AWAY. NEARLY SODOMIZED CASSIDY CLEAN IN *HALF*.
JESUS *CHRIST*, JACKSON.
I'M NOT PROUD OF IT. BUT I *ALWAYS* WANTED TO KNOW MORE, AND THE BASTARD WOULDN'T GIVE IT UP.
WELL, I CAN SEE WHY HE'S *UPSET*.
CHARMING AS EVER, EH, JOHNNY?
YOU MUST BE BEATING THE LADIES OFF WITH A *STICK*.
YOU SHOULD MEET MY FAN CLUB. WELL, WHAT'S *LEFT* OF IT.
WALKER?
WALKER, WHAT'S UP?

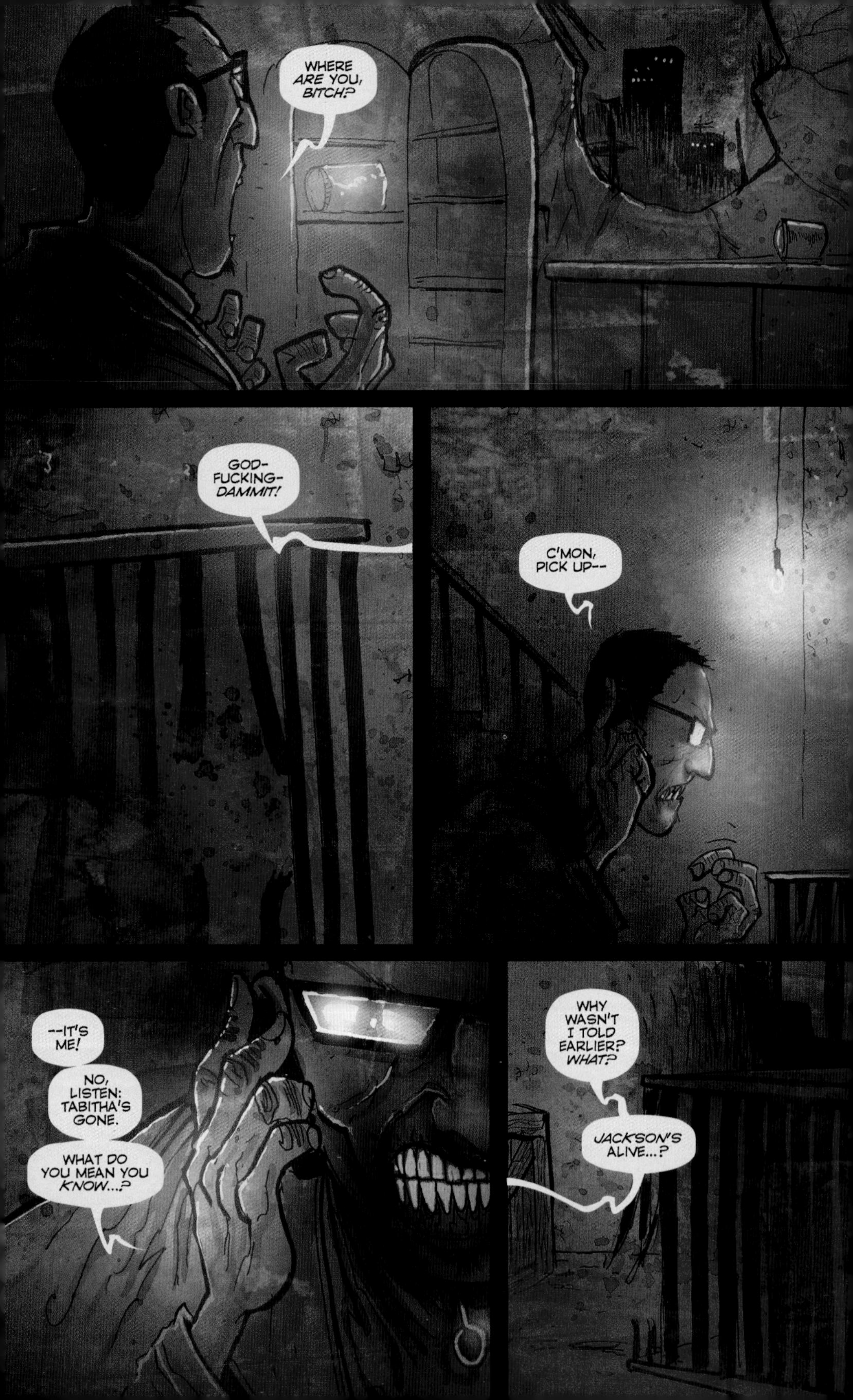
WHERE ARE YOU, BITCH?
GOD-FUCKING-DAMMIT!
C'MON, PICK UP--
--IT'S ME!
NO, LISTEN: TABITHA'S GONE.
WHAT DO YOU MEAN YOU KNOW...?
WHY WASN'T I TOLD EARLIER? WHAT?
JACKSON'S ALIVE...?

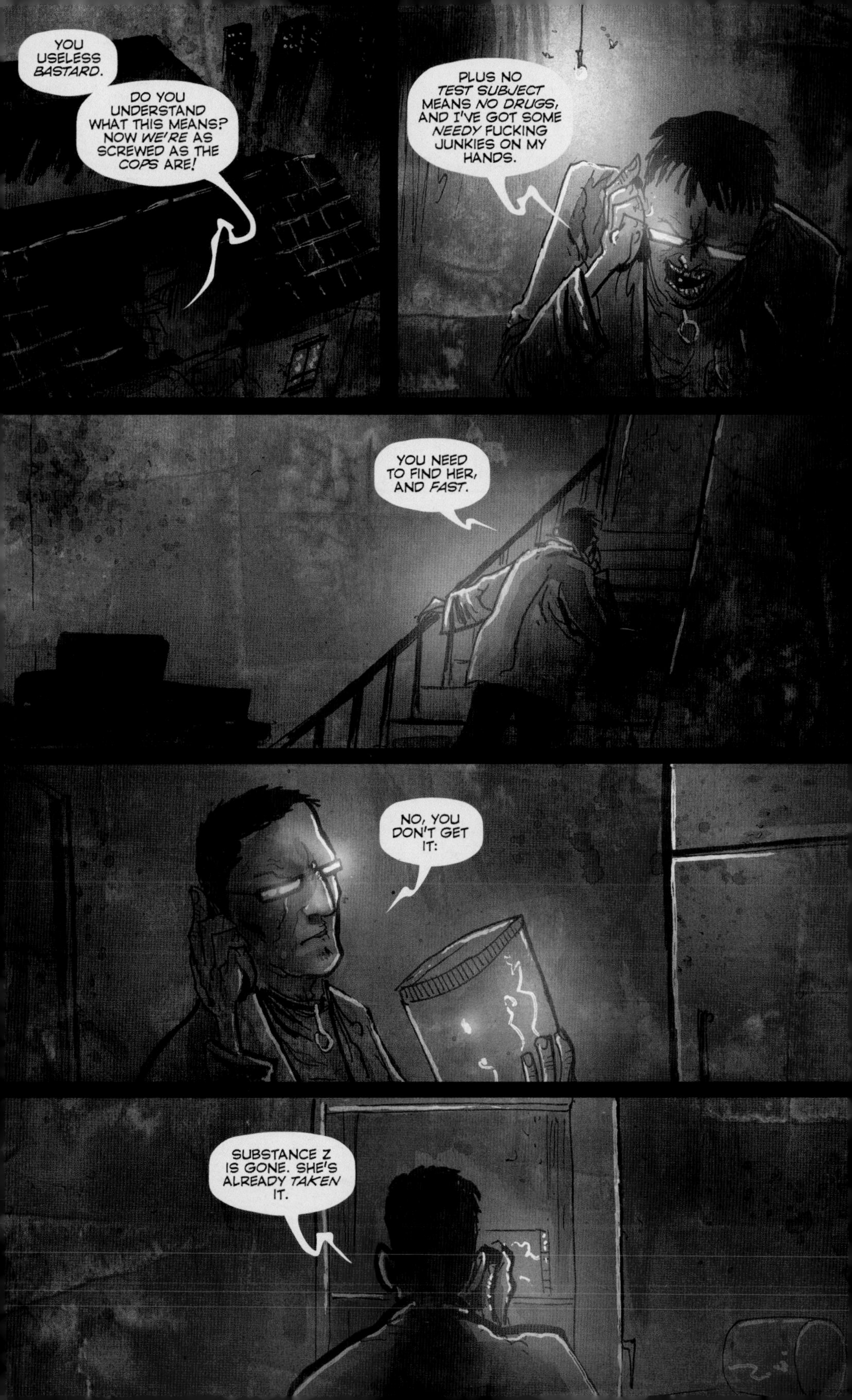
YOU USELESS *BASTARD*.
DO YOU UNDERSTAND WHAT THIS MEANS? NOW *WE'RE* AS SCREWED AS THE *COPS* ARE!
PLUS NO *TEST SUBJECT* MEANS *NO DRUGS*, AND I'VE GOT SOME *NEEDY* FUCKING JUNKIES ON MY HANDS.
YOU NEED TO FIND HER, AND *FAST*.
NO, YOU DON'T GET IT:
SUBSTANCE Z IS GONE. SHE'S ALREADY *TAKEN* IT.

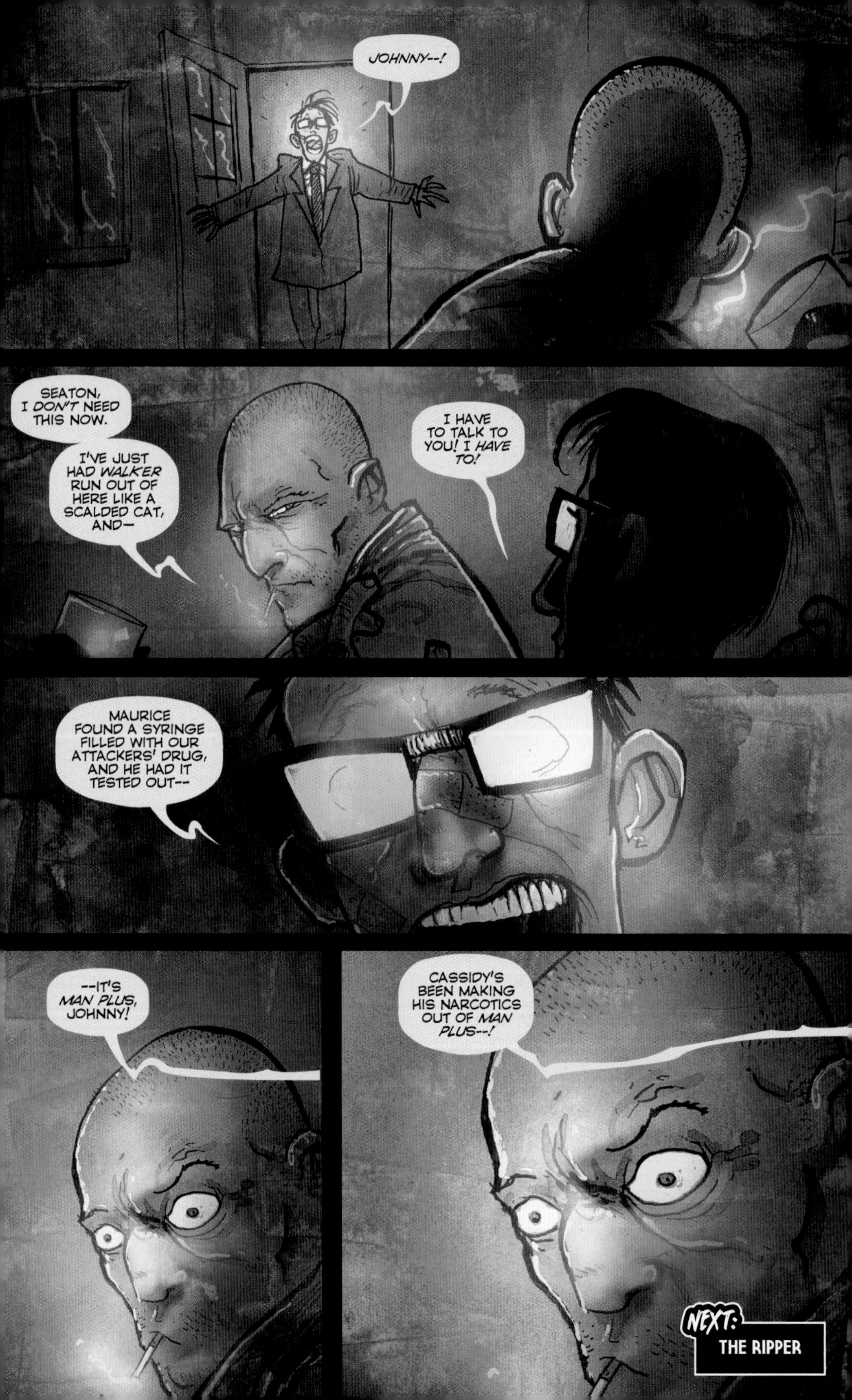
JOHNNY--!
SEATON, I *DON'T* NEED THIS NOW.
I'VE JUST HAD *WALKER* RUN OUT OF HERE LIKE A SCALDED CAT, AND—
I HAVE TO TALK TO YOU! I *HAVE TO!*
MAURICE FOUND A SYRINGE FILLED WITH OUR ATTACKERS' DRUG, AND HE HAD IT TESTED OUT--
--IT'S *MAN PLUS*, JOHNNY!
CASSIDY'S BEEN MAKING HIS NARCOTICS OUT OF *MAN PLUS*--!
NEXT:
THE RIPPER

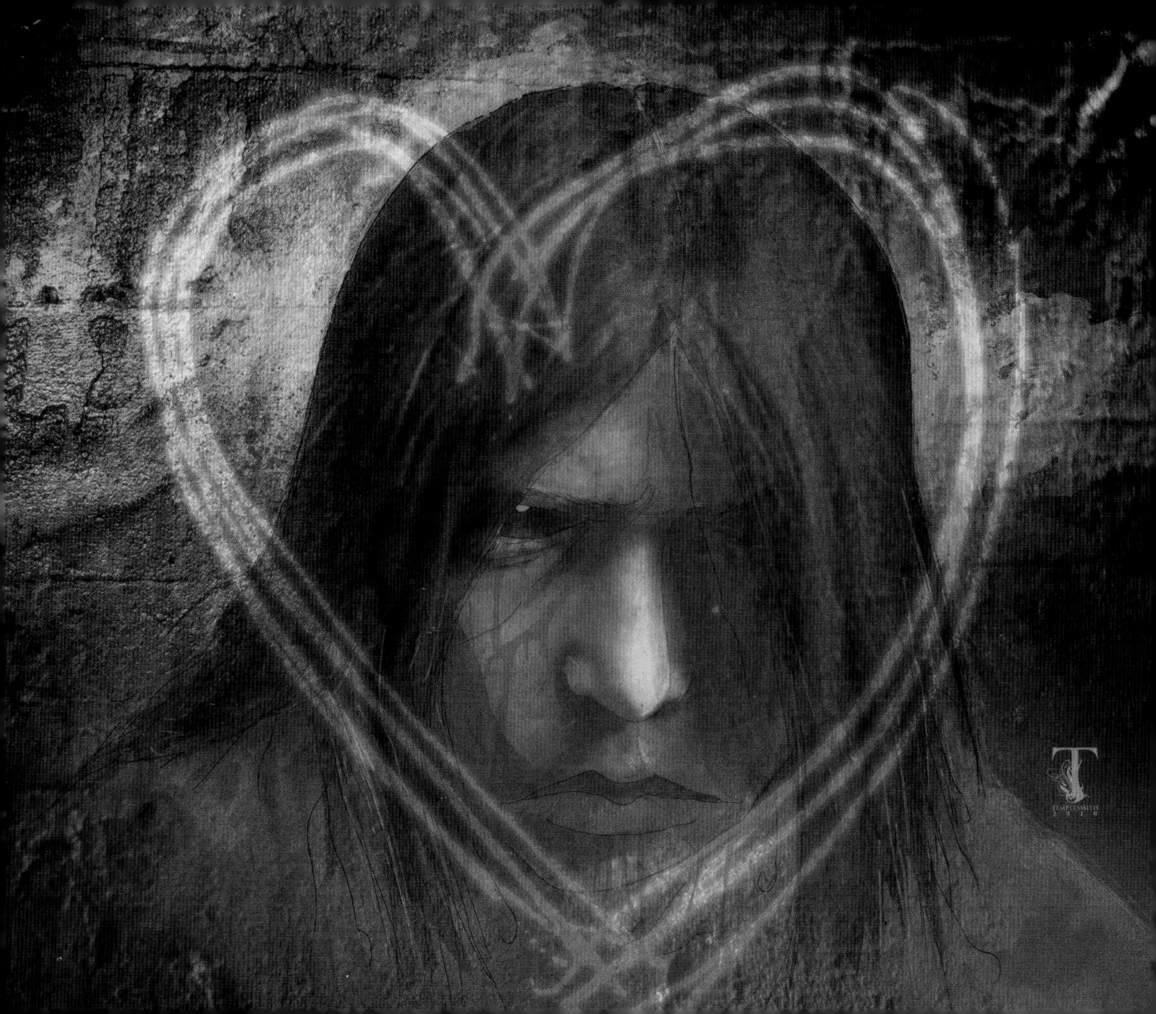

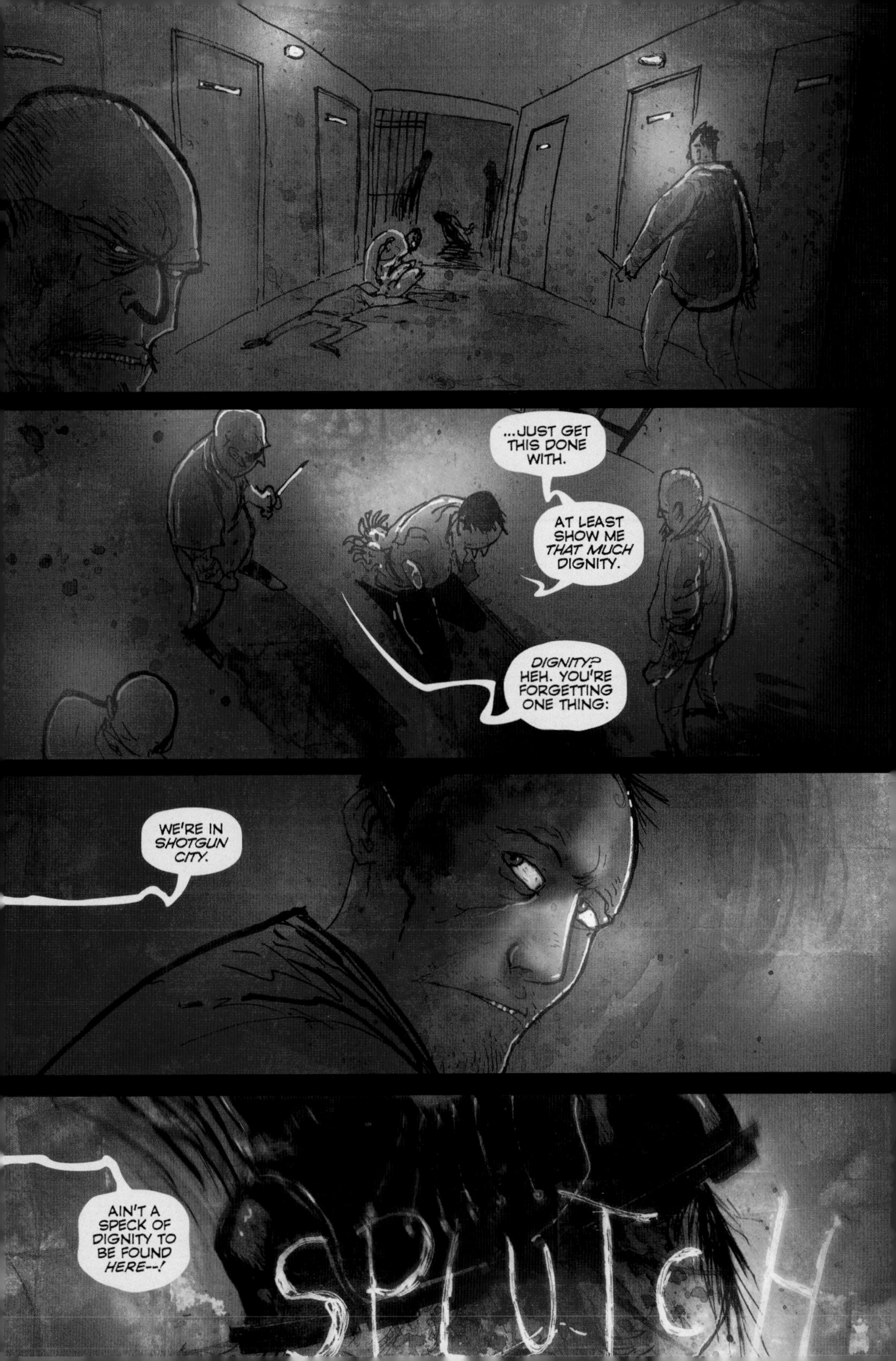
...JUST GET THIS DONE WITH.
AT LEAST SHOW ME *THAT MUCH* DIGNITY.
DIGNITY? HEH. YOU'RE FORGETTING ONE THING:
WE'RE IN *SHOTGUN CITY*.
AIN'T A SPECK OF DIGNITY TO BE FOUND *HERE--!*
SPLUTCH

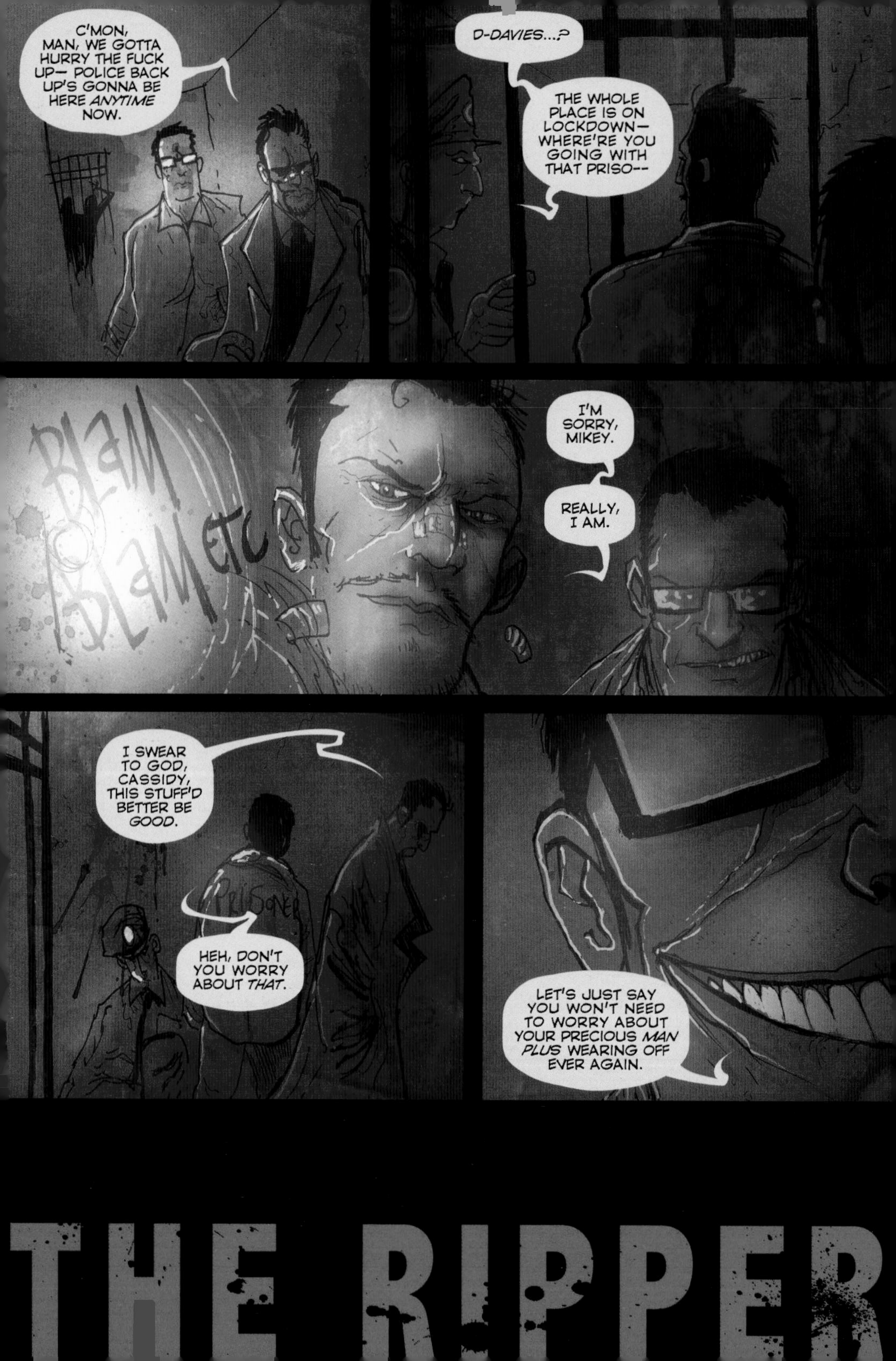
C'MON, MAN, WE GOTTA HURRY THE FUCK UP— POLICE BACK UP'S GONNA BE HERE *ANYTIME* NOW.
D-DAVIES...?
THE WHOLE PLACE IS ON LOCKDOWN— WHERE'RE YOU GOING WITH THAT PRISO--
BLAM BLAM ETC
I'M SORRY, MIKEY.
REALLY, I AM.
I SWEAR TO GOD, CASSIDY, THIS STUFF'D BETTER BE *GOOD*.
PRISONER
HEH, DON'T YOU WORRY ABOUT *THAT*.
LET'S JUST SAY YOU WON'T NEED TO WORRY ABOUT YOUR PRECIOUS *MAN PLUS* WEARING OFF EVER AGAIN.

THE RIPPER

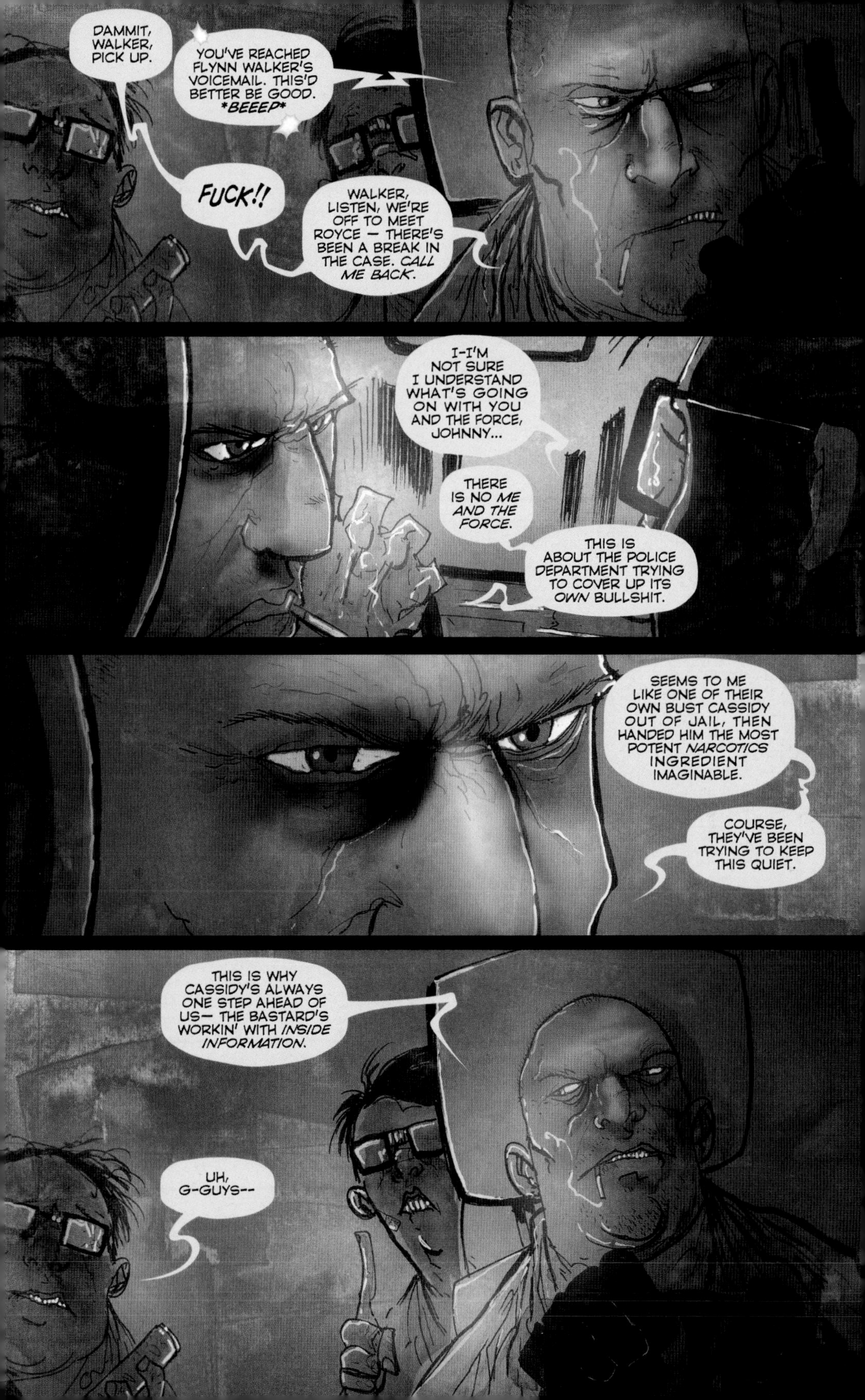

DAMMIT, WALKER, PICK UP.
YOU'VE REACHED FLYNN WALKER'S VOICEMAIL. THIS'D BETTER BE GOOD. *BEEEP*
FUCK!!
WALKER, LISTEN, WE'RE OFF TO MEET ROYCE — THERE'S BEEN A BREAK IN THE CASE. CALL ME BACK.
I-I'M NOT SURE I UNDERSTAND WHAT'S GOING ON WITH YOU AND THE FORCE, JOHNNY...
THERE IS NO ME AND THE FORCE.
THIS IS ABOUT THE POLICE DEPARTMENT TRYING TO COVER UP ITS OWN BULLSHIT.
SEEMS TO ME LIKE ONE OF THEIR OWN BUST CASSIDY OUT OF JAIL, THEN HANDED HIM THE MOST POTENT NARCOTICS INGREDIENT IMAGINABLE.
COURSE, THEY'VE BEEN TRYING TO KEEP THIS QUIET.
THIS IS WHY CASSIDY'S ALWAYS ONE STEP AHEAD OF US— THE BASTARD'S WORKIN' WITH INSIDE INFORMATION.
UH, G-GUYS--

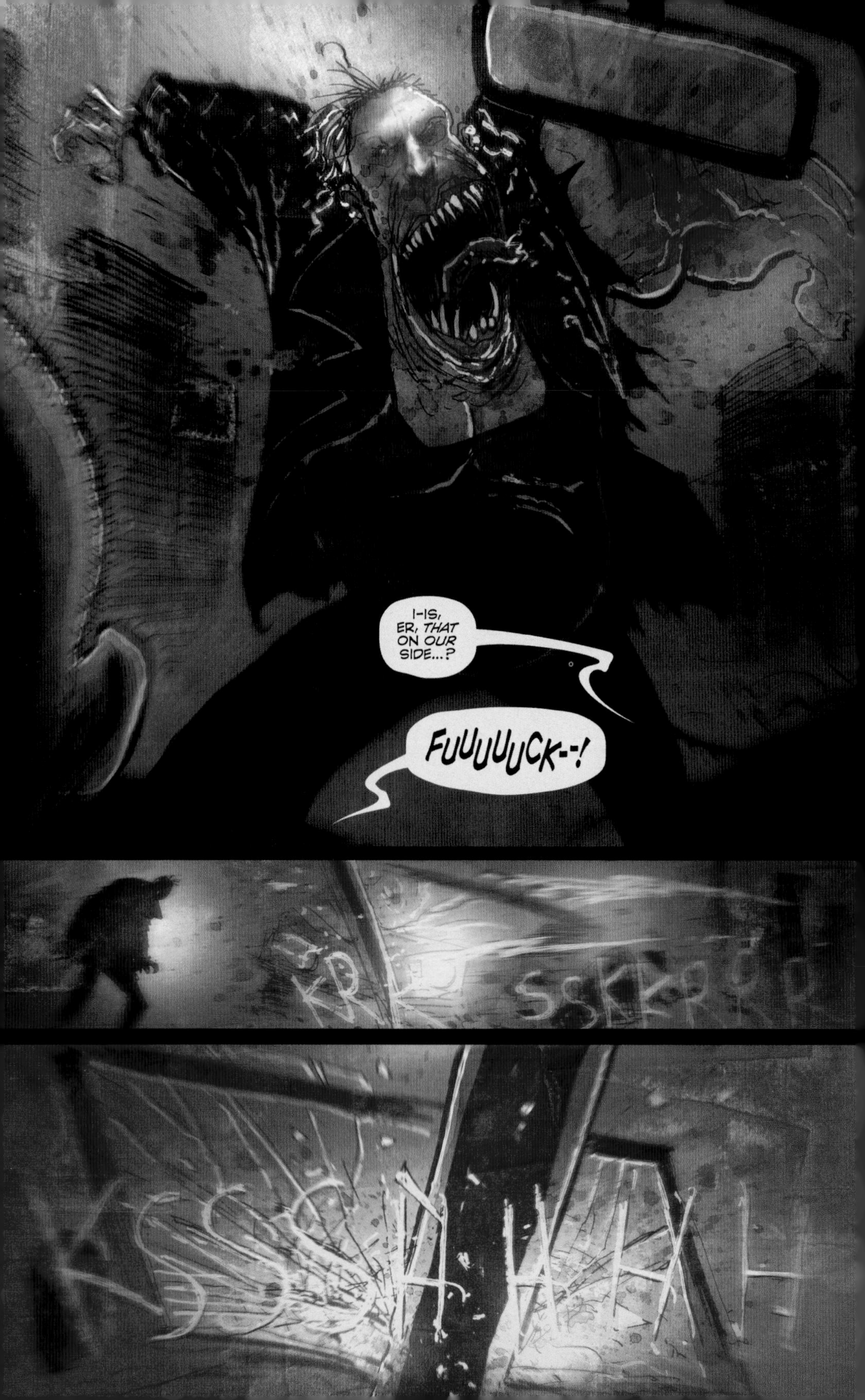
I-IS, ER, *THAT* ON OUR SIDE...?
FUUUUUCK--!

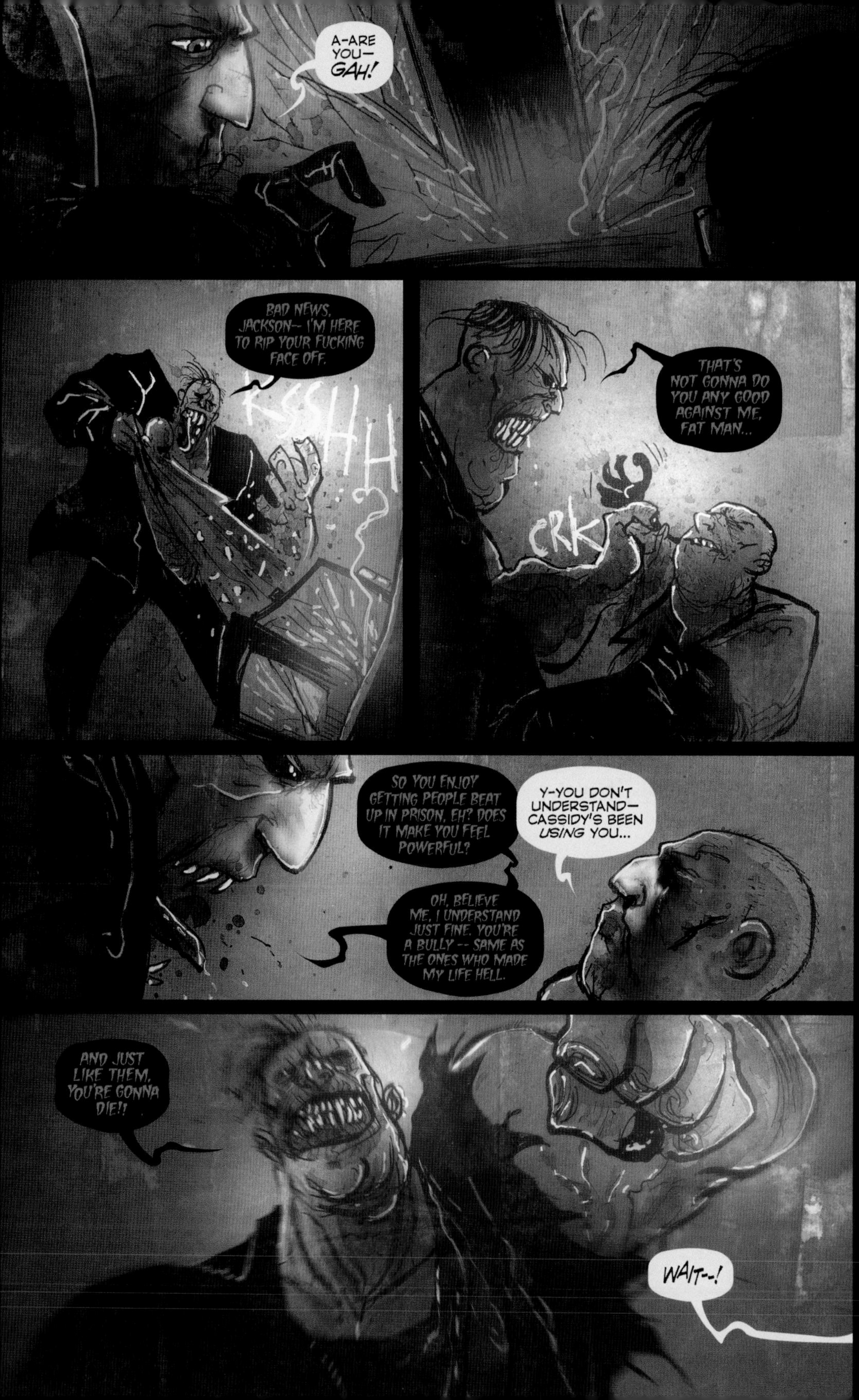
A-ARE YOU—GAH!
BAD NEWS, JACKSON-- I'M HERE TO RIP YOUR FUCKING FACE OFF.
KSSHH
THAT'S NOT GONNA DO YOU ANY GOOD AGAINST ME, FAT MAN...
CRK
SO YOU ENJOY GETTING PEOPLE BEAT UP IN PRISON, EH? DOES IT MAKE YOU FEEL POWERFUL?
Y-YOU DON'T UNDERSTAND—CASSIDY'S BEEN USING YOU...
OH, BELIEVE ME, I UNDERSTAND JUST FINE. YOU'RE A BULLY -- SAME AS THE ONES WHO MADE MY LIFE HELL.
AND JUST LIKE THEM, YOU'RE GONNA DIE!!
WAIT--!

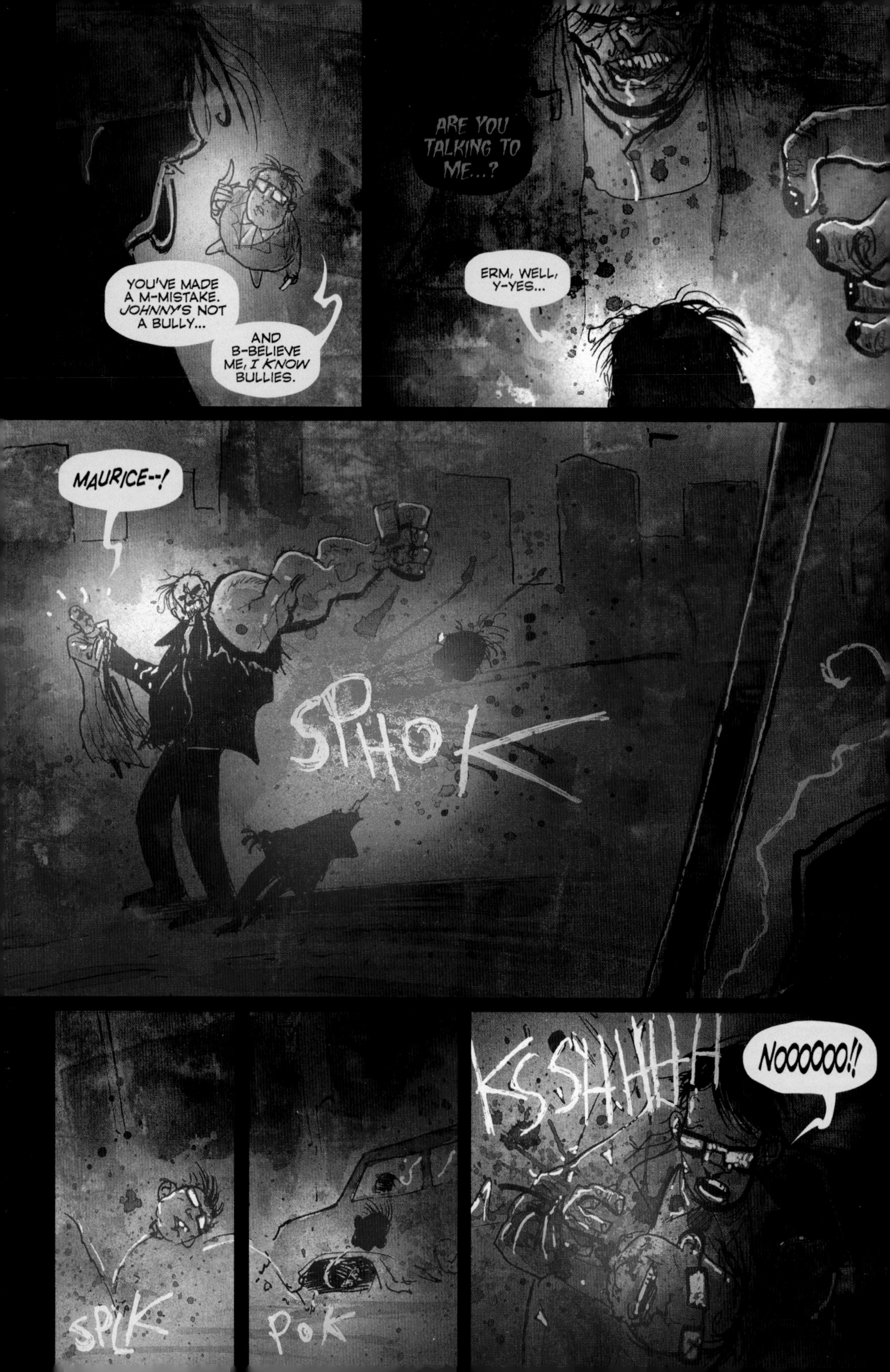
YOU'VE MADE A M-MISTAKE. JOHNNY'S NOT A BULLY...
AND B-BELIEVE ME, I KNOW BULLIES.
ARE YOU TALKING TO ME...?
ERM, WELL, Y-YES...
MAURICE--!
SPHOK
SPLK
POK
KSSHHHH
NOOOOOO!!

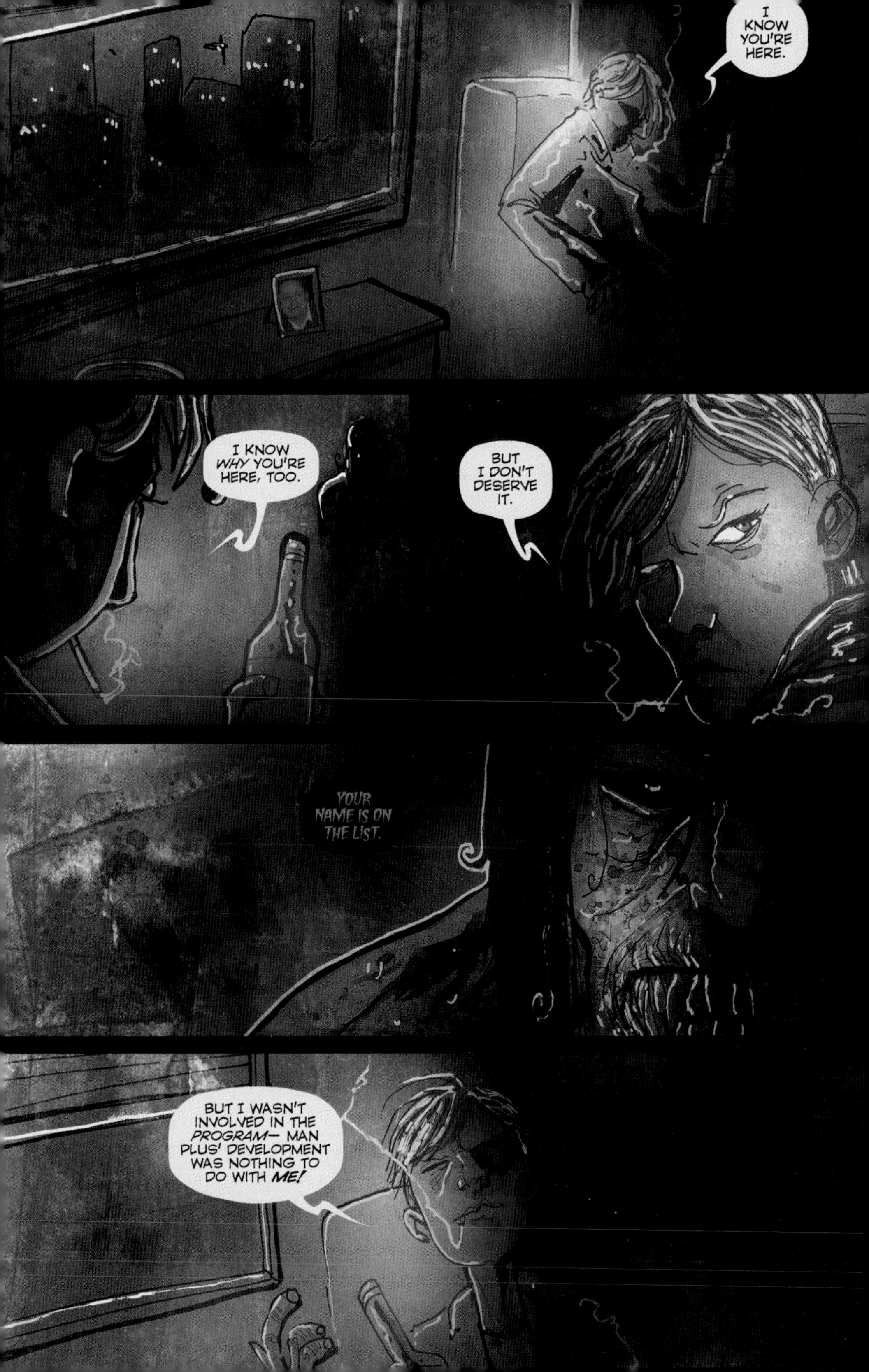
I KNOW YOU'RE HERE.
I KNOW *WHY* YOU'RE HERE, TOO.
BUT I DON'T DESERVE IT.
YOUR NAME IS ON THE LIST.
BUT I WASN'T INVOLVED IN THE *PROGRAM*— MAN PLUS' DEVELOPMENT WAS NOTHING TO DO WITH ***ME!***

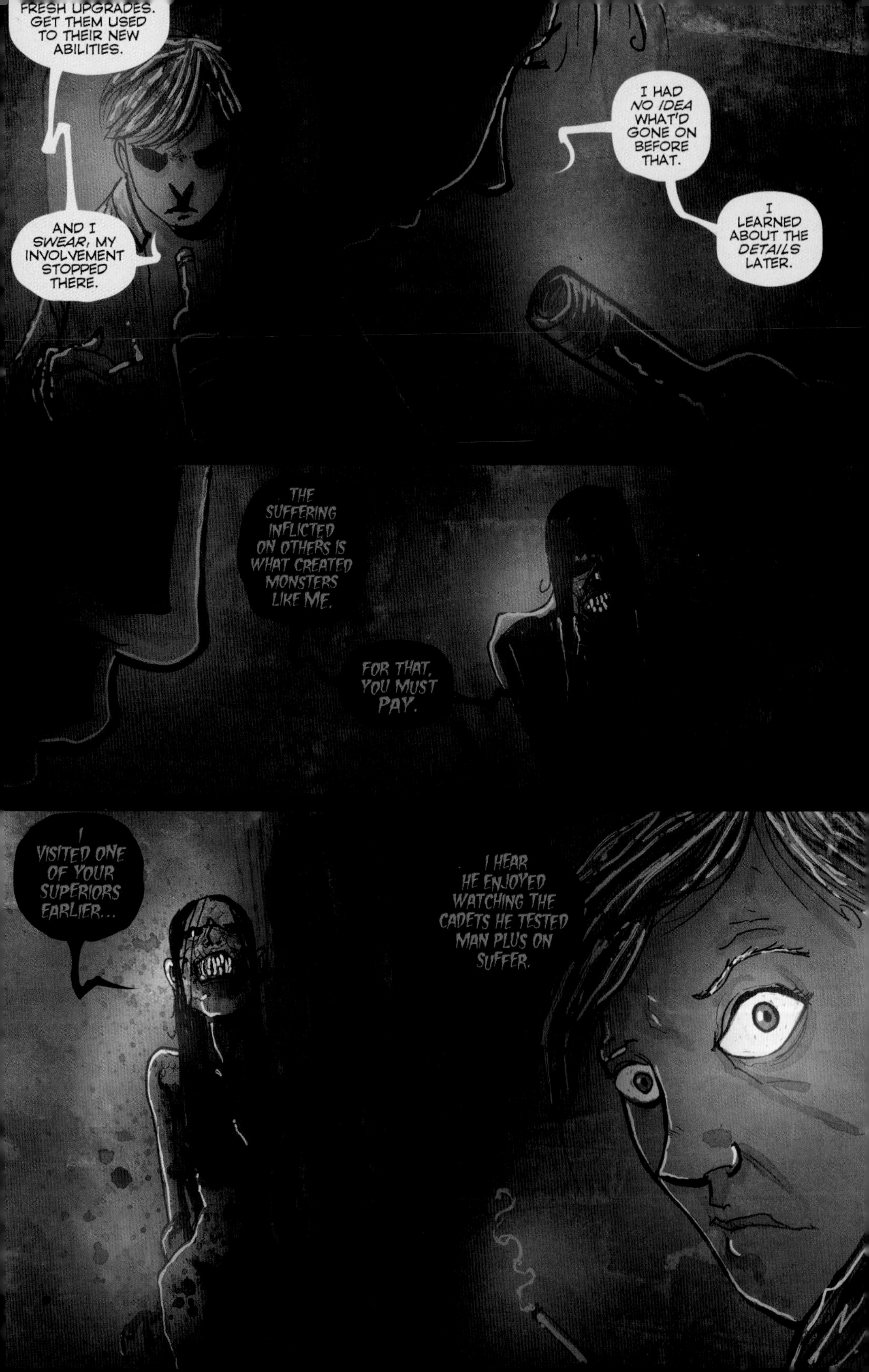
FRESH UPGRADES. GET THEM USED TO THEIR NEW ABILITIES.
AND I SWEAR, MY INVOLVEMENT STOPPED THERE.
I HAD NO IDEA WHAT'D GONE ON BEFORE THAT.
I LEARNED ABOUT THE DETAILS LATER.
THE SUFFERING INFLICTED ON OTHERS IS WHAT CREATED MONSTERS LIKE ME.
FOR THAT, YOU MUST PAY.
I VISITED ONE OF YOUR SUPERIORS EARLIER...
I HEAR HE ENJOYED WATCHING THE CADETS HE TESTED MAN PLUS ON SUFFER.

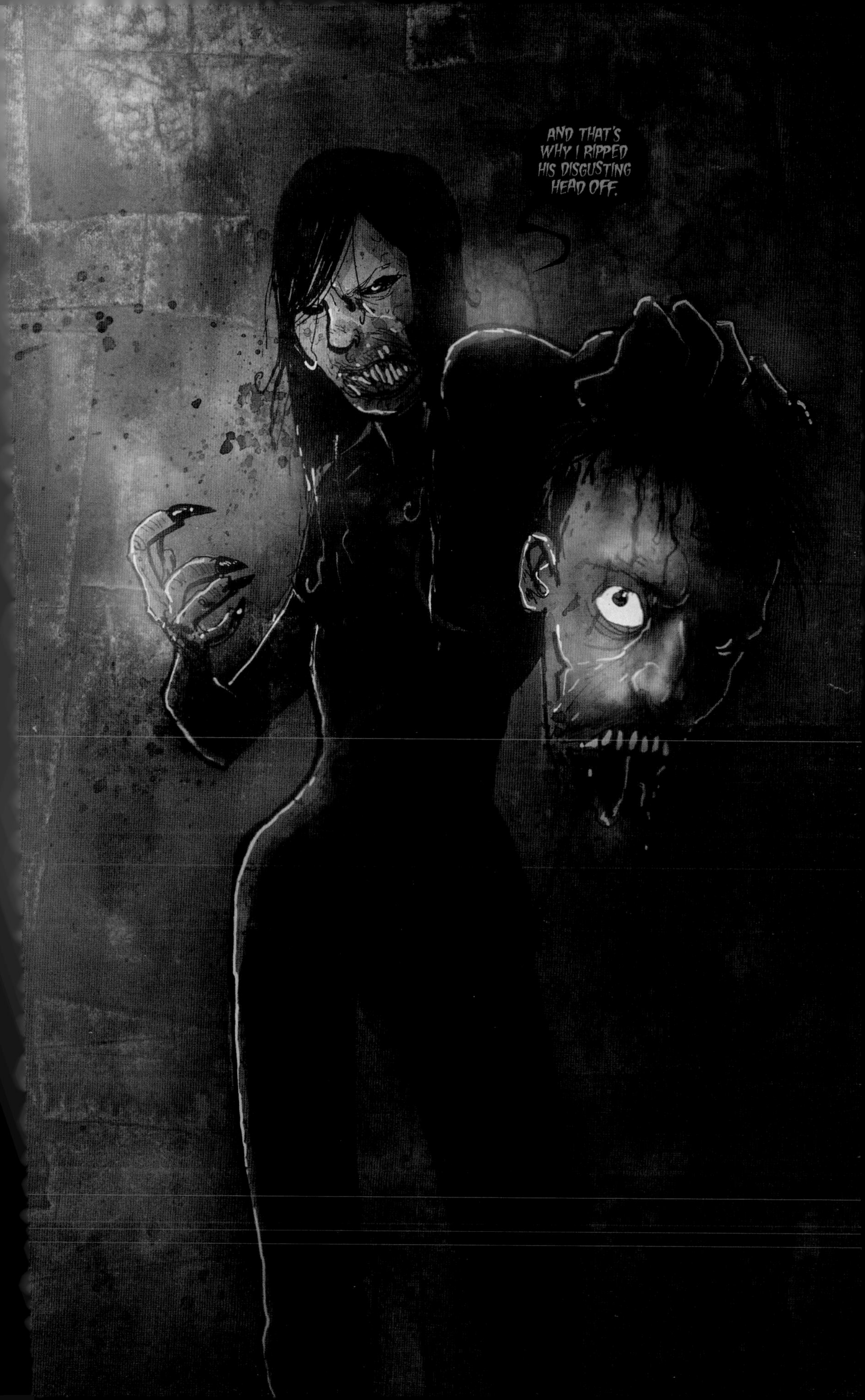
AND THAT'S WHY I RIPPED HIS DISGUSTING HEAD OFF.

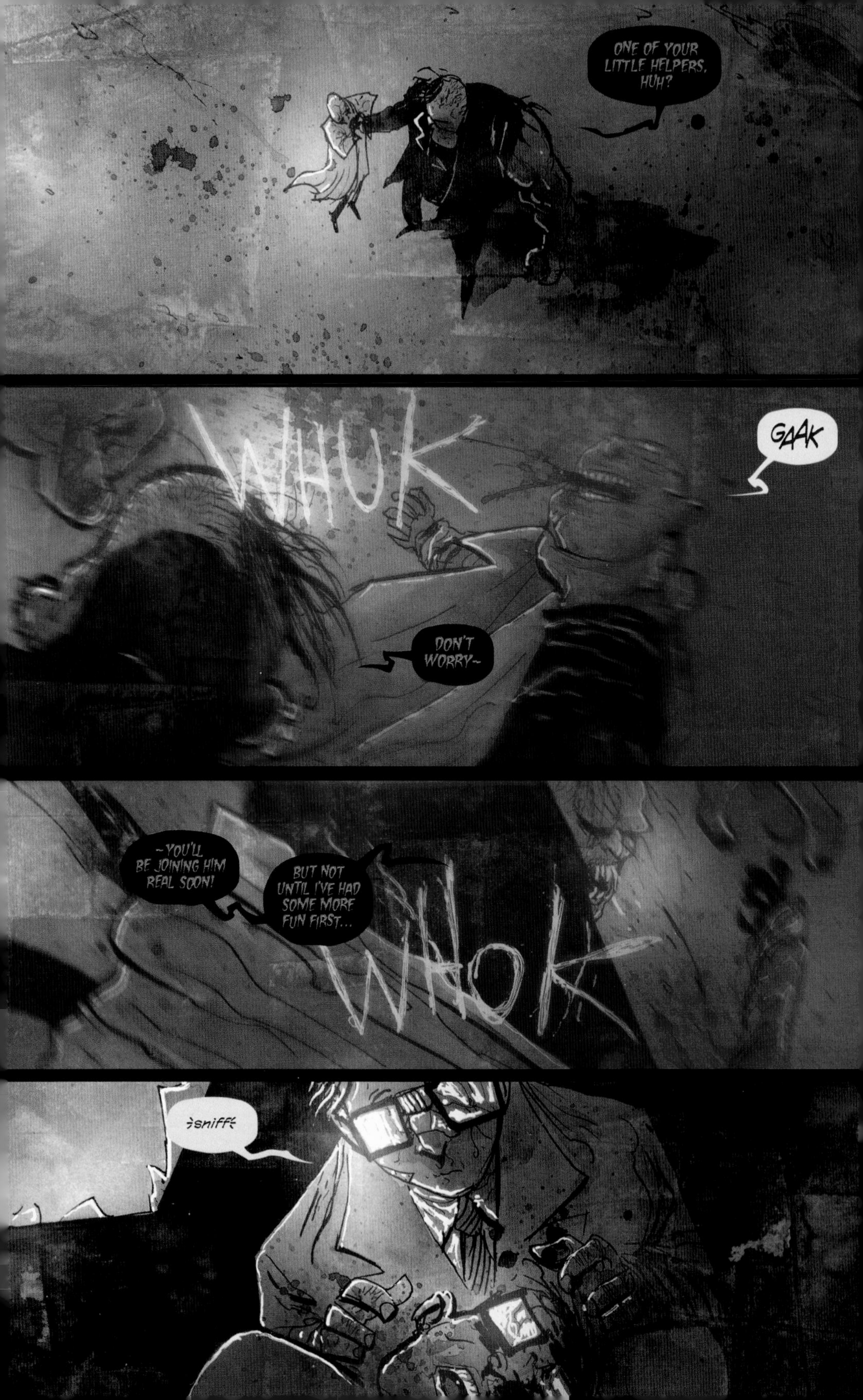
ONE OF YOUR LITTLE HELPERS, HUH?
WHUK
GAAK
DON'T WORRY~
~YOU'LL BE JOINING HIM REAL SOON!
BUT NOT UNTIL I'VE HAD SOME MORE FUN FIRST...
WHOK
sniff

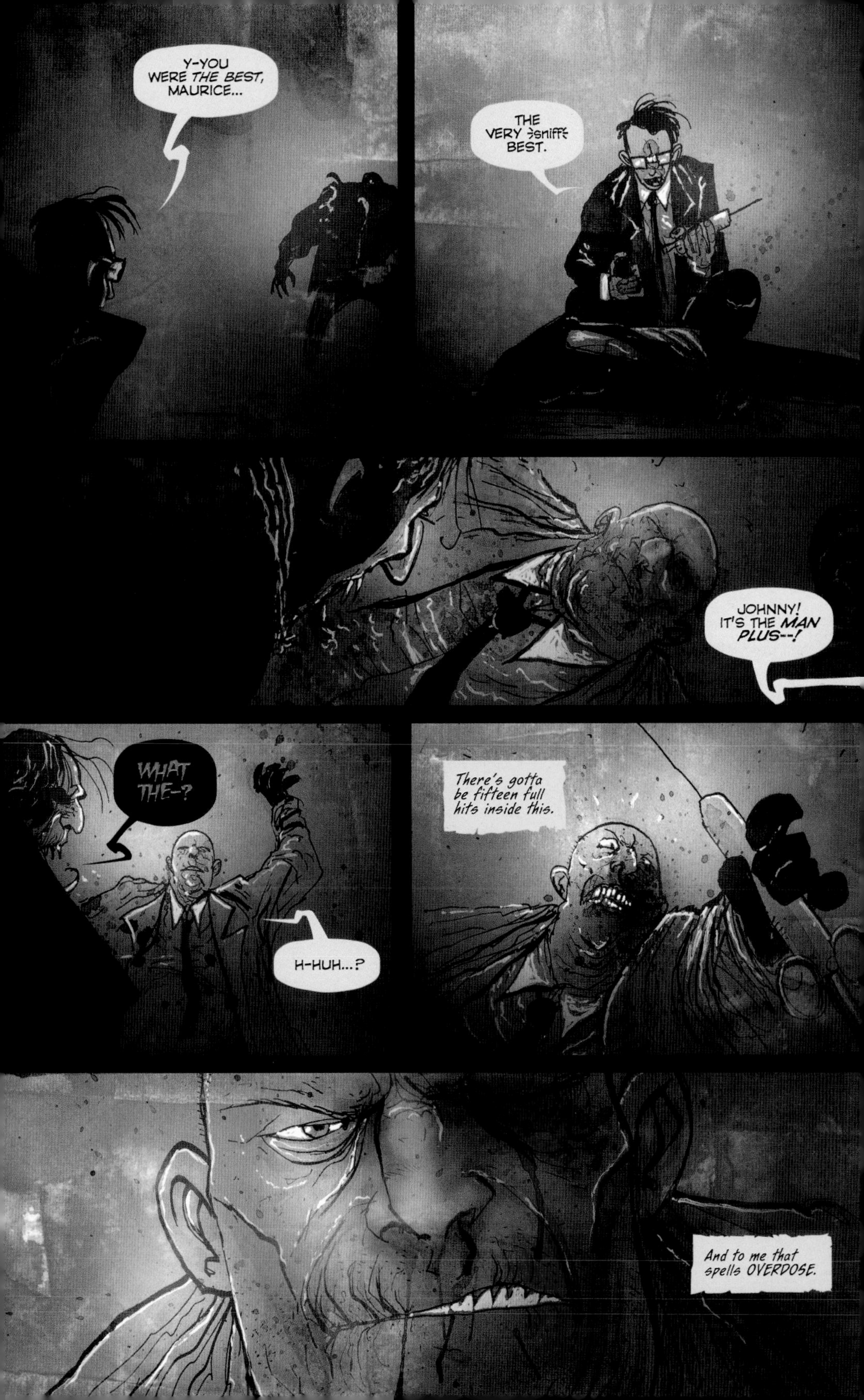
Y-YOU WERE *THE BEST,* MAURICE...
THE VERY ≻sniff≺ BEST.
JOHNNY! IT'S THE ***MAN PLUS--!***
WHAT THE-?
H-HUH...?
There's gotta be fifteen full hits inside this.
And to me that spells OVERDOSE.

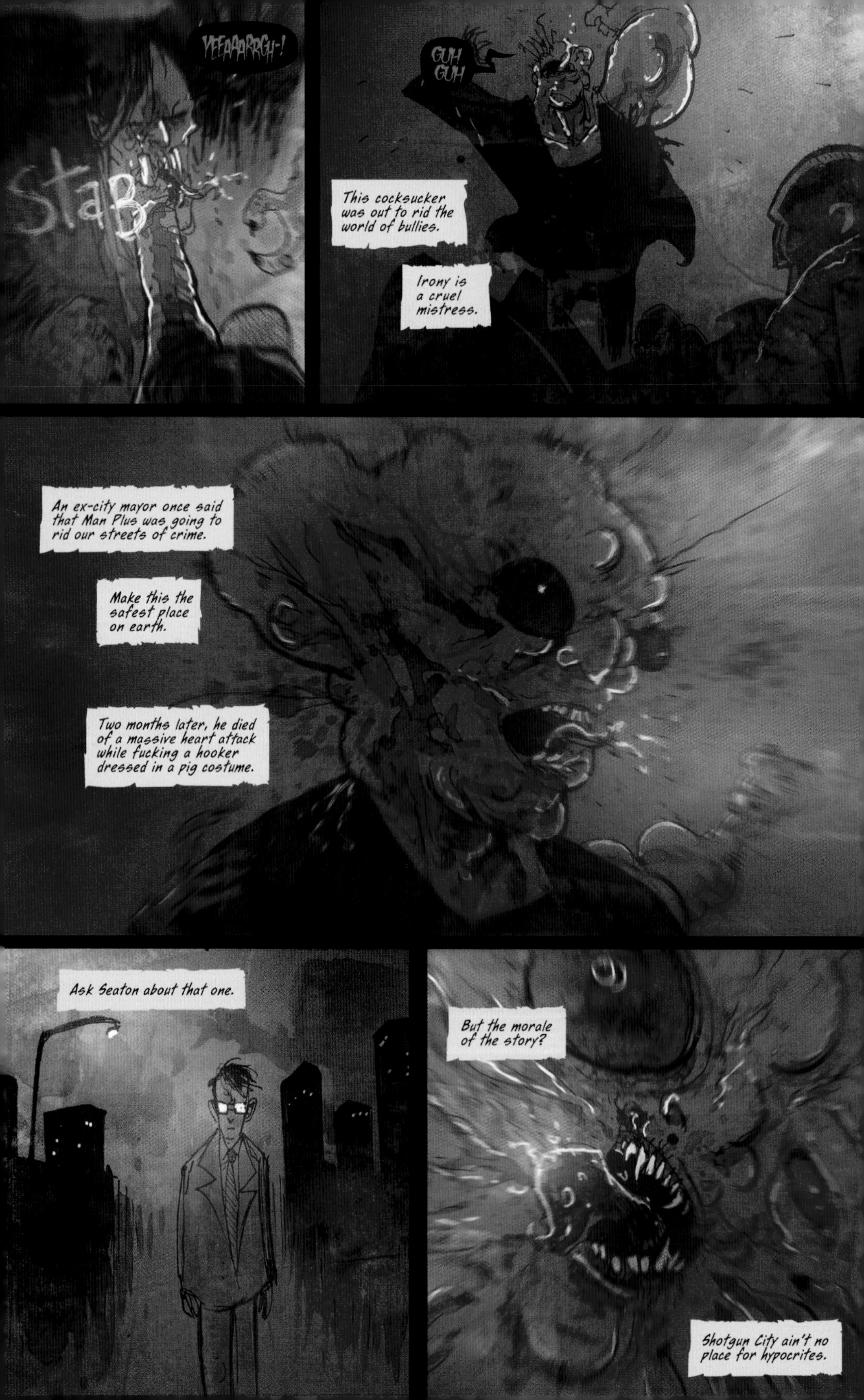
YEEAAARRGH-!
STAB
GUH GUH
This cocksucker was out to rid the world of bullies.
Irony is a cruel mistress.
An ex-city mayor once said that Man Plus was going to rid our streets of crime.
Make this the safest place on earth.
Two months later, he died of a massive heart attack while fucking a hooker dressed in a pig costume.
Ask Seaton about that one.
But the morale of the story?
Shotgun City ain't no place for hypocrites.

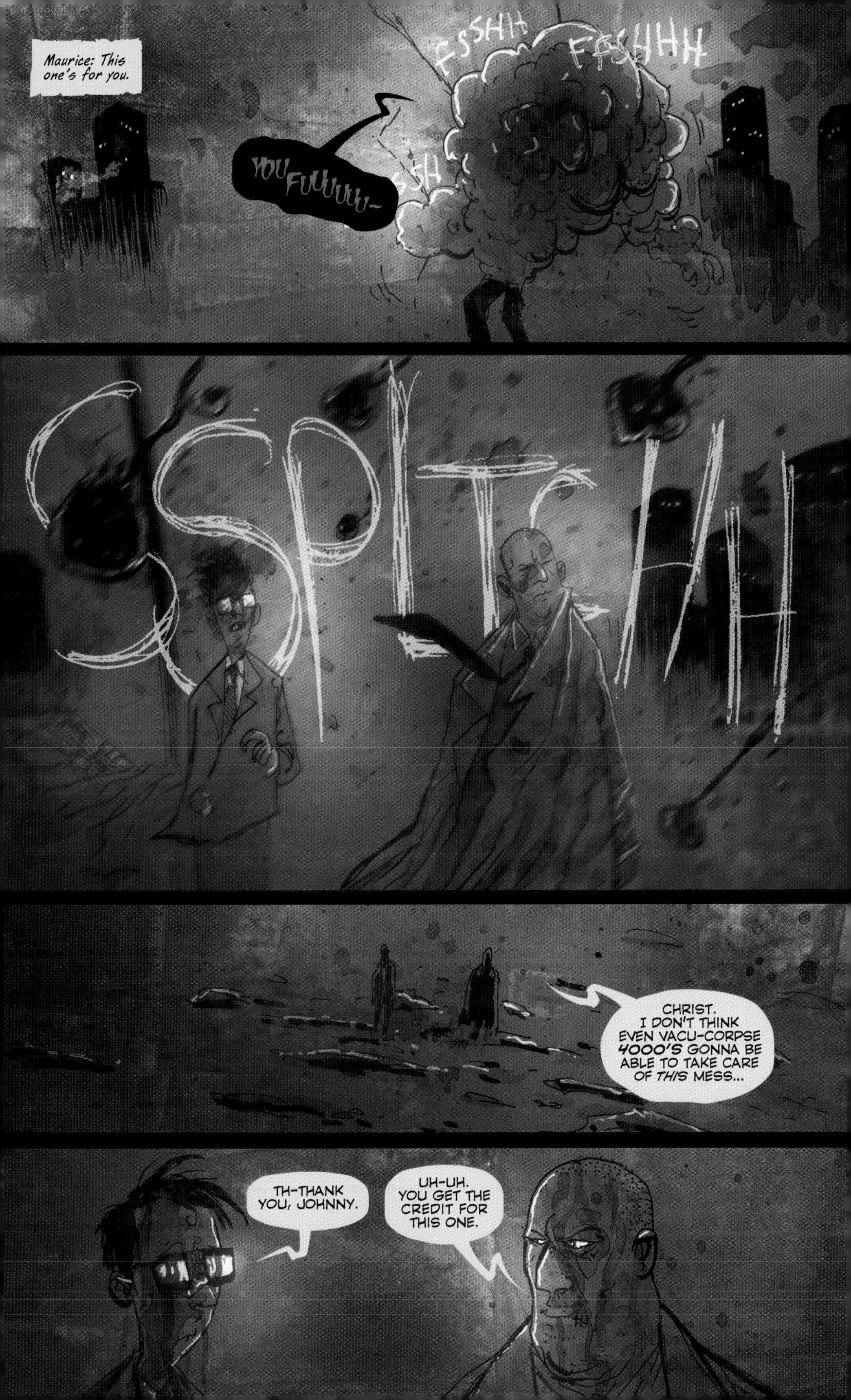
Maurice: This one's for you.
FSSHH
FFSHHH
SSH
YOU FUUUUU-
SPLTCHHH
CHRIST. I DON'T THINK EVEN VACU-CORPSE 4000'S GONNA BE ABLE TO TAKE CARE OF THIS MESS...
TH-THANK YOU, JOHNNY.
UH-UH. YOU GET THE CREDIT FOR THIS ONE.

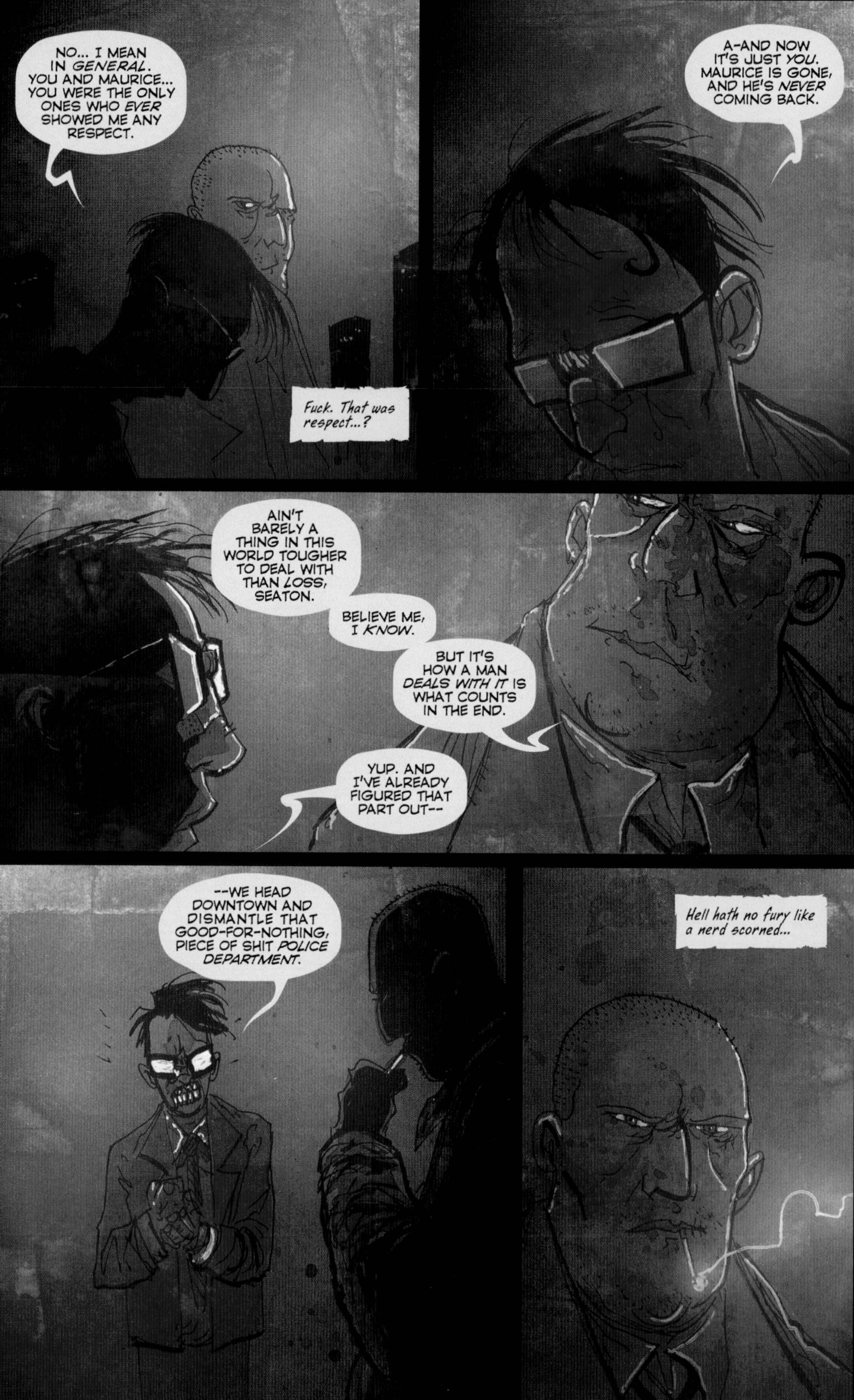
NO... I MEAN IN *GENERAL*. YOU AND MAURICE... YOU WERE THE ONLY ONES WHO *EVER* SHOWED ME ANY RESPECT.
Fuck. That was respect...?
A-AND NOW IT'S JUST *YOU*. MAURICE IS GONE, AND HE'S *NEVER* COMING BACK.
AIN'T BARELY A THING IN THIS WORLD TOUGHER TO DEAL WITH THAN *LOSS*, SEATON.
BELIEVE ME, I *KNOW*.
BUT IT'S HOW A MAN *DEALS WITH IT* IS WHAT COUNTS IN THE END.
YUP. AND I'VE ALREADY FIGURED THAT PART OUT--
--WE HEAD DOWNTOWN AND DISMANTLE THAT GOOD-FOR-NOTHING, PIECE OF SHIT *POLICE DEPARTMENT*.
Hell hath no fury like a nerd scorned...

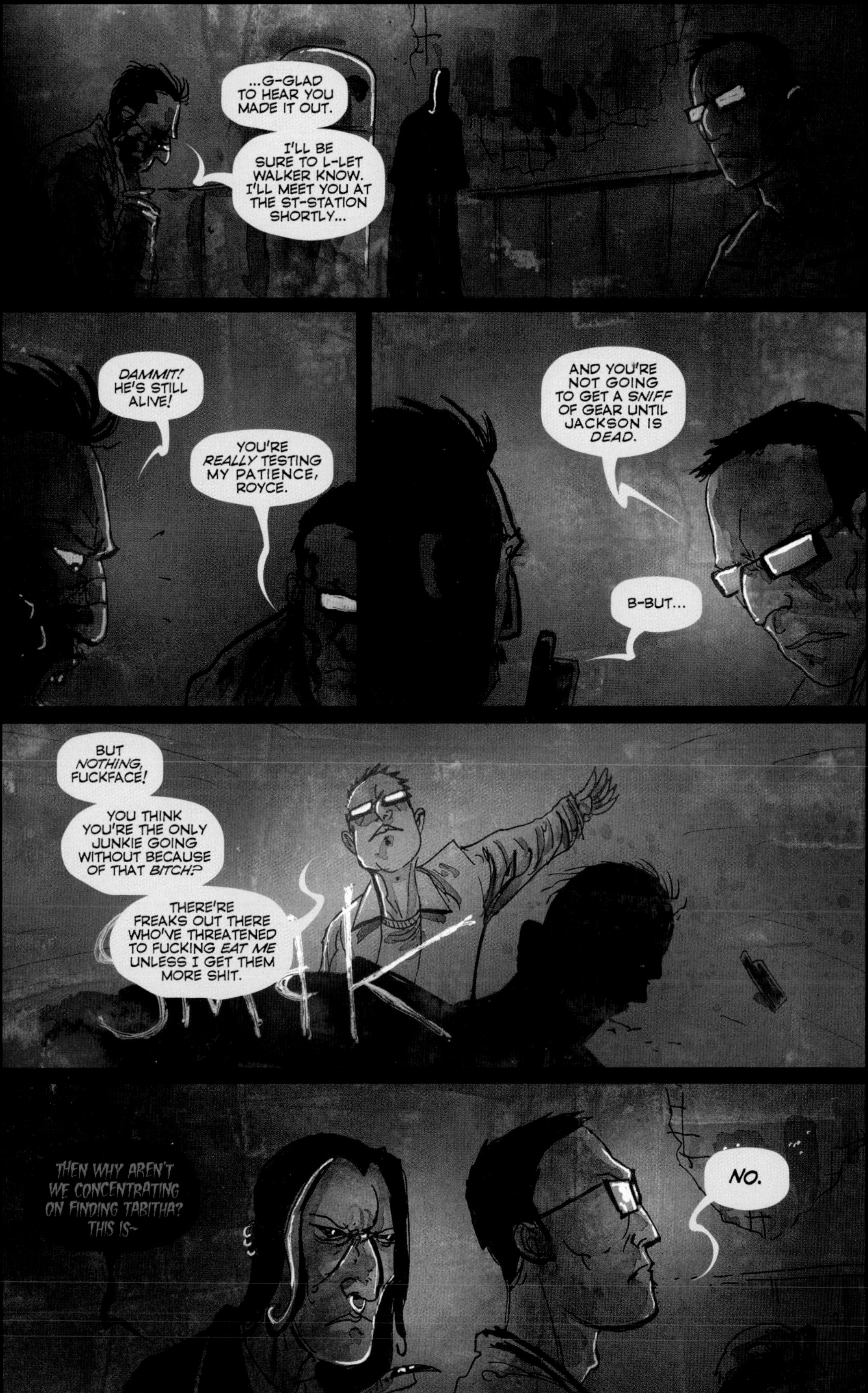
...G-GLAD TO HEAR YOU MADE IT OUT.
I'LL BE SURE TO L-LET WALKER KNOW. I'LL MEET YOU AT THE ST-STATION SHORTLY...
DAMMIT! HE'S STILL *ALIVE!*
YOU'RE *REALLY* TESTING MY PATIENCE, ROYCE.
AND YOU'RE NOT GOING TO GET A *SNIFF* OF GEAR UNTIL JACKSON IS *DEAD*.
B-BUT...
BUT *NOTHING*, FUCKFACE!
YOU THINK YOU'RE THE ONLY JUNKIE GOING WITHOUT BECAUSE OF THAT *BITCH?*
THERE'RE FREAKS OUT THERE WHO'VE THREATENED TO FUCKING *EAT ME* UNLESS I GET THEM MORE SHIT.
THEN WHY AREN'T WE CONCENTRATING ON FINDING TABITHA? THIS IS-
NO.

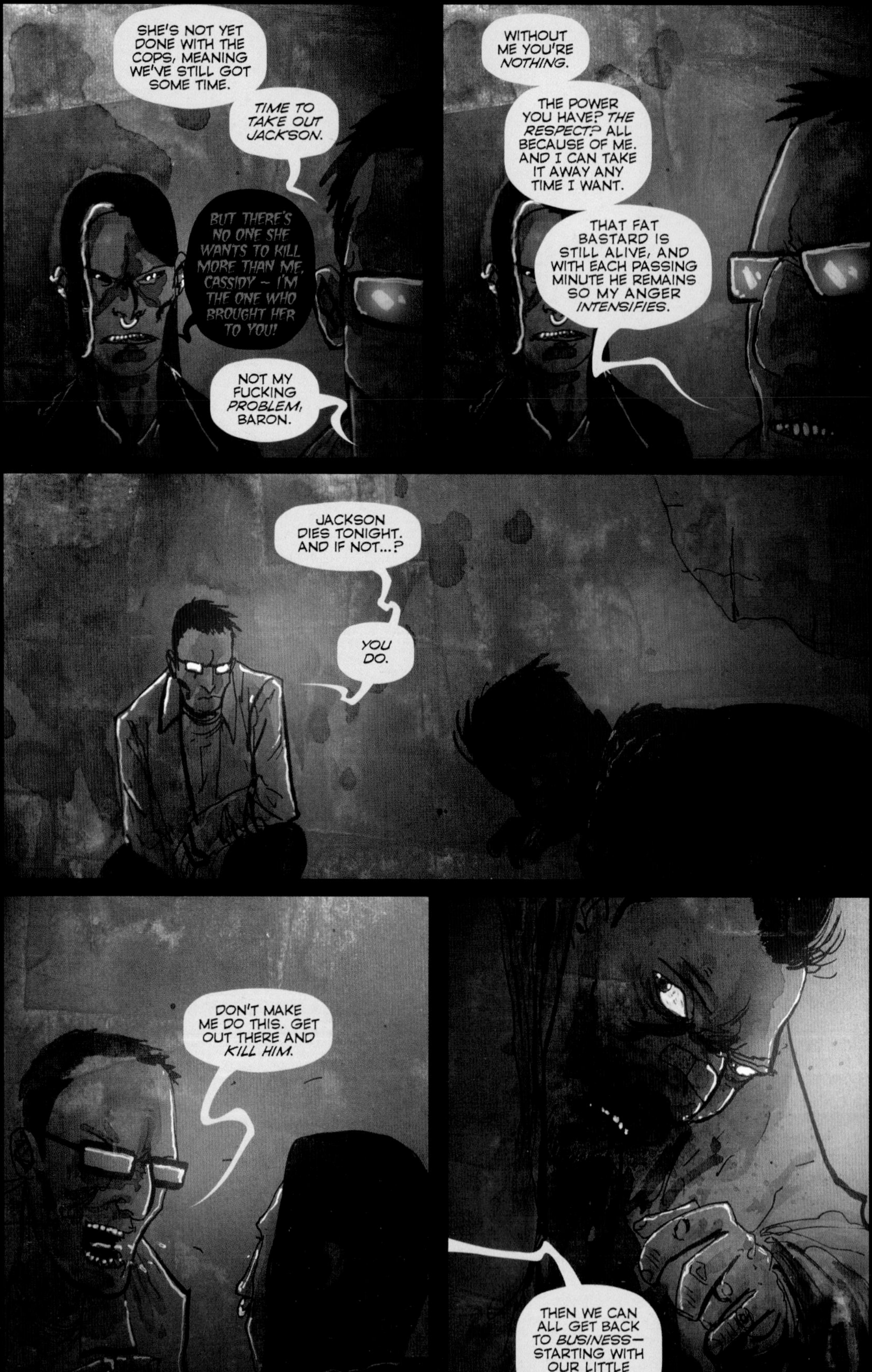
SHE'S NOT YET DONE WITH THE COPS, MEANING WE'VE STILL GOT SOME TIME.
TIME TO TAKE OUT JACKSON.
BUT THERE'S NO ONE SHE WANTS TO KILL MORE THAN ME, CASSIDY ~ I'M THE ONE WHO BROUGHT HER TO YOU!
NOT MY FUCKING PROBLEM, BARON.
WITHOUT ME YOU'RE NOTHING.
THE POWER YOU HAVE? THE RESPECT? ALL BECAUSE OF ME. AND I CAN TAKE IT AWAY ANY TIME I WANT.
THAT FAT BASTARD IS STILL ALIVE, AND WITH EACH PASSING MINUTE HE REMAINS SO MY ANGER INTENSIFIES.
JACKSON DIES TONIGHT. AND IF NOT...?
YOU DO.
DON'T MAKE ME DO THIS. GET OUT THERE AND KILL HIM.
THEN WE CAN ALL GET BACK TO BUSINESS— STARTING WITH OUR LITTLE PROBLEM TABITHA.

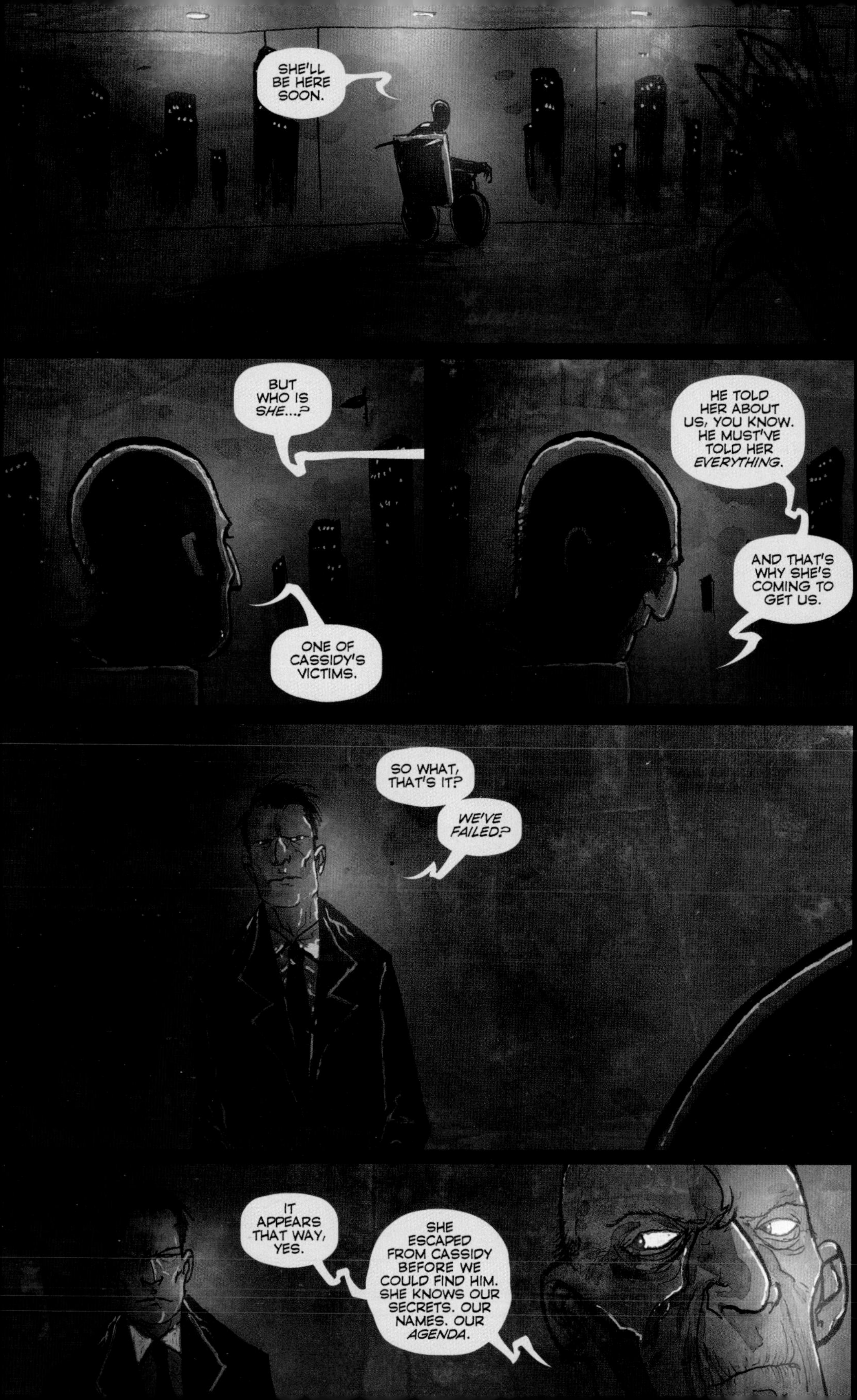

SHE'LL BE HERE SOON.
BUT WHO IS *SHE*...?
ONE OF CASSIDY'S VICTIMS.
HE TOLD HER ABOUT US, YOU KNOW. HE MUST'VE TOLD HER *EVERYTHING*.
AND THAT'S WHY SHE'S COMING TO GET US.
SO WHAT, THAT'S IT?
WE'VE FAILED?
IT APPEARS THAT WAY, YES.
SHE ESCAPED FROM CASSIDY BEFORE WE COULD FIND HIM. SHE KNOWS OUR SECRETS. OUR NAMES. OUR *AGENDA*.

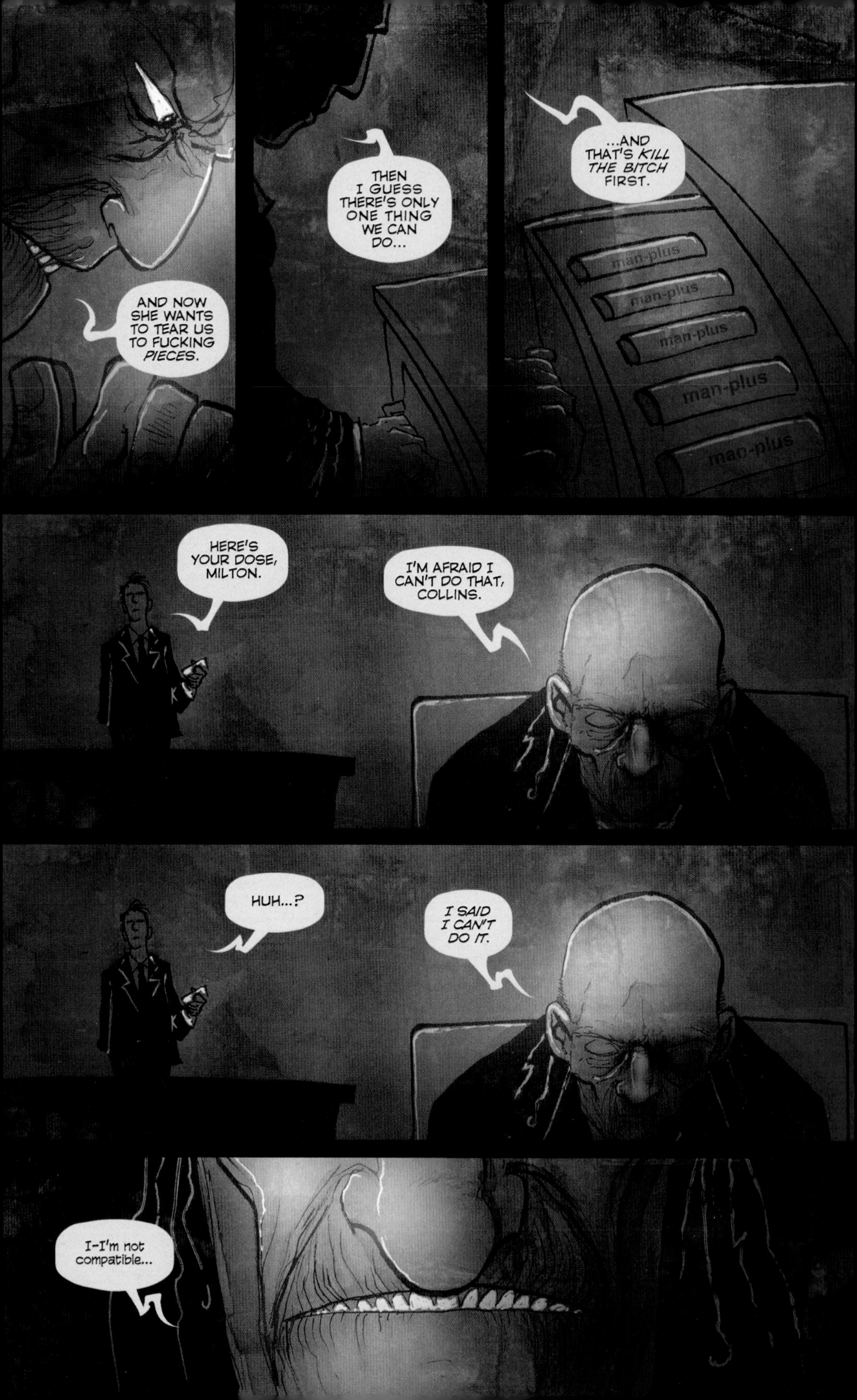
AND NOW SHE WANTS TO TEAR US TO FUCKING *PIECES*.
THEN I GUESS THERE'S ONLY ONE THING WE CAN DO...
...AND THAT'S *KILL THE BITCH* FIRST.
man-plus
man-plus
man-plus
man-plus
man-plus
HERE'S YOUR DOSE, MILTON.
I'M AFRAID I CAN'T DO THAT, COLLINS.
HUH...?
I SAID I CAN'T DO IT.
I-I'm not compatible...

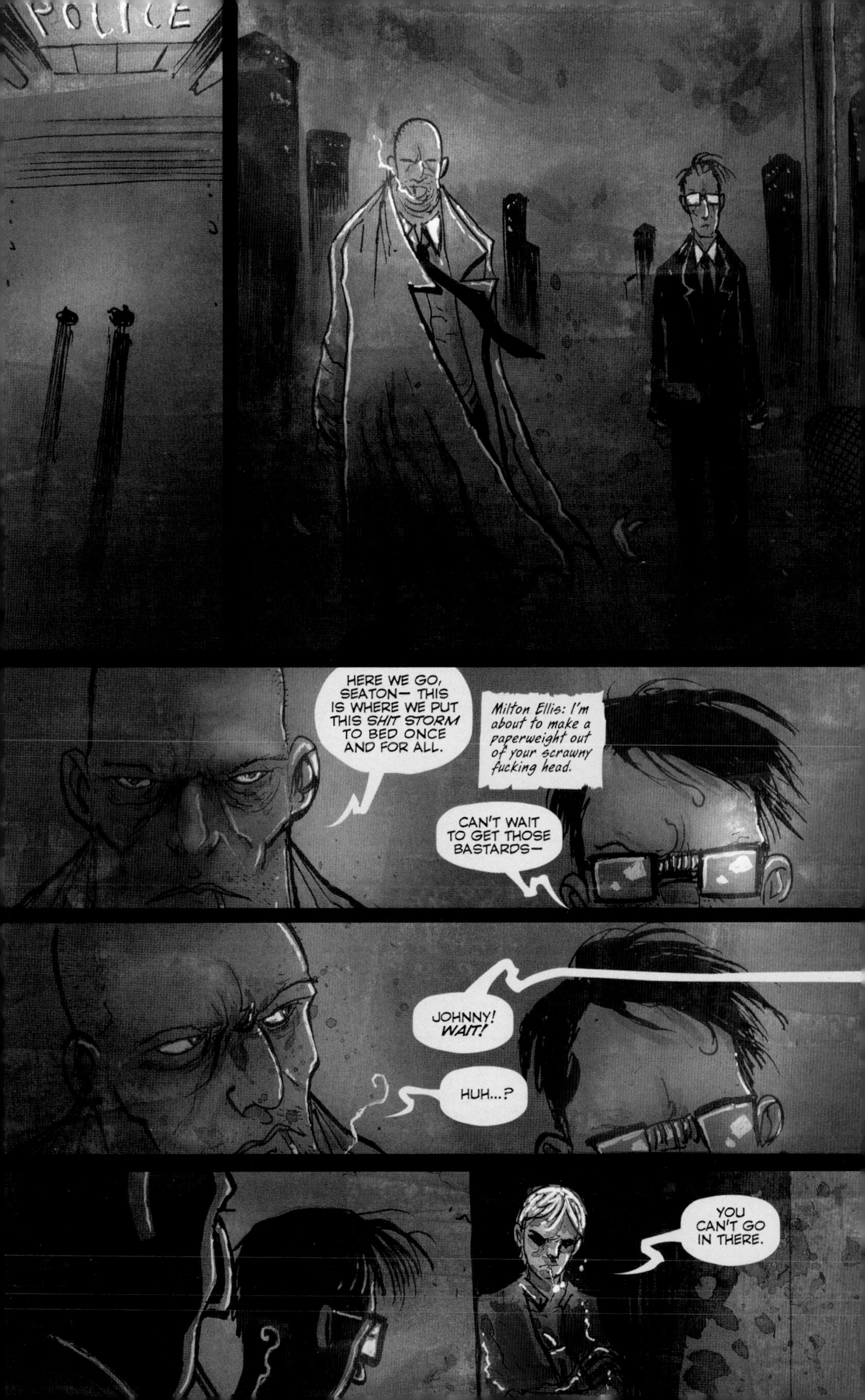
POLICE
HERE WE GO, SEATON— THIS IS WHERE WE PUT THIS SHIT STORM TO BED ONCE AND FOR ALL.
Milton Ellis: I'm about to make a paperweight out of your scrawny fucking head.
CAN'T WAIT TO GET THOSE BASTARDS—
JOHNNY! WAIT!
HUH...?
YOU CAN'T GO IN THERE.

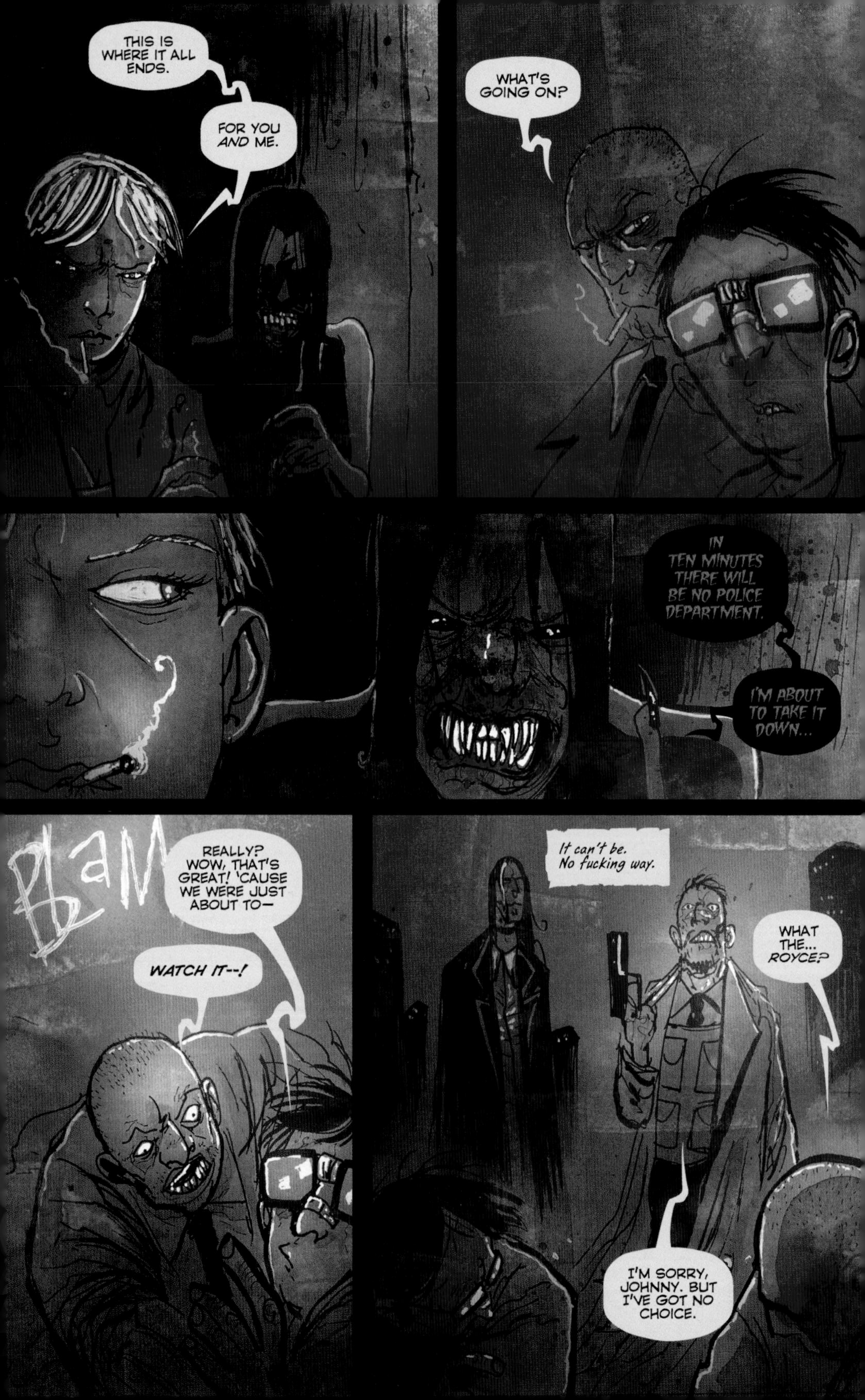
THIS IS WHERE IT ALL ENDS.
FOR YOU AND ME.
WHAT'S GOING ON?
IN TEN MINUTES THERE WILL BE NO POLICE DEPARTMENT.
I'M ABOUT TO TAKE IT DOWN...
Blam
REALLY? WOW, THAT'S GREAT! 'CAUSE WE WERE JUST ABOUT TO—
WATCH IT--!
It can't be. No fucking way.
WHAT THE... ROYCE?
I'M SORRY, JOHNNY. BUT I'VE GOT NO CHOICE.

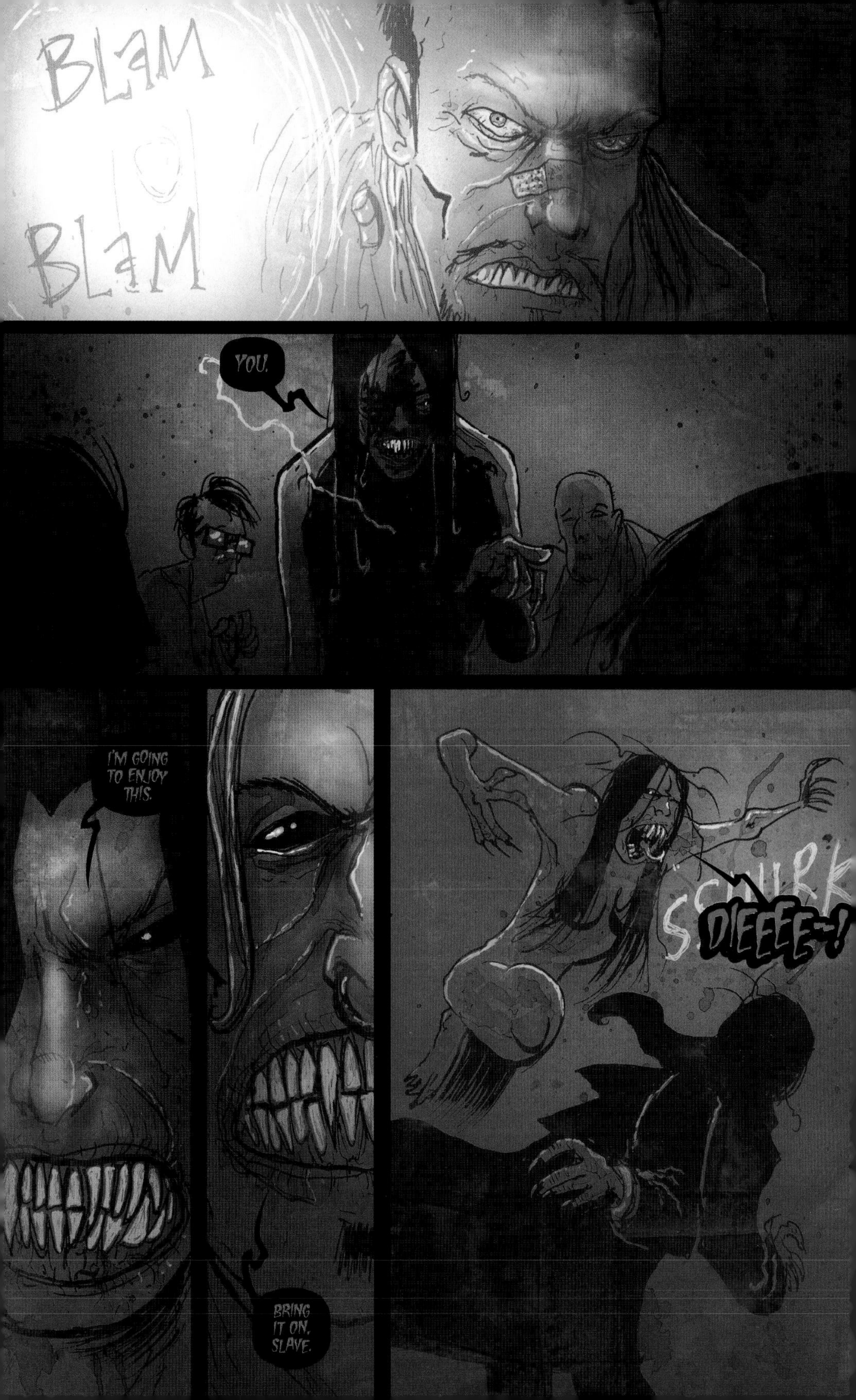
BLAM
BLAM
YOU.
I'M GOING TO ENJOY THIS.
BRING IT ON, SLAVE.
SSHURK
DIEEEE~!

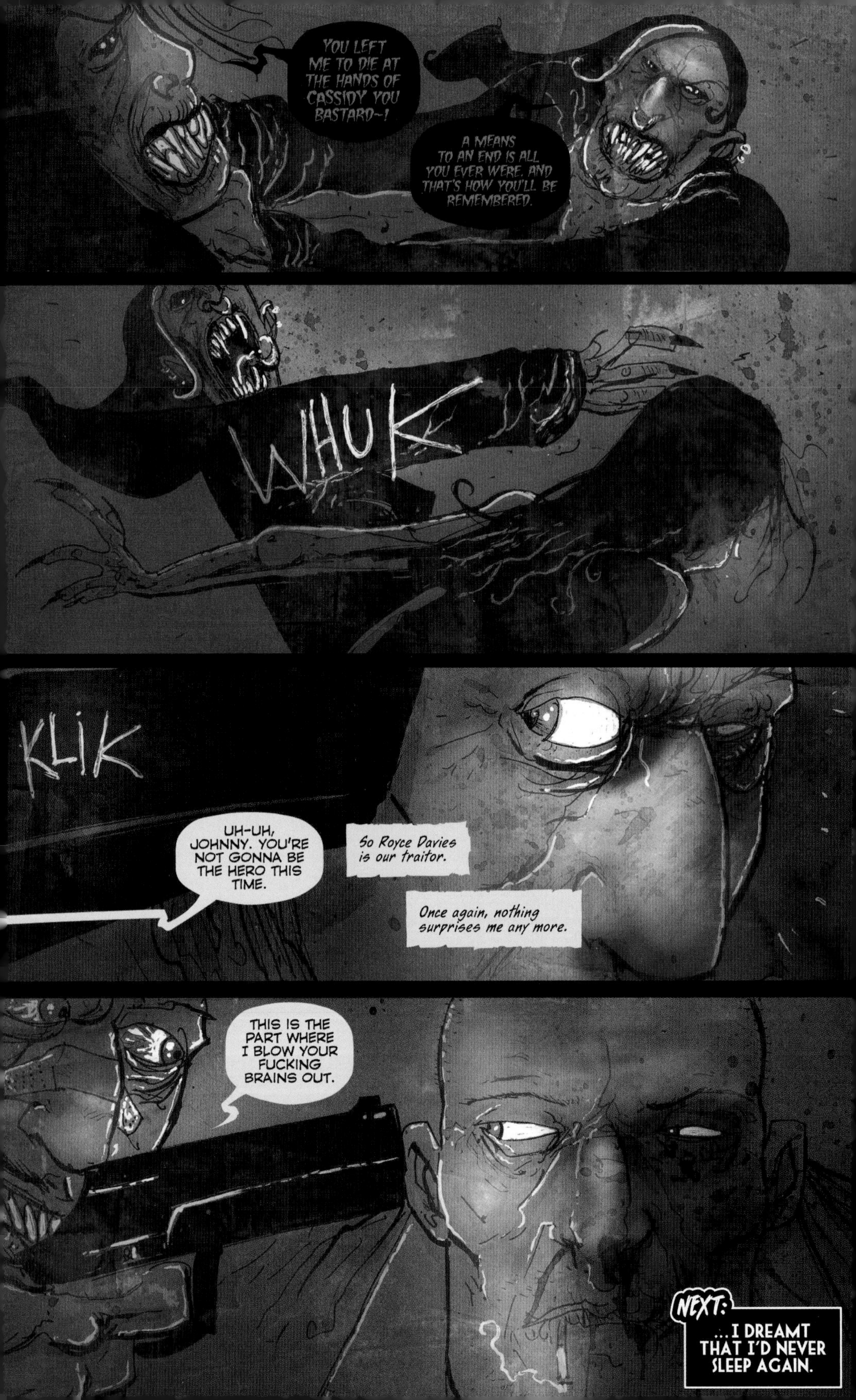
YOU LEFT ME TO DIE AT THE HANDS OF CASSIDY YOU BASTARD~!
A MEANS TO AN END IS ALL YOU EVER WERE. AND THAT'S HOW YOU'LL BE REMEMBERED.
WHUK
KLIK
UH-UH, JOHNNY. YOU'RE NOT GONNA BE THE HERO THIS TIME.
So Royce Davies is our traitor.
Once again, nothing surprises me any more.
THIS IS THE PART WHERE I BLOW YOUR FUCKING BRAINS OUT.
NEXT: ...I DREAMT THAT I'D NEVER SLEEP AGAIN.

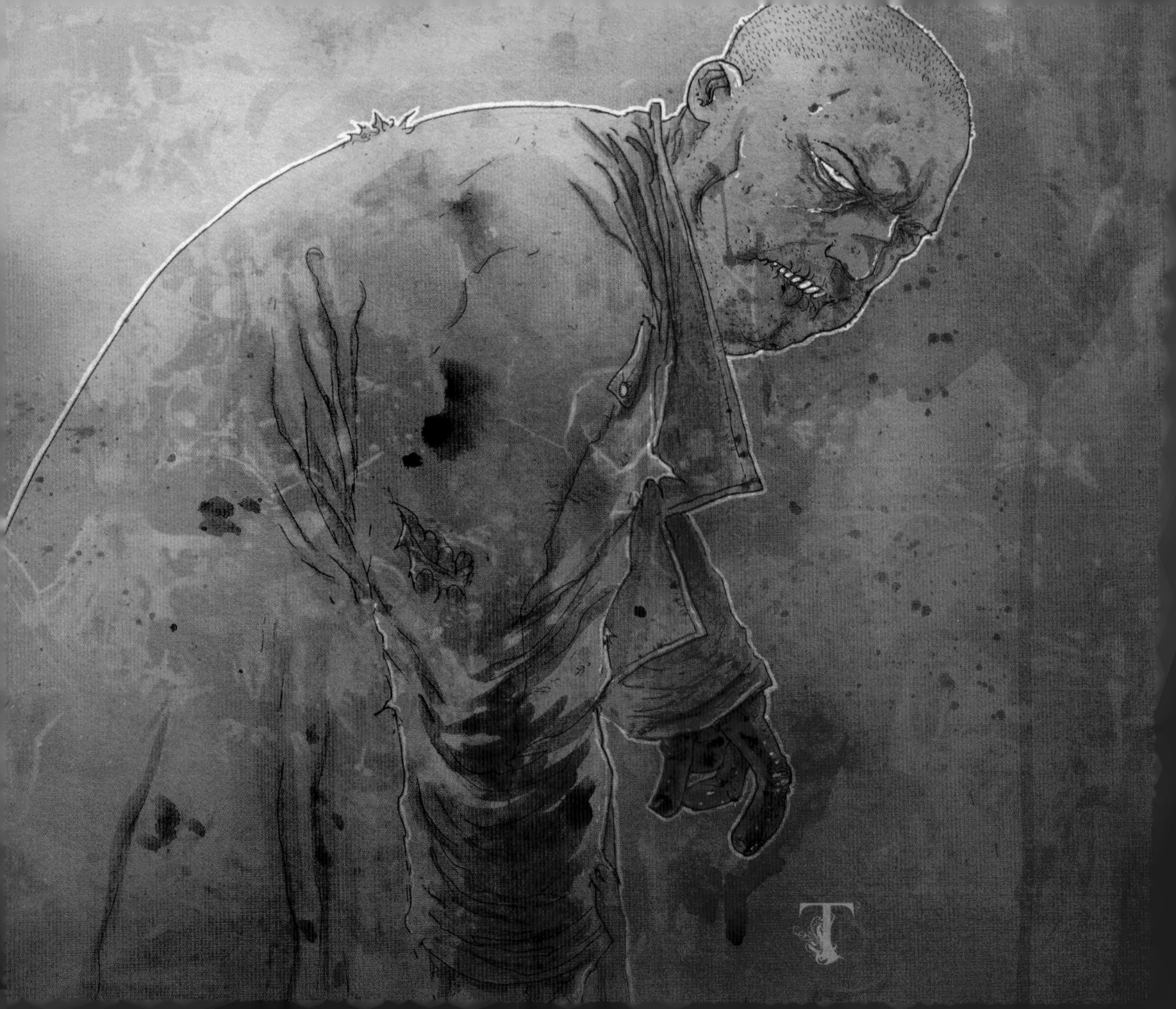

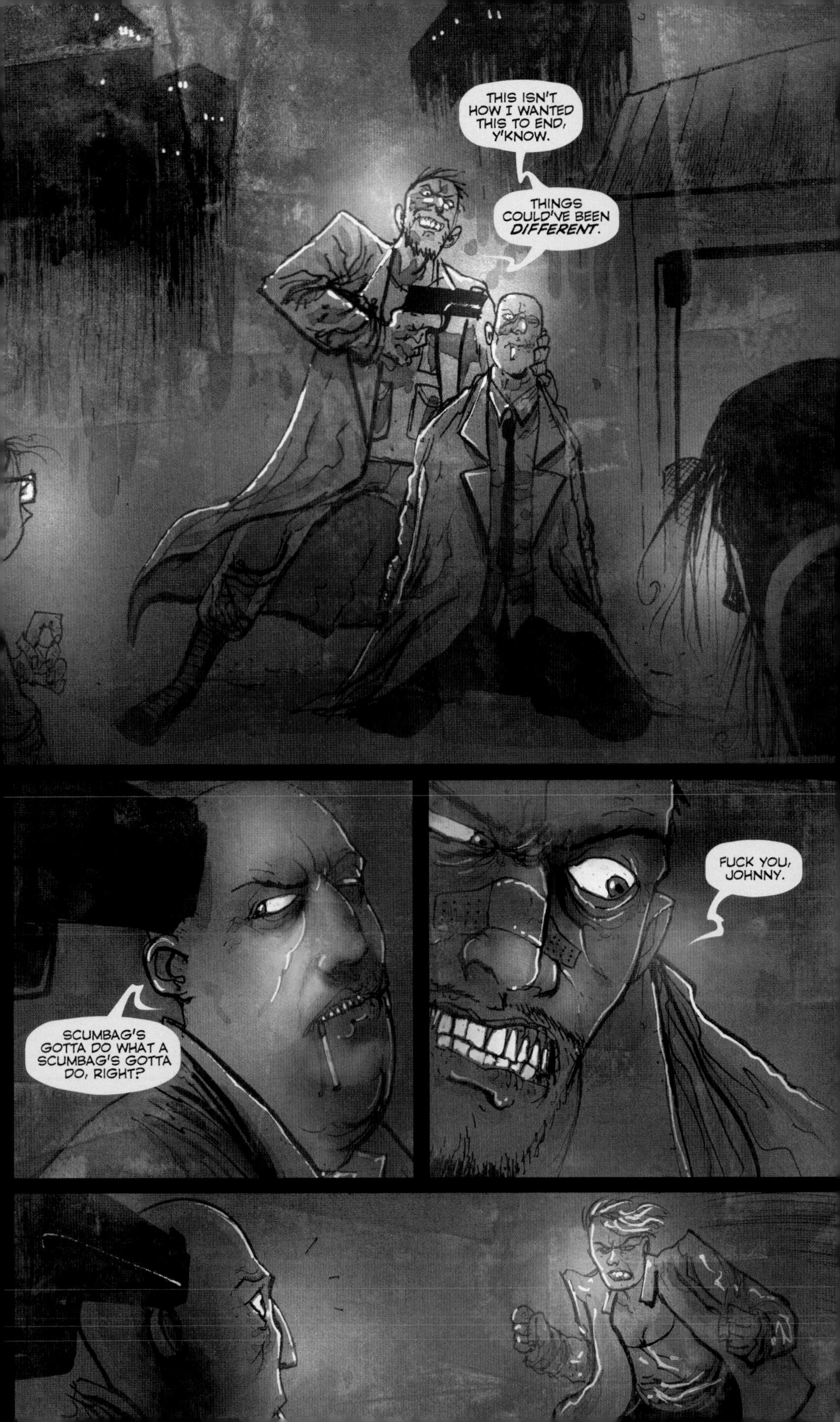

THIS ISN'T HOW I WANTED THIS TO END, Y'KNOW.
THINGS COULD'VE BEEN *DIFFERENT*.
SCUMBAG'S GOTTA DO WHAT A SCUMBAG'S GOTTA DO, RIGHT?
FUCK YOU, JOHNNY.

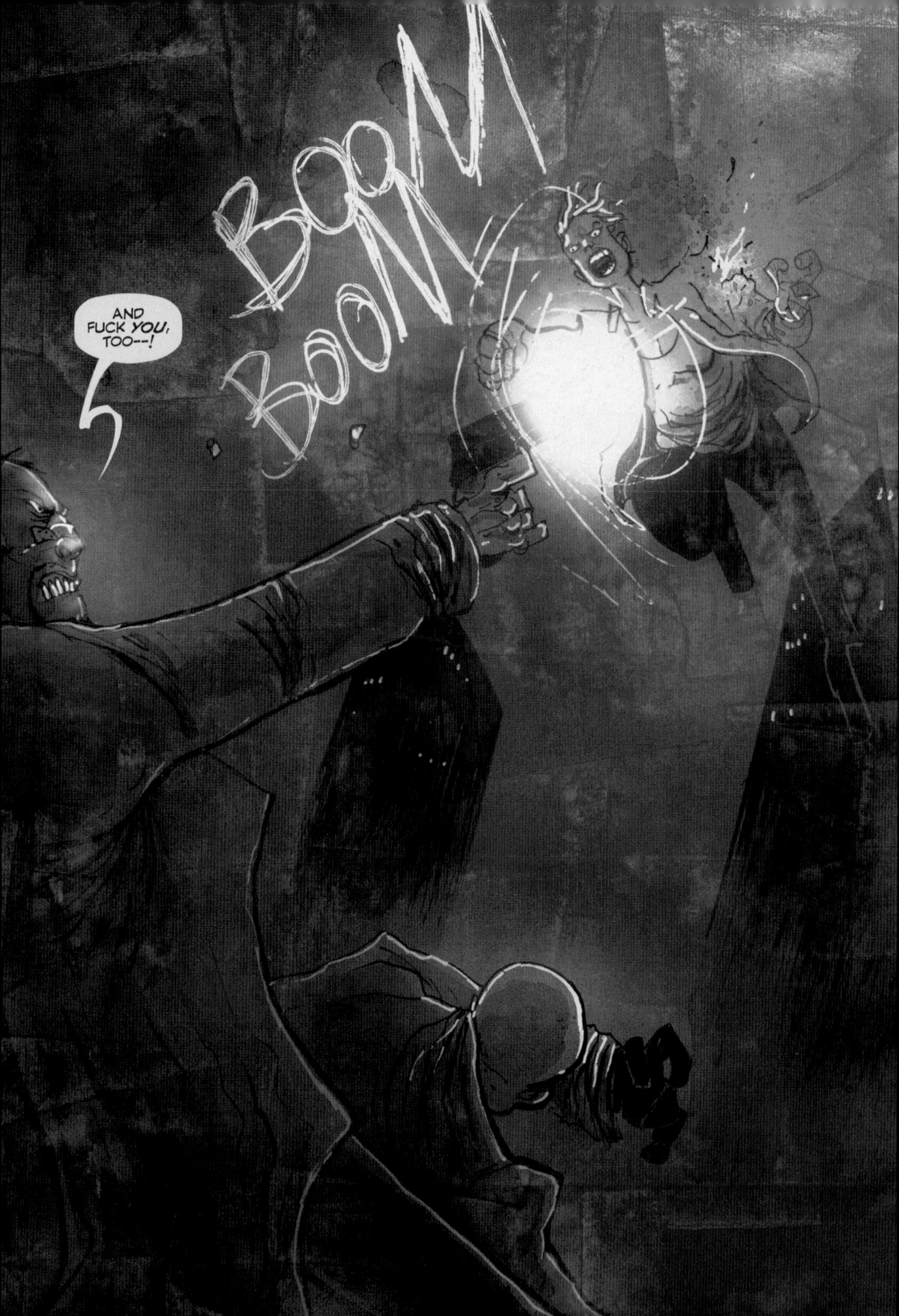
AND FUCK YOU, TOO--!
BOOM
BOOM

"...I DREAMT I'D NEVER SLEEP AGAIN"

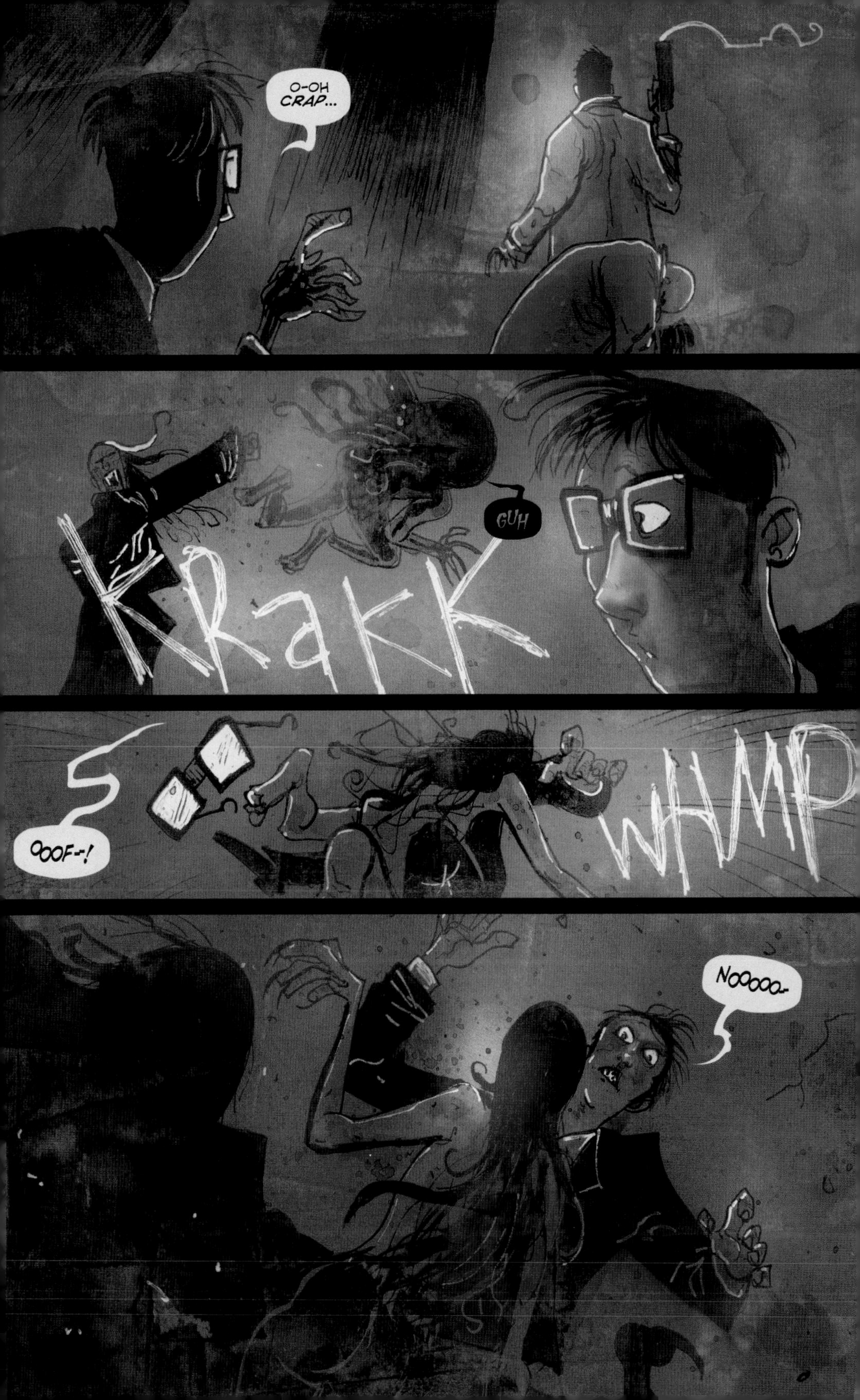
O-OH CRAP...
GUH
KRAKK
OOOF--!
WHMP
NOOOOO--

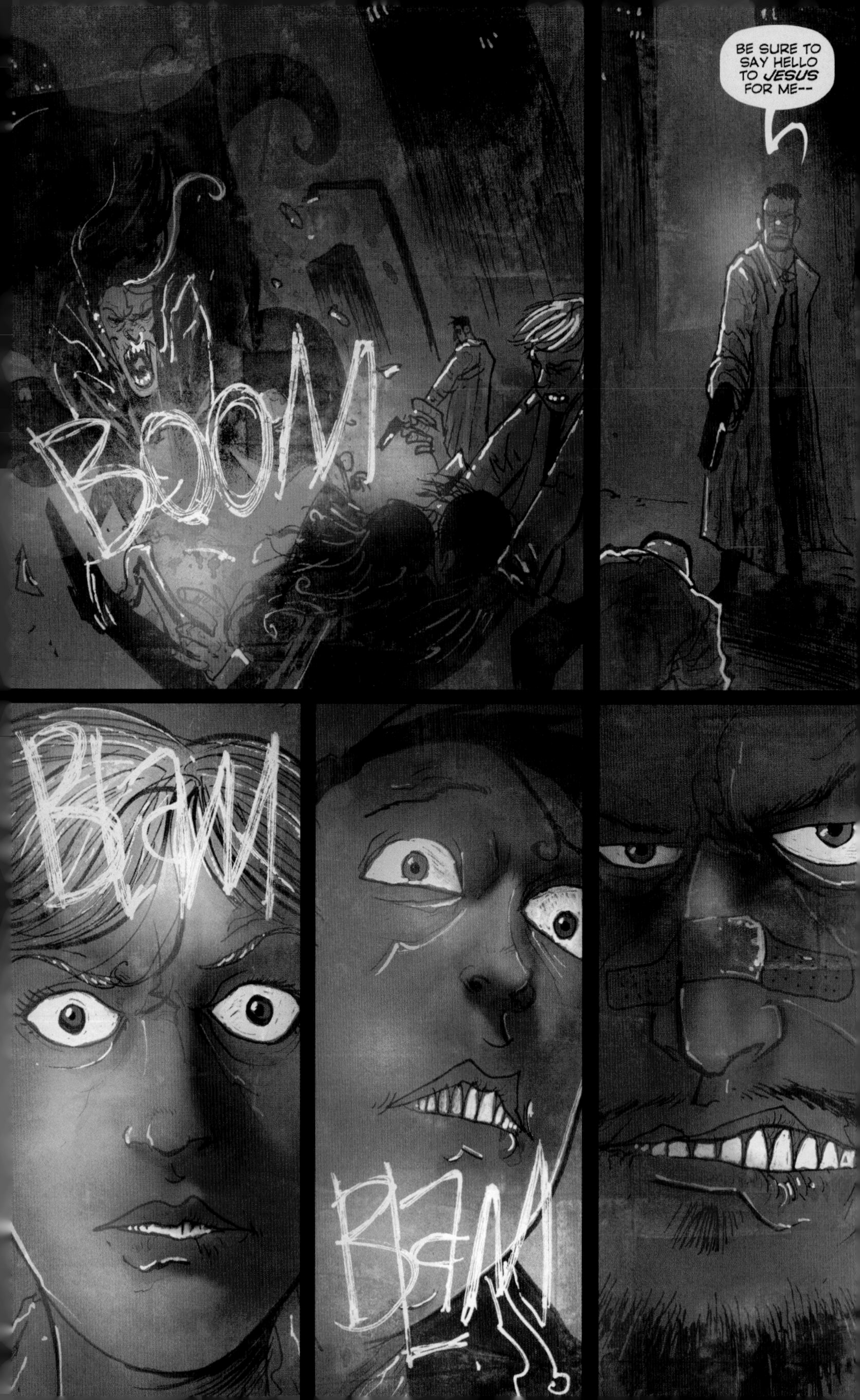
BOOM
BE SURE TO SAY HELLO TO JESUS FOR ME--
BLAM
BLAM

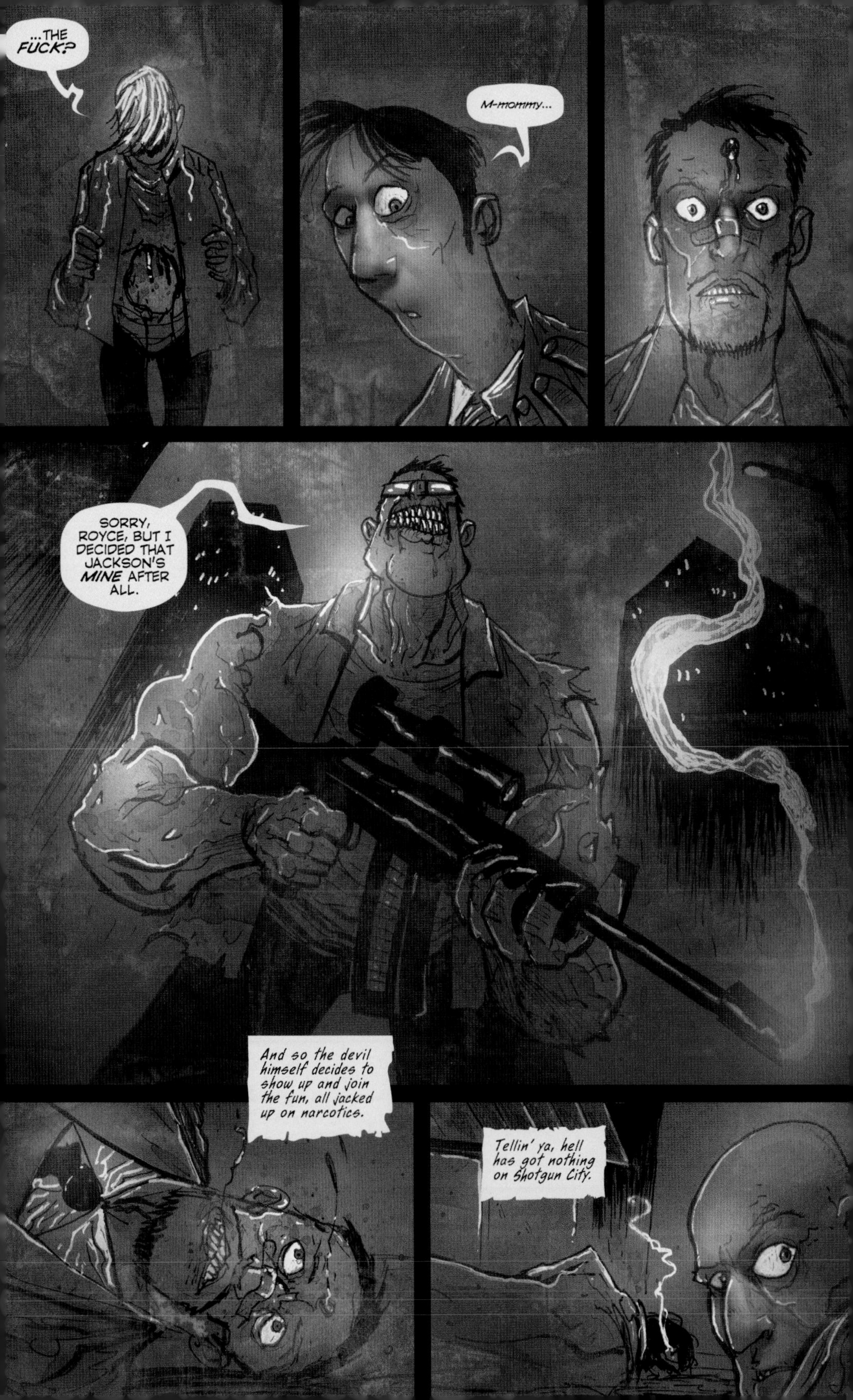
...THE FUCK?
M-mommy...
SORRY, ROYCE, BUT I DECIDED THAT JACKSON'S MINE AFTER ALL.
And so the devil himself decides to show up and join the fun, all jacked up on narcotics.
Tellin' ya, hell has got nothing on Shotgun City.

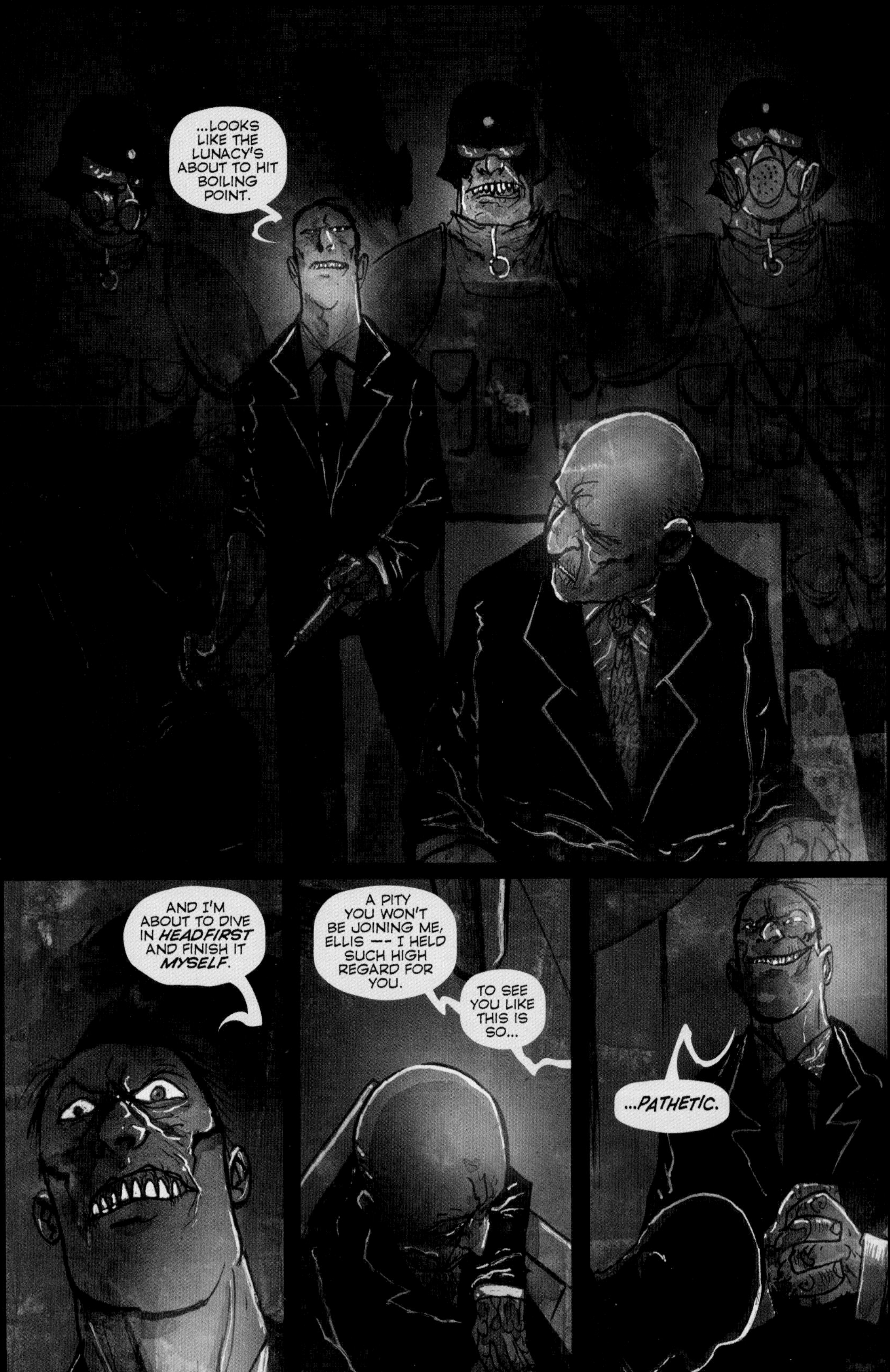
...LOOKS LIKE THE LUNACY'S ABOUT TO HIT BOILING POINT.
AND I'M ABOUT TO DIVE IN *HEADFIRST* AND FINISH IT *MYSELF*.
A PITY YOU WON'T BE JOINING ME, ELLIS -- I HELD SUCH HIGH REGARD FOR YOU.
TO SEE YOU LIKE THIS IS SO...
...*PATHETIC*.

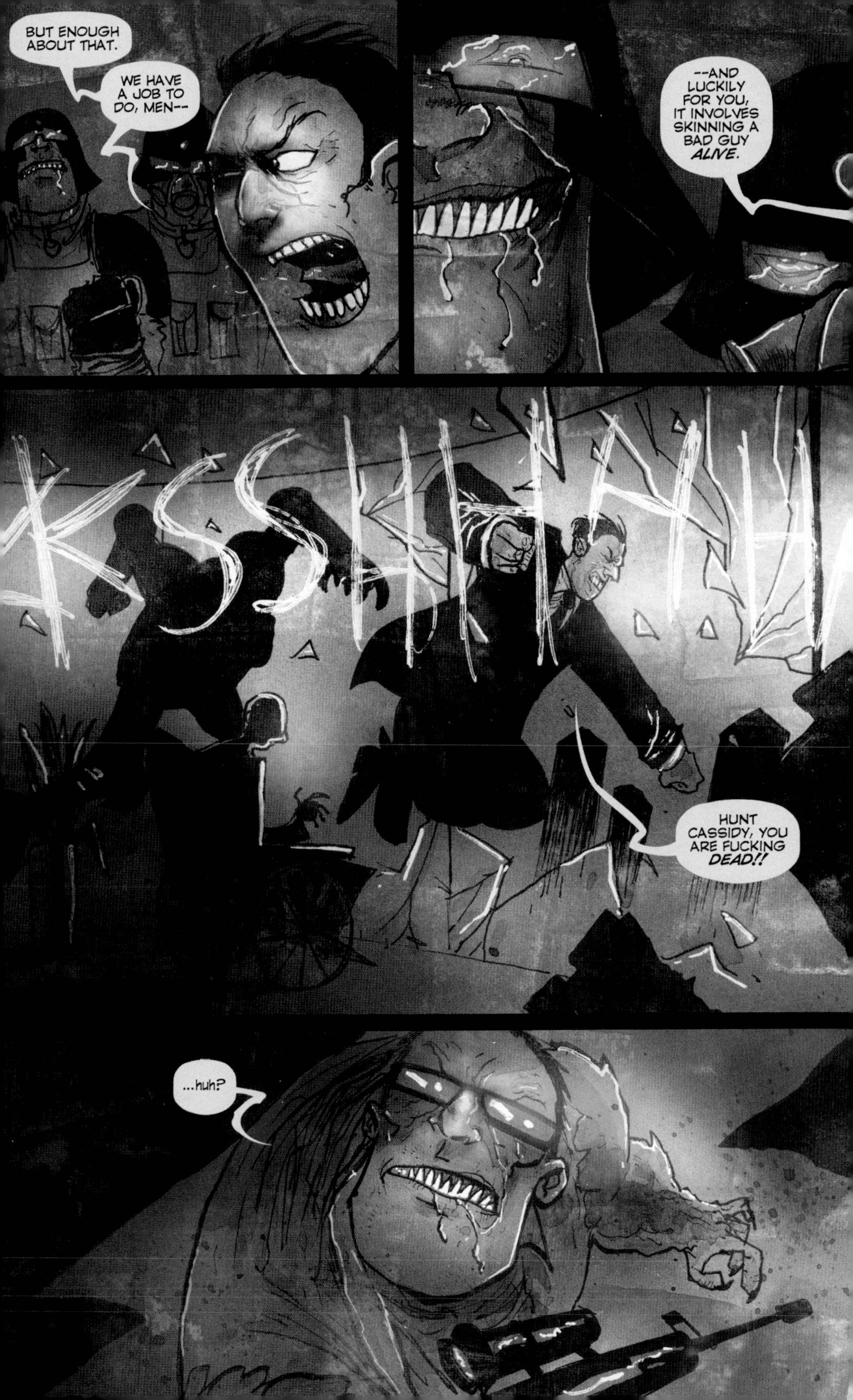
BUT ENOUGH ABOUT THAT.
WE HAVE A JOB TO DO, MEN--
--AND LUCKILY FOR YOU, IT INVOLVES SKINNING A BAD GUY *ALIVE*.
HUNT CASSIDY, YOU ARE FUCKING *DEAD!!*
...huh?

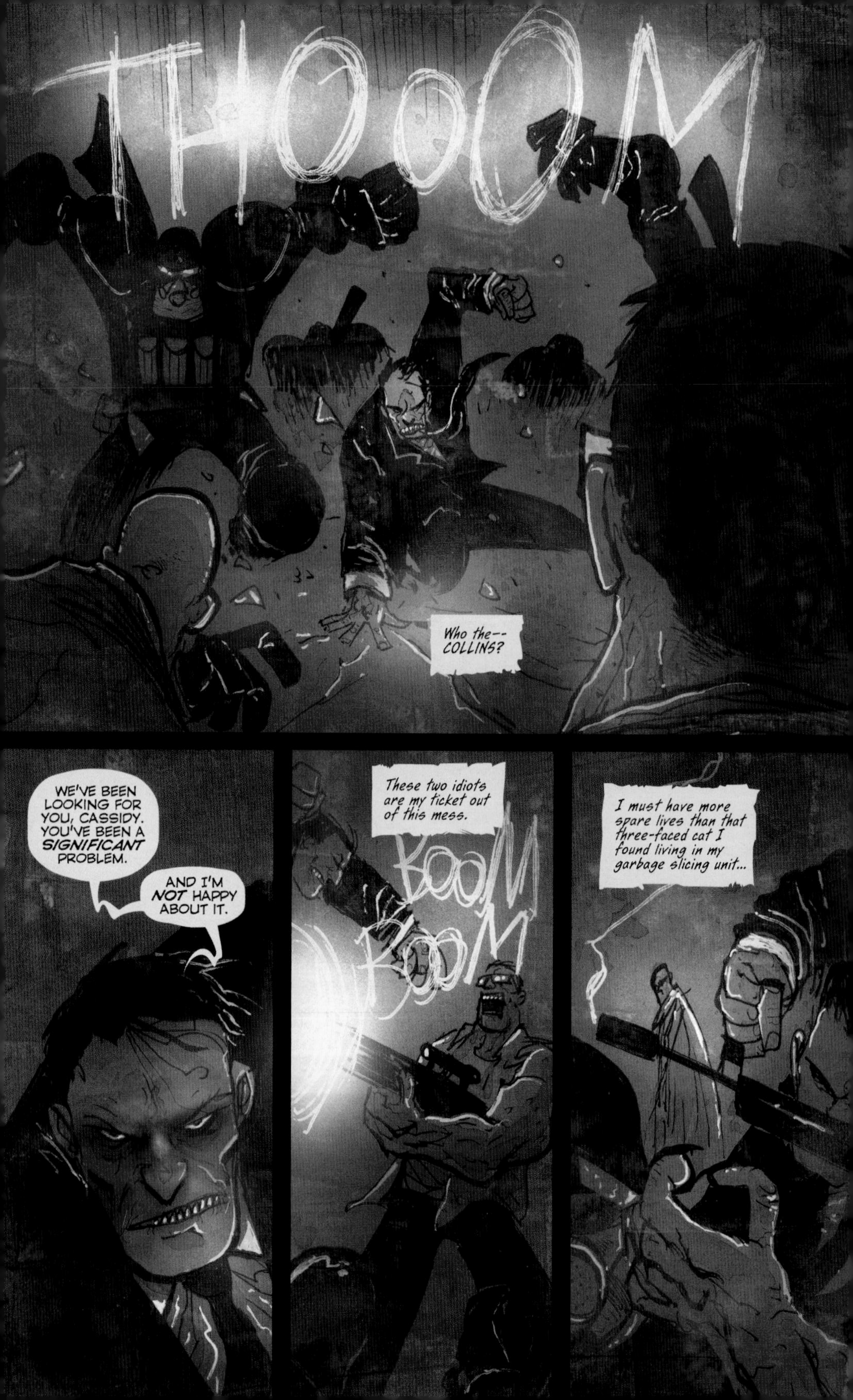
THOOOM
Who the--
COLLINS?
WE'VE BEEN LOOKING FOR YOU, CASSIDY. YOU'VE BEEN A SIGNIFICANT PROBLEM.
AND I'M NOT HAPPY ABOUT IT.
These two idiots are my ticket out of this mess.
BOOM
BOOM
I must have more spare lives than that three-faced cat I found living in my garbage slicing unit...

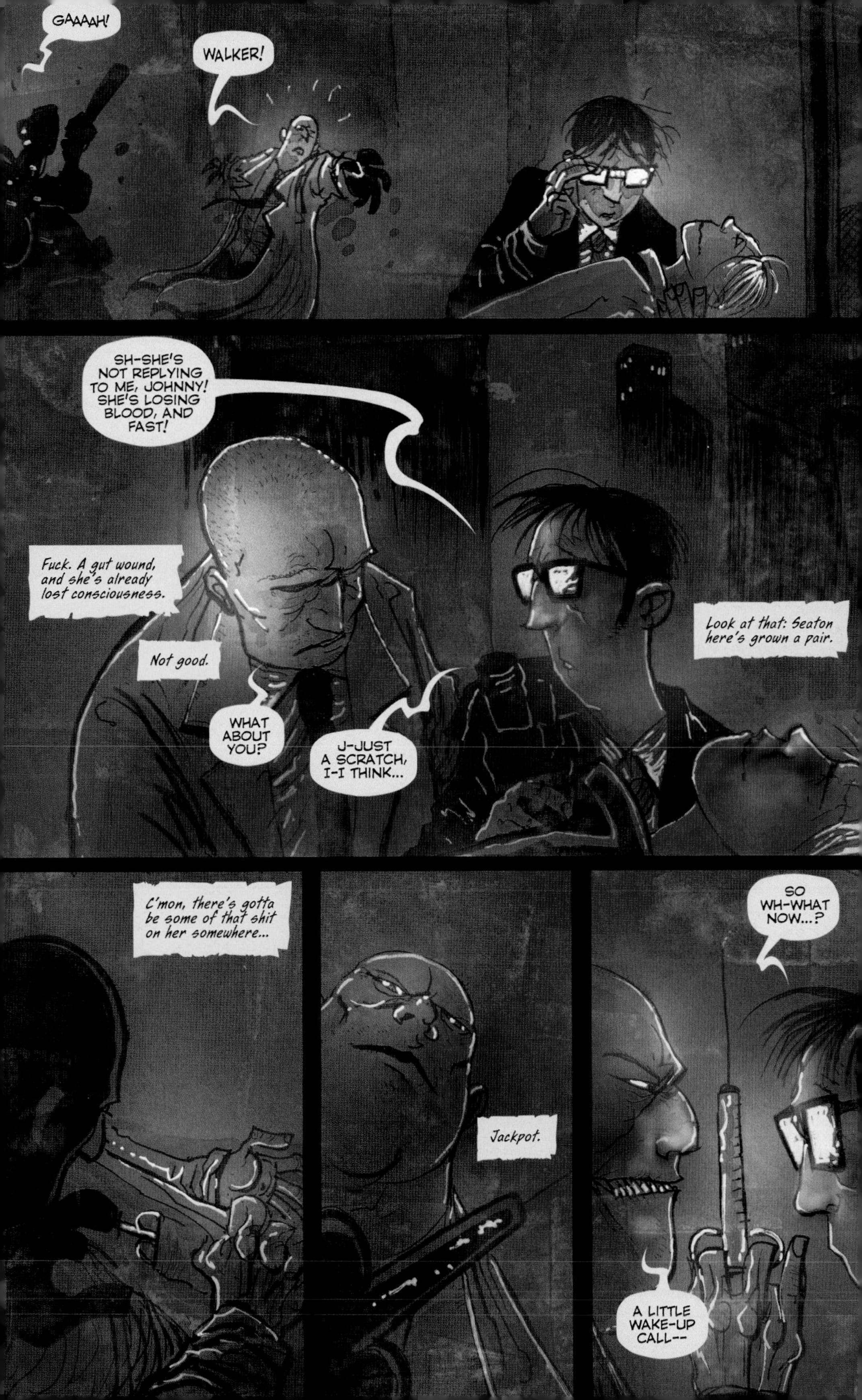
GAAAAH!
WALKER!
SH-SHE'S NOT REPLYING TO ME, JOHNNY! SHE'S LOSING BLOOD, AND FAST!
Fuck. A gut wound, and she's already lost consciousness.
Not good.
Look at that: Seaton here's grown a pair.
WHAT ABOUT YOU?
J-JUST A SCRATCH, I-I THINK...
C'mon, there's gotta be some of that shit on her somewhere...
Jackpot.
SO WH-WHAT NOW...?
A LITTLE WAKE-UP CALL--

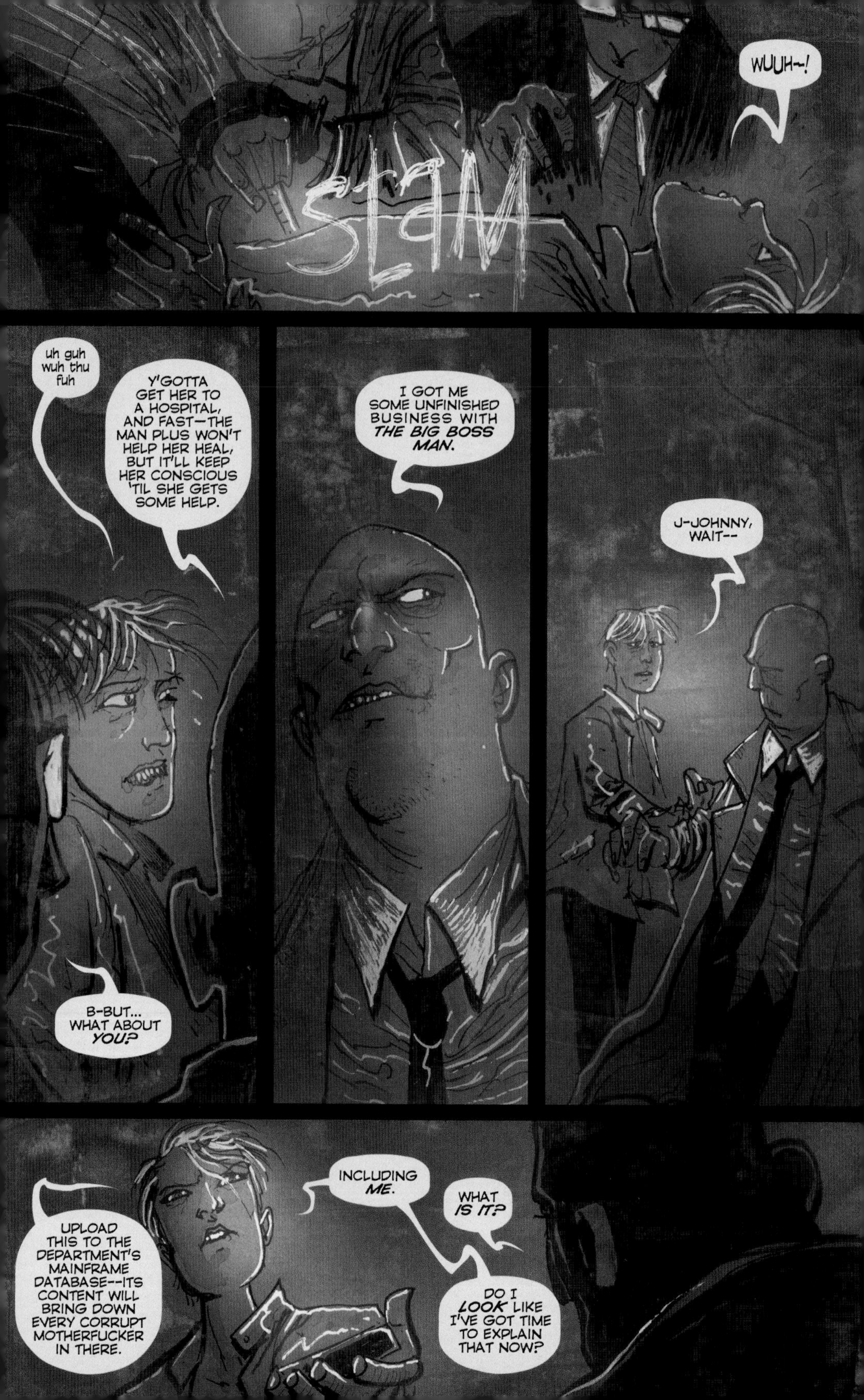
SLAM
WUUH--!
uh guh wuh thu fuh
Y'GOTTA GET HER TO A HOSPITAL, AND FAST—THE MAN PLUS WON'T HELP HER HEAL, BUT IT'LL KEEP HER CONSCIOUS 'TIL SHE GETS SOME HELP.
B-BUT... WHAT ABOUT YOU?
I GOT ME SOME UNFINISHED BUSINESS WITH THE BIG BOSS MAN.
J-JOHNNY, WAIT--
UPLOAD THIS TO THE DEPARTMENT'S MAINFRAME DATABASE--ITS CONTENT WILL BRING DOWN EVERY CORRUPT MOTHERFUCKER IN THERE.
INCLUDING ME.
WHAT IS IT?
DO I LOOK LIKE I'VE GOT TIME TO EXPLAIN THAT NOW?

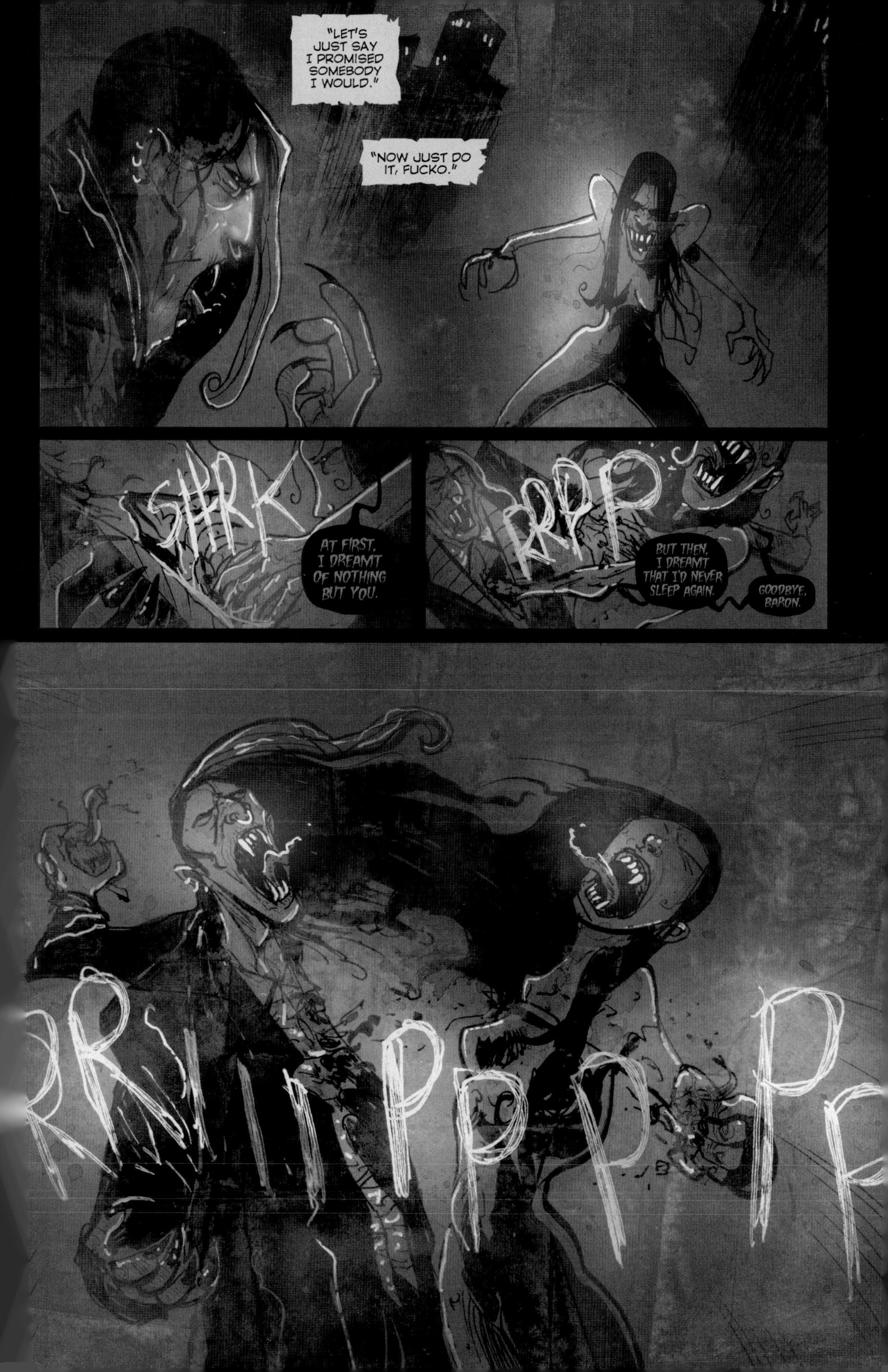

"LET'S JUST SAY I PROMISED SOMEBODY I WOULD."
"NOW JUST DO IT, FUCKO."
SHRK
AT FIRST, I DREAMT OF NOTHING BUT YOU.
RRPP
BUT THEN, I DREAMT THAT I'D NEVER SLEEP AGAIN.
GOODBYE, BARON.
RRIIPPPPP

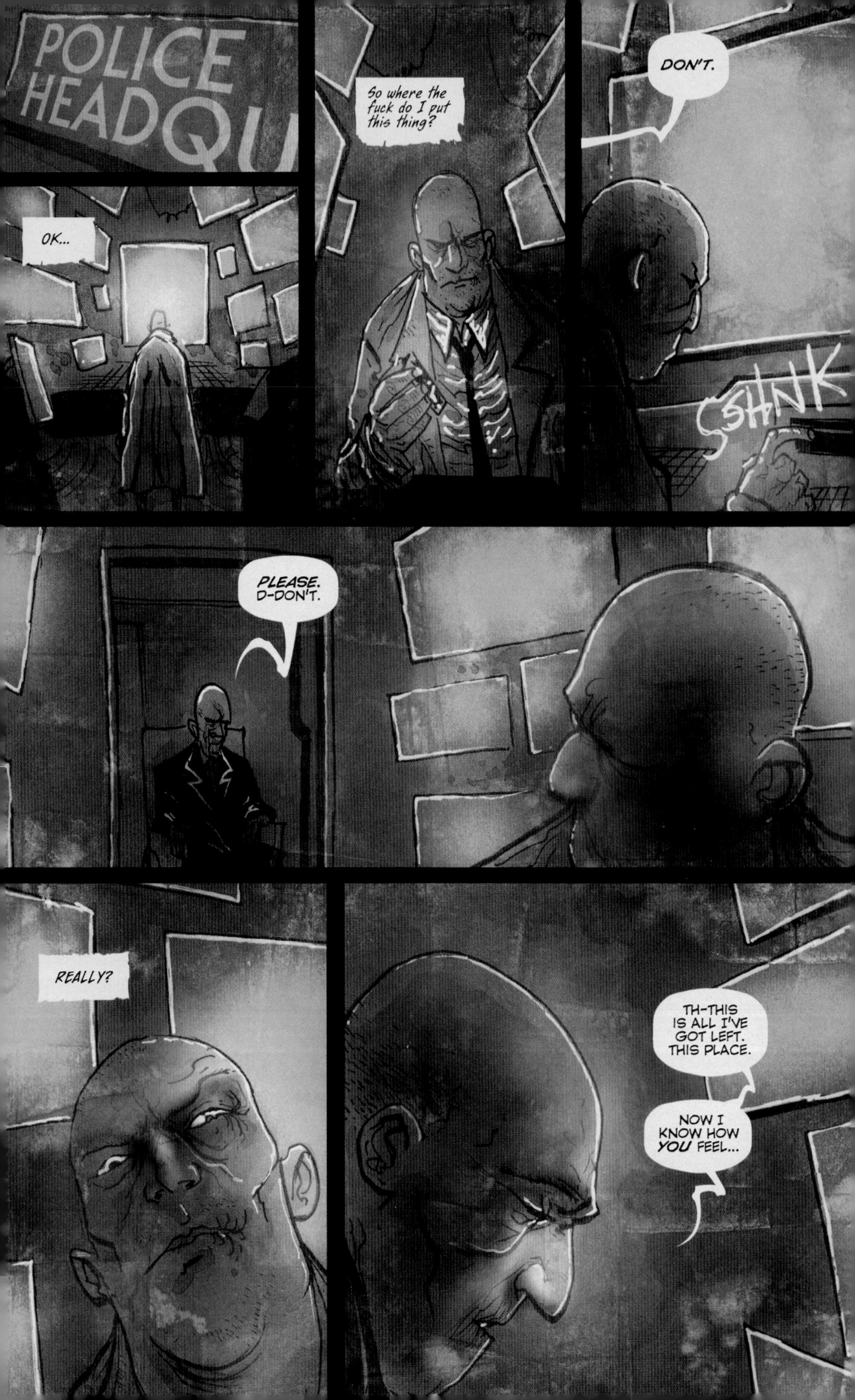
POLICE
HEADQU
OK...
So where the fuck do I put this thing?
DON'T.
SSHNK
PLEASE. D-DON'T.
REALLY?
TH-THIS IS ALL I'VE GOT LEFT. THIS PLACE.
NOW I KNOW HOW YOU FEEL...

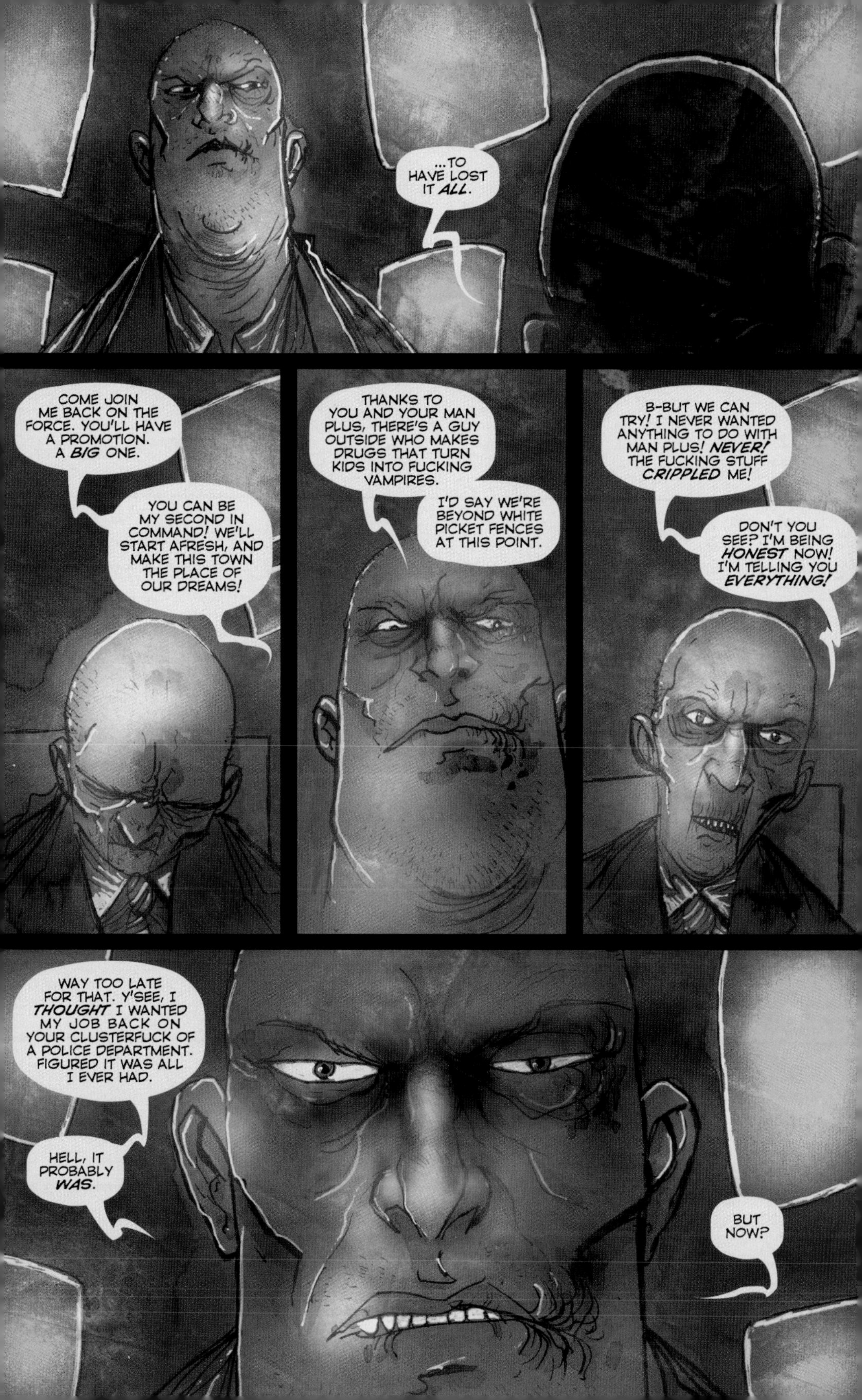
...TO HAVE LOST IT ALL.
COME JOIN ME BACK ON THE FORCE. YOU'LL HAVE A PROMOTION. A BIG ONE.
YOU CAN BE MY SECOND IN COMMAND! WE'LL START AFRESH, AND MAKE THIS TOWN THE PLACE OF OUR DREAMS!
THANKS TO YOU AND YOUR MAN PLUS, THERE'S A GUY OUTSIDE WHO MAKES DRUGS THAT TURN KIDS INTO FUCKING VAMPIRES.
I'D SAY WE'RE BEYOND WHITE PICKET FENCES AT THIS POINT.
B-BUT WE CAN TRY! I NEVER WANTED ANYTHING TO DO WITH MAN PLUS! NEVER! THE FUCKING STUFF CRIPPLED ME!
DON'T YOU SEE? I'M BEING HONEST NOW! I'M TELLING YOU EVERYTHING!
WAY TOO LATE FOR THAT. Y'SEE, I THOUGHT I WANTED MY JOB BACK ON YOUR CLUSTERFUCK OF A POLICE DEPARTMENT. FIGURED IT WAS ALL I EVER HAD.
HELL, IT PROBABLY WAS.
BUT NOW?

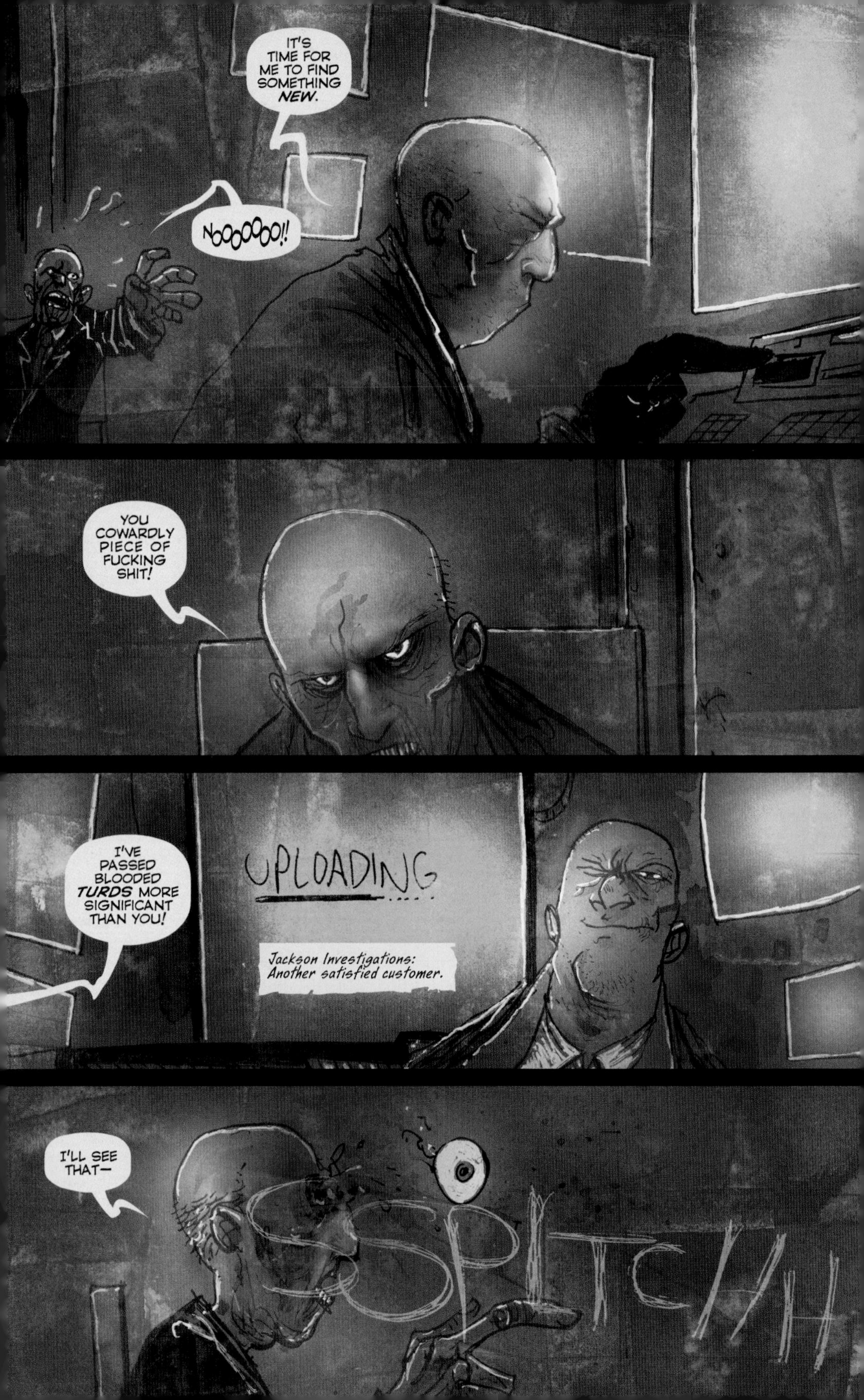
IT'S TIME FOR ME TO FIND SOMETHING *NEW*.
NOOOOOOO!!
YOU COWARDLY PIECE OF FUCKING SHIT!
I'VE PASSED BLOODED *TURDS* MORE SIGNIFICANT THAN YOU!
UPLOADING
Jackson Investigations: Another satisfied customer.
I'LL SEE THAT—
SPLTCHH

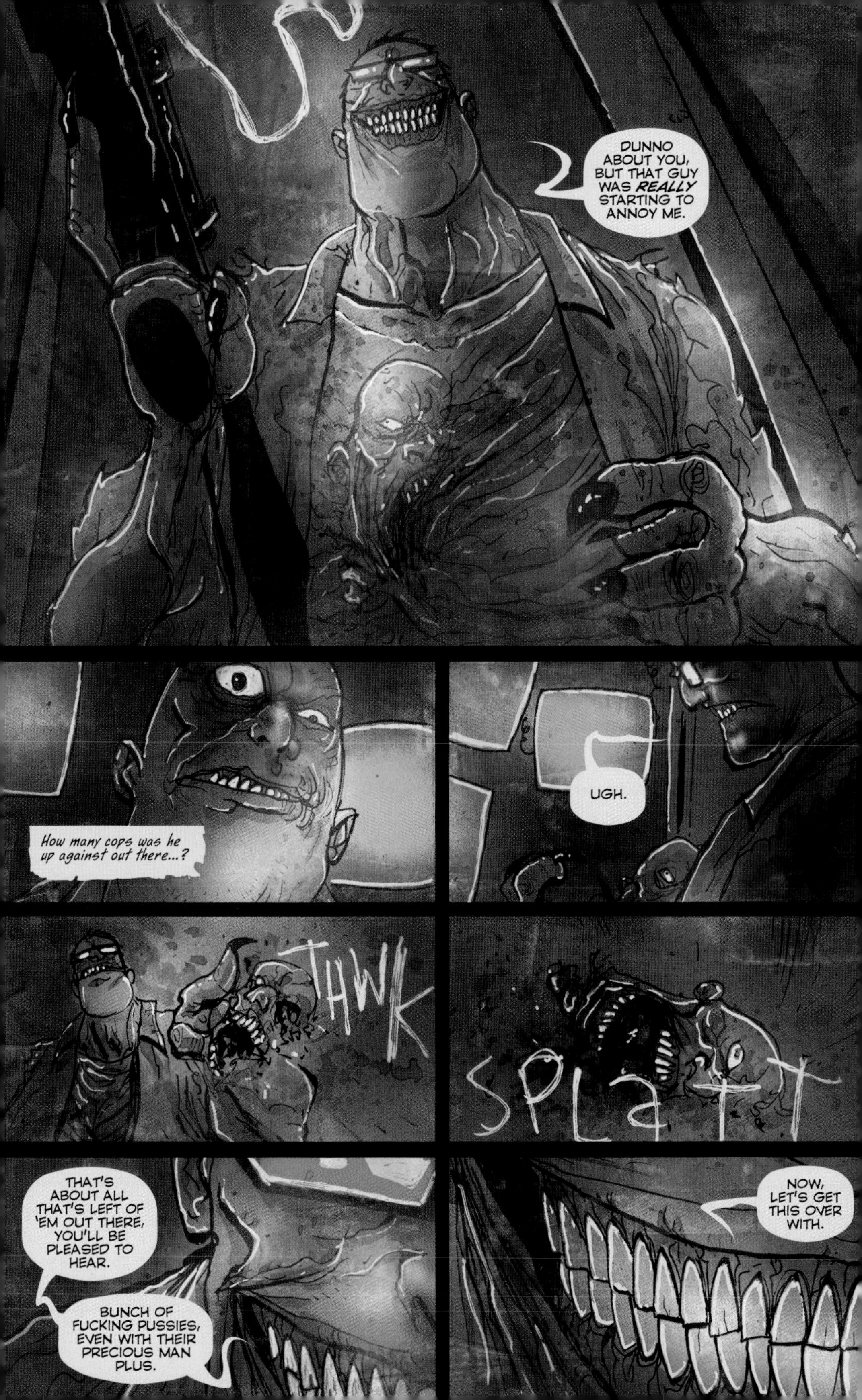

DUNNO ABOUT YOU, BUT THAT GUY WAS *REALLY* STARTING TO ANNOY ME.
How many cops was he up against out there...?
UGH.
THWK
SPLATT
THAT'S ABOUT ALL THAT'S LEFT OF 'EM OUT THERE, YOU'LL BE PLEASED TO HEAR.
BUNCH OF FUCKING PUSSIES, EVEN WITH THEIR PRECIOUS MAN PLUS.
NOW, LET'S GET THIS OVER WITH.

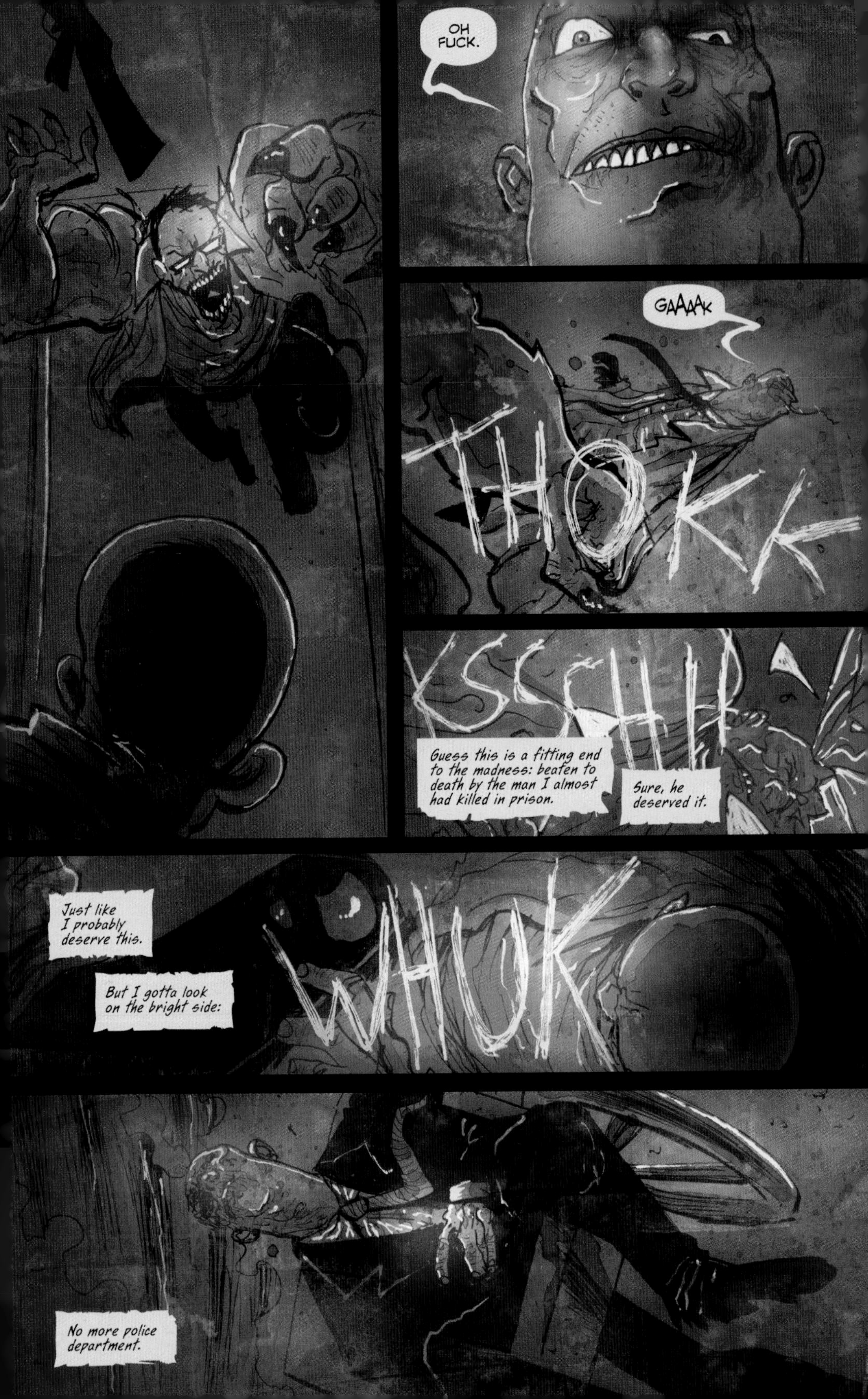
OH FUCK.
GAAAAK
THOKK
KSSCHIP
Guess this is a fitting end to the madness: beaten to death by the man I almost had killed in prison.
Sure, he deserved it.
Just like I probably deserve this.
But I gotta look on the bright side:
WHUK
No more police department.

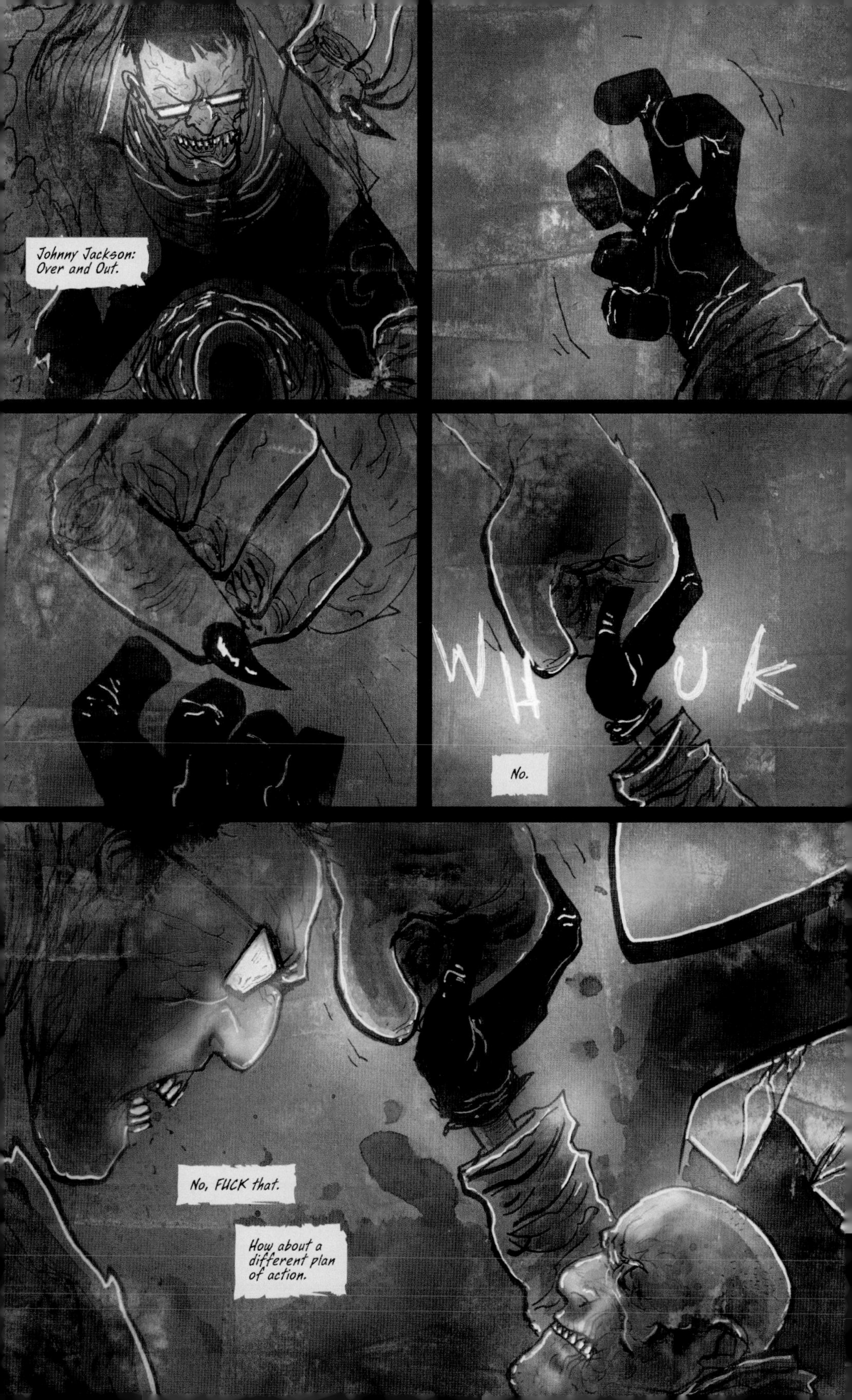

Johnny Jackson: Over and Out.
WH UK
No.
No, FUCK that.
How about a different plan of action.

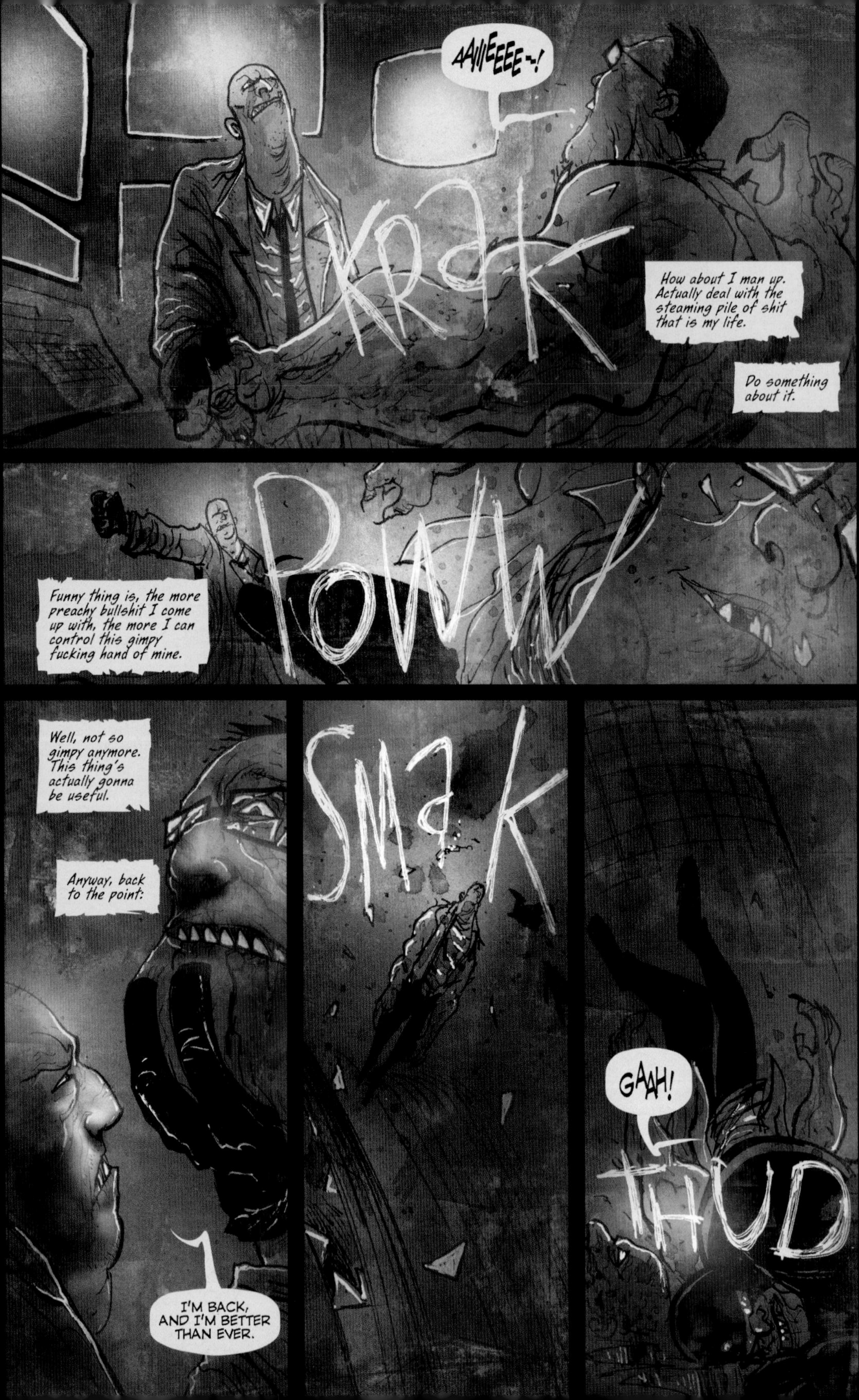
AAIIEEEE~!
KRAK
How about I man up. Actually deal with the steaming pile of shit that is my life.
Do something about it.
POWW
Funny thing is, the more preachy bullshit I come up with, the more I can control this gimpy fucking hand of mine.
Well, not so gimpy anymore. This thing's actually gonna be useful.
Anyway, back to the point:
I'M BACK, AND I'M BETTER THAN EVER.
SMAK
GAAH!
THUD

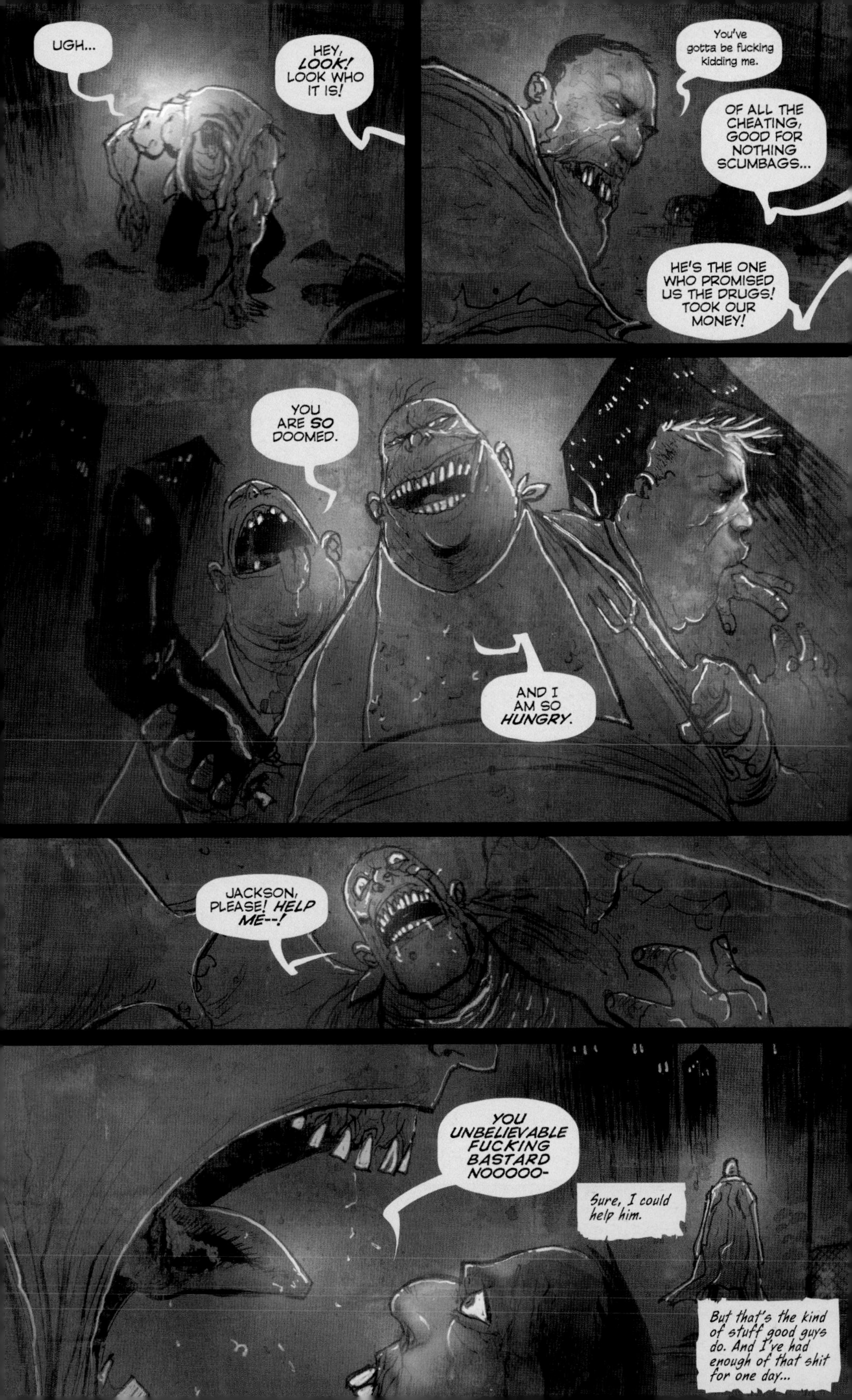
UGH...
HEY, LOOK! LOOK WHO IT IS!
You've gotta be fucking kidding me.
OF ALL THE CHEATING, GOOD FOR NOTHING SCUMBAGS...
HE'S THE ONE WHO PROMISED US THE DRUGS! TOOK OUR MONEY!
YOU ARE SO DOOMED.
AND I AM SO HUNGRY.
JACKSON, PLEASE! HELP ME--!
YOU UNBELIEVABLE FUCKING BASTARD NOOOOO-
Sure, I could help him.
But that's the kind of stuff good guys do. And I've had enough of that shit for one day...

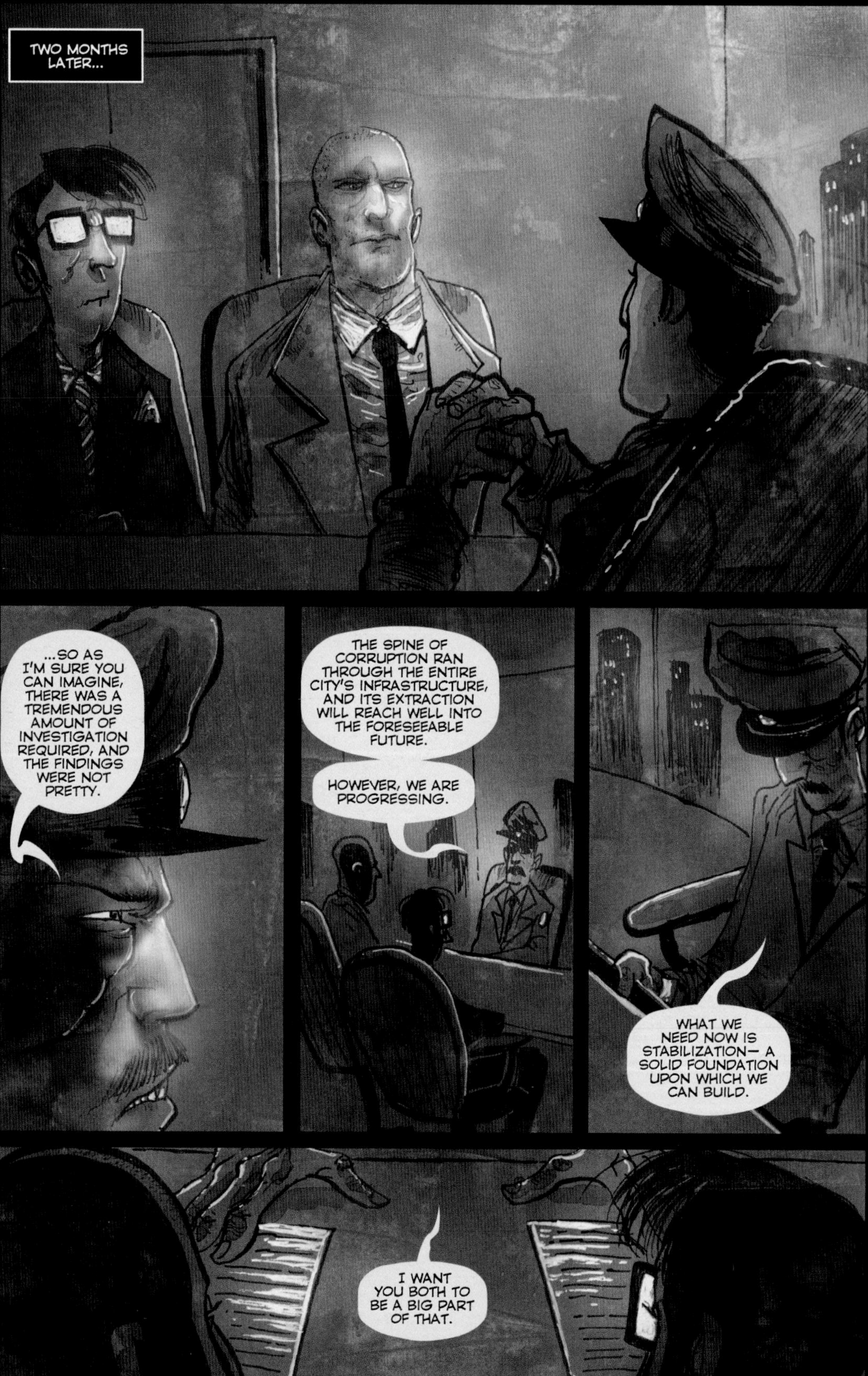
TWO MONTHS LATER...
...SO AS I'M SURE YOU CAN IMAGINE, THERE WAS A TREMENDOUS AMOUNT OF INVESTIGATION REQUIRED, AND THE FINDINGS WERE NOT PRETTY.
THE SPINE OF CORRUPTION RAN THROUGH THE ENTIRE CITY'S INFRASTRUCTURE, AND ITS EXTRACTION WILL REACH WELL INTO THE FORESEEABLE FUTURE.
HOWEVER, WE ARE PROGRESSING.
WHAT WE NEED NOW IS STABILIZATION— A SOLID FOUNDATION UPON WHICH WE CAN BUILD.
I WANT YOU BOTH TO BE A BIG PART OF THAT.

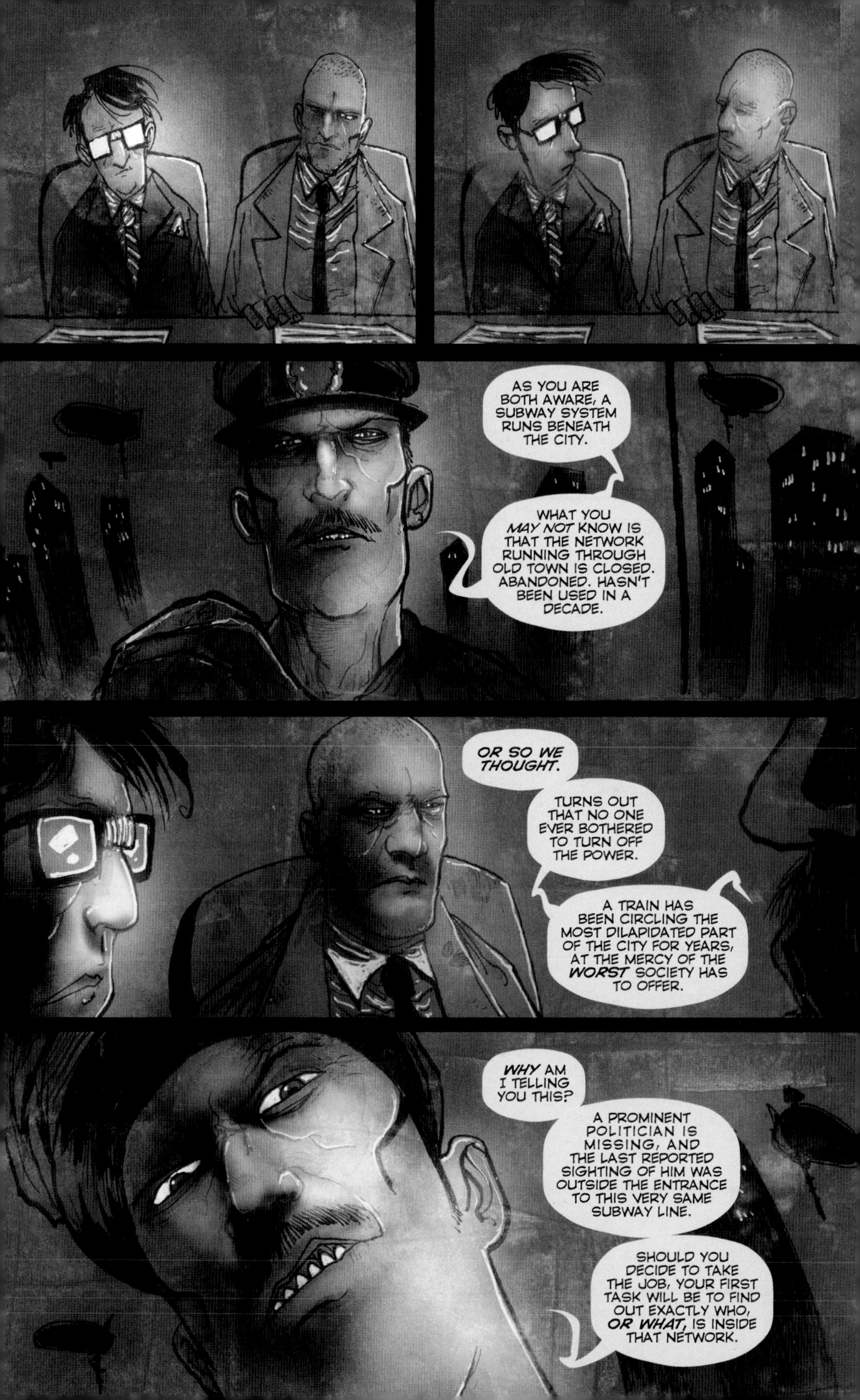
AS YOU ARE BOTH AWARE, A SUBWAY SYSTEM RUNS BENEATH THE CITY.
WHAT YOU *MAY NOT* KNOW IS THAT THE NETWORK RUNNING THROUGH OLD TOWN IS CLOSED. ABANDONED. HASN'T BEEN USED IN A DECADE.
OR SO WE THOUGHT.
TURNS OUT THAT NO ONE EVER BOTHERED TO TURN OFF THE POWER.
A TRAIN HAS BEEN CIRCLING THE MOST DILAPIDATED PART OF THE CITY FOR YEARS, AT THE MERCY OF THE ***WORST*** SOCIETY HAS TO OFFER.
WHY AM I TELLING YOU THIS?
A PROMINENT POLITICIAN IS MISSING, AND THE LAST REPORTED SIGHTING OF HIM WAS OUTSIDE THE ENTRANCE TO THIS VERY SAME SUBWAY LINE.
SHOULD YOU DECIDE TO TAKE THE JOB, YOUR FIRST TASK WILL BE TO FIND OUT EXACTLY WHO, ***OR WHAT,*** IS INSIDE THAT NETWORK.

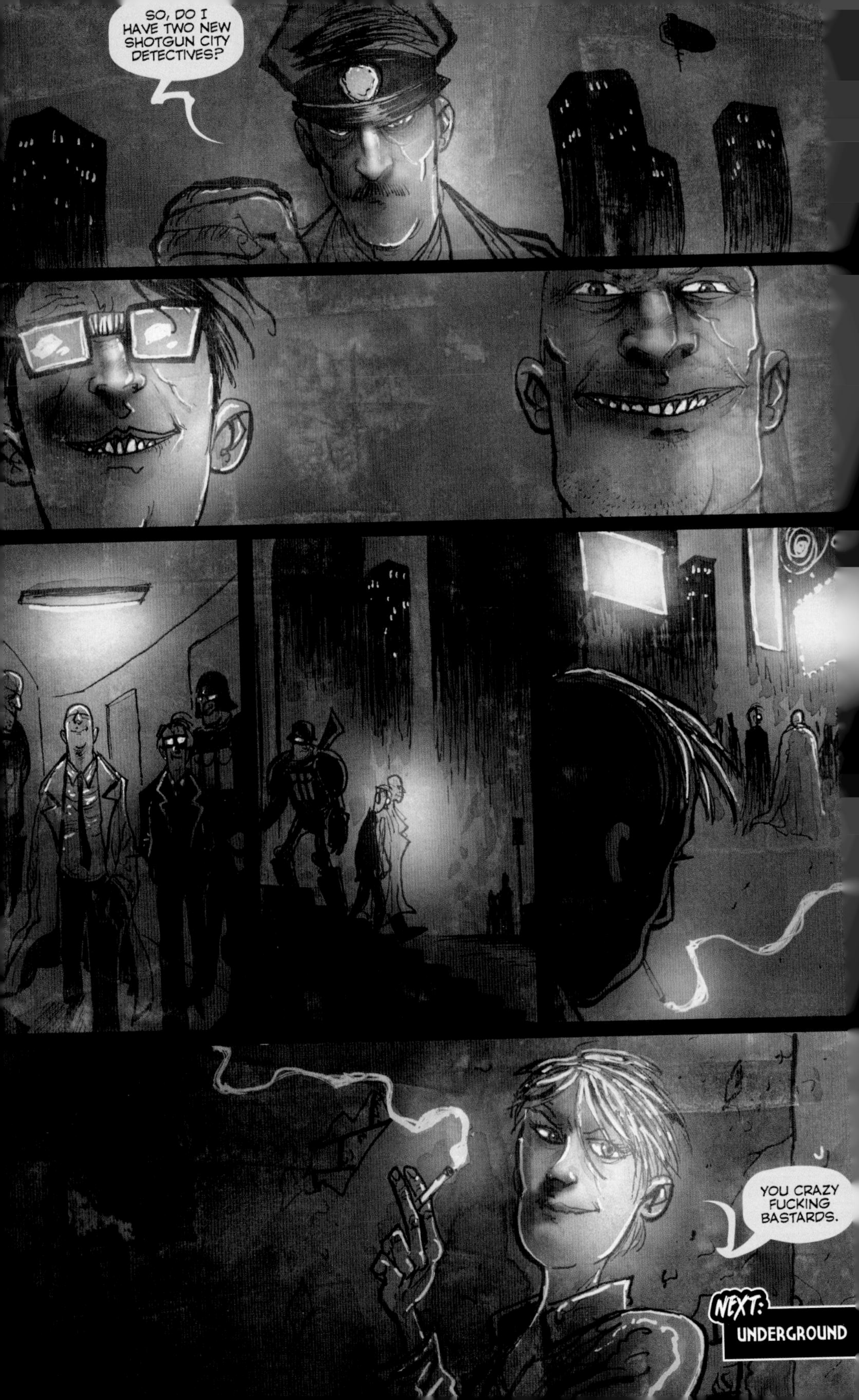
SO, DO I HAVE TWO NEW SHOTGUN CITY DETECTIVES?
YOU CRAZY FUCKING BASTARDS.
NEXT: UNDERGROUND

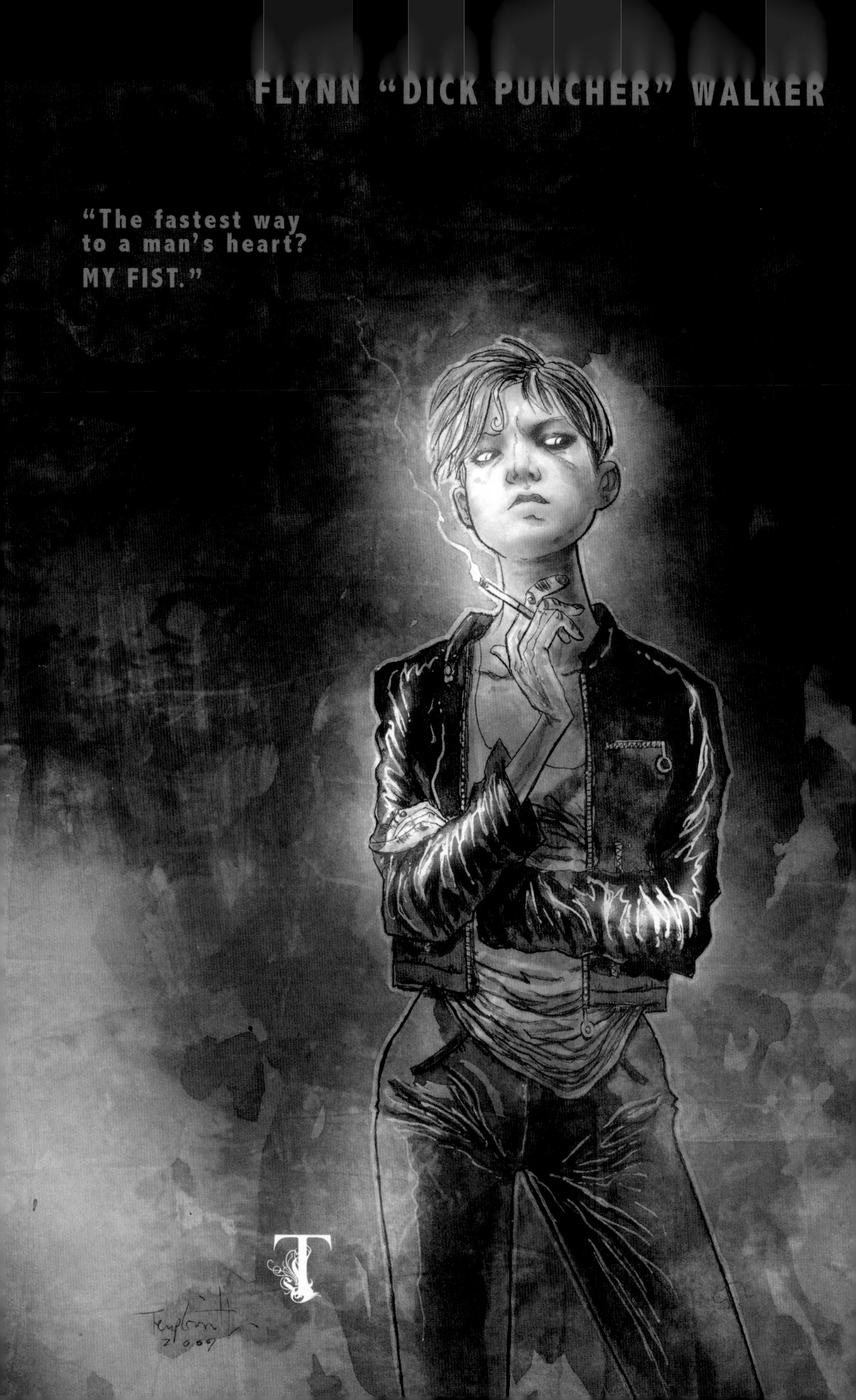
FLYNN "DICK PUNCHER" WALKER
"The fastest way
to a man's heart?
MY FIST."

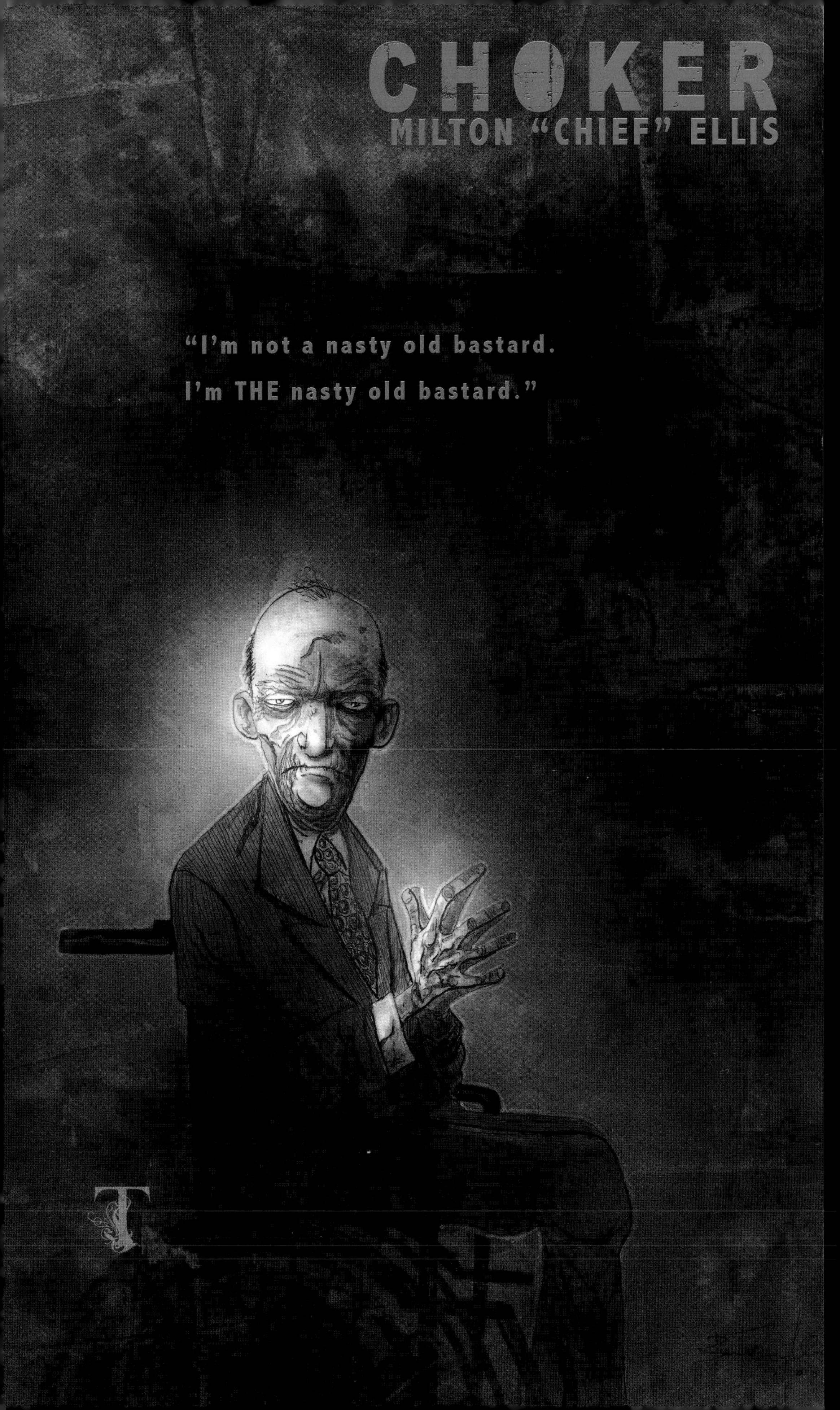
CHOKER
MILTON "CHIEF" ELLIS
"I'm not a nasty old bastard.
I'm THE nasty old bastard."

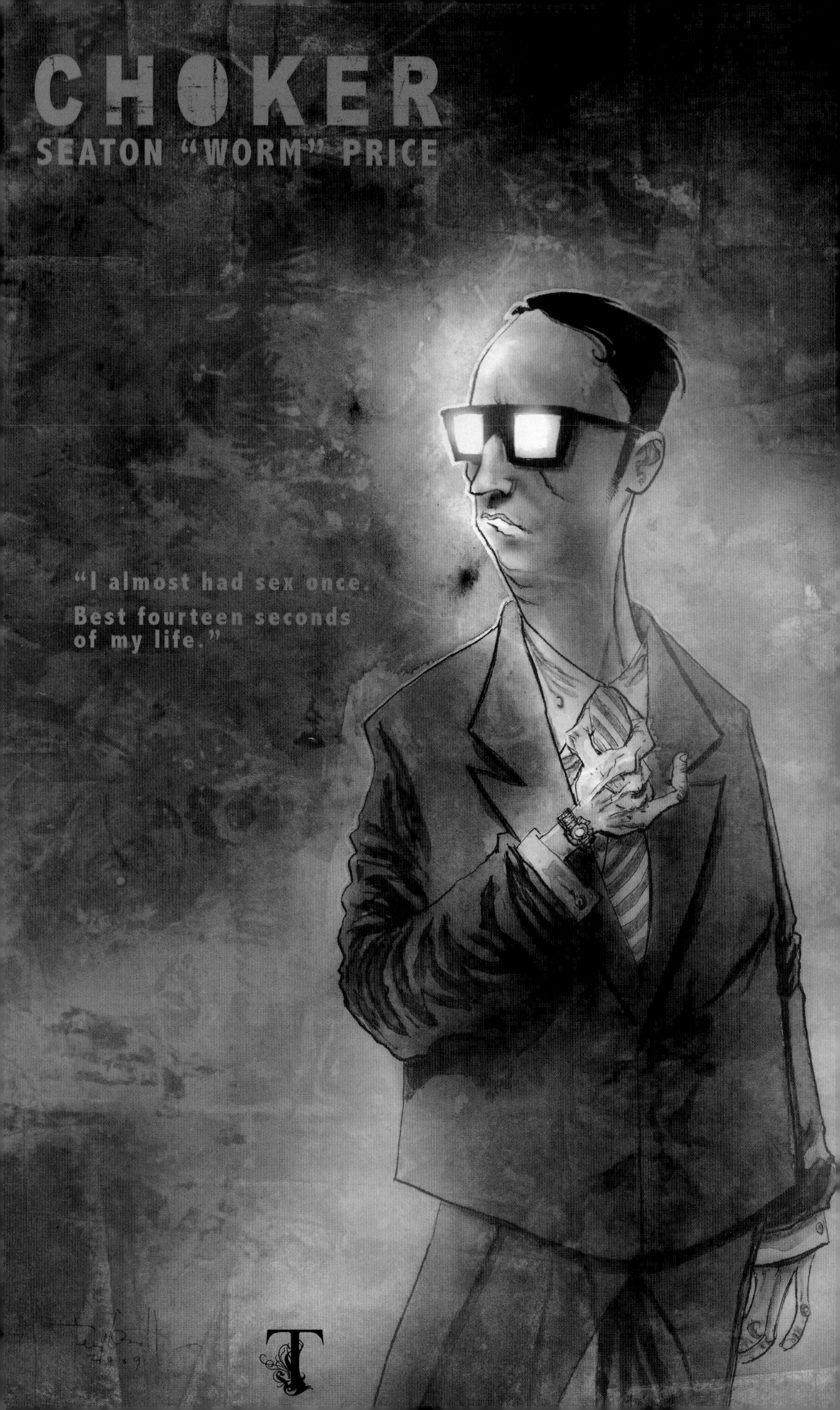
CHOKER
SEATON "WORM" PRICE
"I almost had sex once.
Best fourteen seconds of my life."

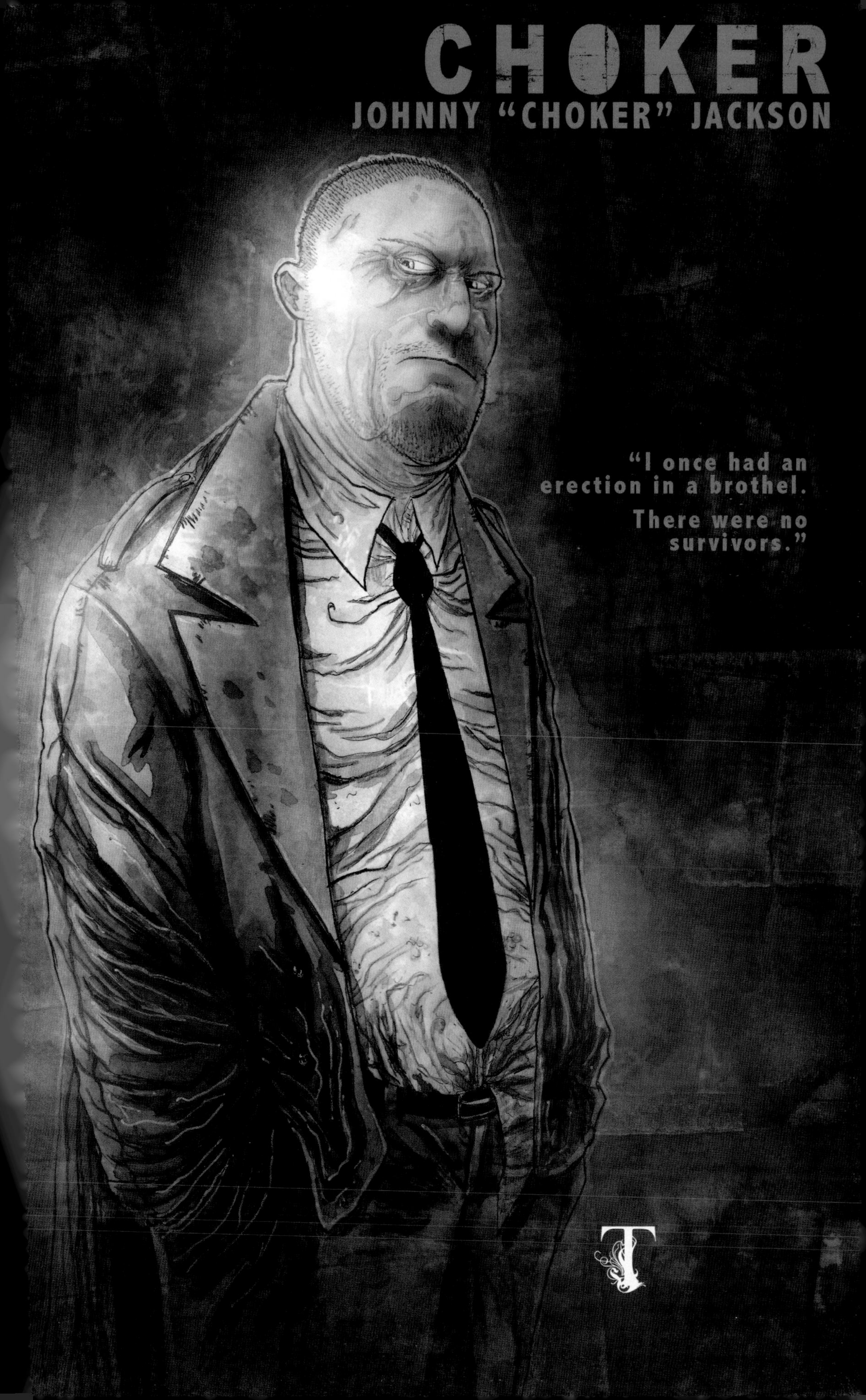
CHOKER
JOHNNY "CHOKER" JACKSON
"I once had an erection in a brothel.
There were no survivors."

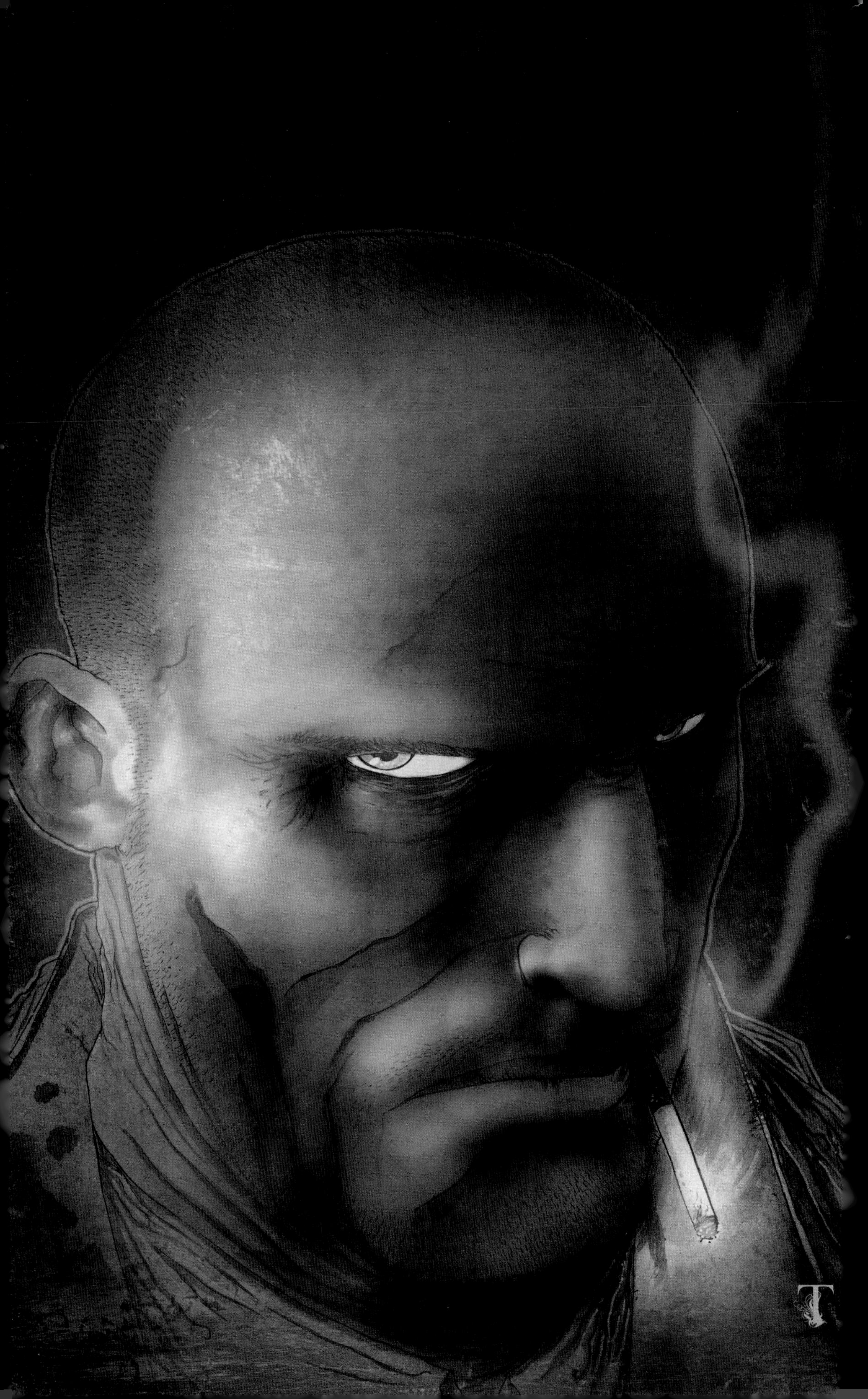

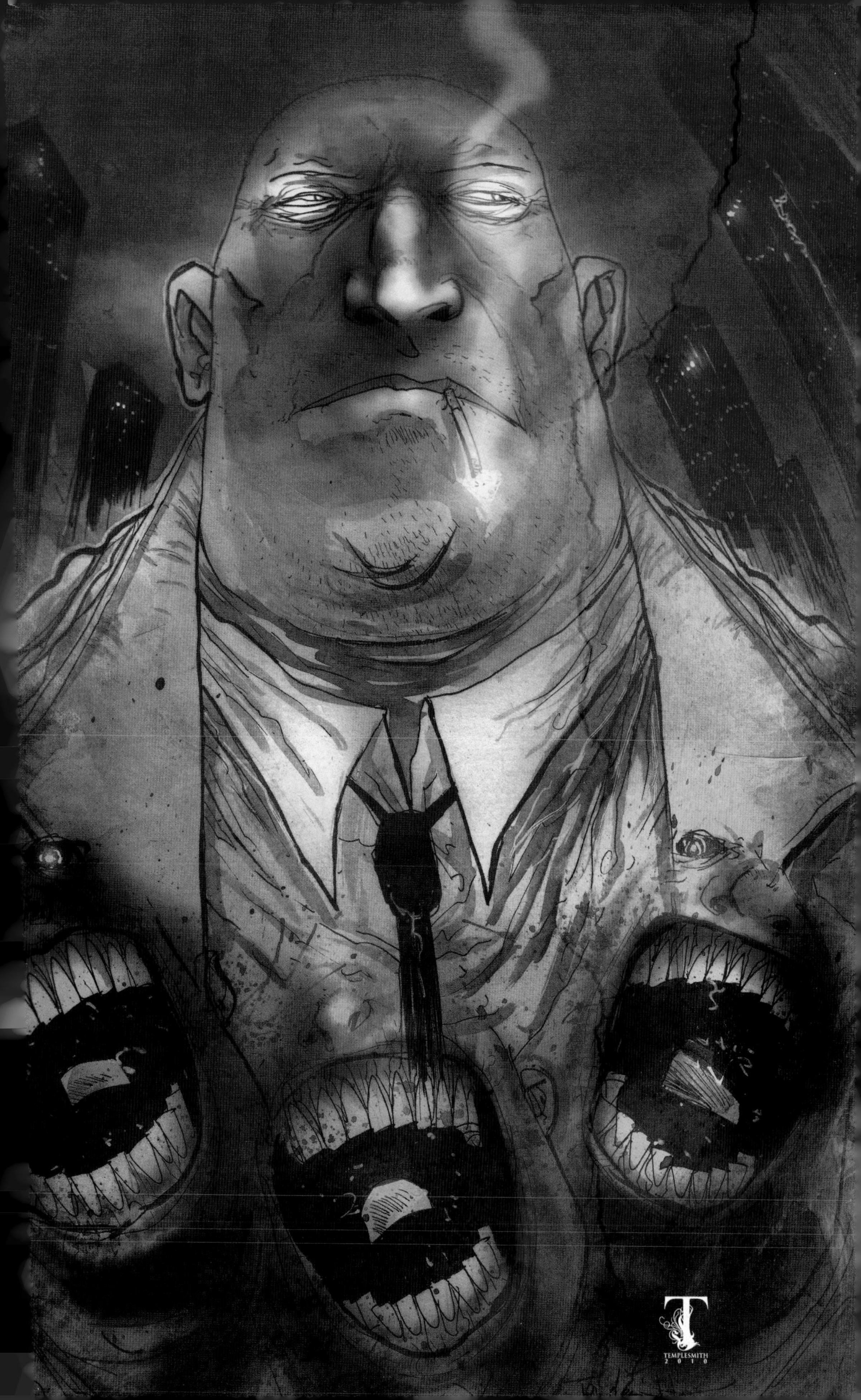
T
TEMPLESMITH
2010

FROM THE DIARY OF JOHNNY JACKSON:

Thursday, December 3rd,

Eugene Collins, the sniveling dicksplash, took a week to crack.

Maybe I'm not as hardnosed as some of the guys at HQ, but if I'm short a confession from the likes of Collins I get IMAGINATIVE.

Detective Jones, ever the diplomat, threatened to remove his eyelids with toenail clippers. Collins didn't buy it. He knows the rules. See, Shotgun City's Police Brutality License is only good on the streets, so once we've got high-level suspects in custody we have to play pussy cat; judges want the REAL bastards fit to stand trial.

But I wasn't going to give Collins a chance to duck justice. Not again.

We took a ride uptown and introduced him to a well-known vigilante. Makes malevolence look like an art form. I made clear that Eugene had been a bad boy in the past, so when little girls started going missing we figured he might be involved. Also, that this breach of procedure was as redundant as Collins' pleas for justice: we clarified (check: falsified) that he no longer was IN custody; he'd escaped from his holding cell two hours earlier. We even had (check: fabricated) a police report to confirm it. Hell, for all WE knew, he could be out raping MORE little girls. Our tyrant of integrity outlined Collins' bleak outlook, as well as lack of legal protection, which fashioned tears, soiled pants, and a full admission of guilt. Can't blame the bastard; I wouldn't much like to eat my own nutsack either.

Am I proud of this? Is this the way it should be? Doesn't matter.

Because in Shotgun City's Police Department, lying and cheating WORKS.

HOW IT'S DONE:

One of the things that still puzzles me to this day, 8 years after getting what they term "a career" doing this drawing for a living thing, is when people assume I "do it all in the computer". There's still a few guys out there that think there's perhaps a magical button one can press and it all happens instantaneously, no real work required. Sadly, this isn't the case.

Truth is, now more than ever, I work in the real world, physically drawing and painting up the pages and covers, ironically, much more so than many "traditional" styled books what with the advent of digital inking and colours on the computer and what not. For me, there's nothing better than a physical piece of art, as artefact, at the end of the process. Don't think I'll ever be one to literally draw on the computer, even if I have a Cintiq I'm slowly figuring out what to do with.

I get asked about process a lot, so tend to post quite a few shots of work in progress as I go of images on my blog but I don't think that reaches everyone who actually reads my work so here's a brief rundown of

So, the cover was basically done on some Rives BFK, 11x17 inches or thereabouts. Always starts with a pencil drawing. I rarely do anything but a basic compositional idea or two before I chow down on the main drawing. No blue pencils for me either. Just plain old lead.

As you can see from the photo though, I do use a mechanical pencil. HB leads.

Next up I get to inking the sucker. Primarily I use uni-ball pens as well as anything decent with a chisel tip and more recently a bit of the brush pen action. For some reason I always start with medium line weights, then the fine lines with maybe a micron, followed by the thicker more important lines at the end.

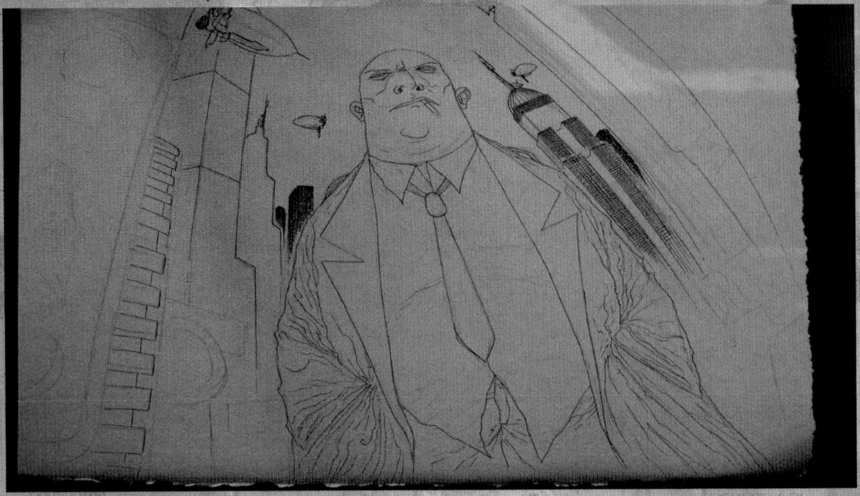

The whole time I'm doing this by the way, I've already got in mind what I want to do with the colours when on computer. In this case, Johnny is walking through the city, with a bunch of neon type signs around him, some of the colour playing off him a little. A bunch of this will come together a little further along.

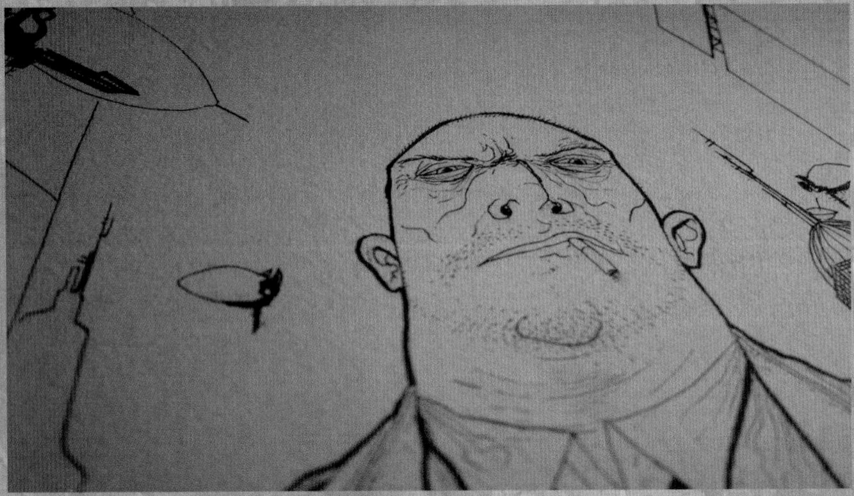

Tones come next. Because I work on tinted paper, I can work both darker and lighter much more easily, so I use water colour quite a lot, followed by maybe a little white acylic paint and more often than not, a bunch of white pen (called Signo pens) these days.

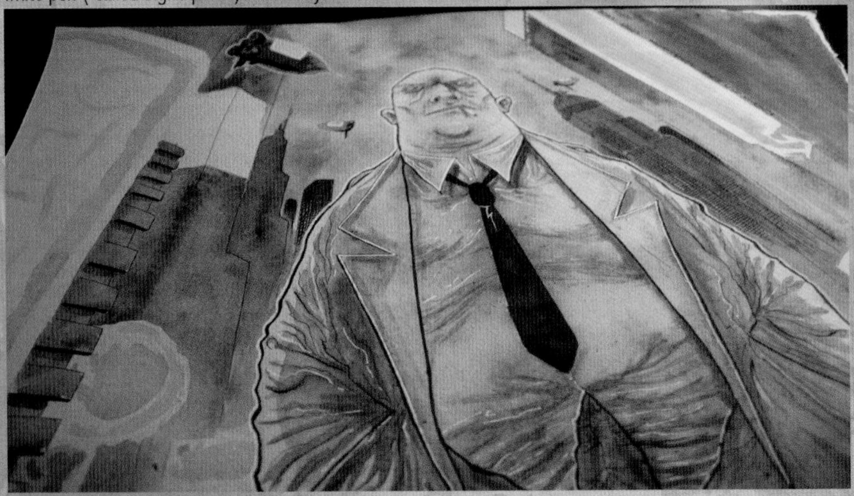

So here's what I end up with, after I scan it in at 600DPI, greyscale. Basically a good 80% of the work is done.

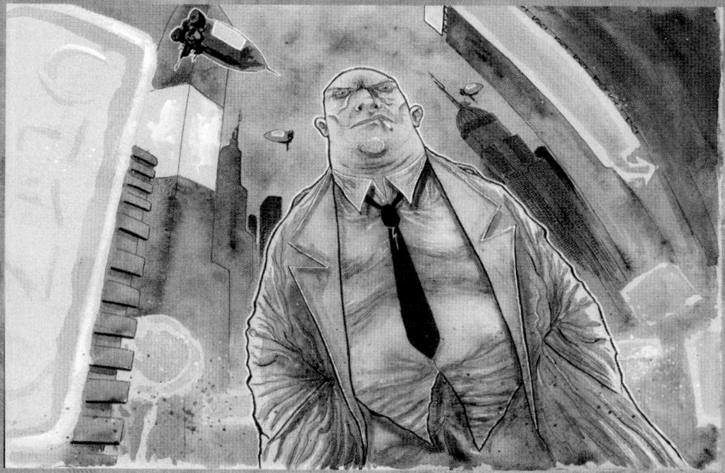

Next I get to adding some textures in, from my extensive collection of photos and self made painterly, collage type things I've made up myself and scanned in. On top of that, I add an overlay of another couple drawings I did, by hand, and invert the linework to give me all the white sign lines.

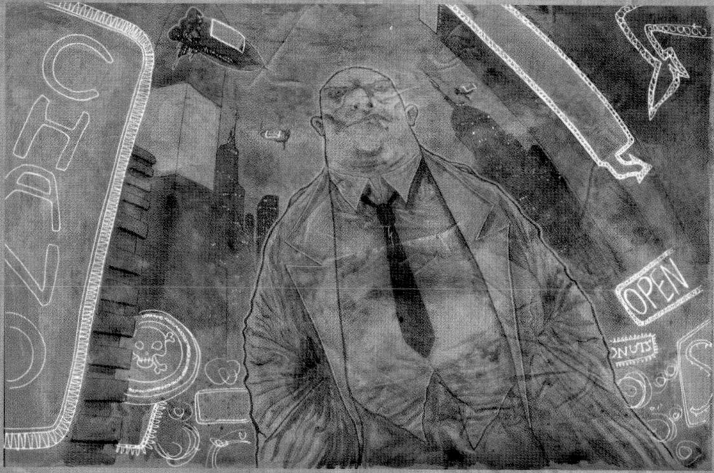
OPEN

Finally, with a couple easy Photoshop tricks I colour the signs, add some blur/glow to them and use the "colour" function to add hints of the neon on Johnny himself. Final stage is where I add "lighting effects" under the render option and add an overall colour tone to the piece, kind of meshing it all together. I go for blues and also add his cigarette smoke trail at this point with simple airbrush. And then it's done, apart from adding it to the cover logo design.

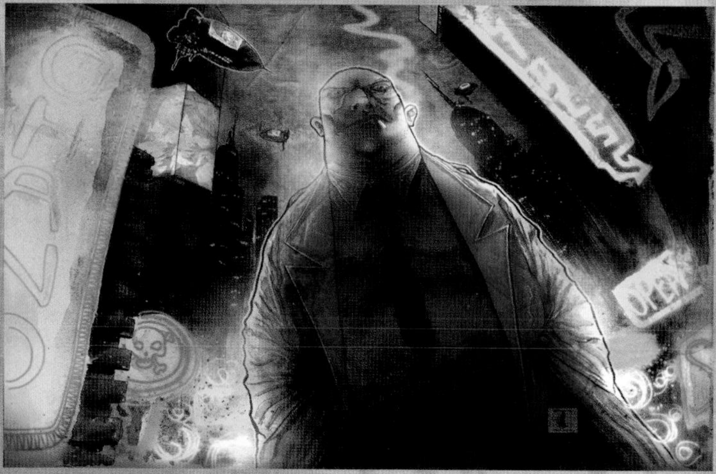

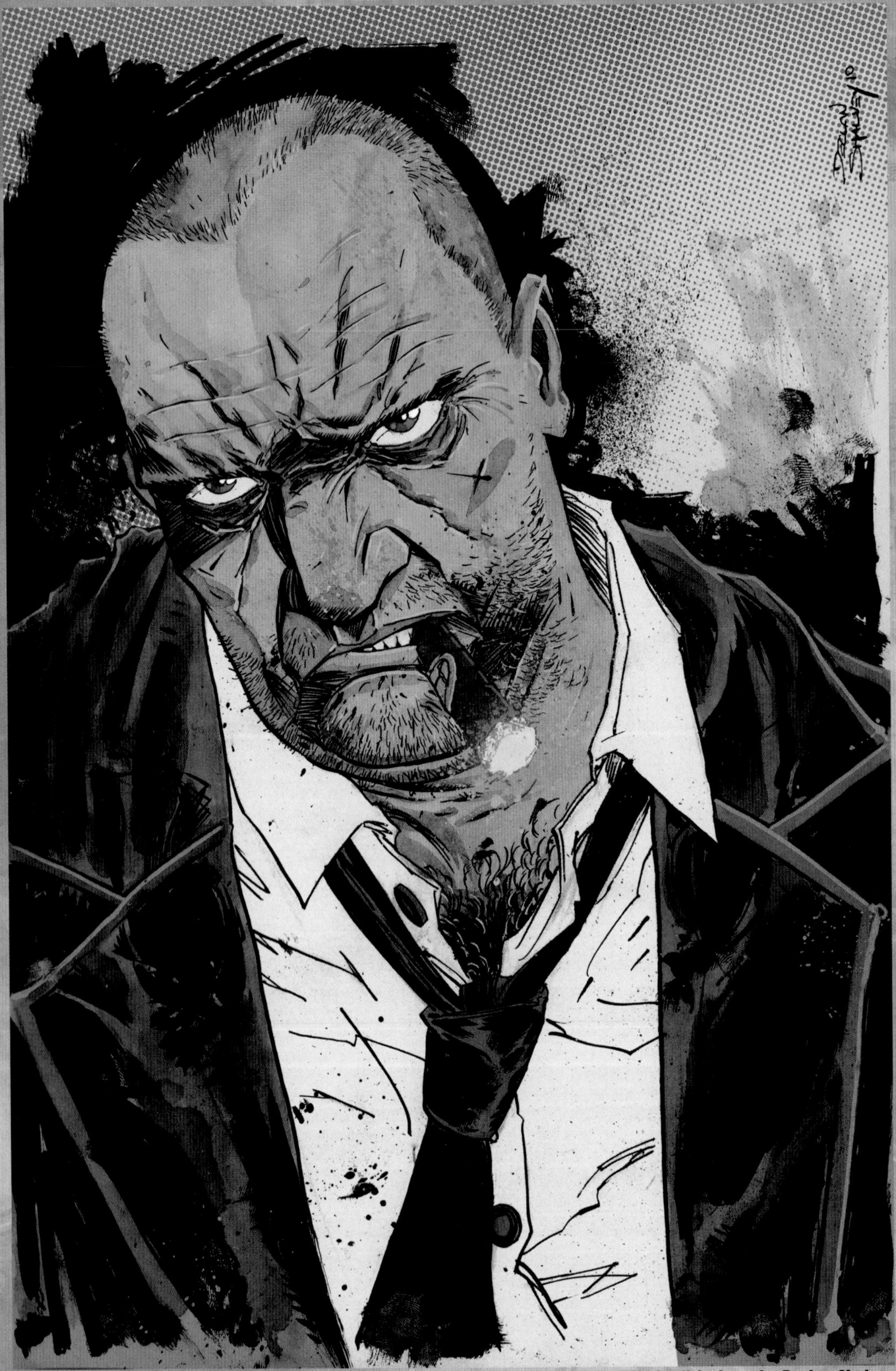

Johnny "Choker" Jackson by Declan Shalvey

THE CHOKER SIGNING TOUR...

Shortly after arriving in Phoenix, Arizona, myself and Ben T decided to do something daft. It didn't take us long to settle on the idea of getting tattoos, and so retail maestro Mike Malve (owner of the ridiculously awesome ATOMIC COMICS) arranged for some painful inking.

Once the signing was complete, Atomic Comics' Mesa store became a tattoo parlour and I had an original piece of Templesmith art emblazoned upon my leg. Mike's customers looked a little... baffled.

See? Irresponsible behaviour is FUN!

--Ben McCool

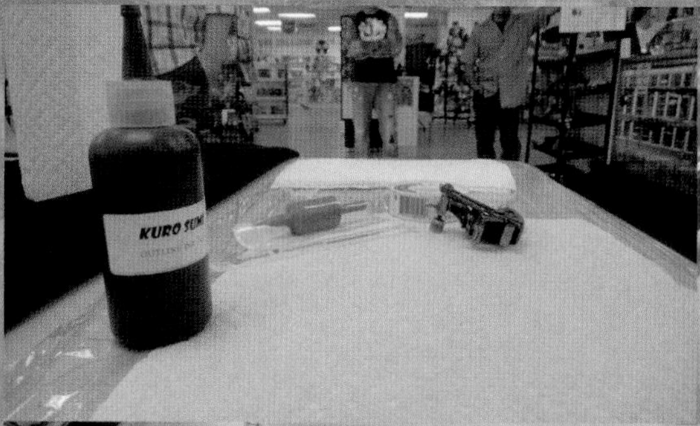
KURO SUMI

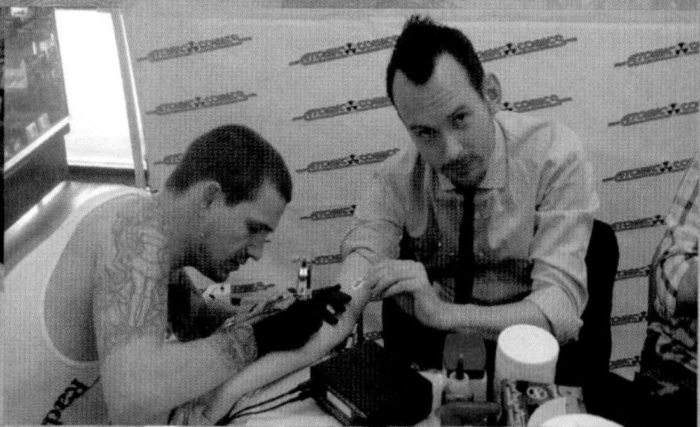

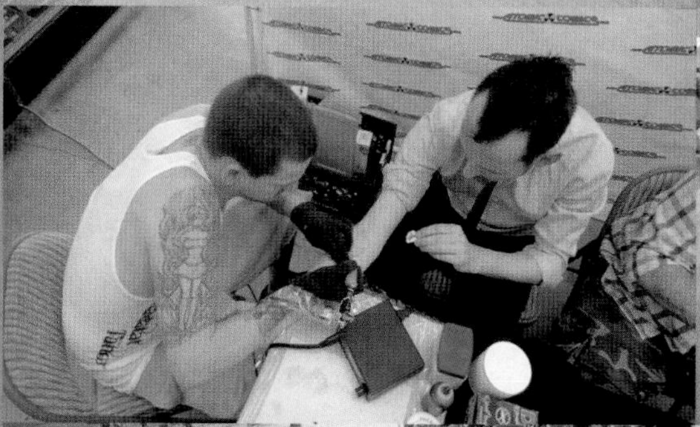

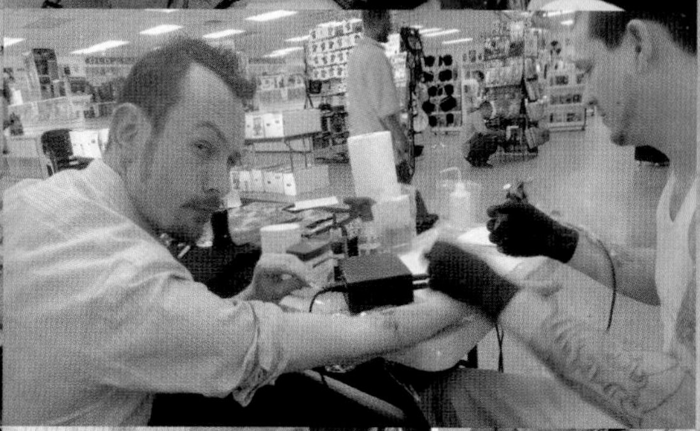

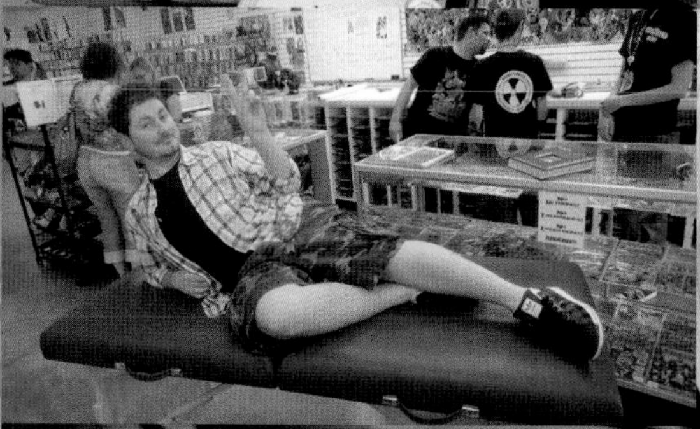

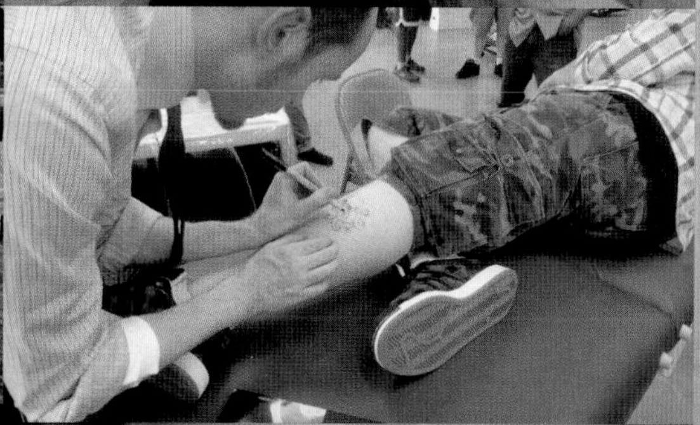

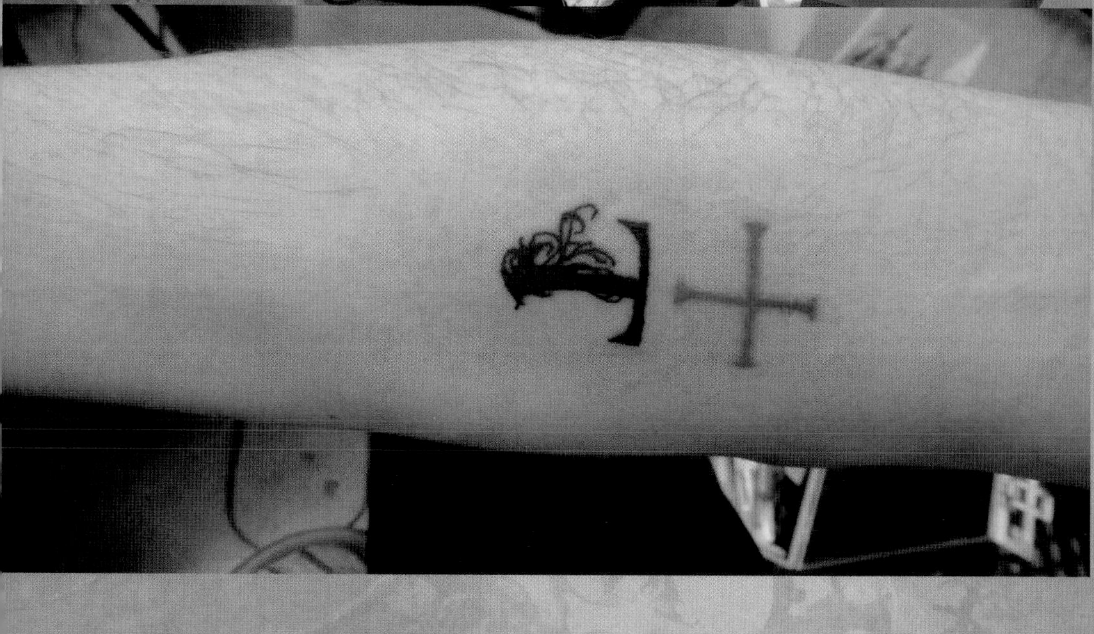

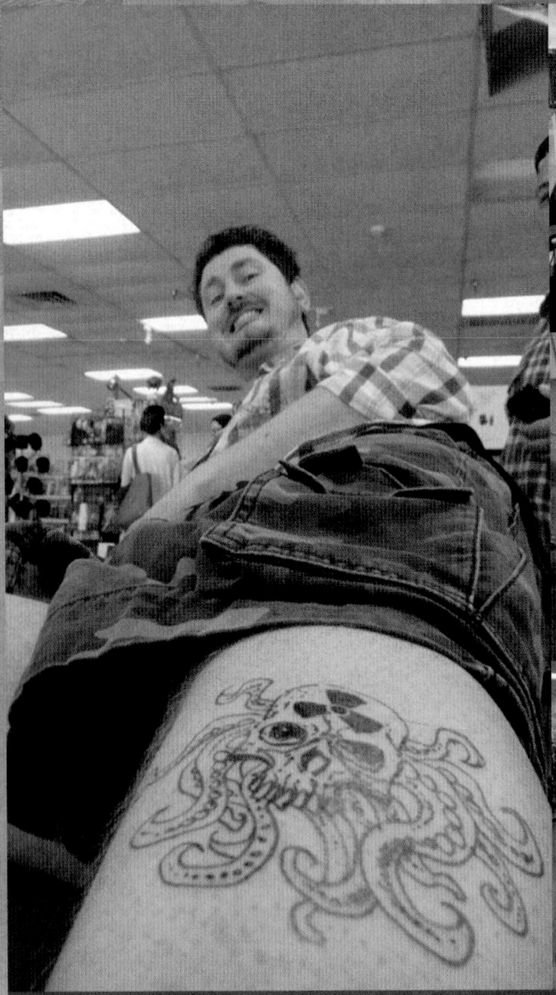
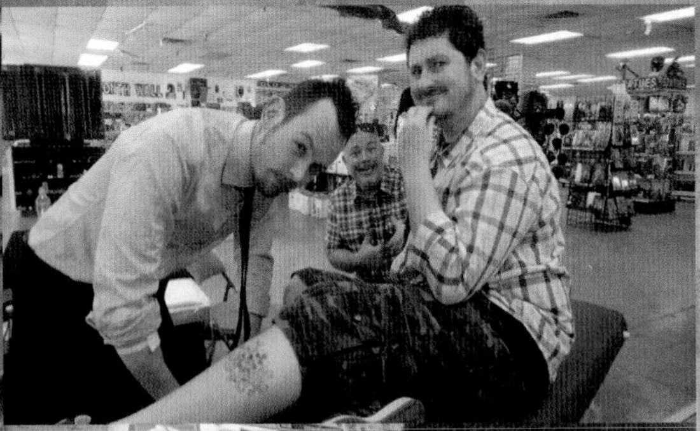
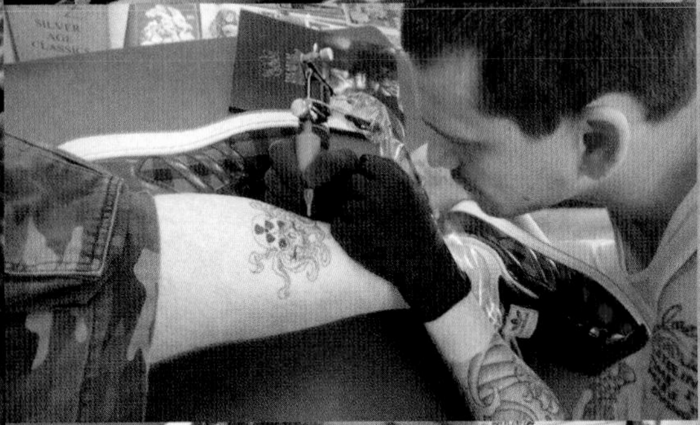
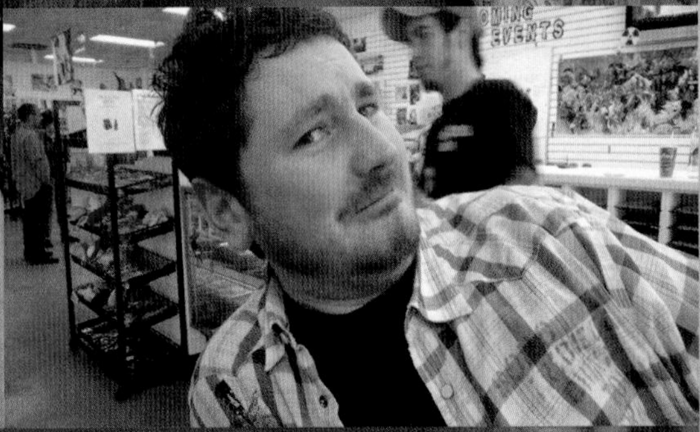
EVENTS
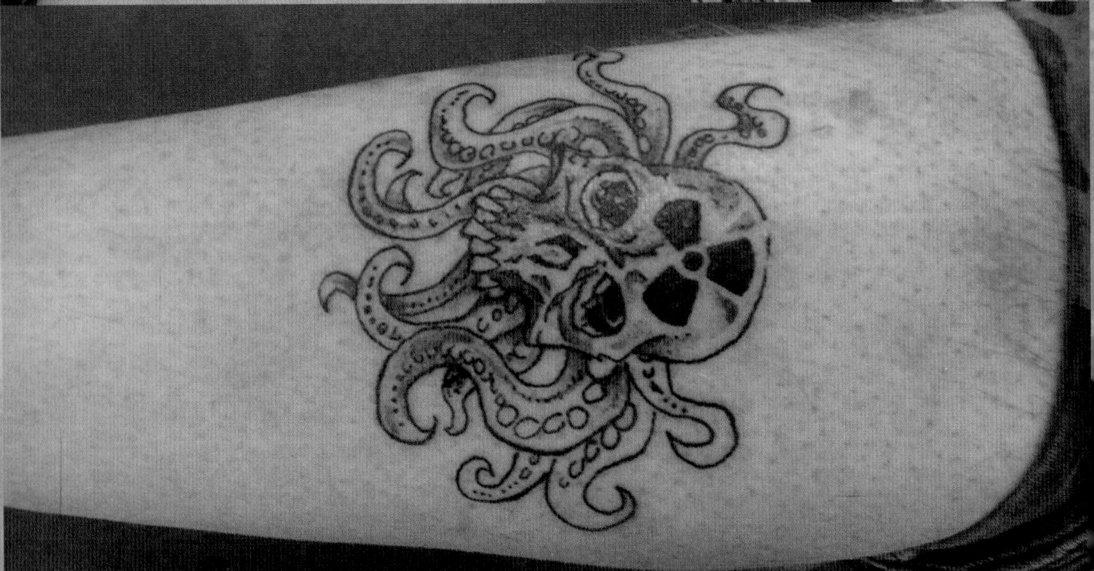

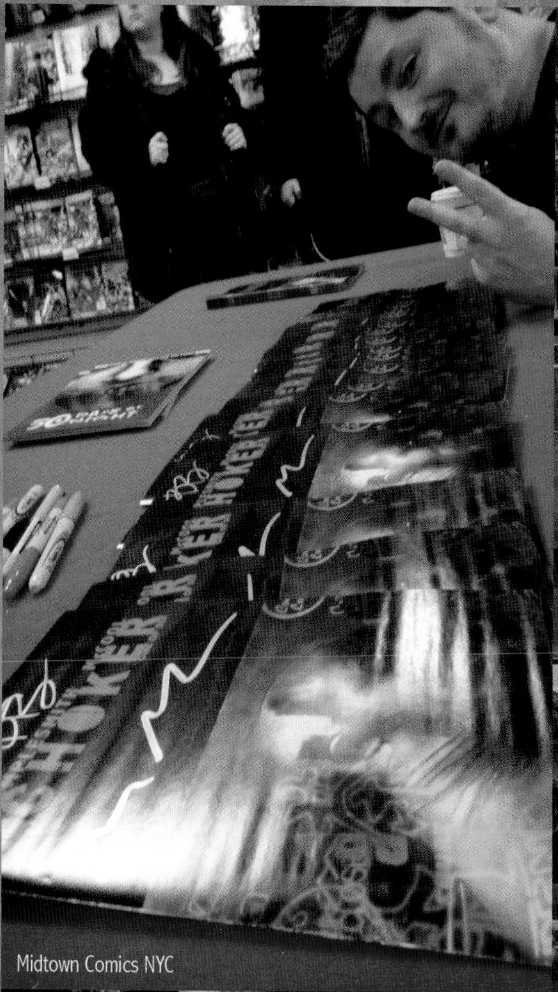

Midtown Comics NYC

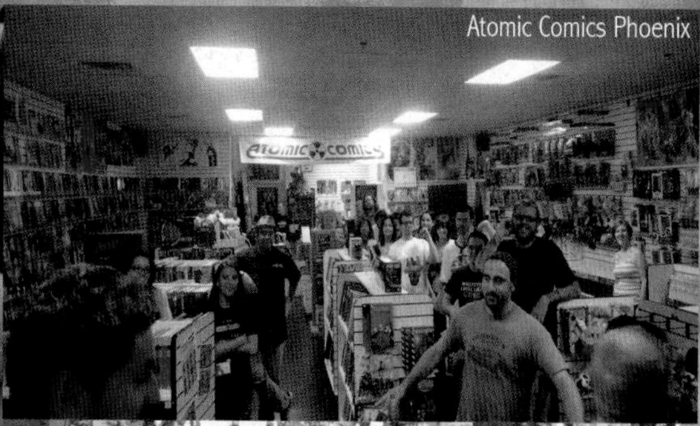
ATOMIC COMICS

Atomic Comics Phoenix

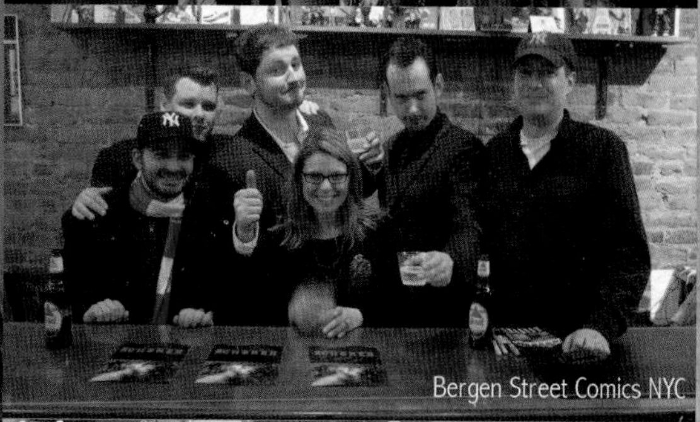

Bergen Street Comics NYC

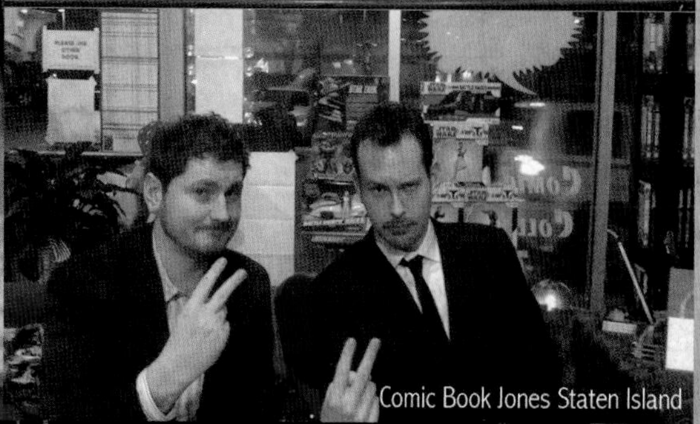

Comic Book Jones Staten Island

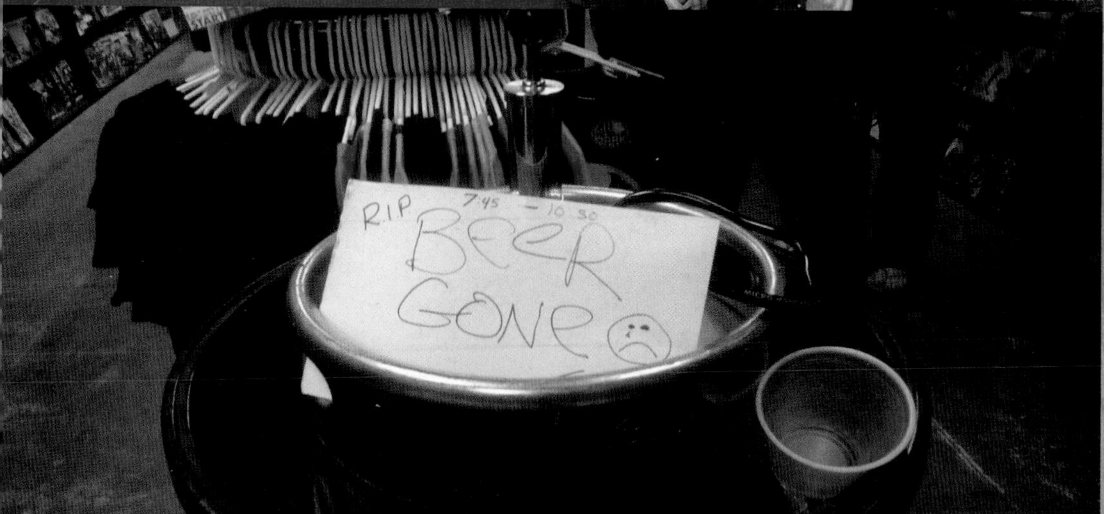
R.I.P.
7:45 – 10:30
BEER
GONE

A Comic Shop Orlando

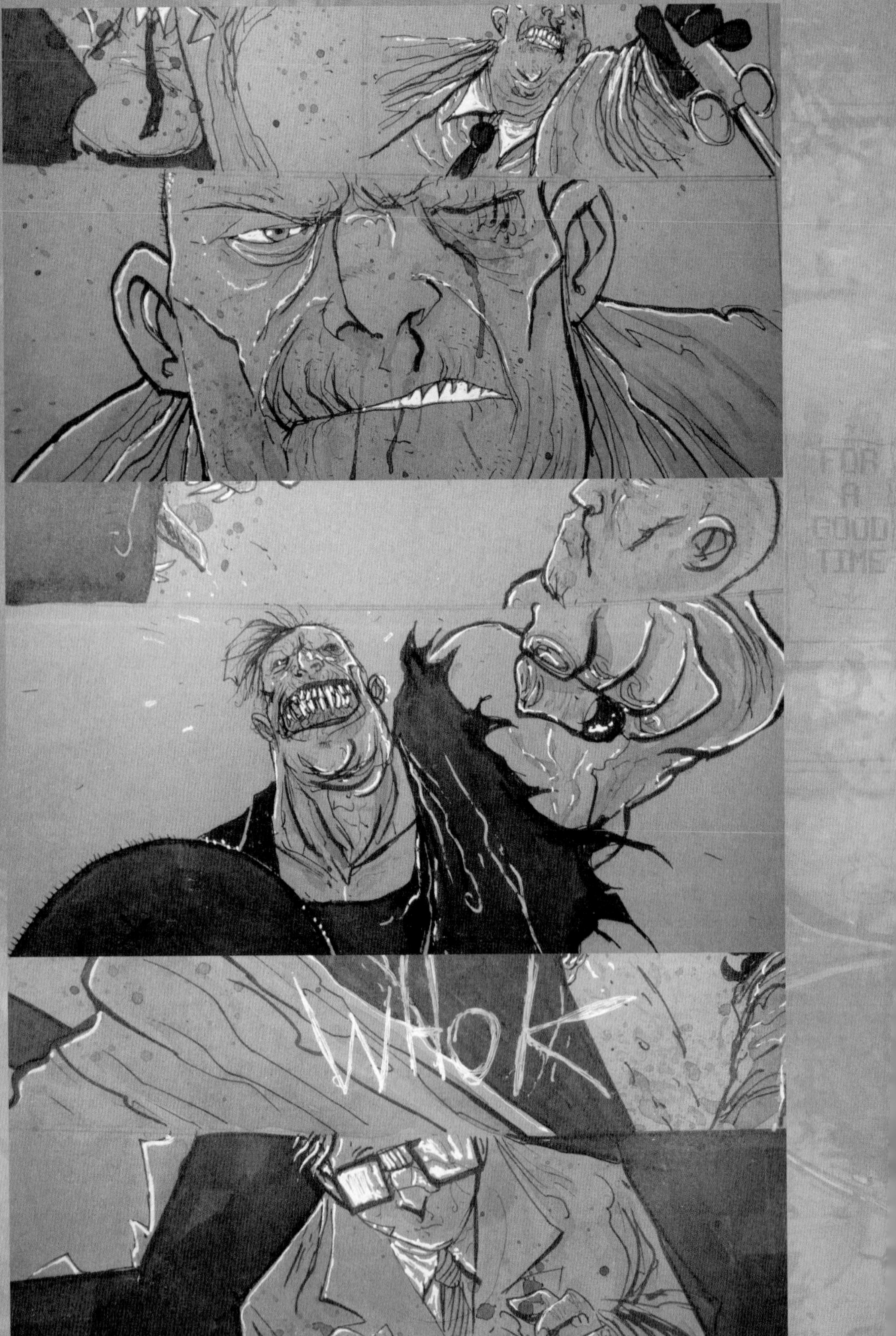
FOR A GOOD TIME
WHOK